Yuto Tsukuda

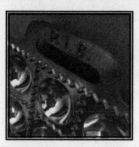

Let me explain how *Food Wars!* is created each week, using cooking as an example:

① Ms. Morisaki prepares a bunch of fresh ingredients and rare seasonings.

② Tsukuda racks his brain to come up with a recipe based on those ingredients.

③ The editor, Mr. Nakaji, reviews the recipe (occasionally tossing the whole thing out).

④ Head Chef Saeki and his staff take the recipe and prepare it to beautiful perfection.

Oh hey! That turned out kinda neat, don't ya think? Huh? Don't ya?

Shun Saeki

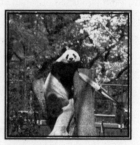

At Ueno Zoo... Apparently, pandas were forced to adapt to eating bamboo because of stuff like environmental changes and competing predators. I wonder what they would eat if they hadn't had to do that. Meat maybe?

About the authors

Yuto Tsukuda won the 34th Jump Juniketsu Newcomers' Manga Award for his one-shot story *Kiba ni Naru*. He made his *Weekly Shonen Jump* debut in 2010 with the series *Shonen Shikku*. His follow-up series, *Food Wars!: Shokugeki no Soma*, is his first English-language release.

Shun Saeki made his *Jump NEXT!* debut in 2011 with the one-shot story *Kimi to Watashi no Renai Soudan*. *Food Wars!: Shokugeki no Soma* is his first *Shonen Jump* series.

DEC 1 5 2015

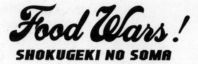

Food Wars!
SHOKUGEKI NO SOMA

Volume 8
Shonen Jump Manga Edition
Story by Yuto Tsukuda, Art by Shun Saeki
Contributor Yuki Morisaki

Translation: Adrienne Beck
Touch-Up Art & Lettering: NRP Studios
Design: Izumi Evers
Editor: Jennifer LeBlanc

Printed in the U.S.A.

Published by VIZ Media, LLC
P.O. Box 77010
San Francisco, CA 94107

10 9 8 7 6 5 4 3 2 1
First printing, October 2015

THE WORLD'S MOST
CUTTING-EDGE MANGA

SHONEN JUMP
ADVANCED
www.shonenjump.com

www.viz.com

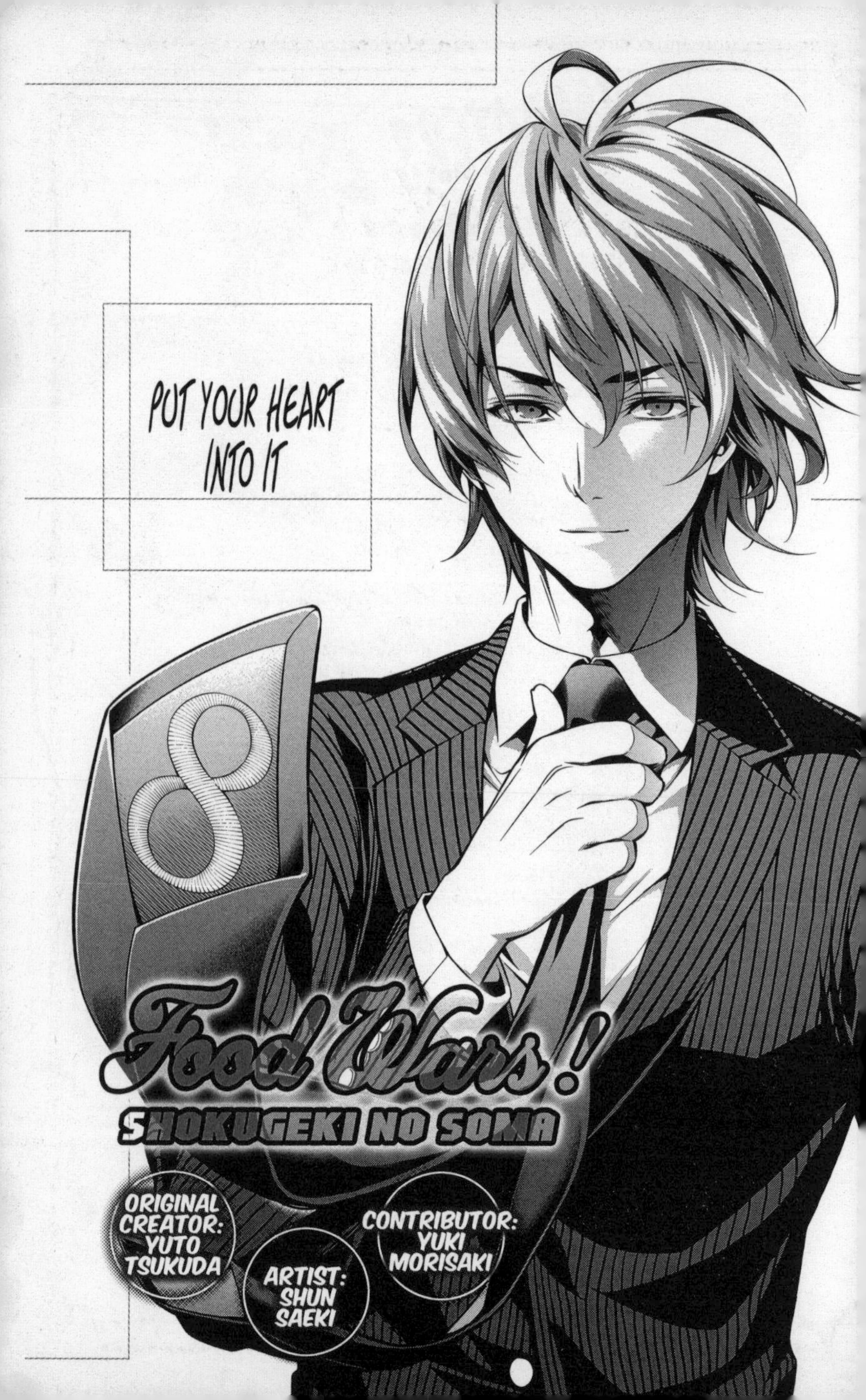

PUT YOUR HEART INTO IT
Food Wars!
SHOKUGEKI NO SOMA
ORIGINAL CREATOR: YUTO TSUKUDA
CONTRIBUTOR: YUKI MORISAKI
ARTIST: SHUN SAEKI

CHARACTERS

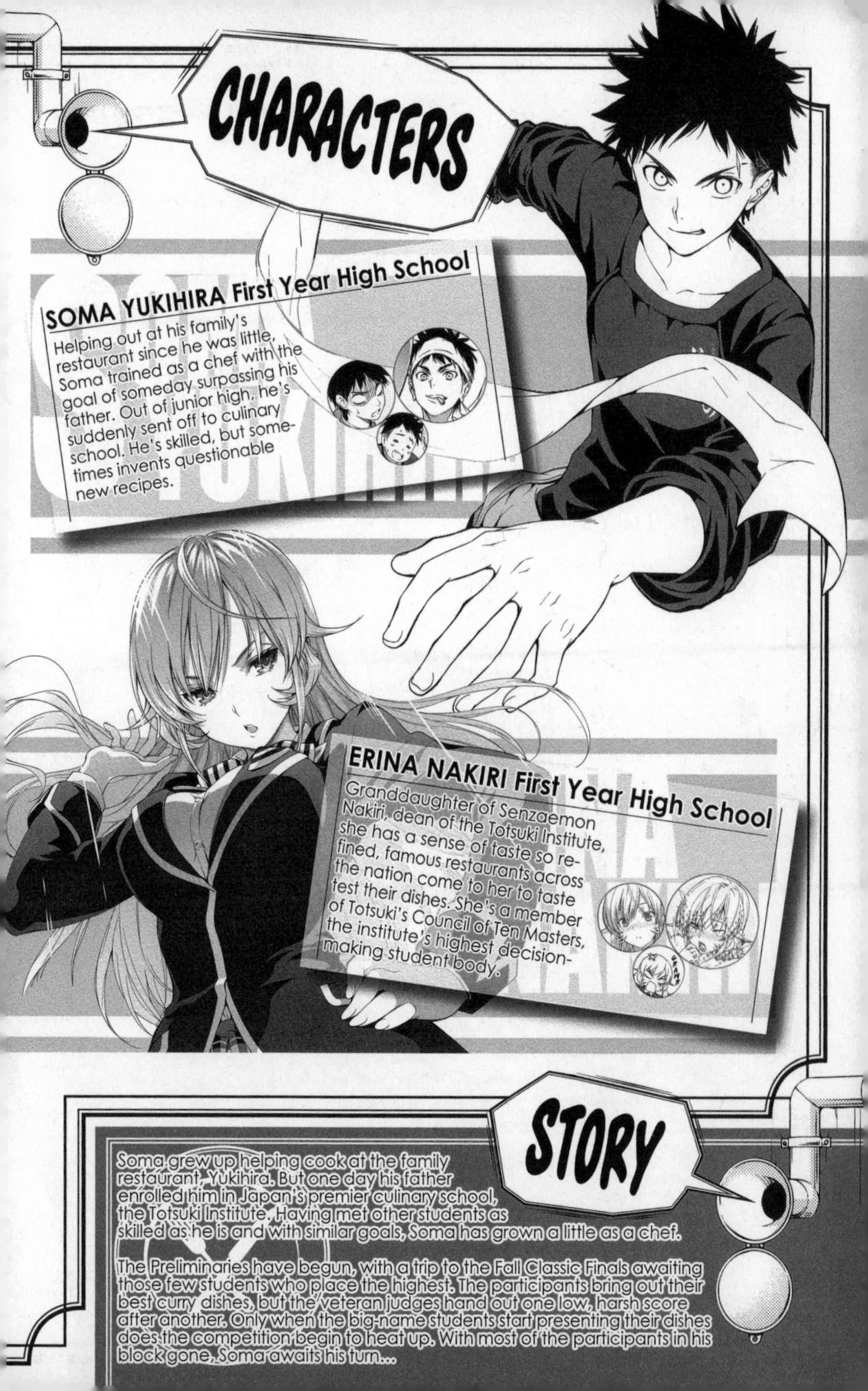

SOMA YUKIHIRA First Year High School

Helping out at his family's restaurant since he was little, Soma trained as a chef with the goal of someday surpassing his father. Out of junior high, he's suddenly sent off to culinary school. He's skilled, but sometimes invents questionable new recipes.

ERINA NAKIRI First Year High School

Granddaughter of Senzaemon Nakiri, dean of the Totsuki Institute, she has a sense of taste so refined, famous restaurants across the nation come to her to taste test their dishes. She's a member of Totsuki's Council of Ten Masters, the institute's highest decision-making student body.

STORY

Soma grew up helping cook at the family restaurant, Yukihira. But one day his father enrolled him in Japan's premier culinary school, the Totsuki Institute. Having met other students as skilled as he is and with similar goals, Soma has grown a little as a chef.

The Preliminaries have begun, with a trip to the Fall Classic Finals awaiting those few students who place the highest. The participants bring out their best curry dishes, but the veteran judges hand out one low, harsh score after another. Only when the big-name students start presenting their dishes does the competition begin to heat up. With most of the participants in his block gone, Soma awaits his turn...

—The Fall Classic Preliminaries—

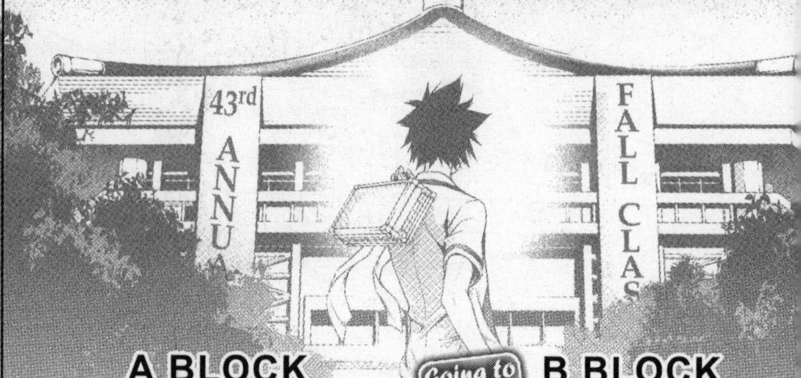
43rd ANNUA
FALL CLAS

Going to Finals

A BLOCK

Rank	Name	Points
1st	RYO KUROKIBA	93pts
2nd	MARUI ZENJI	88pts
2nd	SHUN IBUSAKI	88pts
4th	IKUMI MITO	86pts
4th	RYOKO SAKAKI	86pts
	Soma Yukihira	- - - pts
	Akira Hayama	- - - pts

B BLOCK

Rank	Name	Points
1st	ALICE NAKIRI	95pts
2nd	HISAKO ARATO	92pts
3rd	TAKUMI ALDINI	90pts
4th	MEGUMI TADOKORO	88pts
5th	Miyoko Hojo	87pts
5th	Isami Aldini	87pts
7th	Yuki Yoshino	86pts
8th	Nao Sadatsuka	84pts

*The top four in each block advance to the Finals.

Food Wars! SHOKUGEKI NO SOMA

8

Table of Contents

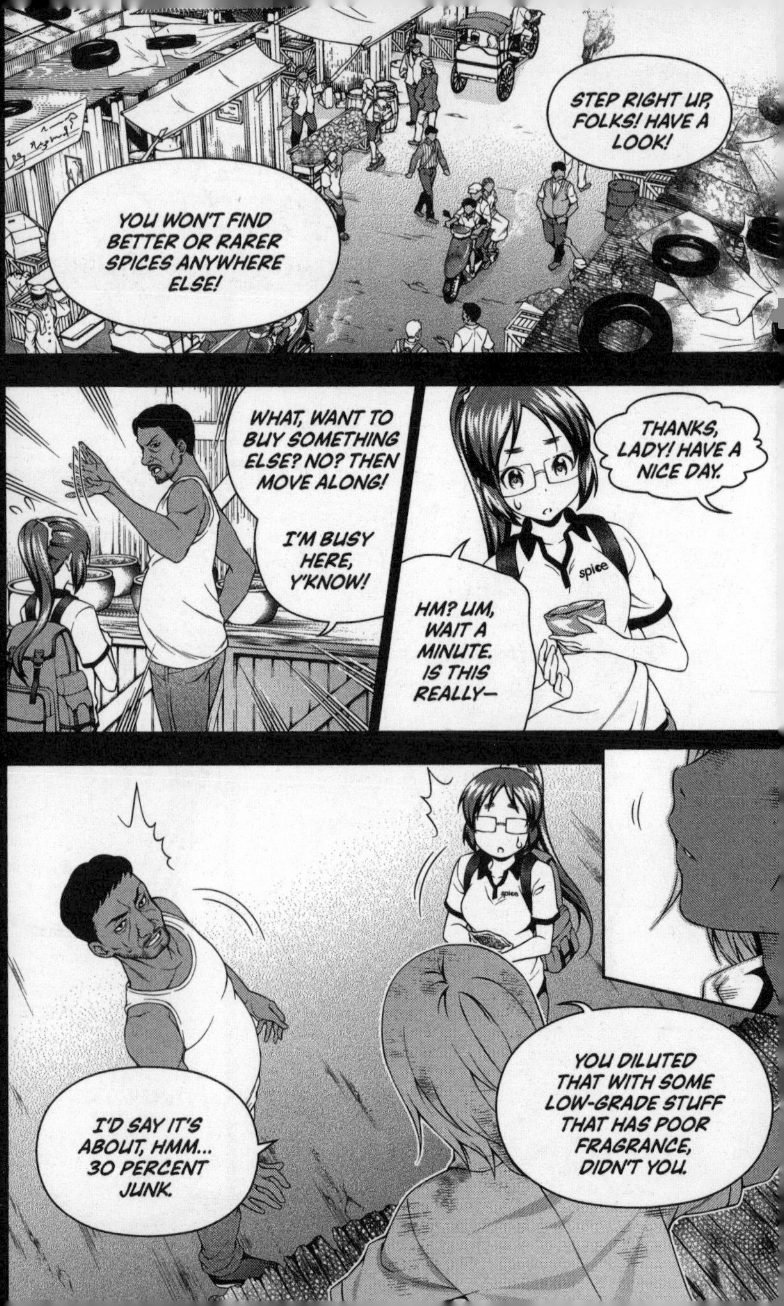
STEP RIGHT UP, FOLKS! HAVE A LOOK!
YOU WON'T FIND BETTER OR RARER SPICES ANYWHERE ELSE!
THANKS, LADY! HAVE A NICE DAY.
HM? UM, WAIT A MINUTE. IS THIS REALLY—
WHAT, WANT TO BUY SOMETHING ELSE? NO? THEN MOVE ALONG!
I'M BUSY HERE, Y'KNOW!
YOU DILUTED THAT WITH SOME LOW-GRADE STUFF THAT HAS POOR FRAGRANCE, DIDN'T YOU.
I'D SAY IT'S ABOUT, HMM... 30 PERCENT JUNK.

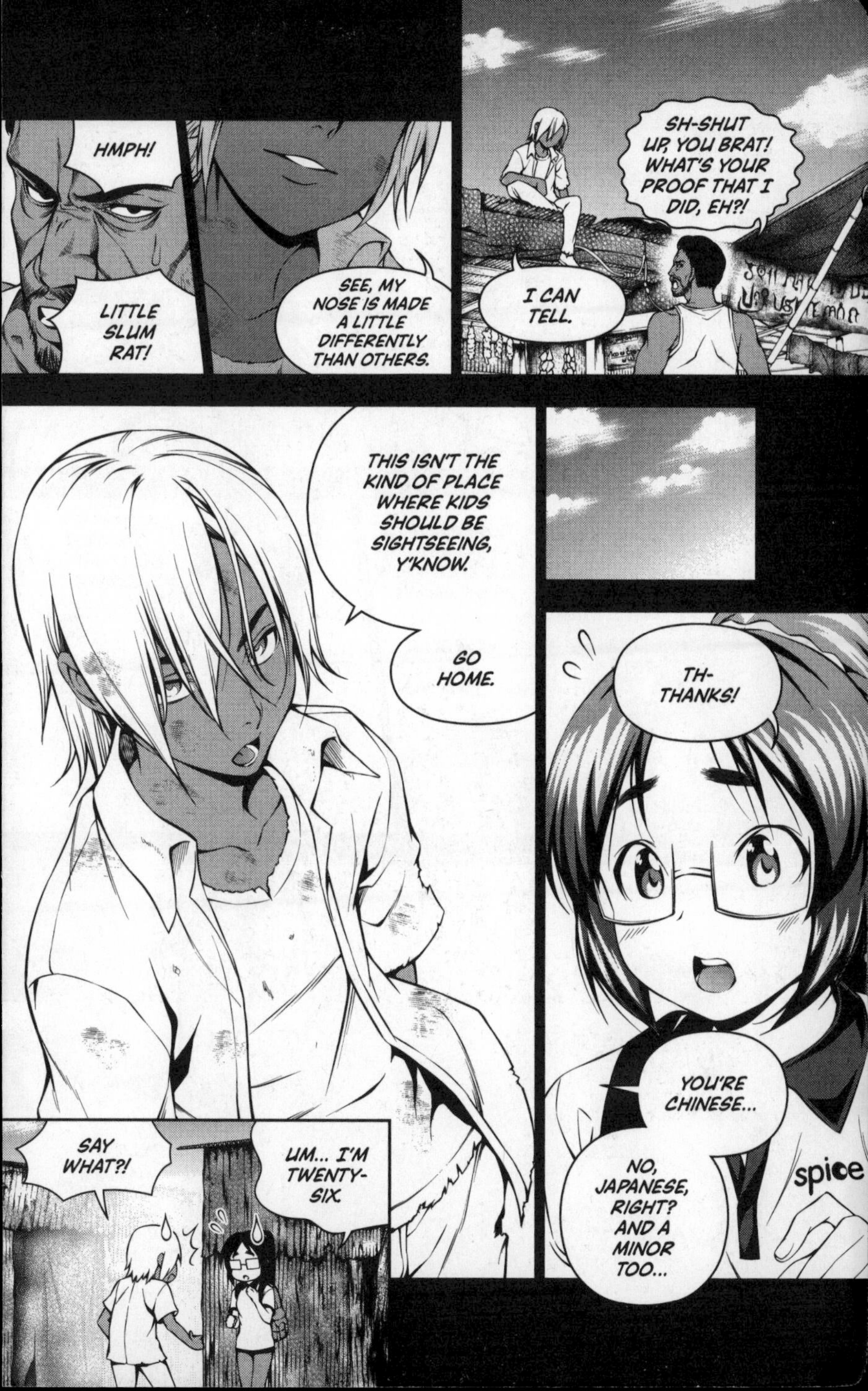
SH-SHUT UP, YOU BRAT! WHAT'S YOUR PROOF THAT I DID, EH?!
I CAN TELL.
SEE, MY NOSE IS MADE A LITTLE DIFFERENTLY THAN OTHERS.
HMPH!
LITTLE SLUM RAT!
TH-THANKS!
YOU'RE CHINESE...
NO, JAPANESE, RIGHT? AND A MINOR TOO...
spice
THIS ISN'T THE KIND OF PLACE WHERE KIDS SHOULD BE SIGHTSEEING, Y'KNOW.
GO HOME.
UM... I'M TWENTY-SIX.
SAY WHAT?!

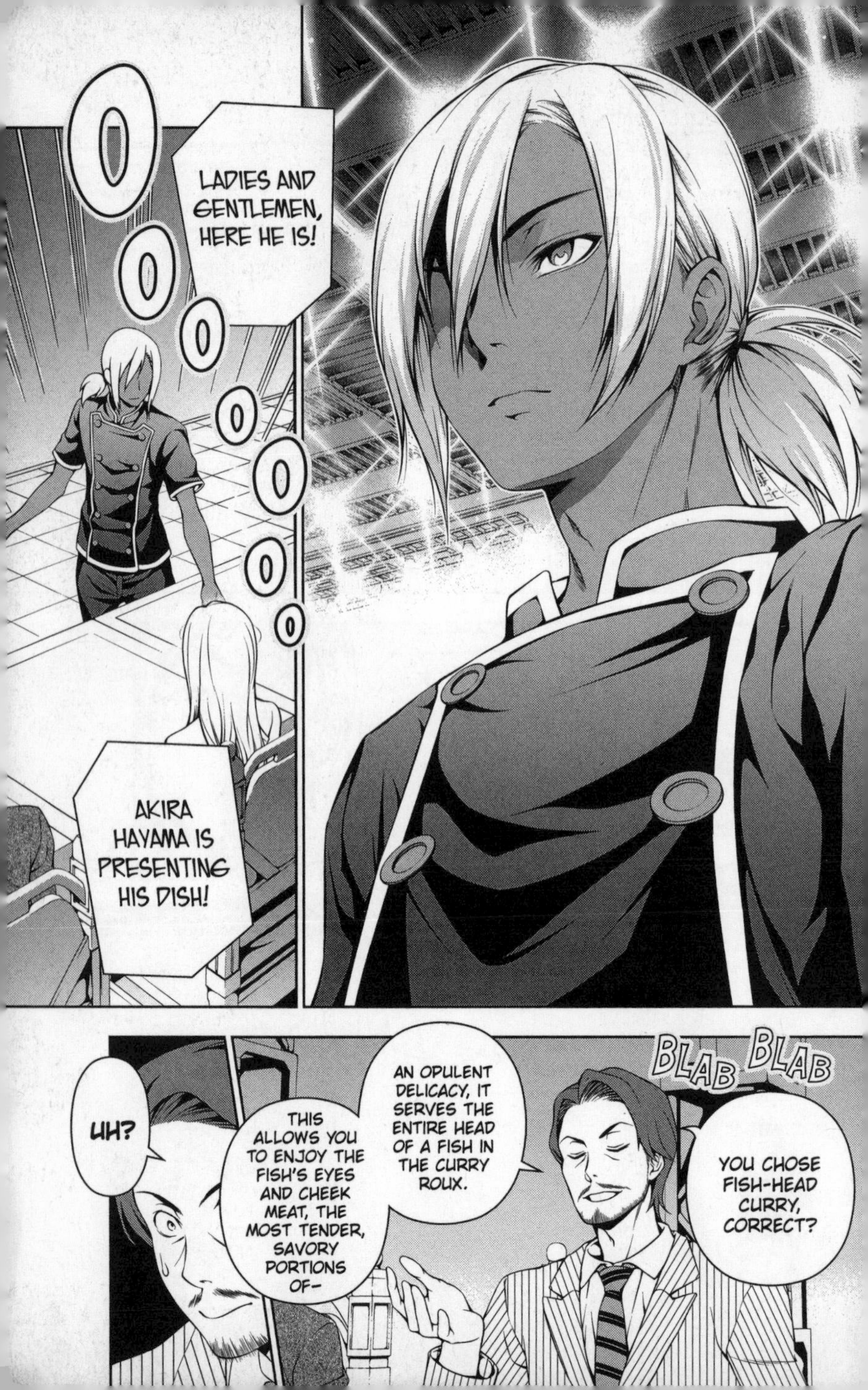

OOOOOOOO
LADIES AND GENTLEMEN, HERE HE IS!
AKIRA HAYAMA IS PRESENTING HIS DISH!
BLAB BLAB
YOU CHOSE FISH-HEAD CURRY, CORRECT?
AN OPULENT DELICACY, IT SERVES THE ENTIRE HEAD OF A FISH IN THE CURRY ROUX.
THIS ALLOWS YOU TO ENJOY THE FISH'S EYES AND CHEEK MEAT, THE MOST TENDER, SAVORY PORTIONS OF-
UH?

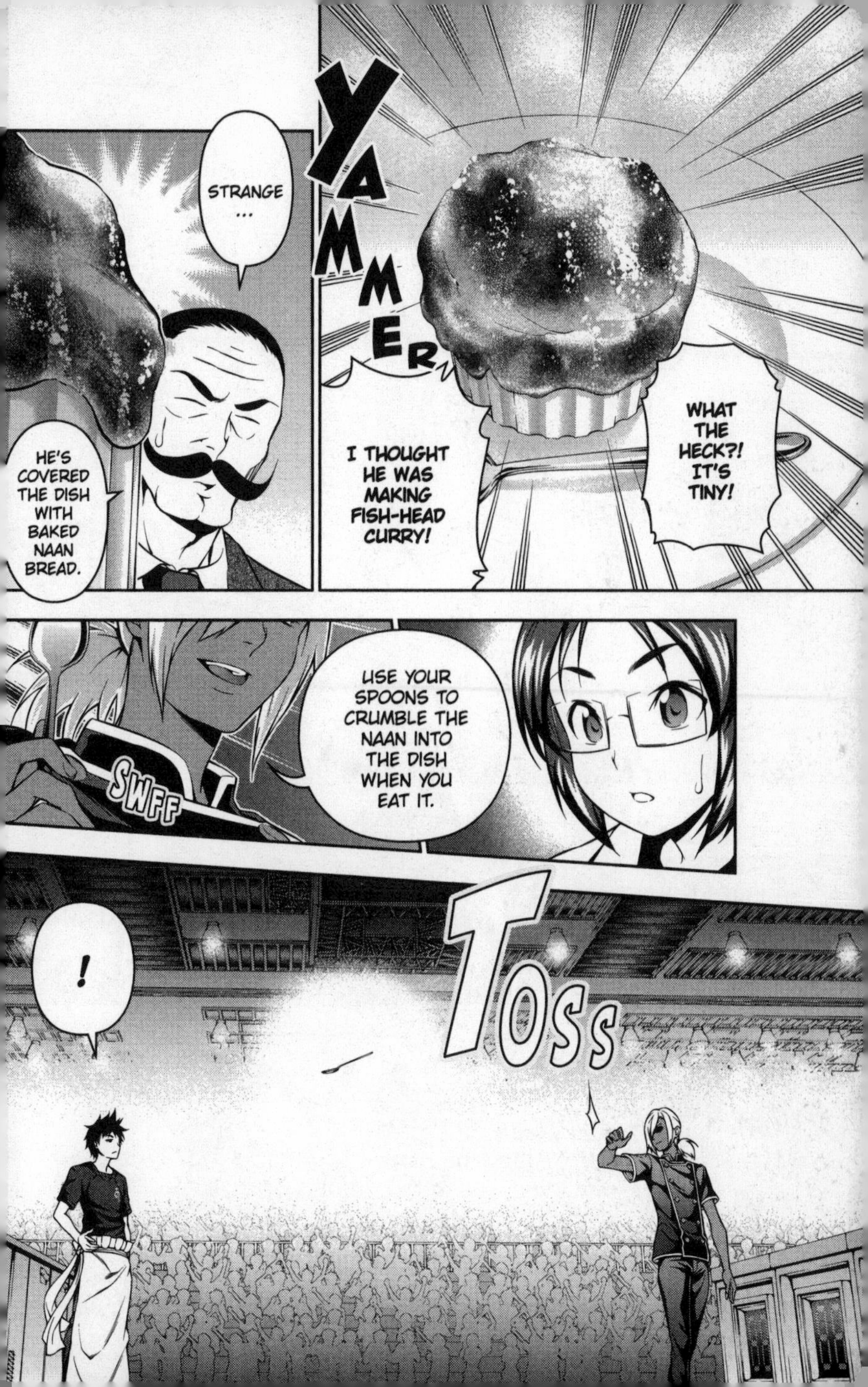
YAMMER
WHAT THE HECK?! IT'S TINY!
I THOUGHT HE WAS MAKING FISH-HEAD CURRY!
STRANGE ...
HE'S COVERED THE DISH WITH BAKED NAAN BREAD.
USE YOUR SPOONS TO CRUMBLE THE NAAN INTO THE DISH WHEN YOU EAT IT.
SWFF
TOSS
!

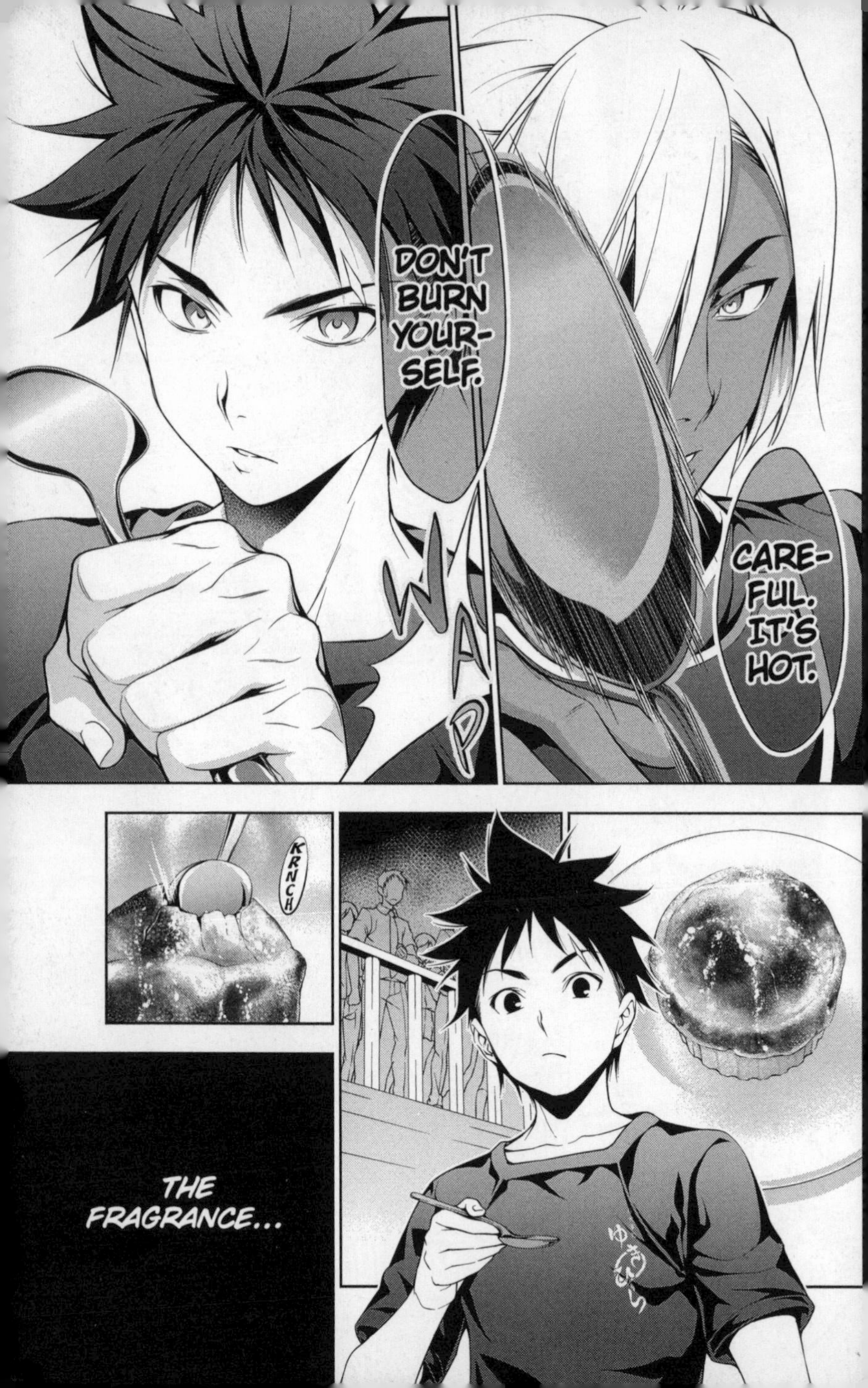
DON'T BURN YOUR-SELF.
CARE-FUL. IT'S HOT.
WAP
KRNCH
THE FRAGRANCE...

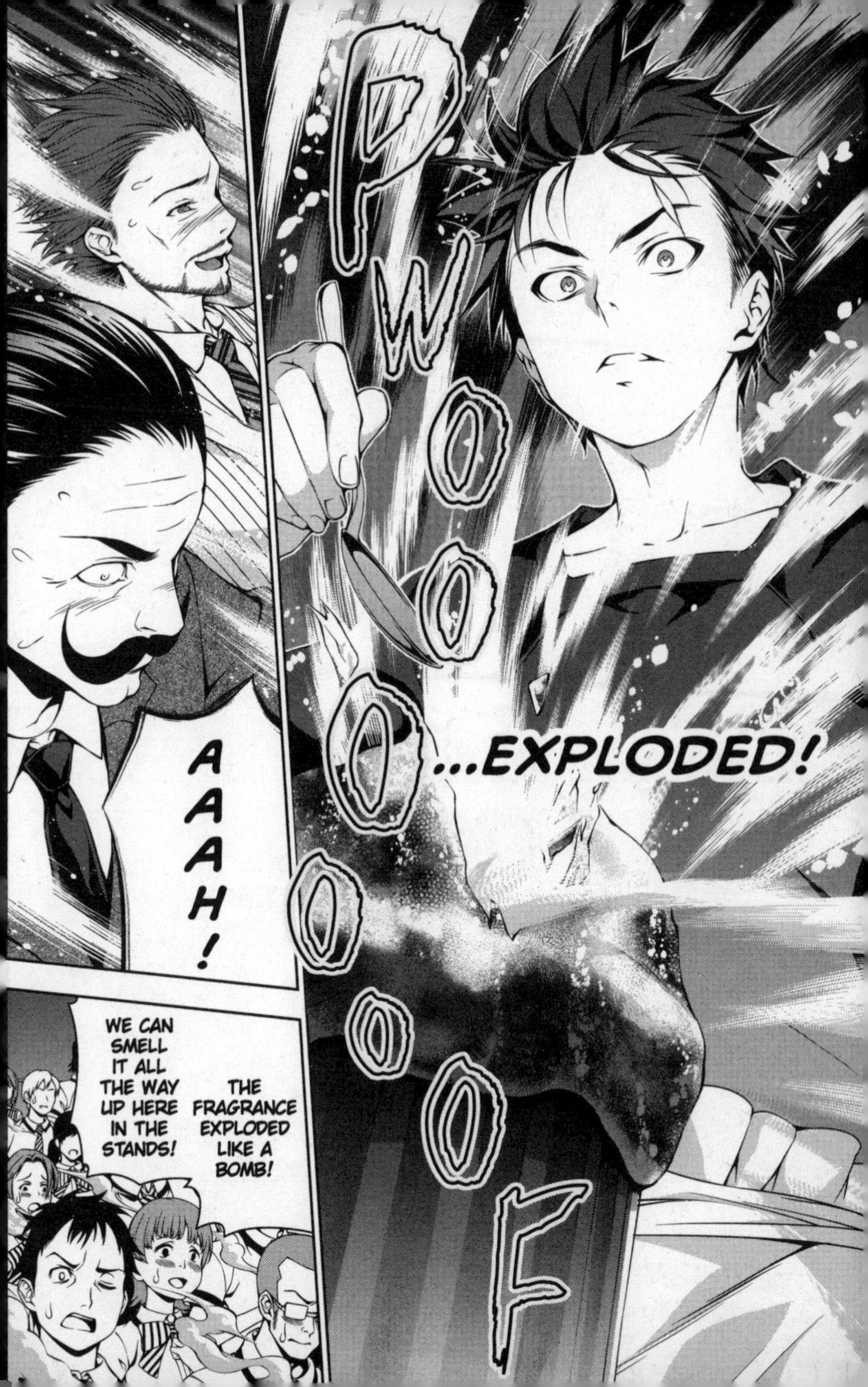
POWOOOOOOOOF
...EXPLODED!
AAAAH!
THE FRAGRANCE EXPLODED LIKE A BOMB!
WE CAN SMELL IT ALL THE WAY UP HERE IN THE STANDS!

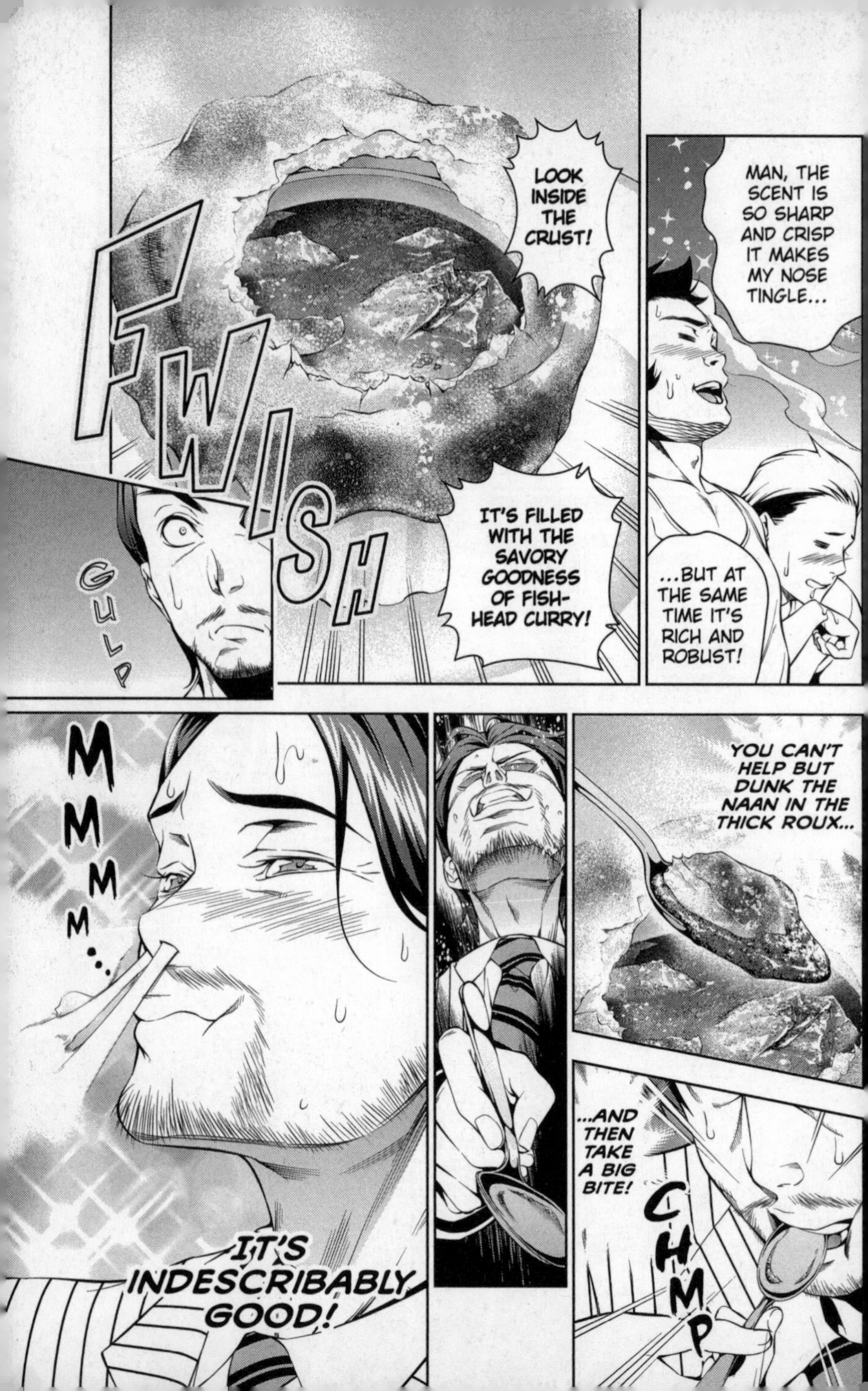
MAN, THE SCENT IS SO SHARP AND CRISP IT MAKES MY NOSE TINGLE...
...BUT AT THE SAME TIME IT'S RICH AND ROBUST!
LOOK INSIDE THE CRUST!
FWISH
IT'S FILLED WITH THE SAVORY GOODNESS OF FISH-HEAD CURRY!
GULP
YOU CAN'T HELP BUT DUNK THE NAAN IN THE THICK ROUX...
...AND THEN TAKE A BIG BITE!
CHMP
MMMM...
IT'S INDESCRIBABLY GOOD!

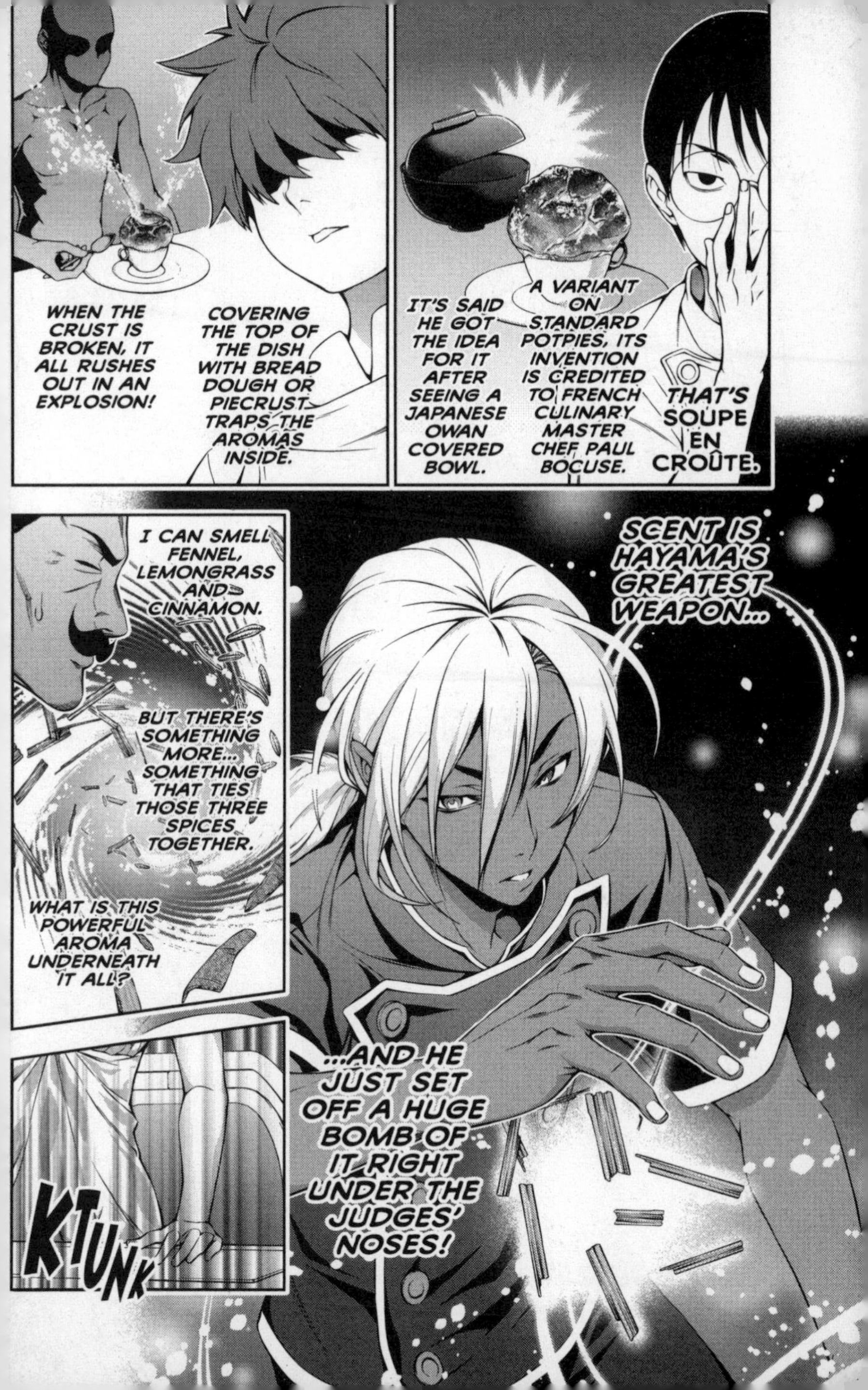
THAT'S SOUPE EN CROÛTE.
A VARIANT ON STANDARD POTPIES, ITS INVENTION IS CREDITED TO FRENCH CULINARY MASTER CHEF PAUL BOCUSE.
IT'S SAID HE GOT THE IDEA FOR IT AFTER SEEING A JAPANESE OWAN COVERED BOWL.
COVERING THE TOP OF THE DISH WITH BREAD DOUGH OR PIECRUST TRAPS THE AROMAS INSIDE.
WHEN THE CRUST IS BROKEN, IT ALL RUSHES OUT IN AN EXPLOSION!
SCENT IS HAYAMA'S GREATEST WEAPON...
...AND HE JUST SET OFF A HUGE BOMB OF IT RIGHT UNDER THE JUDGES' NOSES!
I CAN SMELL FENNEL, LEMONGRASS AND CINNAMON.
BUT THERE'S SOMETHING MORE... SOMETHING THAT TIES THOSE THREE SPICES TOGETHER.
WHAT IS THIS POWERFUL AROMA UNDERNEATH IT ALL?
KTUNK

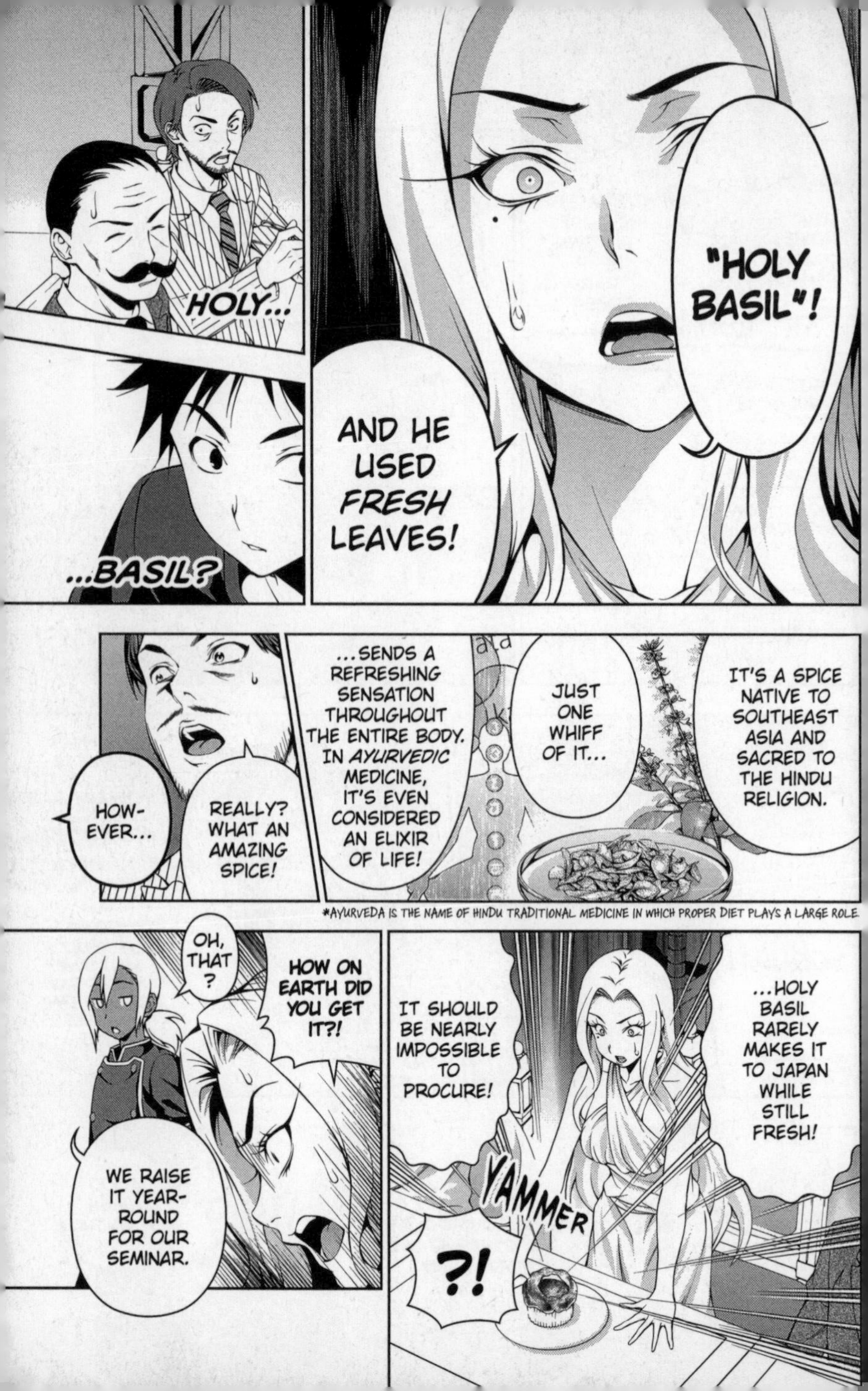
"HOLY BASIL"!
AND HE USED FRESH LEAVES!
HOLY...
...BASIL?
IT'S A SPICE NATIVE TO SOUTHEAST ASIA AND SACRED TO THE HINDU RELIGION.
JUST ONE WHIFF OF IT...
...SENDS A REFRESHING SENSATION THROUGHOUT THE ENTIRE BODY. IN AYURVEDIC MEDICINE, IT'S EVEN CONSIDERED AN ELIXIR OF LIFE!
REALLY? WHAT AN AMAZING SPICE!
HOW-EVER...
...HOLY BASIL RARELY MAKES IT TO JAPAN WHILE STILL FRESH!
IT SHOULD BE NEARLY IMPOSSIBLE TO PROCURE!
YAMMER
?!
HOW ON EARTH DID YOU GET IT?!
OH, THAT?
WE RAISE IT YEAR-ROUND FOR OUR SEMINAR.

*AYURVEDA IS THE NAME OF HINDU TRADITIONAL MEDICINE IN WHICH PROPER DIET PLAYS A LARGE ROLE.

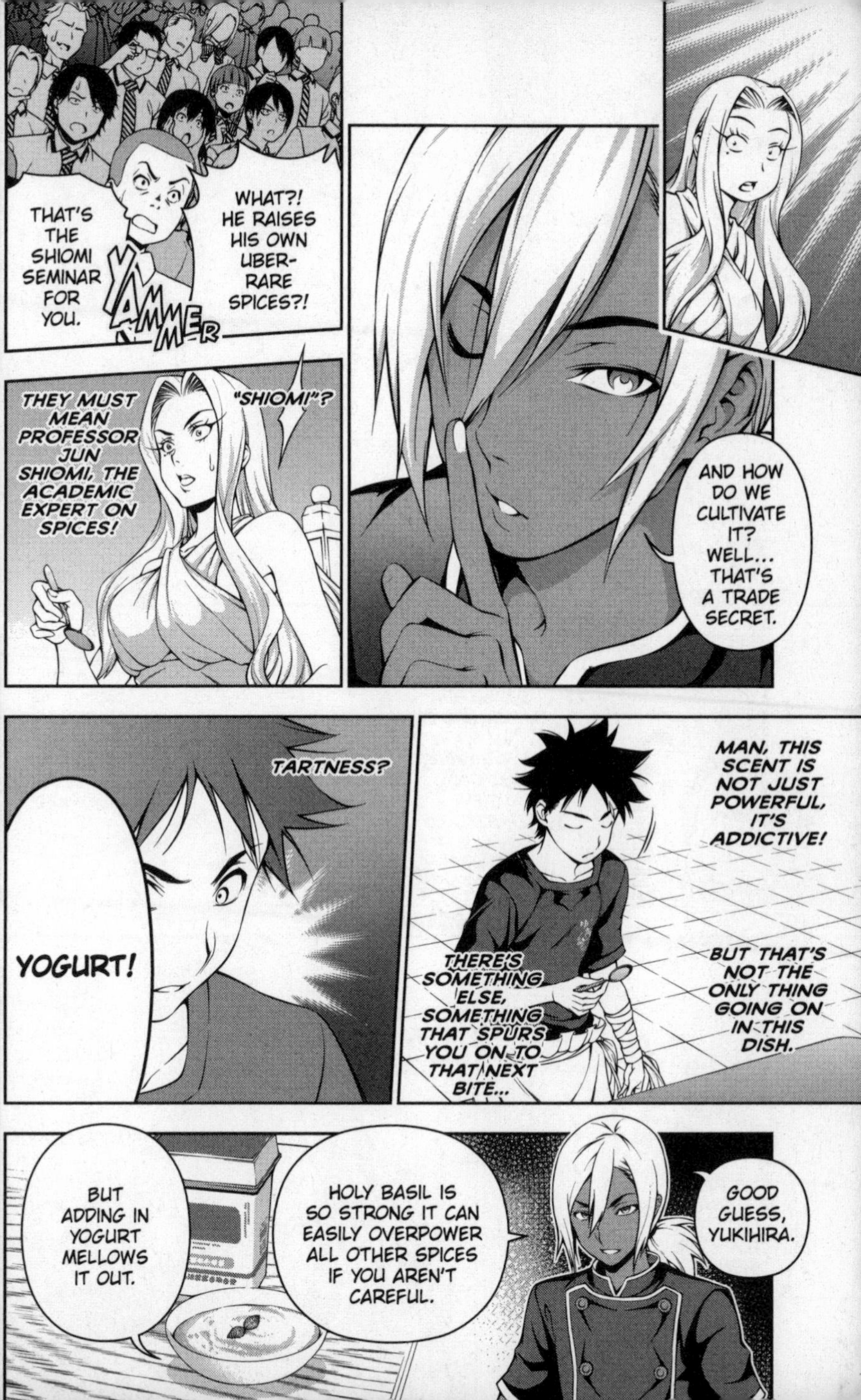
AND HOW DO WE CULTIVATE IT? WELL... THAT'S A TRADE SECRET.
WHAT?! HE RAISES HIS OWN UBER-RARE SPICES?!
YAMMER YAMMER
THAT'S THE SHIOMI SEMINAR FOR YOU.
"SHIOMI"?
THEY MUST MEAN PROFESSOR JUN SHIOMI, THE ACADEMIC EXPERT ON SPICES!
MAN, THIS SCENT IS NOT JUST POWERFUL, IT'S ADDICTIVE!
BUT THAT'S NOT THE ONLY THING GOING ON IN THIS DISH.
THERE'S SOMETHING ELSE, SOMETHING THAT SPURS YOU ON TO THAT NEXT BITE...
TARTNESS?
YOGURT!
GOOD GUESS, YUKIHIRA.
HOLY BASIL IS SO STRONG IT CAN EASILY OVERPOWER ALL OTHER SPICES IF YOU AREN'T CAREFUL.
BUT ADDING IN YOGURT MELLOWS IT OUT.

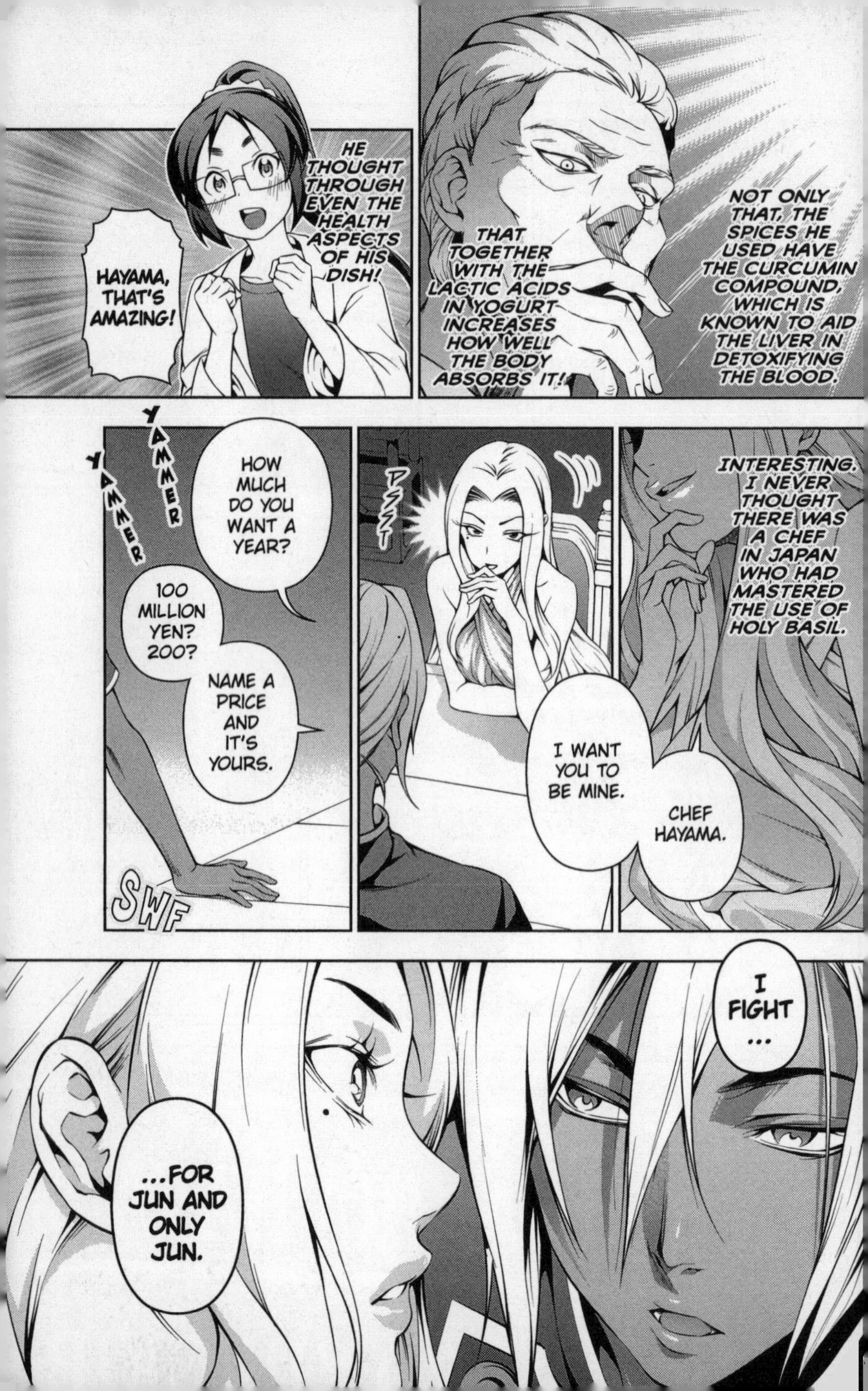
NOT ONLY THAT, THE SPICES HE USED HAVE THE CURCUMIN COMPOUND, WHICH IS KNOWN TO AID THE LIVER IN DETOXIFYING THE BLOOD.
THAT TOGETHER WITH THE LACTIC ACIDS IN YOGURT INCREASES HOW WELL THE BODY ABSORBS IT!
HE THOUGHT THROUGH EVEN THE HEALTH ASPECTS OF HIS DISH!
HAYAMA, THAT'S AMAZING!
INTERESTING. I NEVER THOUGHT THERE WAS A CHEF IN JAPAN WHO HAD MASTERED THE USE OF HOLY BASIL.
I WANT YOU TO BE MINE.
CHEF HAYAMA.
PSST
YAMMER
YAMMER
HOW MUCH DO YOU WANT A YEAR?
100 MILLION YEN? 200?
NAME A PRICE AND IT'S YOURS.
SWF
I FIGHT...
...FOR JUN AND ONLY JUN.

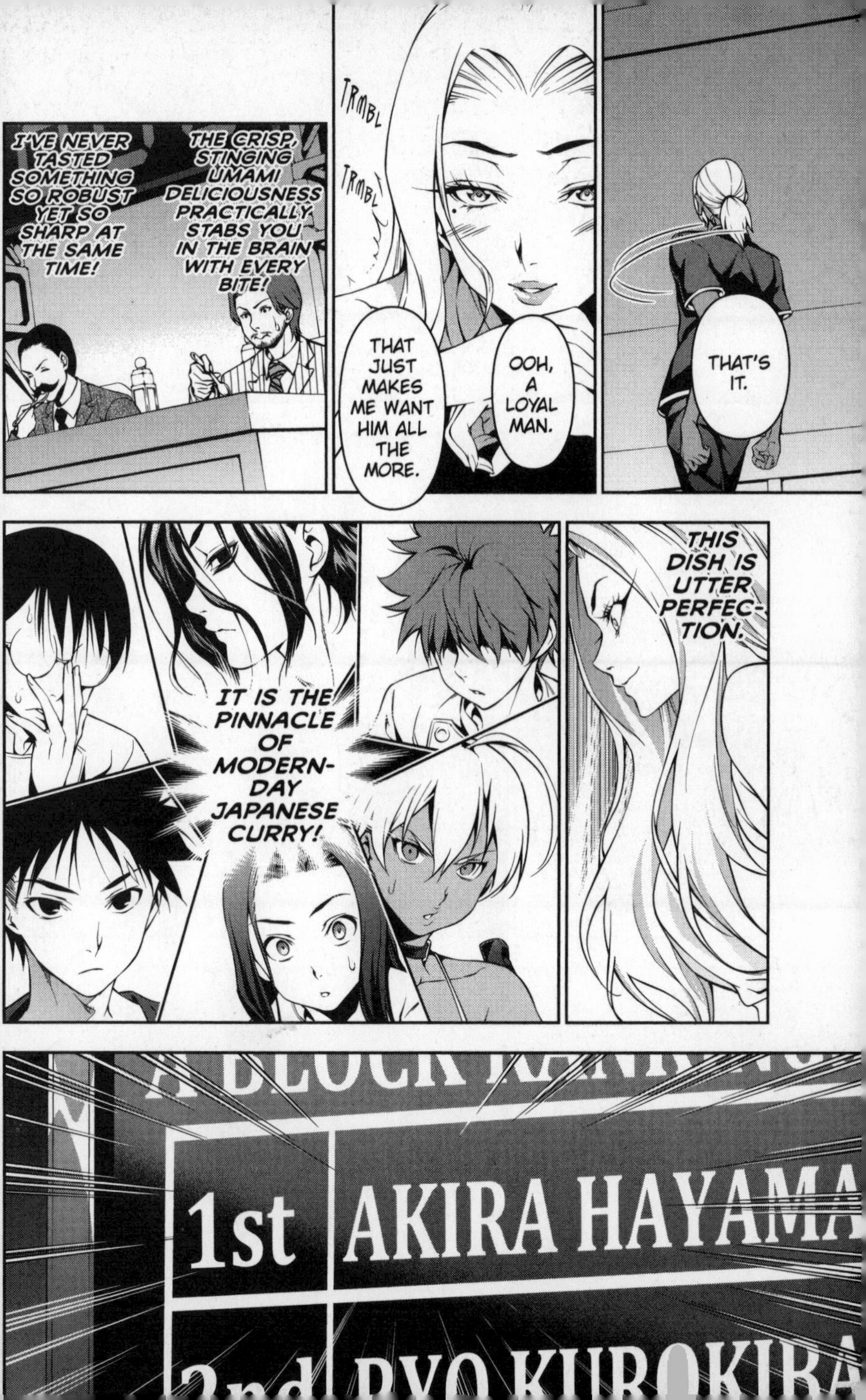
THAT'S IT.
TRMBL
TRMBL
OOH, A LOYAL MAN.
THAT JUST MAKES ME WANT HIM ALL THE MORE.
THE CRISP, STINGING UMAMI DELICIOUSNESS PRACTICALLY STABS YOU IN THE BRAIN WITH EVERY BITE!
I'VE NEVER TASTED SOMETHING SO ROBUST YET SO SHARP AT THE SAME TIME!
THIS DISH IS UTTER PERFEC-TION.
IT IS THE PINNACLE OF MODERN-DAY JAPANESE CURRY!
1st
AKIRA HAYAMA

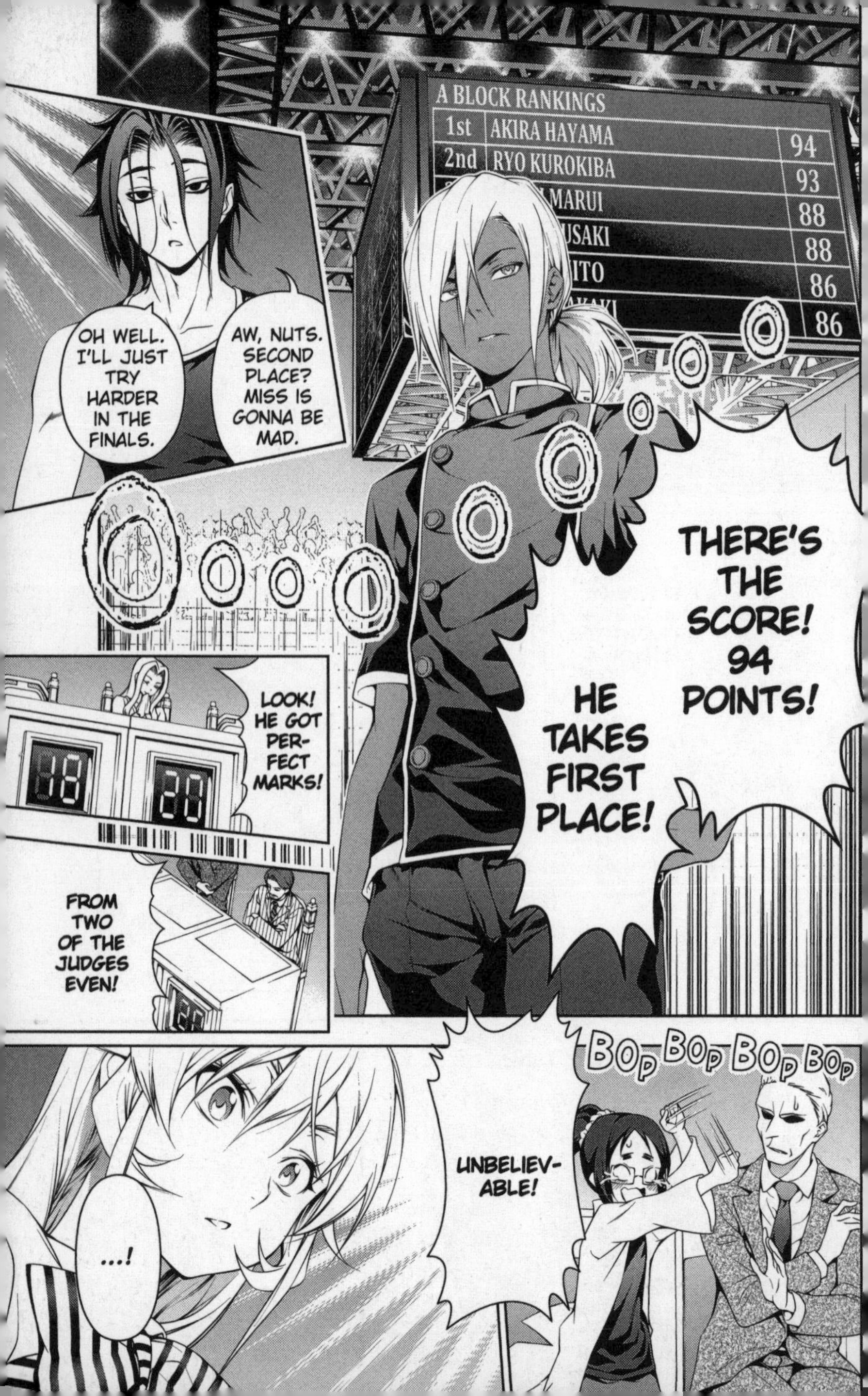
A BLOCK RANKINGS
1st AKIRA HAYAMA 94
2nd RYO KUROKIBA 93
THERE'S THE SCORE! 94 POINTS!
HE TAKES FIRST PLACE!
AW, NUTS. SECOND PLACE? MISS IS GONNA BE MAD.
OH WELL. I'LL JUST TRY HARDER IN THE FINALS.
LOOK! HE GOT PERFECT MARKS!
FROM TWO OF THE JUDGES EVEN!
BOP BOP BOP BOP
UNBELIEV-ABLE!
...!

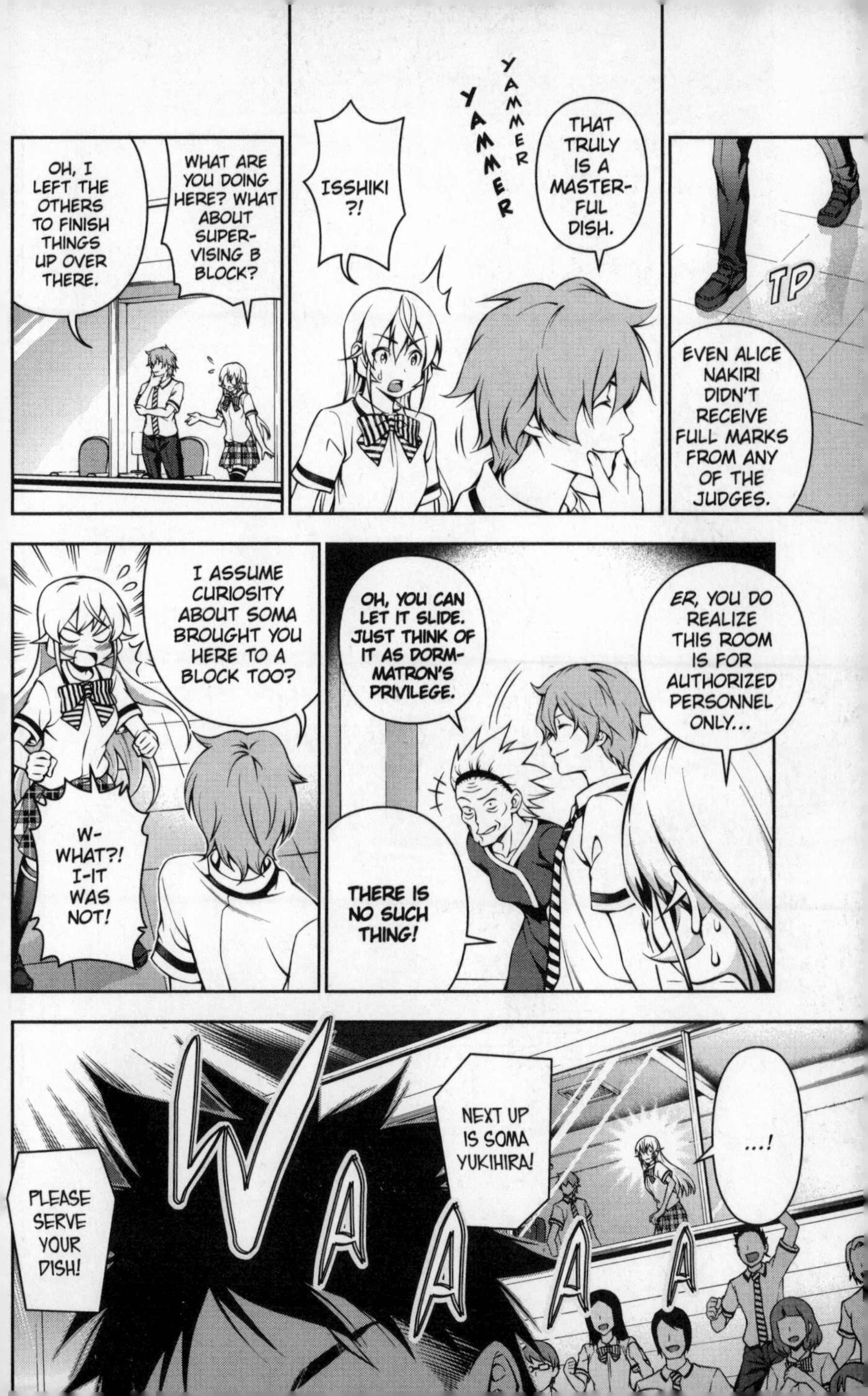
TP
EVEN ALICE NAKIRI DIDN'T RECEIVE FULL MARKS FROM ANY OF THE JUDGES.
THAT TRULY IS A MASTER-FUL DISH.
YAMMER YAMMER
ISSHIKI ?!
WHAT ARE YOU DOING HERE? WHAT ABOUT SUPER-VISING B BLOCK?
OH, I LEFT THE OTHERS TO FINISH THINGS UP OVER THERE.
ER, YOU DO REALIZE THIS ROOM IS FOR AUTHORIZED PERSONNEL ONLY...
OH, YOU CAN LET IT SLIDE. JUST THINK OF IT AS DORM-MATRON'S PRIVILEGE.
THERE IS NO SUCH THING!
I ASSUME CURIOSITY ABOUT SOMA BROUGHT YOU HERE TO A BLOCK TOO?
W-WHAT?! I-IT WAS NOT!
...!
NEXT UP IS SOMA YUKIHIRA!
WAAAAAA
PLEASE SERVE YOUR DISH!

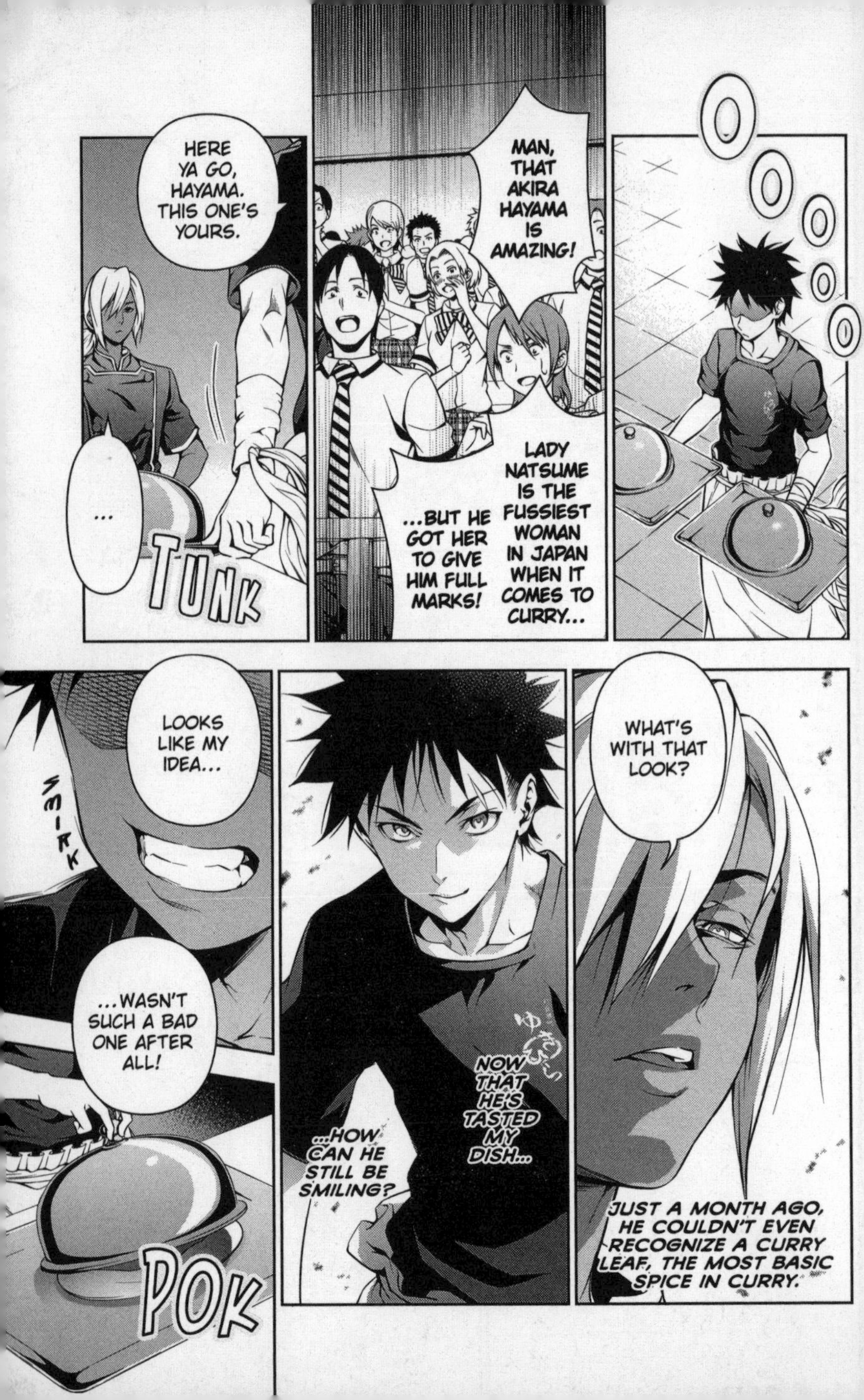
MAN, THAT AKIRA HAYAMA IS AMAZING!
LADY NATSUME IS THE FUSSIEST WOMAN IN JAPAN WHEN IT COMES TO CURRY...
...BUT HE GOT HER TO GIVE HIM FULL MARKS!
HERE YA GO, HAYAMA. THIS ONE'S YOURS.
...
TUNK
WHAT'S WITH THAT LOOK?
JUST A MONTH AGO, HE COULDN'T EVEN RECOGNIZE A CURRY LEAF, THE MOST BASIC SPICE IN CURRY.
NOW THAT HE'S TASTED MY DISH...
...HOW CAN HE STILL BE SMILING?
LOOKS LIKE MY IDEA...
SMIRK
...WASN'T SUCH A BAD ONE AFTER ALL!
POK

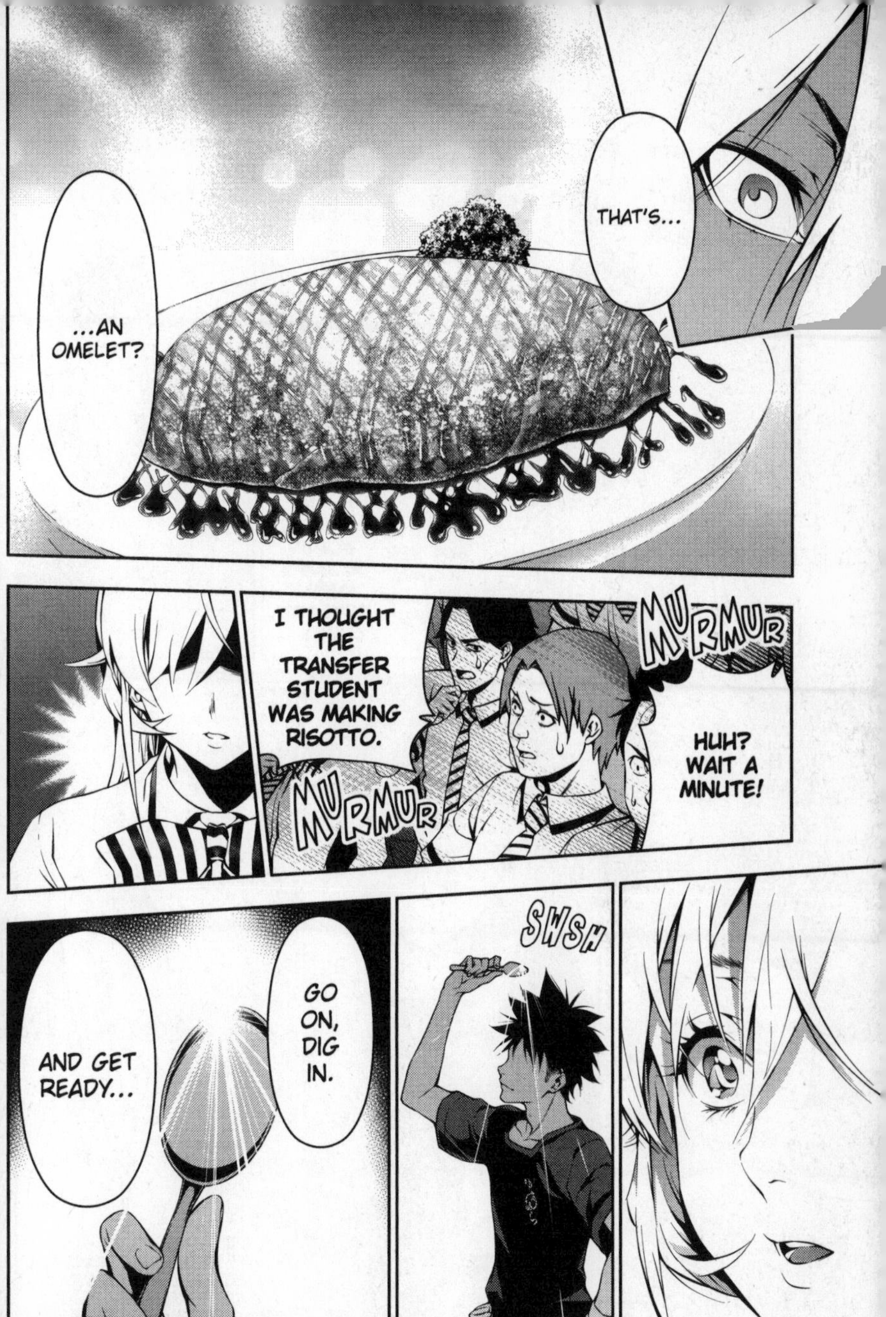
THAT'S...
...AN OMELET?
MURMUR
I THOUGHT THE TRANSFER STUDENT WAS MAKING RISOTTO.
HUH? WAIT A MINUTE!
MURMUR
SWSH
GO ON, DIG IN.
AND GET READY...

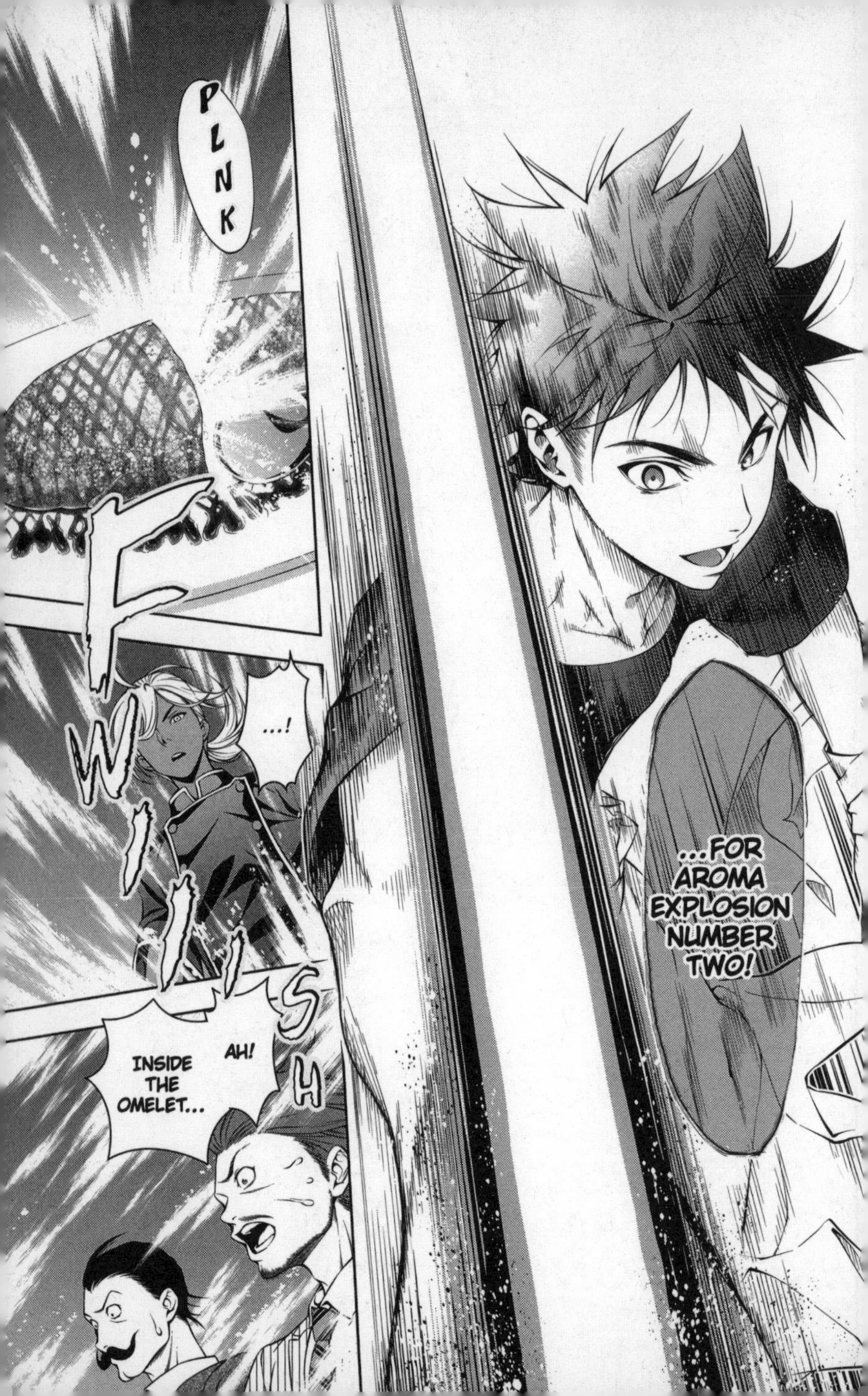

...FOR AROMA EXPLOSION NUMBER TWO!
PLNK
FWISH
...!
AH!
INSIDE THE OMELET...

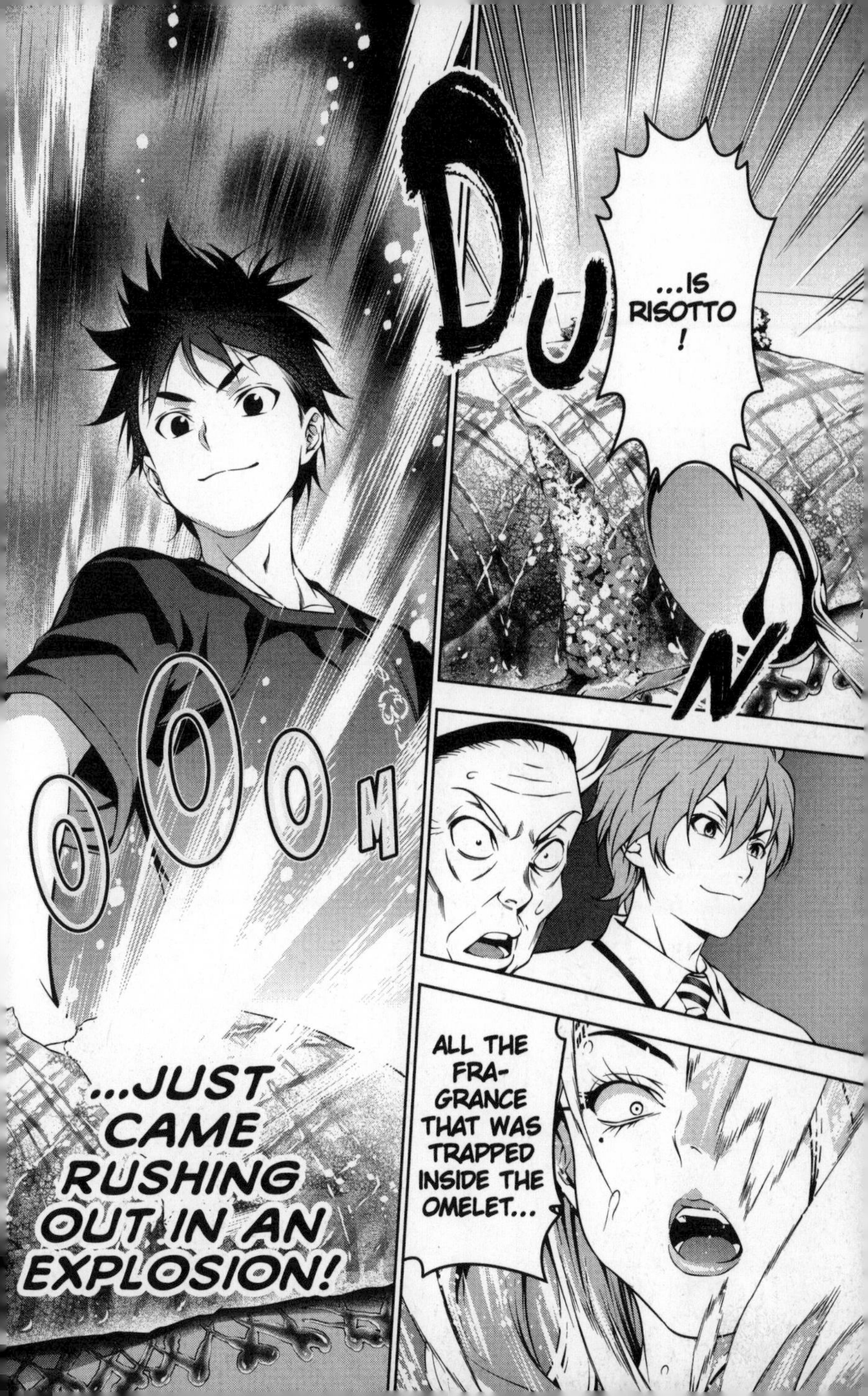
...IS RISOTTO!
DUN
ALL THE FRA-GRANCE THAT WAS TRAPPED INSIDE THE OMELET...
OOOOM
...JUST CAME RUSHING OUT IN AN EXPLOSION!

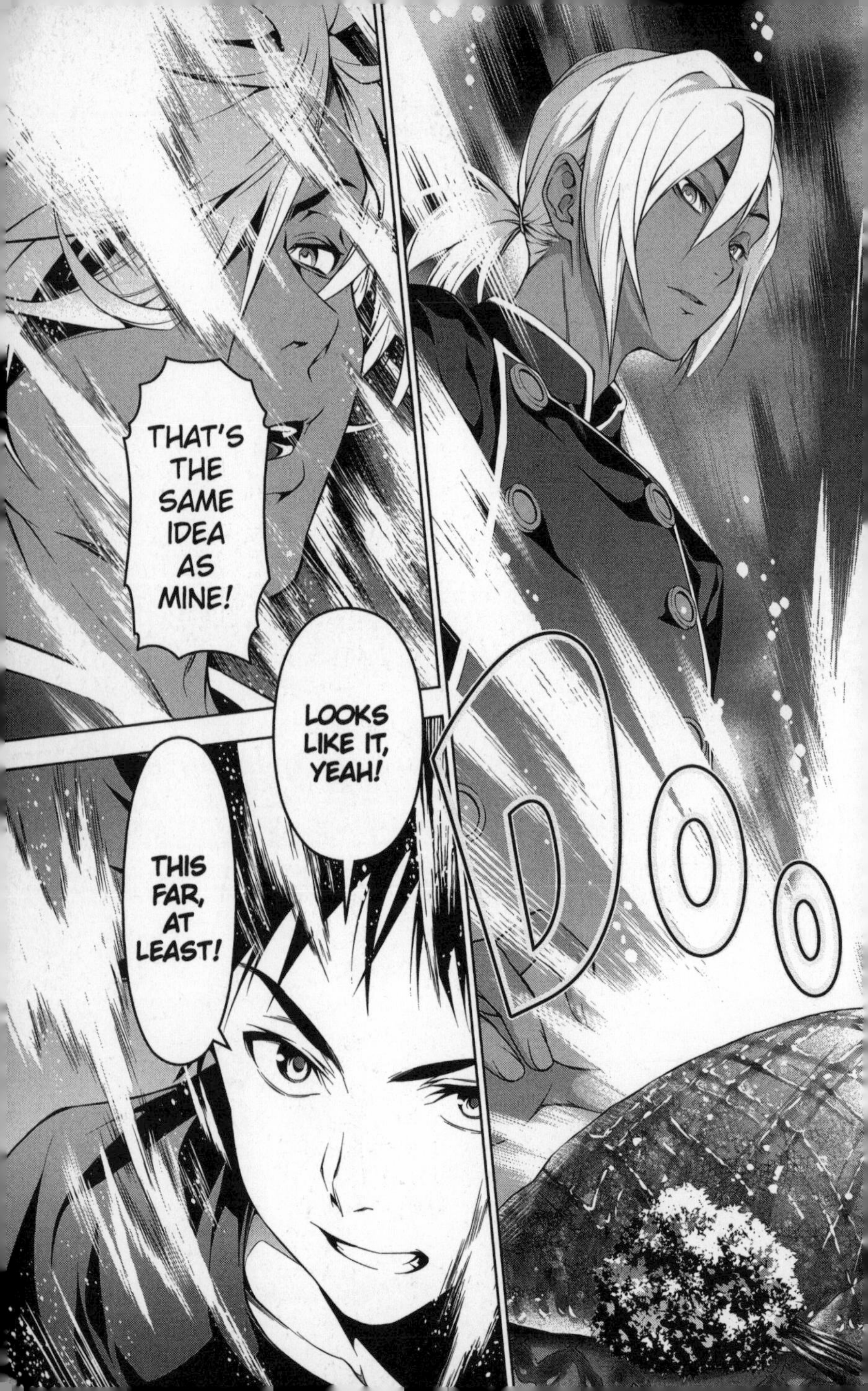
THAT'S THE SAME IDEA AS MINE!
LOOKS LIKE IT, YEAH!
THIS FAR, AT LEAST!
DOOO

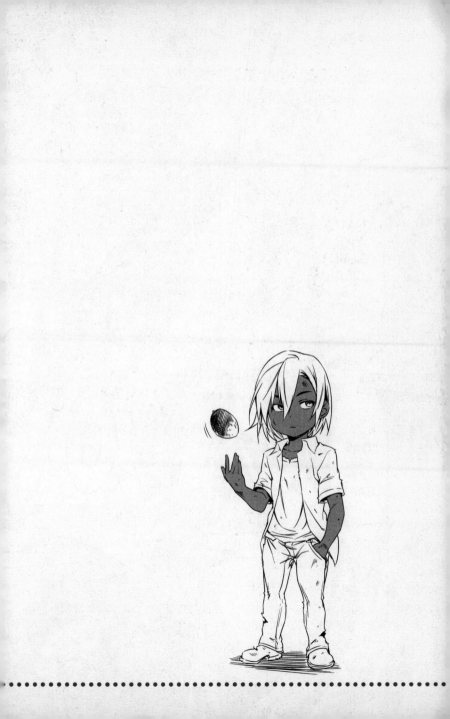

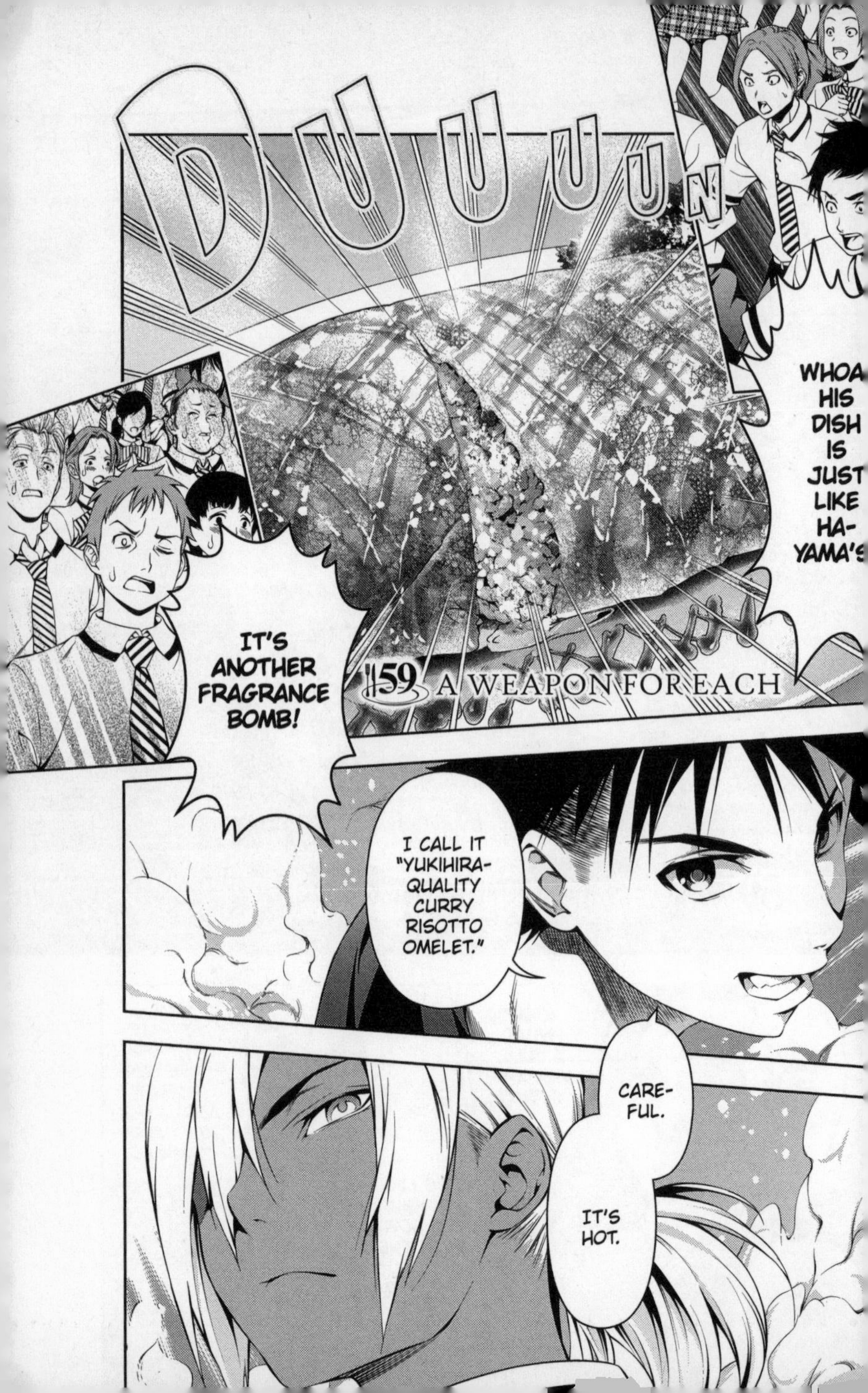
DUUUUN
WHOA HIS DISH IS JUST LIKE HA-YAMA'S
IT'S ANOTHER FRAGRANCE BOMB!
159 A WEAPON FOR EACH
I CALL IT "YUKIHIRA-QUALITY CURRY RISOTTO OMELET."
CARE-FUL.
IT'S HOT.

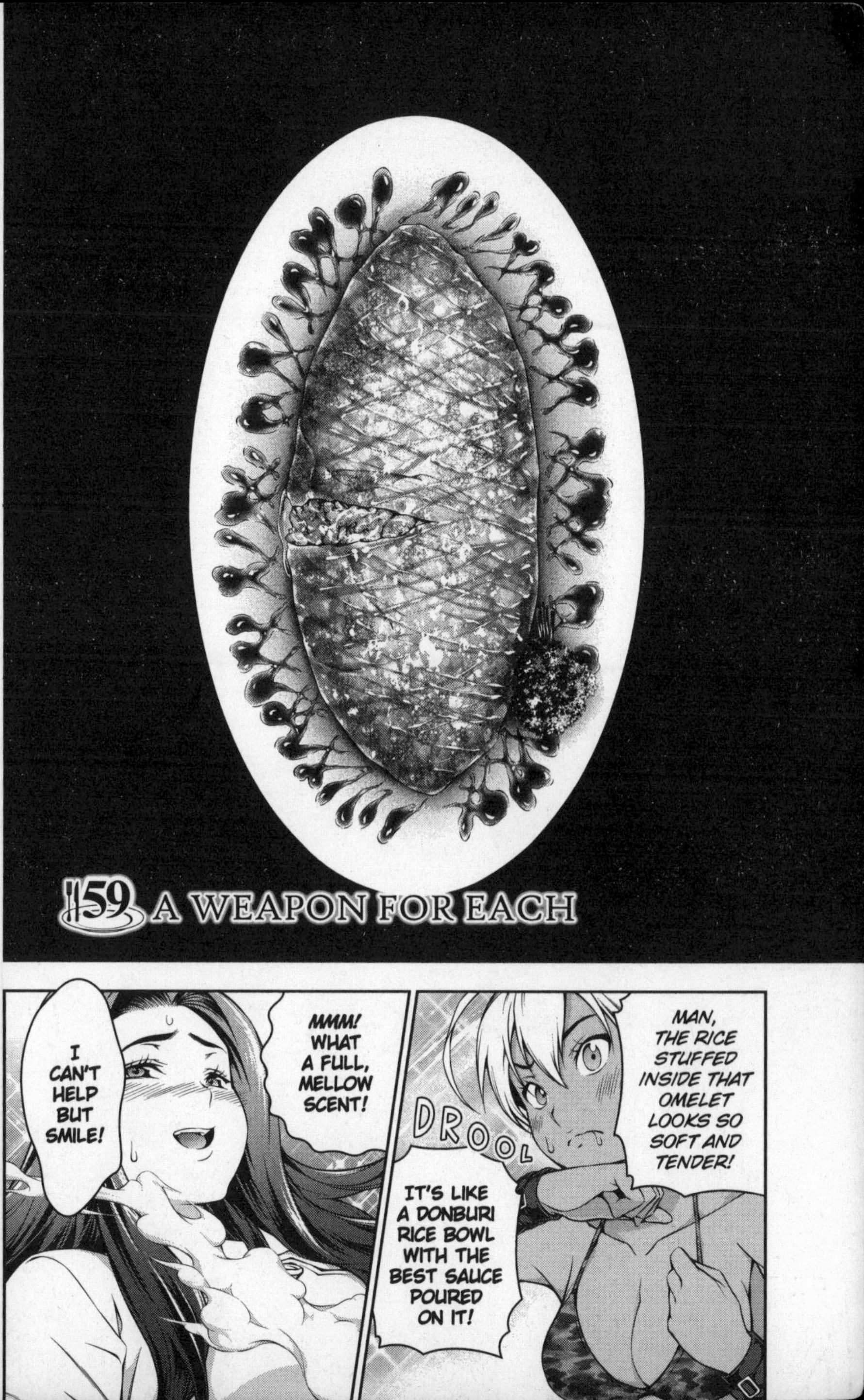
159 A WEAPON FOR EACH
MAN, THE RICE STUFFED INSIDE THAT OMELET LOOKS SO SOFT AND TENDER!
DROOL
IT'S LIKE A DONBURI RICE BOWL WITH THE BEST SAUCE POURED ON IT!
MMM! WHAT A FULL, MELLOW SCENT!
I CAN'T HELP BUT SMILE!

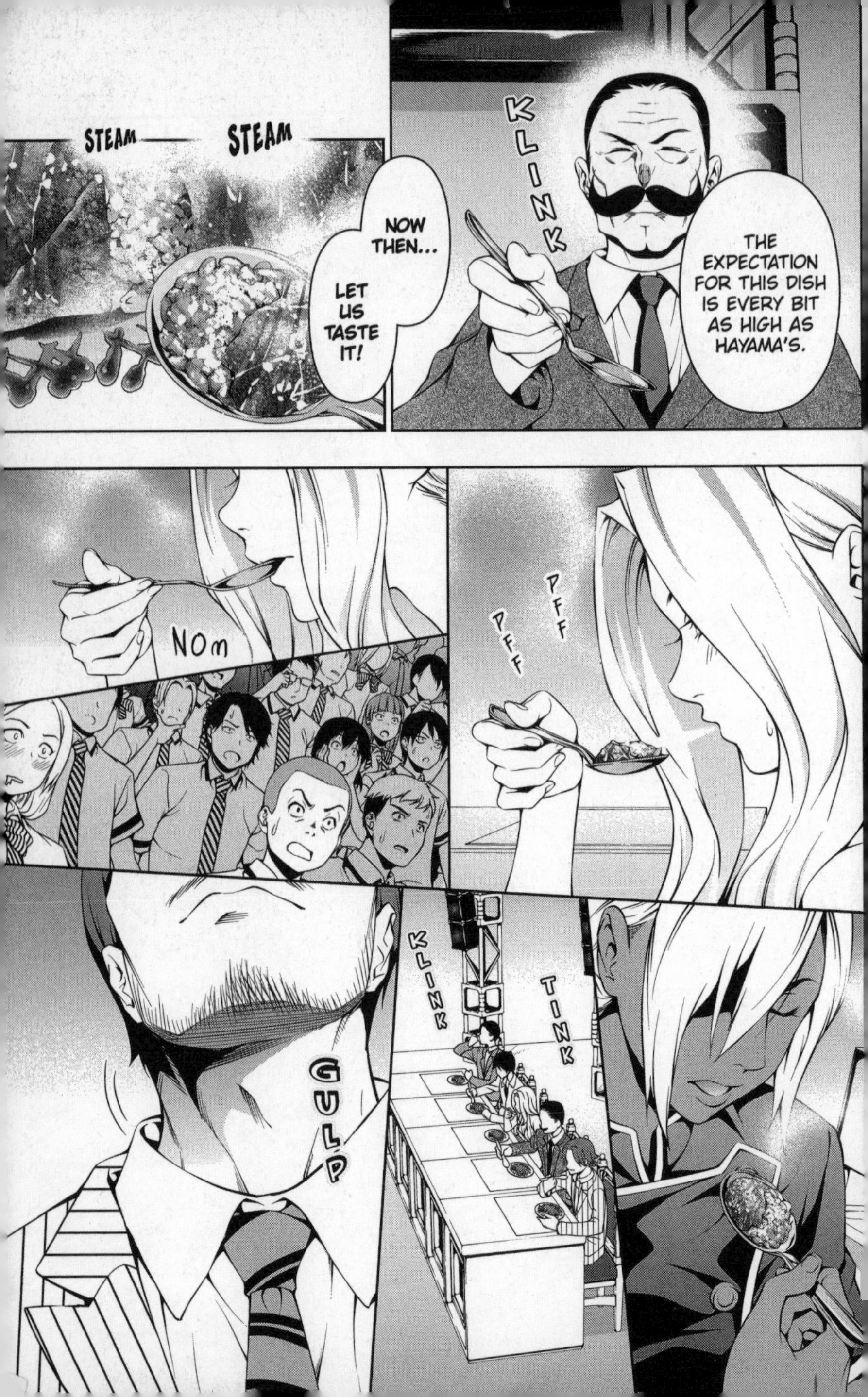
THE EXPECTATION FOR THIS DISH IS EVERY BIT AS HIGH AS HAYAMA'S.
KLINK
NOW THEN...
LET US TASTE IT!
STEAM
STEAM
PFF
PFF
NOM
TINK
KLINK
GULP

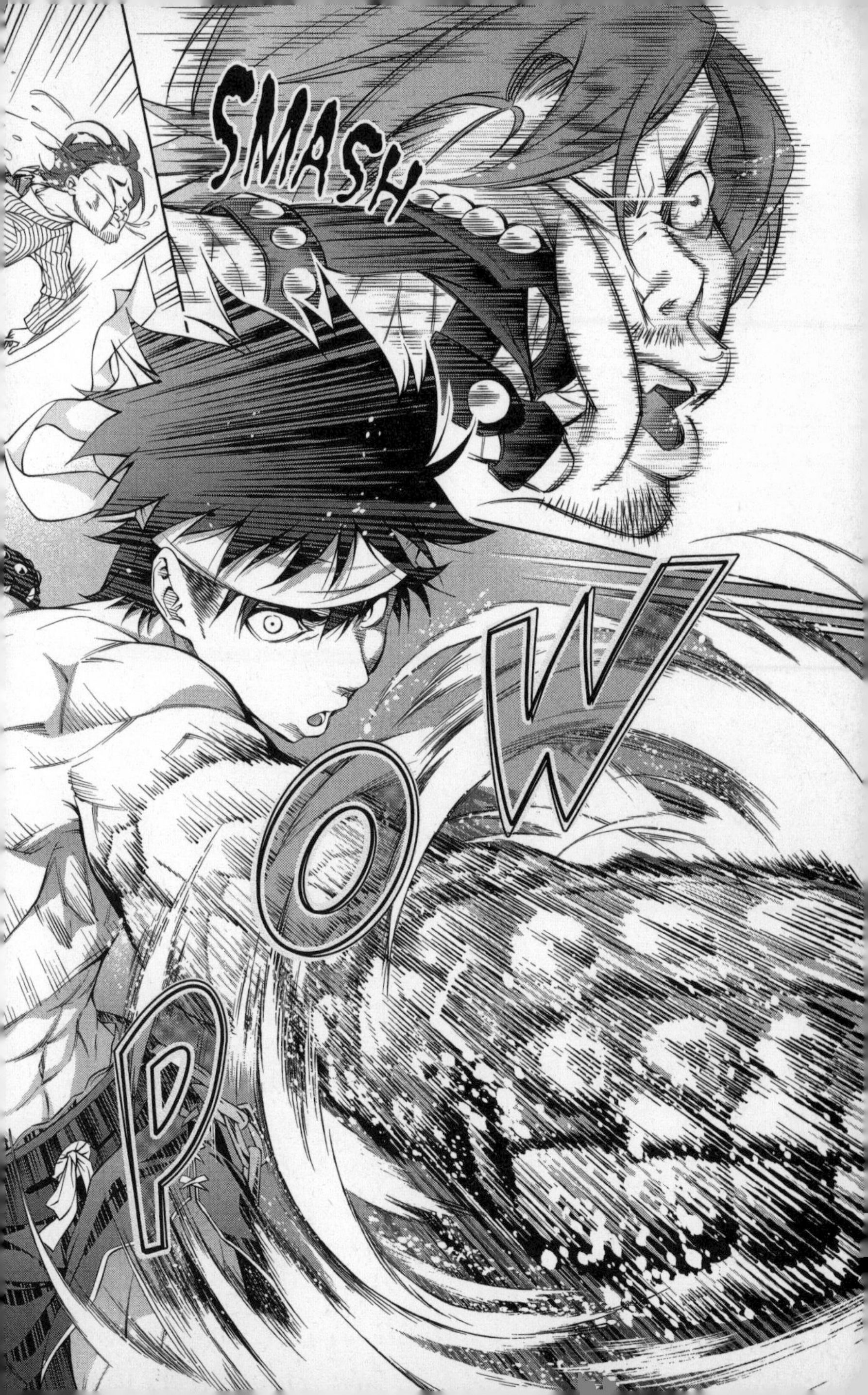
SMASH
POW

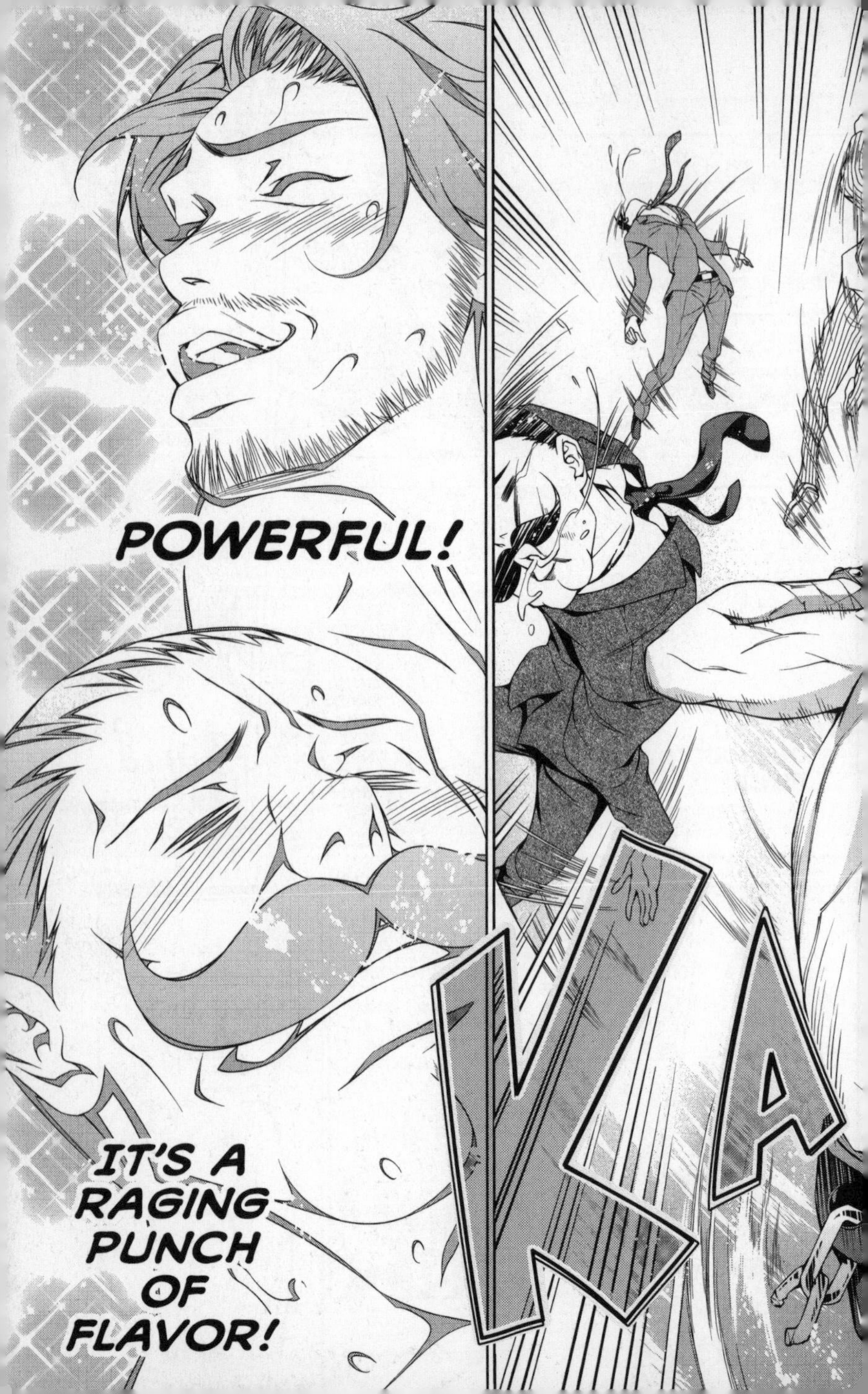
POWERFUL!
IT'S A RAGING PUNCH OF FLAVOR!

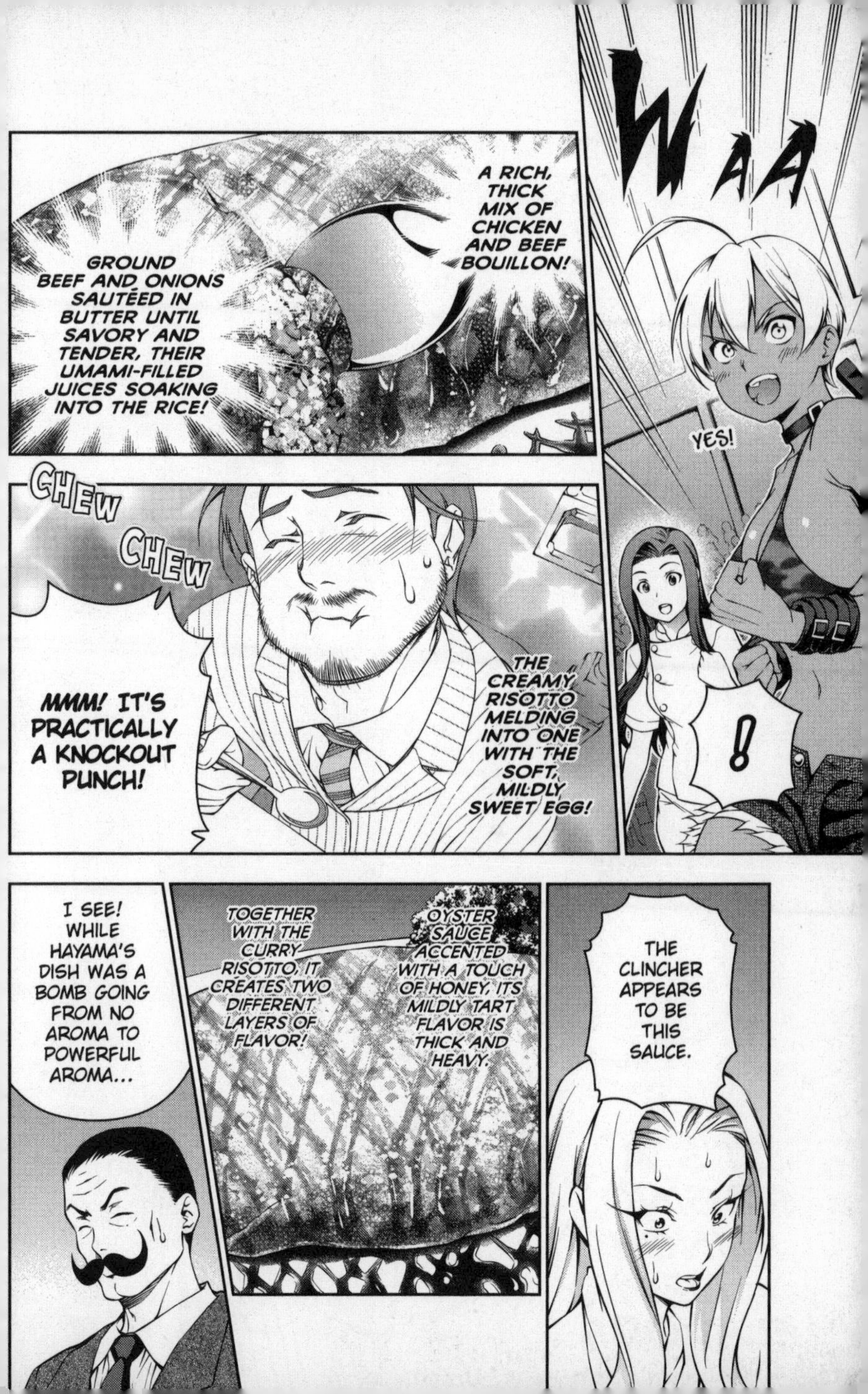
WAAA
YES!
!
A RICH, THICK MIX OF CHICKEN AND BEEF BOUILLON!
GROUND BEEF AND ONIONS SAUTÉED IN BUTTER UNTIL SAVORY AND TENDER, THEIR UMAMI-FILLED JUICES SOAKING INTO THE RICE!
CHEW CHEW
THE CREAMY RISOTTO MELDING INTO ONE WITH THE SOFT, MILDLY SWEET EGG!
MMM! IT'S PRACTICALLY A KNOCKOUT PUNCH!
THE CLINCHER APPEARS TO BE THIS SAUCE.
OYSTER SAUCE ACCENTED WITH A TOUCH OF HONEY, ITS MILDLY TART FLAVOR IS THICK AND HEAVY.
TOGETHER WITH THE CURRY RISOTTO, IT CREATES TWO DIFFERENT LAYERS OF FLAVOR!
I SEE! WHILE HAYAMA'S DISH WAS A BOMB GOING FROM NO AROMA TO POWERFUL AROMA...

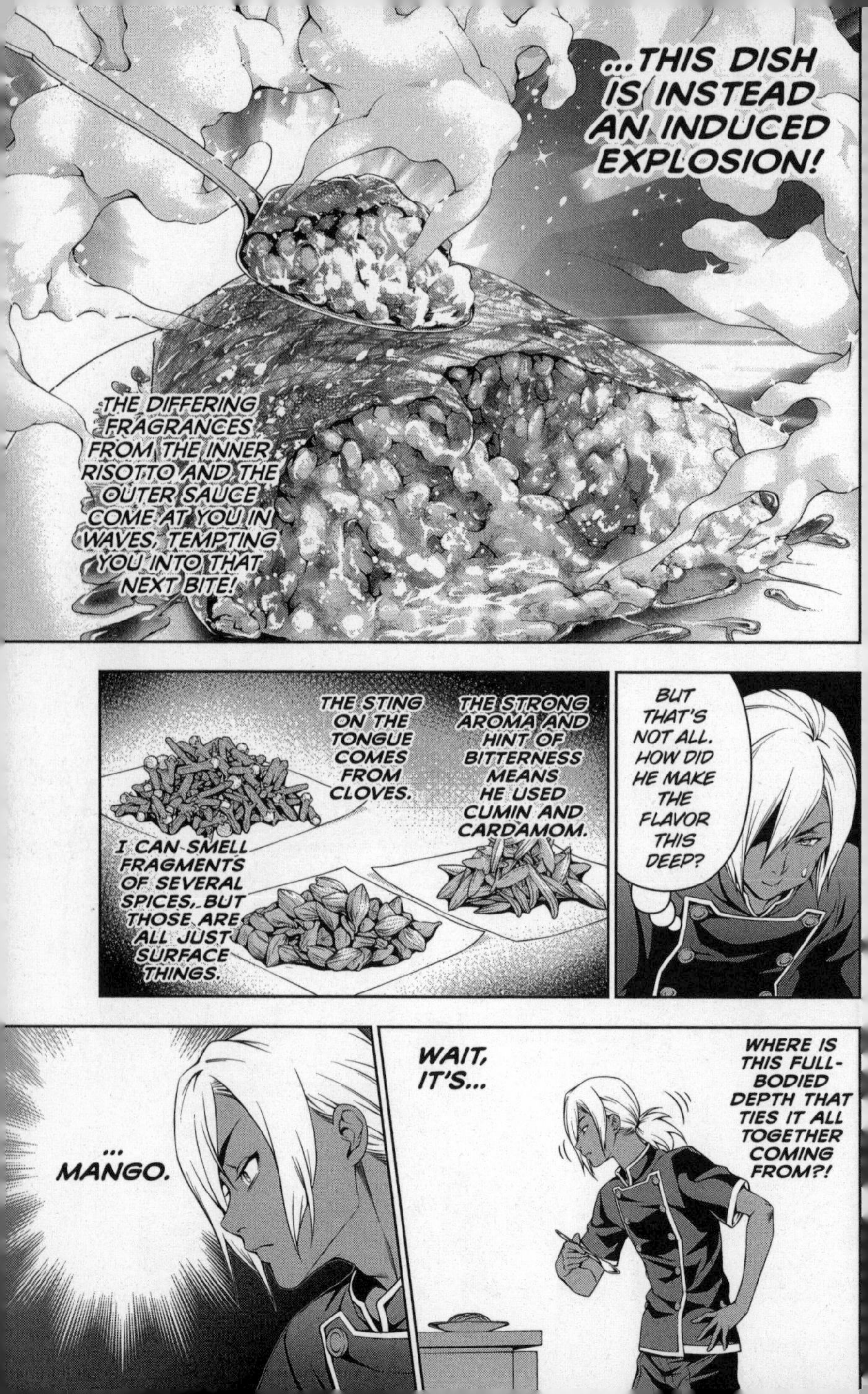
...THIS DISH IS INSTEAD AN INDUCED EXPLOSION!
THE DIFFERING FRAGRANCES FROM THE INNER RISOTTO AND THE OUTER SAUCE COME AT YOU IN WAVES, TEMPTING YOU INTO THAT NEXT BITE!
BUT THAT'S NOT ALL. HOW DID HE MAKE THE FLAVOR THIS DEEP?
THE STRONG AROMA AND HINT OF BITTERNESS MEANS HE USED CUMIN AND CARDAMOM.
THE STING ON THE TONGUE COMES FROM CLOVES.
I CAN SMELL FRAGMENTS OF SEVERAL SPICES, BUT THOSE ARE ALL JUST SURFACE THINGS.
WHERE IS THIS FULL-BODIED DEPTH THAT TIES IT ALL TOGETHER COMING FROM?!
WAIT, IT'S...
... MANGO.

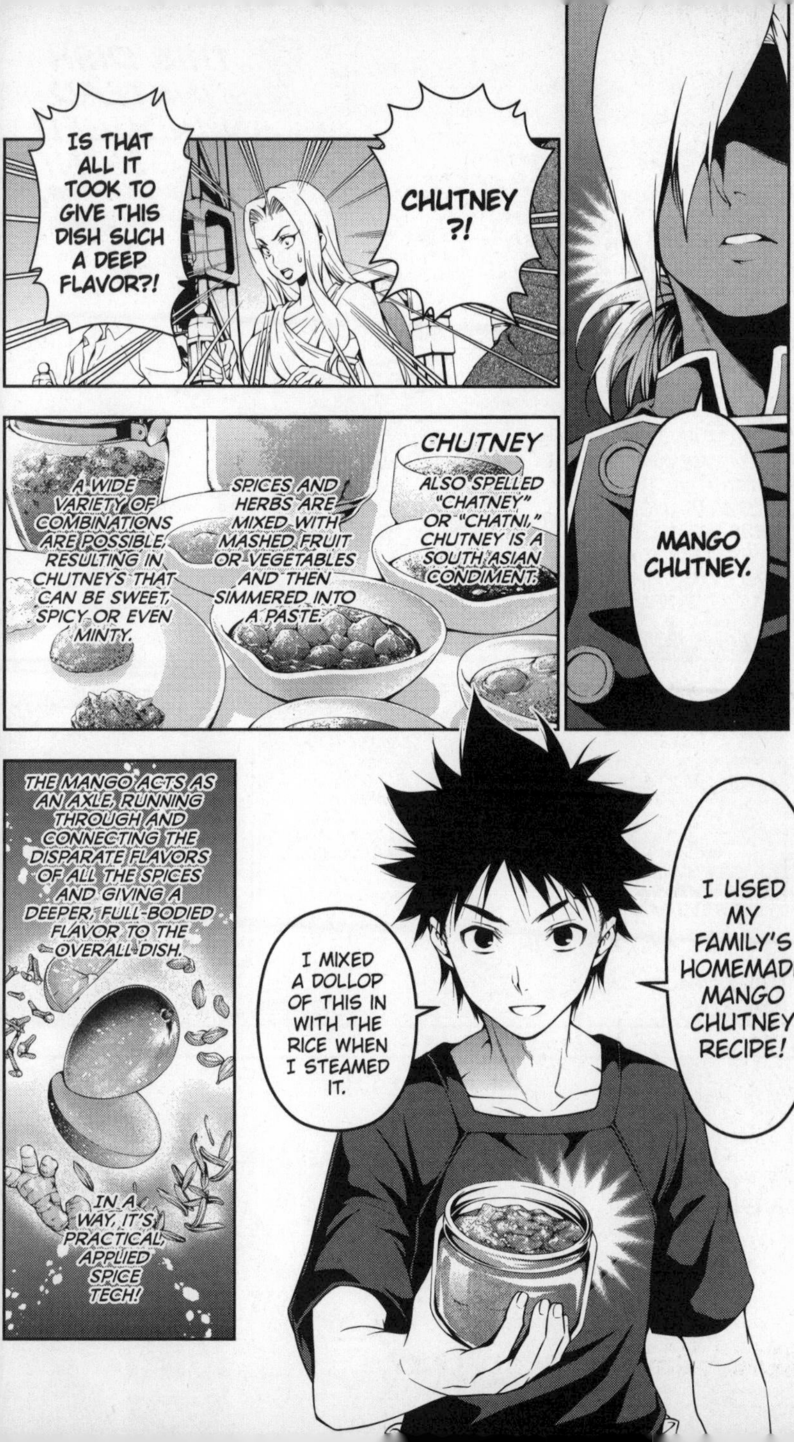
MANGO CHUTNEY.
CHUTNEY ?!
IS THAT ALL IT TOOK TO GIVE THIS DISH SUCH A DEEP FLAVOR?!
CHUTNEY
ALSO SPELLED "CHATNEY" OR "CHATNI," CHUTNEY IS A SOUTH ASIAN CONDIMENT.
SPICES AND HERBS ARE MIXED WITH MASHED FRUIT OR VEGETABLES AND THEN SIMMERED INTO A PASTE.
A WIDE VARIETY OF COMBINATIONS ARE POSSIBLE, RESULTING IN CHUTNEYS THAT CAN BE SWEET, SPICY OR EVEN MINTY.
I USED MY FAMILY'S HOMEMADE MANGO CHUTNEY RECIPE!
I MIXED A DOLLOP OF THIS IN WITH THE RICE WHEN I STEAMED IT.
THE MANGO ACTS AS AN AXLE, RUNNING THROUGH AND CONNECTING THE DISPARATE FLAVORS OF ALL THE SPICES AND GIVING A DEEPER, FULL-BODIED FLAVOR TO THE OVERALL DISH.
IN A WAY, IT'S PRACTICAL, APPLIED SPICE TECH!

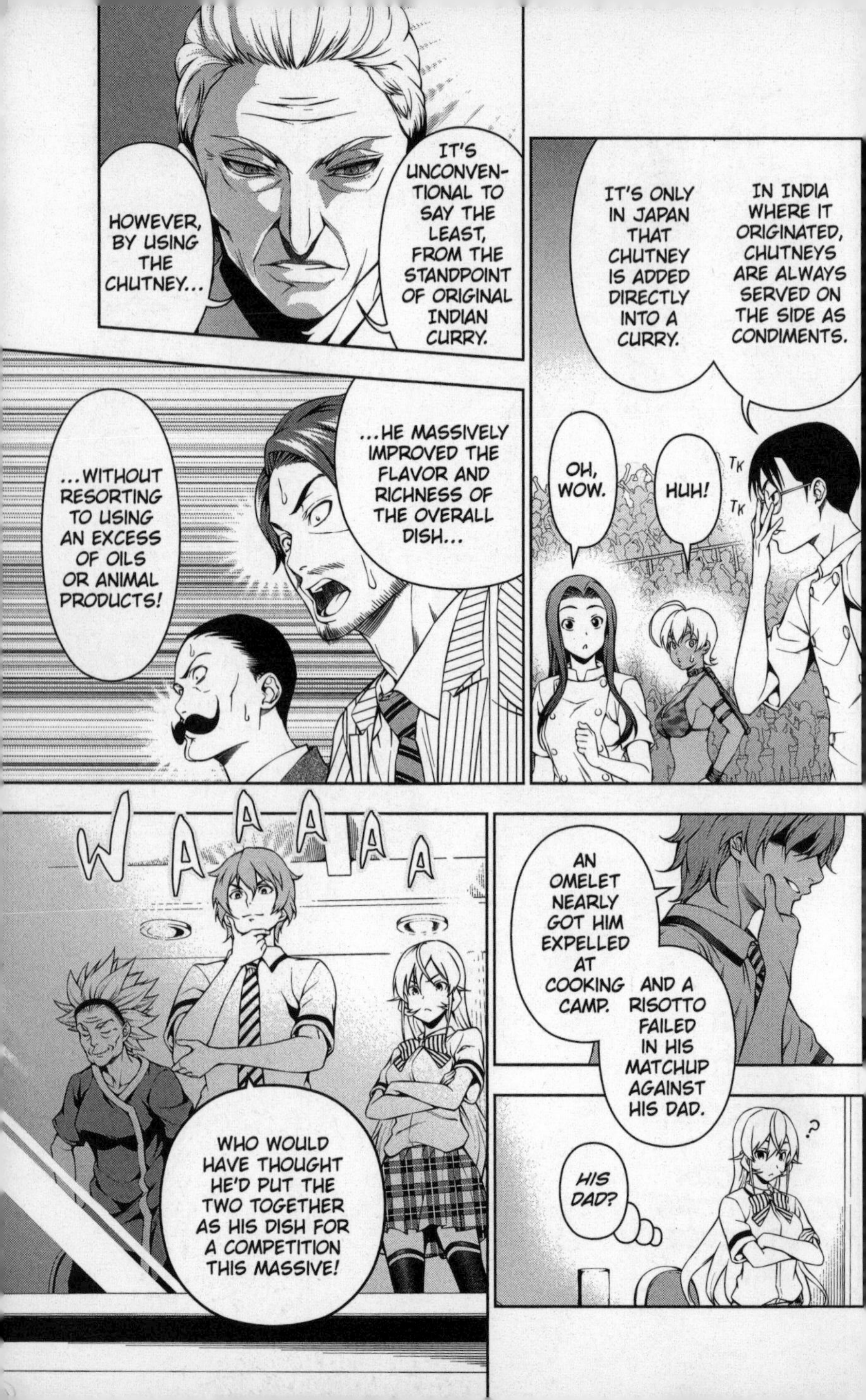
IN INDIA WHERE IT ORIGINATED, CHUTNEYS ARE ALWAYS SERVED ON THE SIDE AS CONDIMENTS.
IT'S ONLY IN JAPAN THAT CHUTNEY IS ADDED DIRECTLY INTO A CURRY.
TK
TK
HUH!
OH, WOW.
IT'S UNCONVENTIONAL TO SAY THE LEAST, FROM THE STANDPOINT OF ORIGINAL INDIAN CURRY.
HOWEVER, BY USING THE CHUTNEY...
...HE MASSIVELY IMPROVED THE FLAVOR AND RICHNESS OF THE OVERALL DISH...
...WITHOUT RESORTING TO USING AN EXCESS OF OILS OR ANIMAL PRODUCTS!
AN OMELET NEARLY GOT HIM EXPELLED AT COOKING CAMP.
AND A RISOTTO FAILED IN HIS MATCHUP AGAINST HIS DAD.
?
HIS DAD?
WAAAAAA
WHO WOULD HAVE THOUGHT HE'D PUT THE TWO TOGETHER AS HIS DISH FOR A COMPETITION THIS MASSIVE!

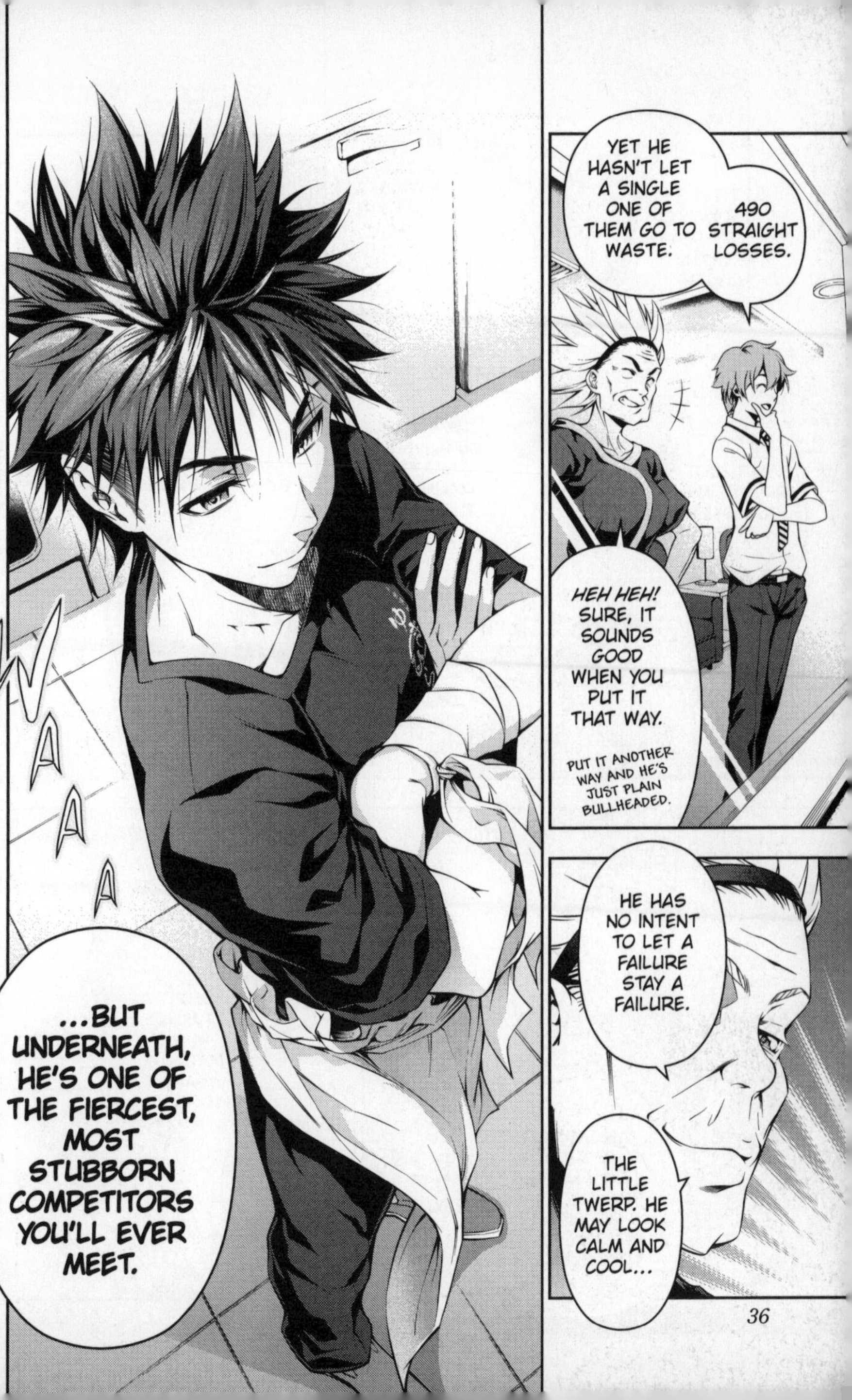
490 STRAIGHT LOSSES.
YET HE HASN'T LET A SINGLE ONE OF THEM GO TO WASTE.
HEH HEH! SURE, IT SOUNDS GOOD WHEN YOU PUT IT THAT WAY.
PUT IT ANOTHER WAY AND HE'S JUST PLAIN BULLHEADED.
HE HAS NO INTENT TO LET A FAILURE STAY A FAILURE.
THE LITTLE TWERP. HE MAY LOOK CALM AND COOL...
WAAAA
...BUT UNDERNEATH, HE'S ONE OF THE FIERCEST, MOST STUBBORN COMPETITORS YOU'LL EVER MEET.

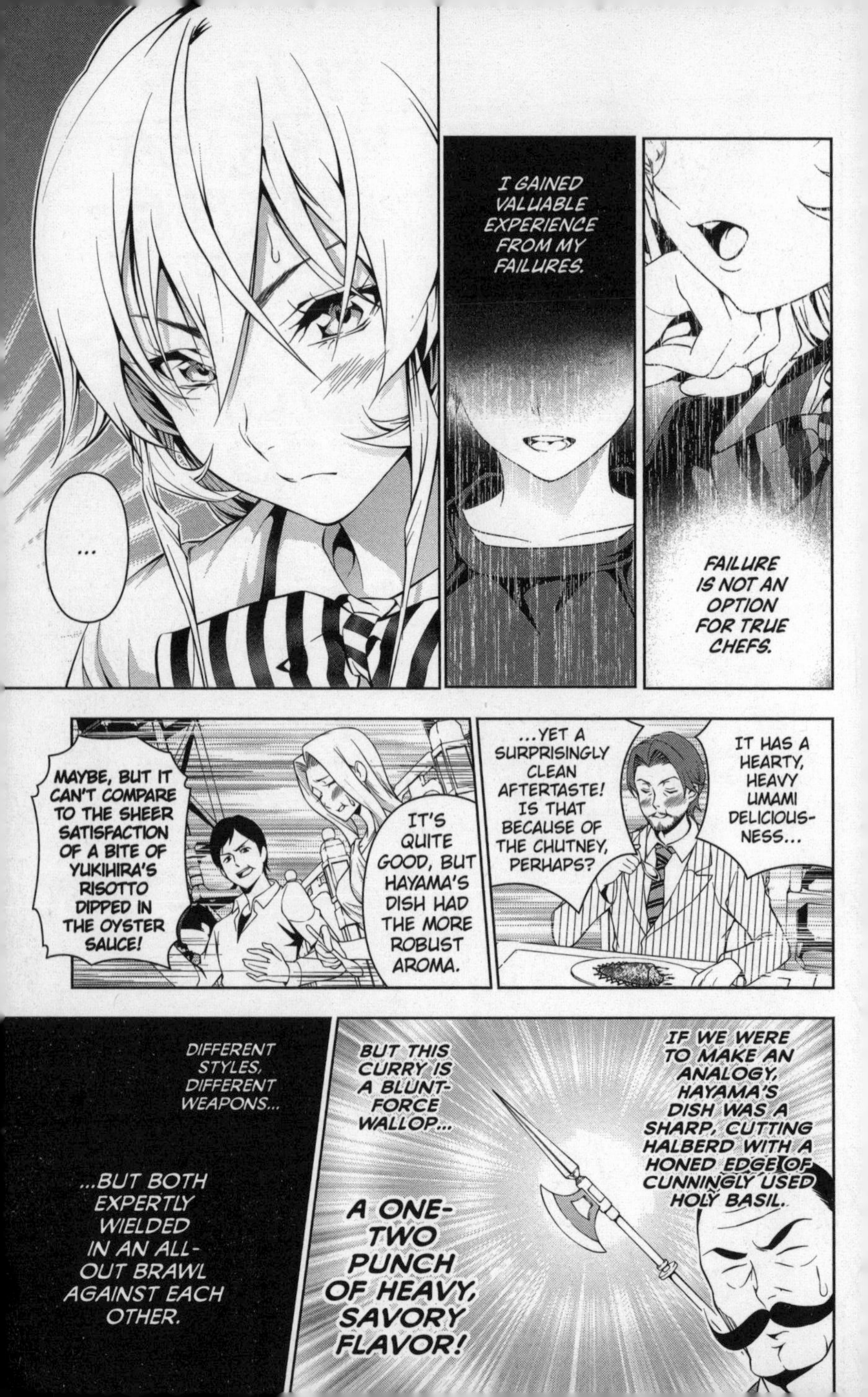
FAILURE IS NOT AN OPTION FOR TRUE CHEFS.
I GAINED VALUABLE EXPERIENCE FROM MY FAILURES.
...
IT HAS A HEARTY, HEAVY UMAMI DELICIOUSNESS...
...YET A SURPRISINGLY CLEAN AFTERTASTE! IS THAT BECAUSE OF THE CHUTNEY, PERHAPS?
IT'S QUITE GOOD, BUT HAYAMA'S DISH HAD THE MORE ROBUST AROMA.
MAYBE, BUT IT CAN'T COMPARE TO THE SHEER SATISFACTION OF A BITE OF YUKIHIRA'S RISOTTO DIPPED IN THE OYSTER SAUCE!
IF WE WERE TO MAKE AN ANALOGY, HAYAMA'S DISH WAS A SHARP, CUTTING HALBERD WITH A HONED EDGE OF CUNNINGLY USED HOLY BASIL.
BUT THIS CURRY IS A BLUNT-FORCE WALLOP...
A ONE-TWO PUNCH OF HEAVY, SAVORY FLAVOR!
DIFFERENT STYLES, DIFFERENT WEAPONS...
...BUT BOTH EXPERTLY WIELDED IN AN ALL-OUT BRAWL AGAINST EACH OTHER.

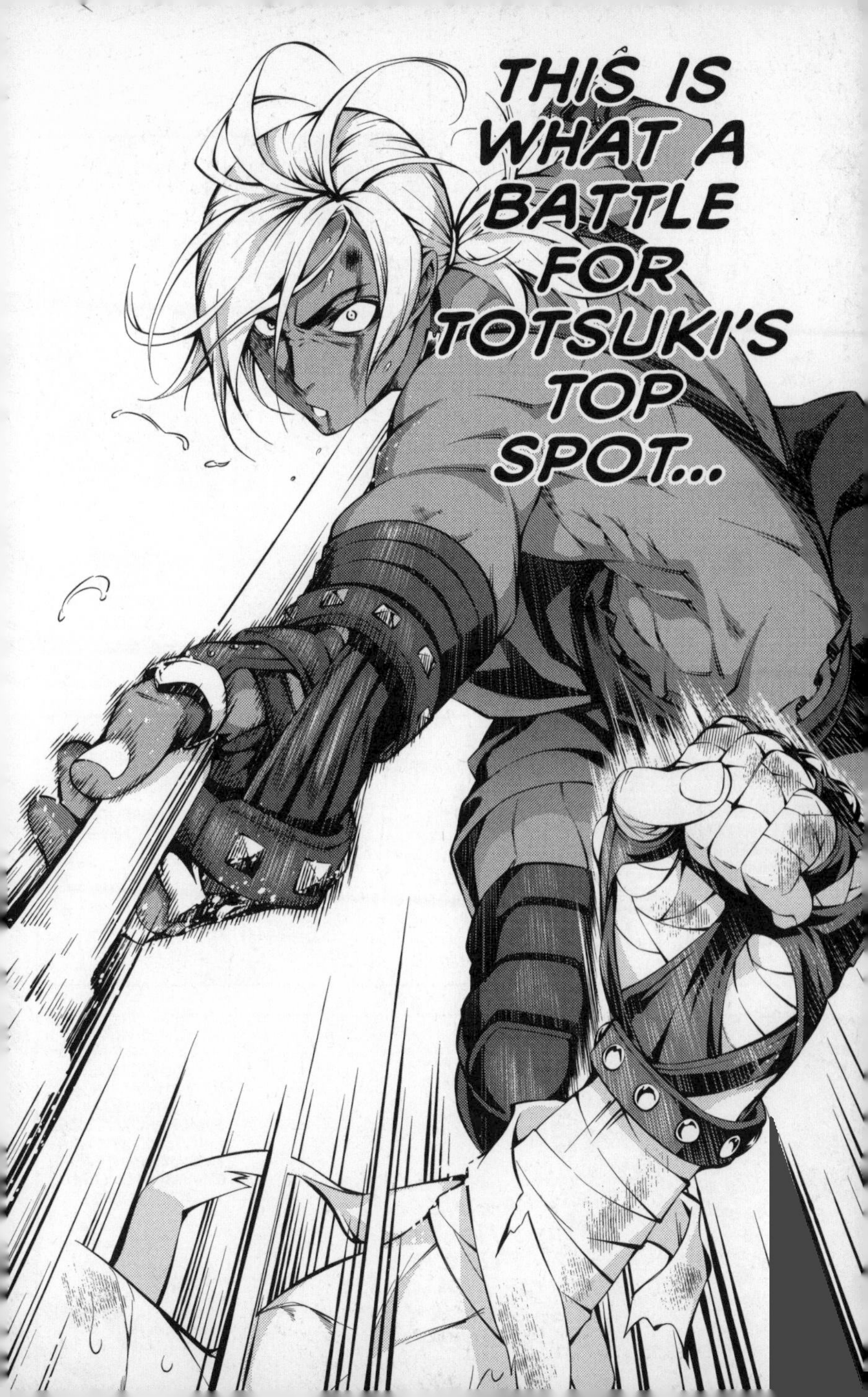
THIS IS WHAT A BATTLE FOR TOTSUKI'S TOP SPOT...

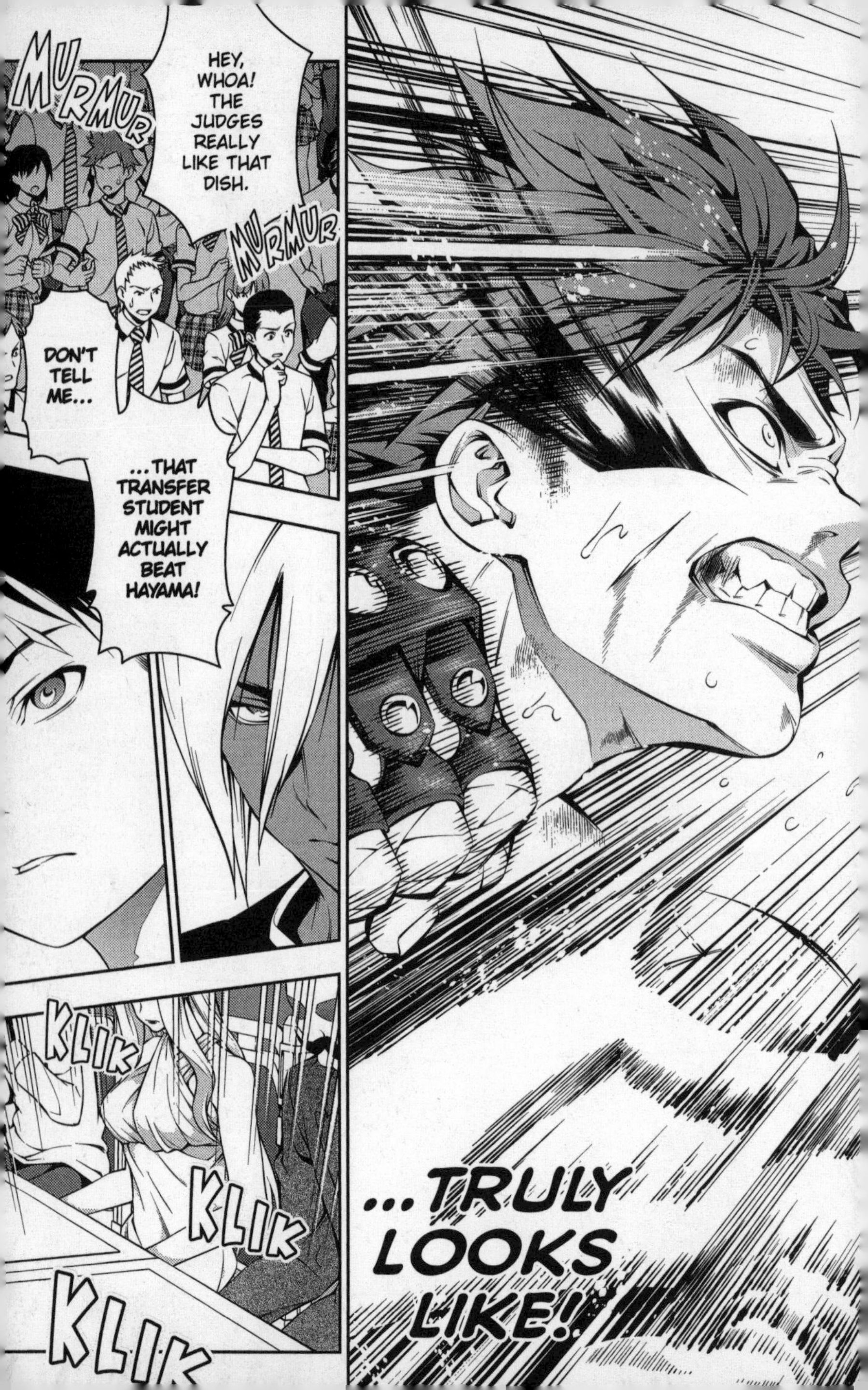
...TRULY LOOKS LIKE!
HEY, WHOA! THE JUDGES REALLY LIKE THAT DISH.
MURMUR
MURMUR
DON'T TELL ME...
...THAT TRANSFER STUDENT MIGHT ACTUALLY BEAT HAYAMA!
KLIK
KLIK
KLIK

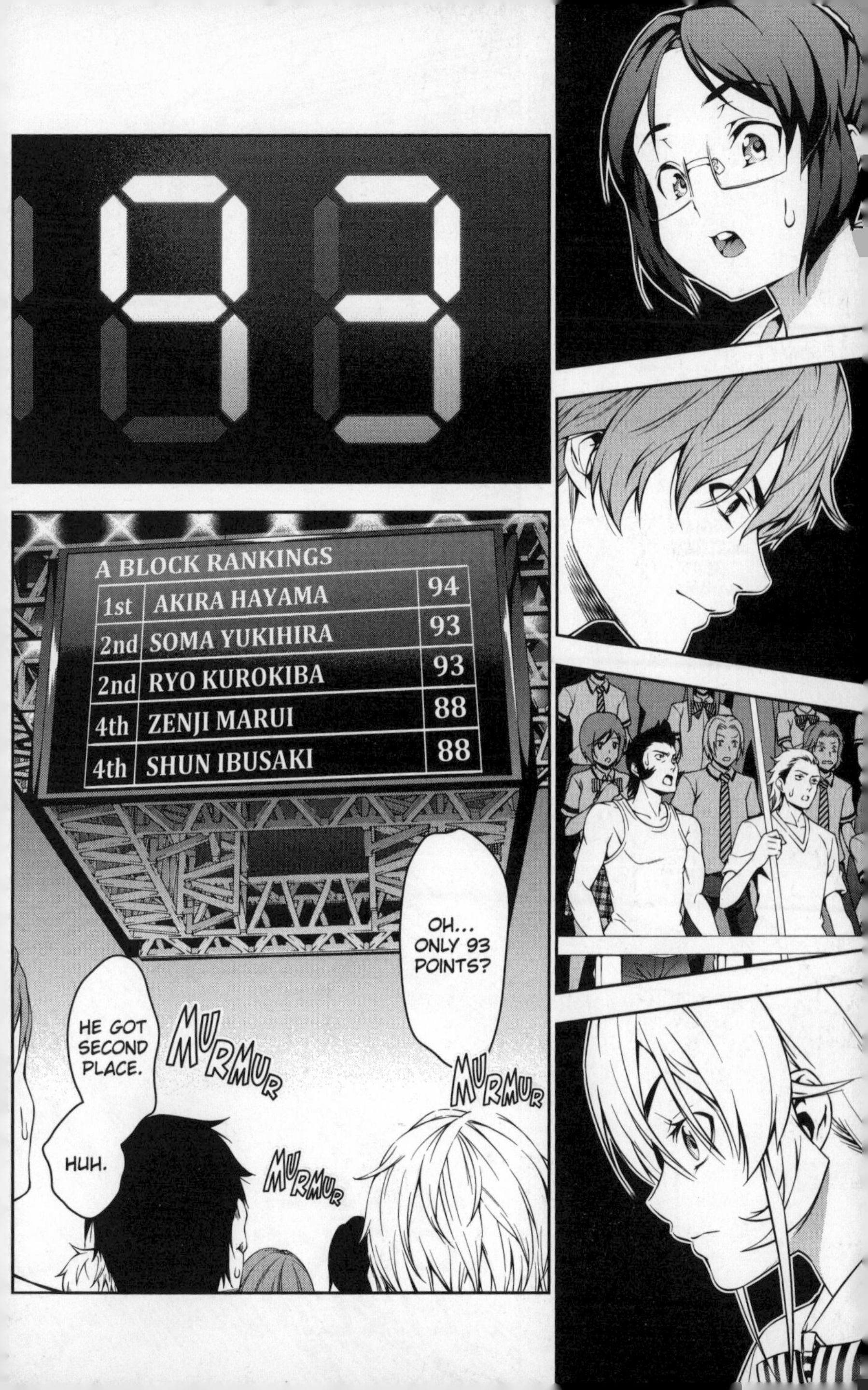

A BLOCK RANKINGS
1st AKIRA HAYAMA 94
2nd SOMA YUKIHIRA 93
2nd RYO KUROKIBA 93
4th ZENJI MARUI 88
4th SHUN IBUSAKI 88
OH... ONLY 93 POINTS?
MURMUR
MURMUR
HE GOT SECOND PLACE.
MURMUR
HUH.

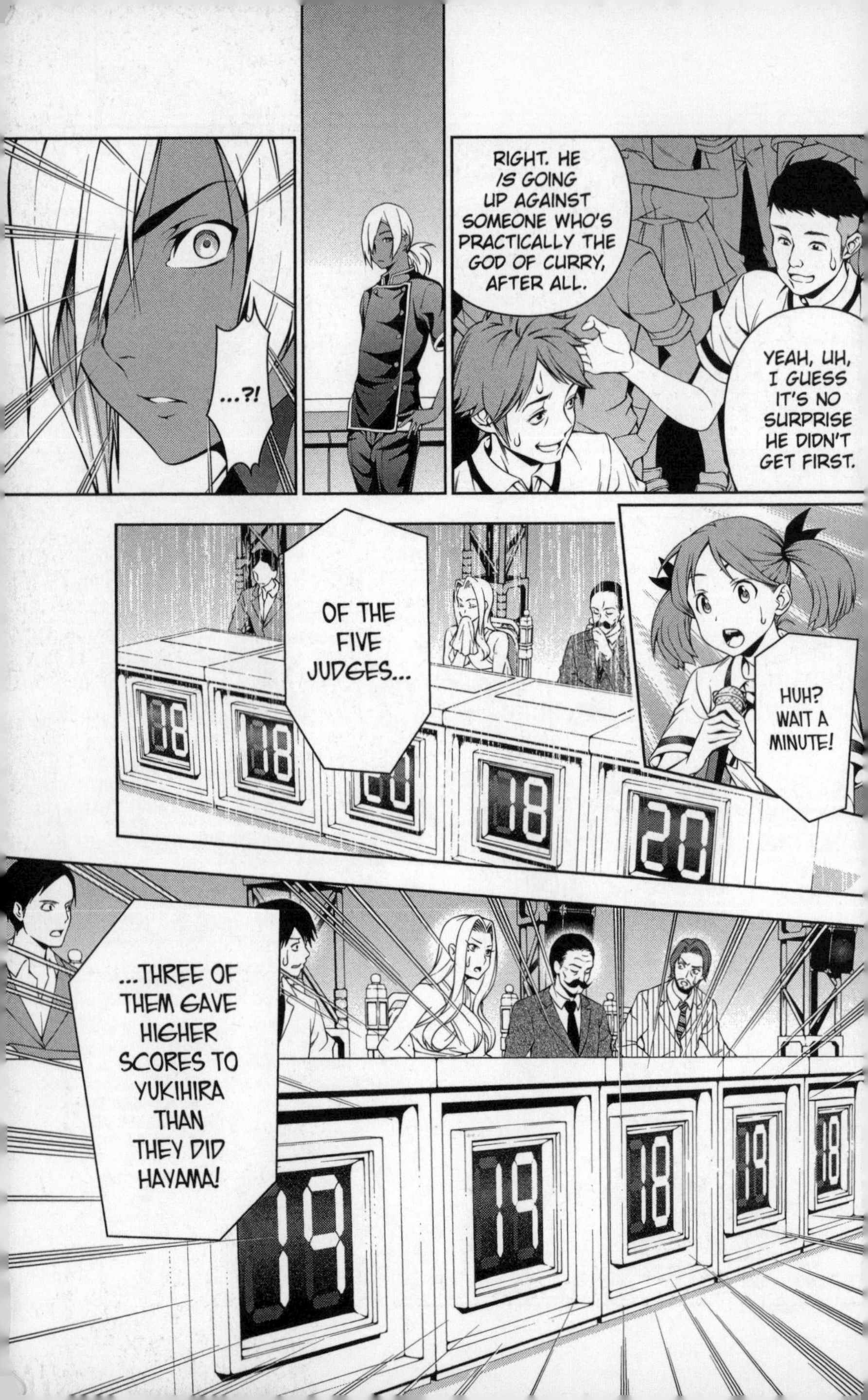
YEAH, UH, I GUESS IT'S NO SURPRISE HE DIDN'T GET FIRST.
RIGHT. HE IS GOING UP AGAINST SOMEONE WHO'S PRACTICALLY THE GOD OF CURRY, AFTER ALL.
...?!
HUH? WAIT A MINUTE!
OF THE FIVE JUDGES...
...THREE OF THEM GAVE HIGHER SCORES TO YUKIHIRA THAN THEY DID HAYAMA!

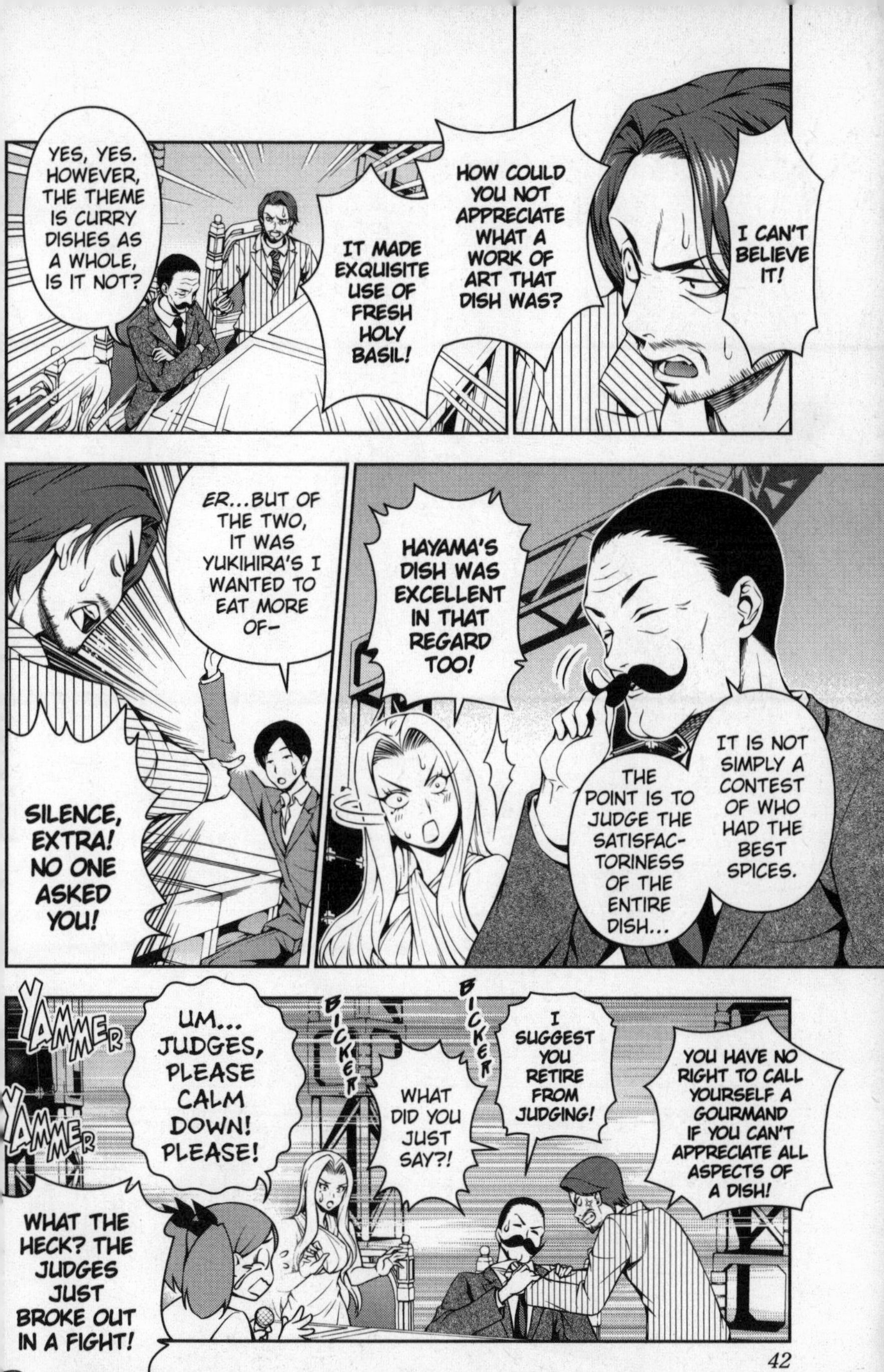
I CAN'T BELIEVE IT!
HOW COULD YOU NOT APPRECIATE WHAT A WORK OF ART THAT DISH WAS?
IT MADE EXQUISITE USE OF FRESH HOLY BASIL!
YES, YES. HOWEVER, THE THEME IS CURRY DISHES AS A WHOLE, IS IT NOT?
IT IS NOT SIMPLY A CONTEST OF WHO HAD THE BEST SPICES.
THE POINT IS TO JUDGE THE SATISFACTORINESS OF THE ENTIRE DISH...
HAYAMA'S DISH WAS EXCELLENT IN THAT REGARD TOO!
ER...BUT OF THE TWO, IT WAS YUKIHIRA'S I WANTED TO EAT MORE OF–
SILENCE, EXTRA! NO ONE ASKED YOU!
YOU HAVE NO RIGHT TO CALL YOURSELF A GOURMAND IF YOU CAN'T APPRECIATE ALL ASPECTS OF A DISH!
I SUGGEST YOU RETIRE FROM JUDGING!
BICKER
WHAT DID YOU JUST SAY?!
BICKER
UM... JUDGES, PLEASE CALM DOWN! PLEASE!
YAMMER
YAMMER
WHAT THE HECK? THE JUDGES JUST BROKE OUT IN A FIGHT!

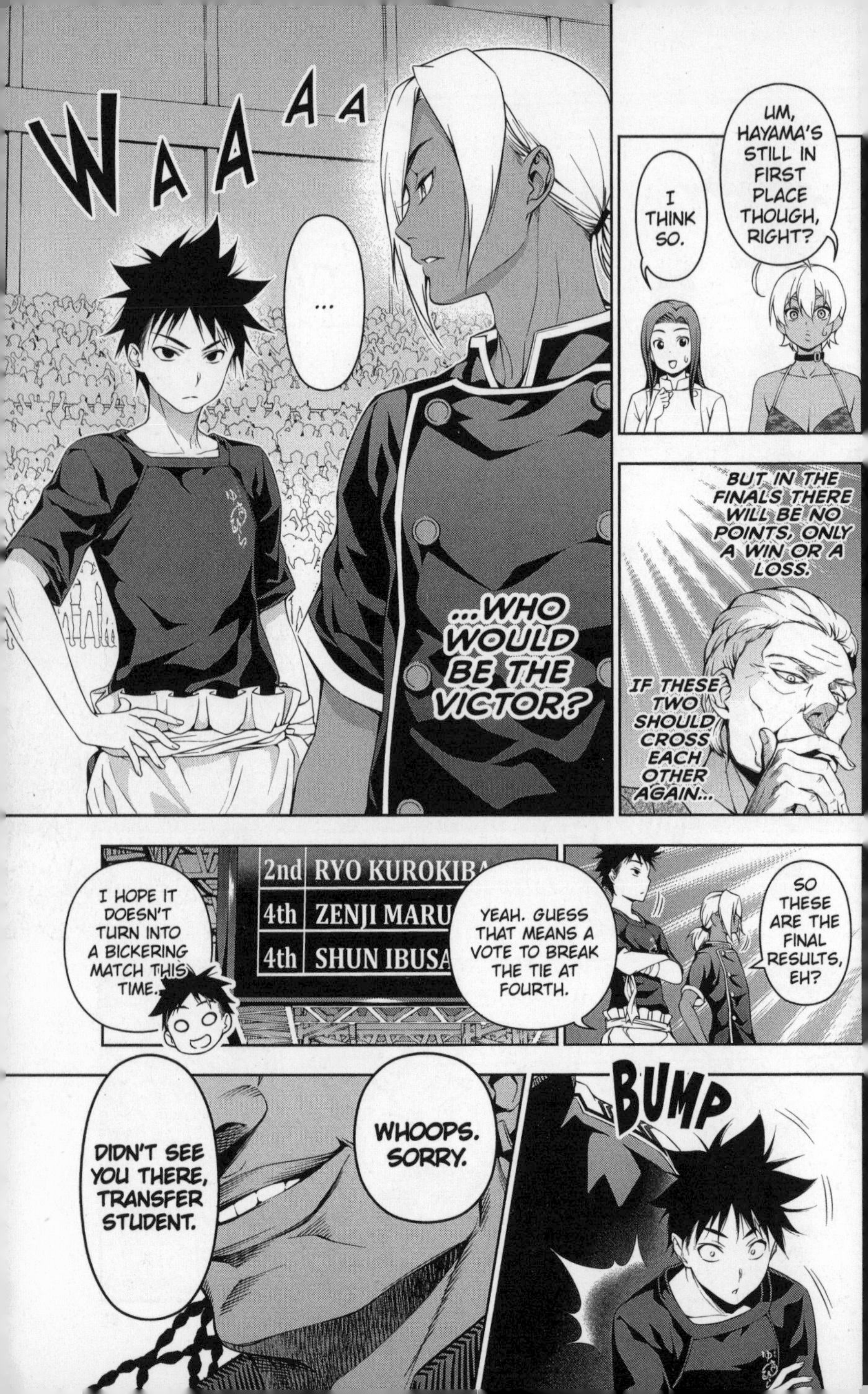
UM, HAYAMA'S STILL IN FIRST PLACE THOUGH, RIGHT?
I THINK SO.
BUT IN THE FINALS THERE WILL BE NO POINTS, ONLY A WIN OR A LOSS.
IF THESE TWO SHOULD CROSS EACH OTHER AGAIN...
WAAAAA
...
...WHO WOULD BE THE VICTOR?
SO THESE ARE THE FINAL RESULTS, EH?
YEAH. GUESS THAT MEANS A VOTE TO BREAK THE TIE AT FOURTH.
2nd RYO KUROKIBA
4th ZENJI MARU
4th SHUN IBUSA
I HOPE IT DOESN'T TURN INTO A BICKERING MATCH THIS TIME.
BUMP
WHOOPS. SORRY.
DIDN'T SEE YOU THERE, TRANSFER STUDENT.

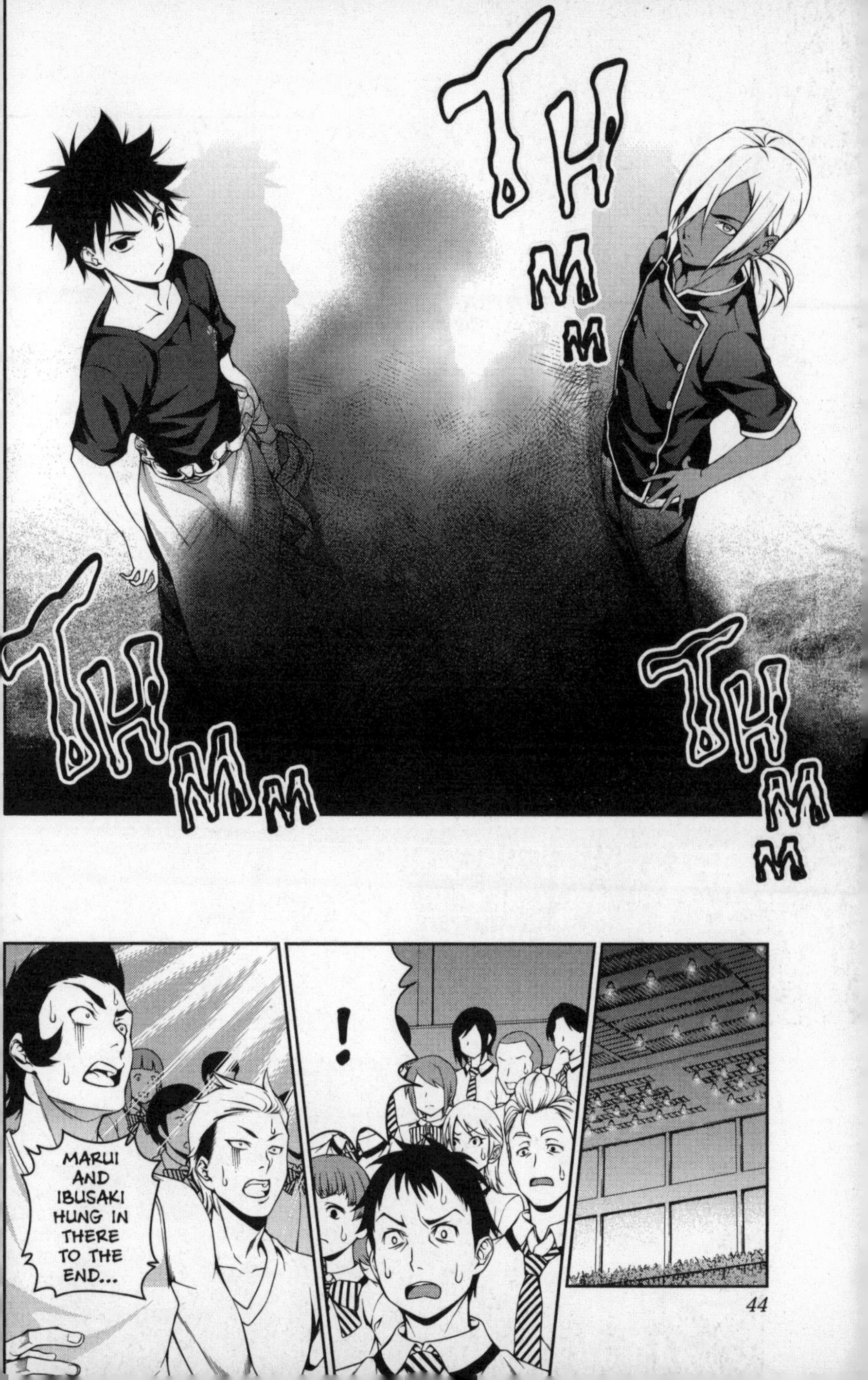
THUMM
THUMM
THUMM
!
MARUI AND IBUSAKI HUNG IN THERE TO THE END...

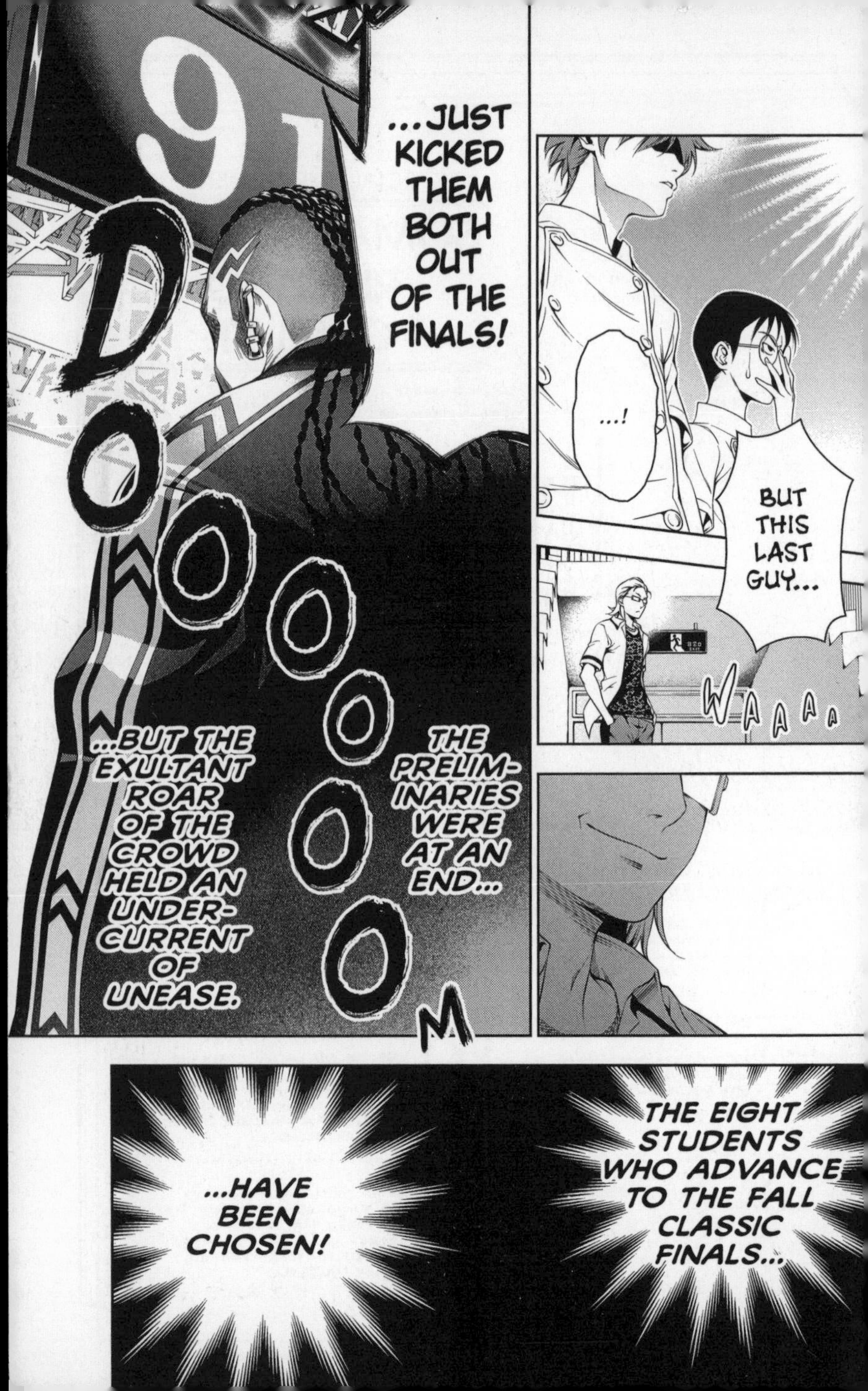
...!
BUT THIS LAST GUY...
WAAAA
...JUST KICKED THEM BOTH OUT OF THE FINALS!
DOOOOOOOM
THE PRELIMINARIES WERE AT AN END...
...BUT THE EXULTANT ROAR OF THE CROWD HELD AN UNDERCURRENT OF UNEASE.
THE EIGHT STUDENTS WHO ADVANCE TO THE FALL CLASSIC FINALS...
...HAVE BEEN CHOSEN!

RECIPE BY: YUKI MORISAKI

PRACTICAL RECIPE #1

VOLUME 8
SPECIAL SUPPLEMENT!

SOMA'S CURRY RISOTTO OMELET

THE OYSTER SAUCE IS ADDICT-ING!

ARTIST: YUTO TSUKUDA

INGREDIENTS SERVES 4

- 1 CUP UNCOOKED RICE
- 150 GRAMS GROUND BEEF
- 1/2 ONION
- 1 1/2 TABLESPOONS CURRY POWDER
- 1 TABLESPOON MANGO CHUTNEY (SUBSTITUTES: MARMALADE OR JAM)
- 2 TABLESPOONS BUTTER
- 2 TEASPOONS GRATED GINGER
- A
  - 1 TABLESPOON GRANULATED CONSOMMÉ
  - 1 LITER WATER
- 50 GRAMS PIZZA CHEESE
- SALT, PEPPER, PARSLEY

★ EGG BATTER

- 8 EGGS
- 2 TABLESPOONS EACH MILK AND CREAM
- 4 TABLESPOONS BUTTER
- SALT, PEPPER

★ SAUCE

- 2 TABLESPOONS EACH OYSTER SAUCE AND COOKING SAKE
- 1 TABLESPOON SOY SAUCE
- 1 TEASPOON SUGAR

1. DICE THE ONION.
2. MELT THE BUTTER IN A POT AND ADD THE DICED ONION AND GRATED GINGER. SAUTÉ UNTIL THE ONIONS ARE TRANSLUCENT AND TENDER. ADD THE GROUND BEEF AND CURRY POWDER AND COOK UNTIL FRAGRANT.
3. ADD THE RICE TO (2) AND SAUTÉ. ADD THE MANGO CHUTNEY. MIX (A) TOGETHER AND ADD JUST ENOUGH TO SUBMERGE THE MIXTURE.
4. HEAT (3) TO BOILING AND THEN REDUCE TO LOW HEAT. SIMMER ON LOW HEAT FOR FIFTEEN MINUTES, ADDING MORE OF (A) IF ALL THE LIQUID GETS ABSORBED.
5. ADD THE PIZZA CHEESE TO (4) AND STIR. SEASON TO TASTE WITH SALT AND PEPPER.
6. MAKE THE EGG BATTER. CRACK THE EGGS INTO A BOWL AND BEAT TO BREAK THE YOLKS. ADD THE MILK AND CREAM, SEASON WITH SALT AND PEPPER AND THEN WHIP UNTIL THOROUGHLY BLENDED.
7. HEAT 1 TABLESPOON OF BUTTER IN A FRYING PAN AND POUR IN 1/4 OF (6) WHILE QUICKLY STIRRING IT WITH A FORK. ONCE THE EGG HAS SET ON THE BOTTOM, POUR 1/4 OF (4) ON TOP. USE A FORK TO FOLD THE FAR EDGE OF THE COOKED EGG OVER TOP OF IT. EASE THE OMELET TO THE EDGE OF THE PAN AND THEN FLIP IT ONTO A PLATE AND GENTLY MOLD INTO SHAPE. REPEAT THIS PROCESS THREE TIMES WITH THE REMAINING 3/4.
8. MIX THE SAUCE INGREDIENTS AND POUR IT INTO THE PAN THAT WAS USED FOR (7). HEAT TO BOILING AND THEN QUICKLY REMOVE FROM HEAT. DRIZZLE OVER (7), SIDE WITH PARSLEY, AND DONE!

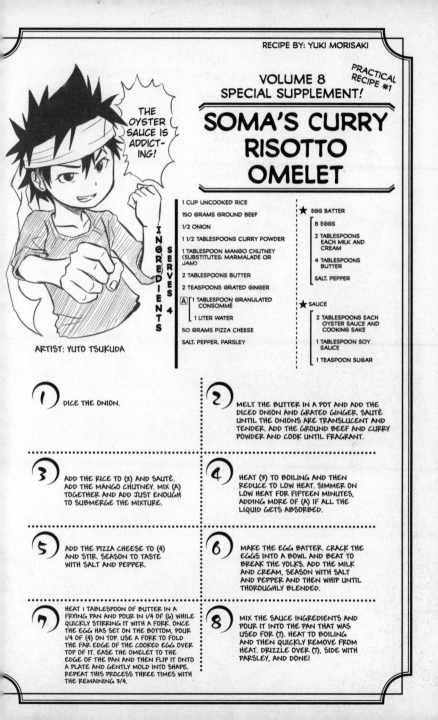

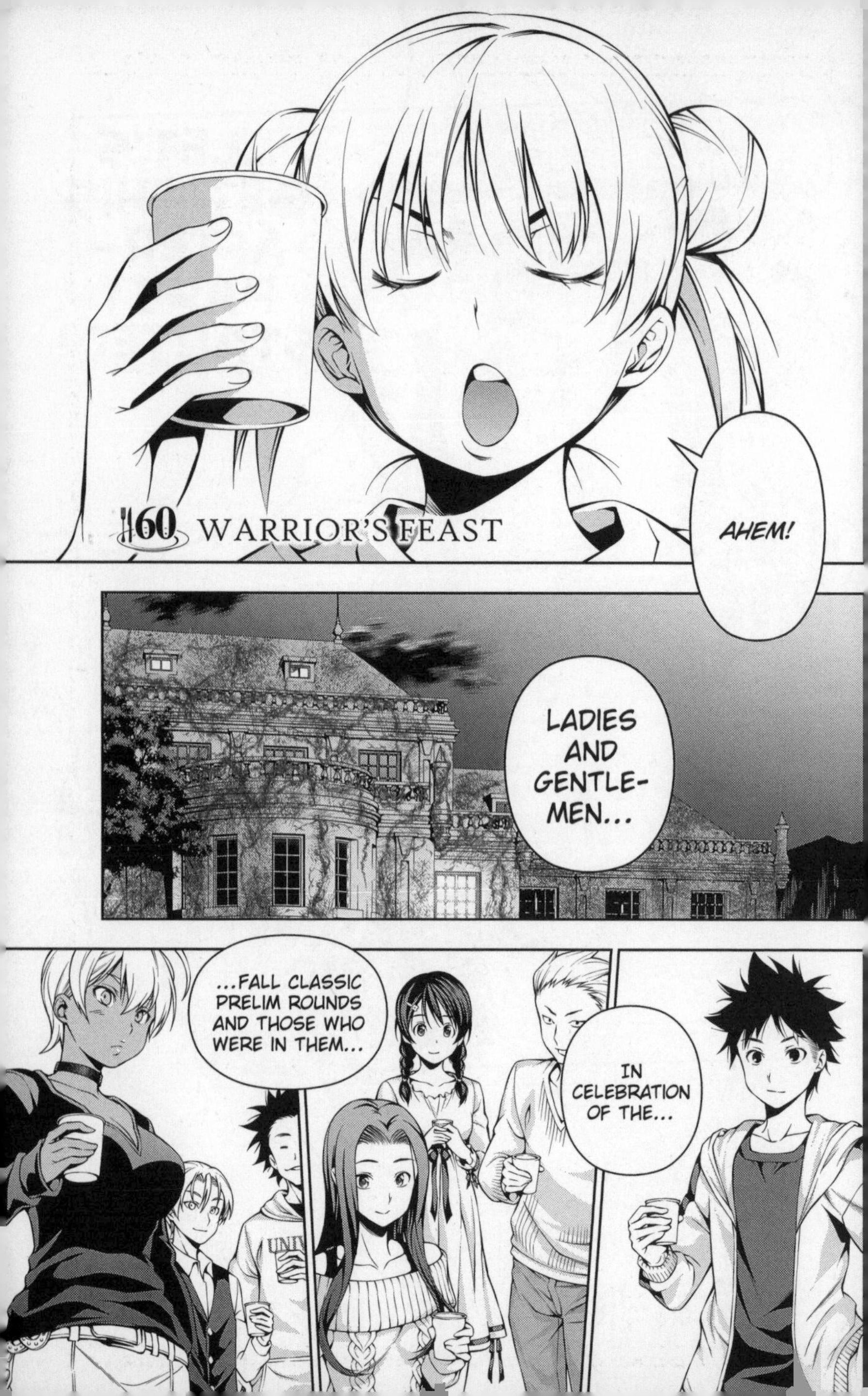
AHEM!
160 WARRIOR'S FEAST
LADIES AND GENTLE-MEN...
IN CELEBRATION OF THE...
...FALL CLASSIC PRELIM ROUNDS AND THOSE WHO WERE IN THEM...

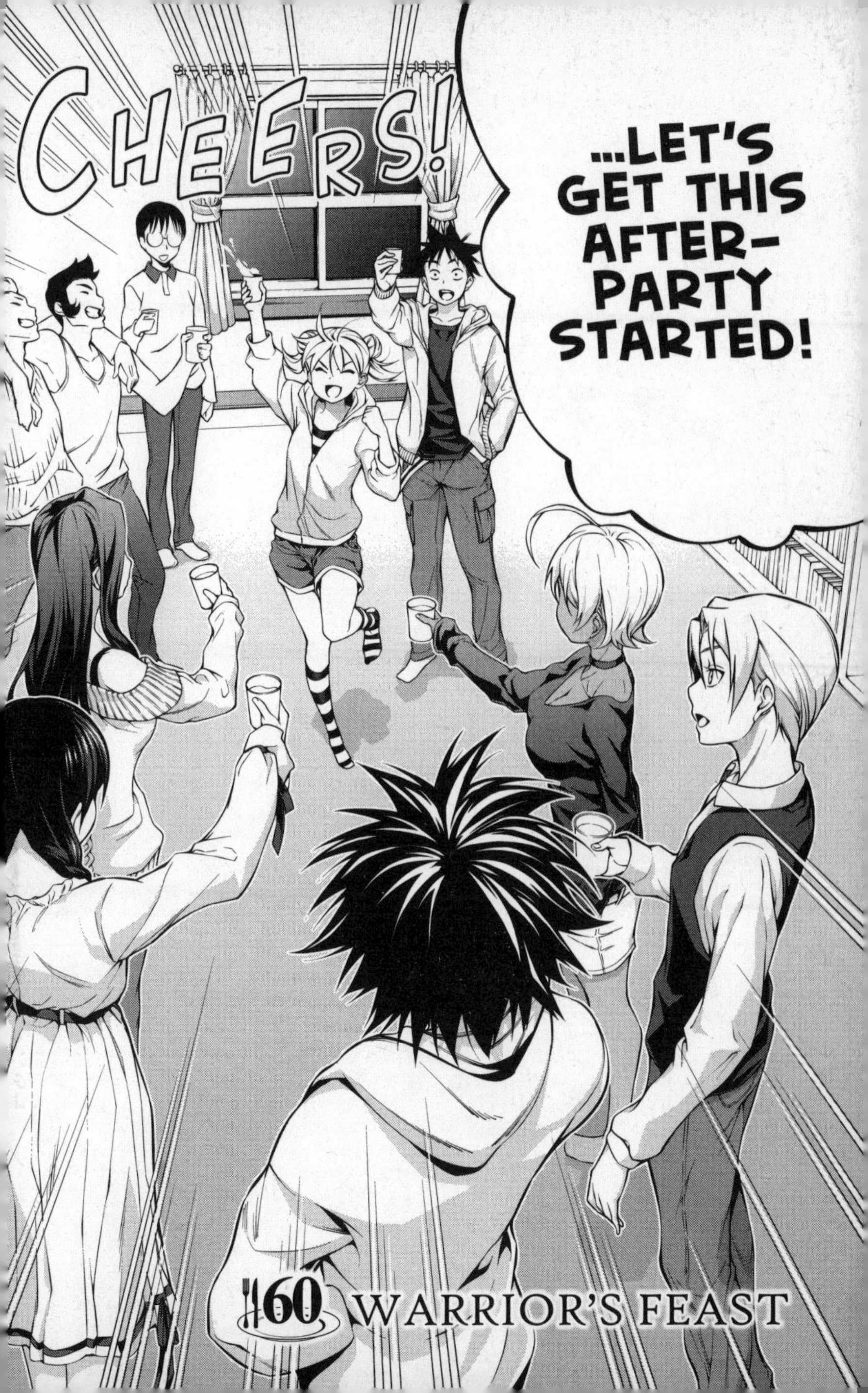
...LET'S GET THIS AFTER-PARTY STARTED!
CHEERS!
60 WARRIOR'S FEAST

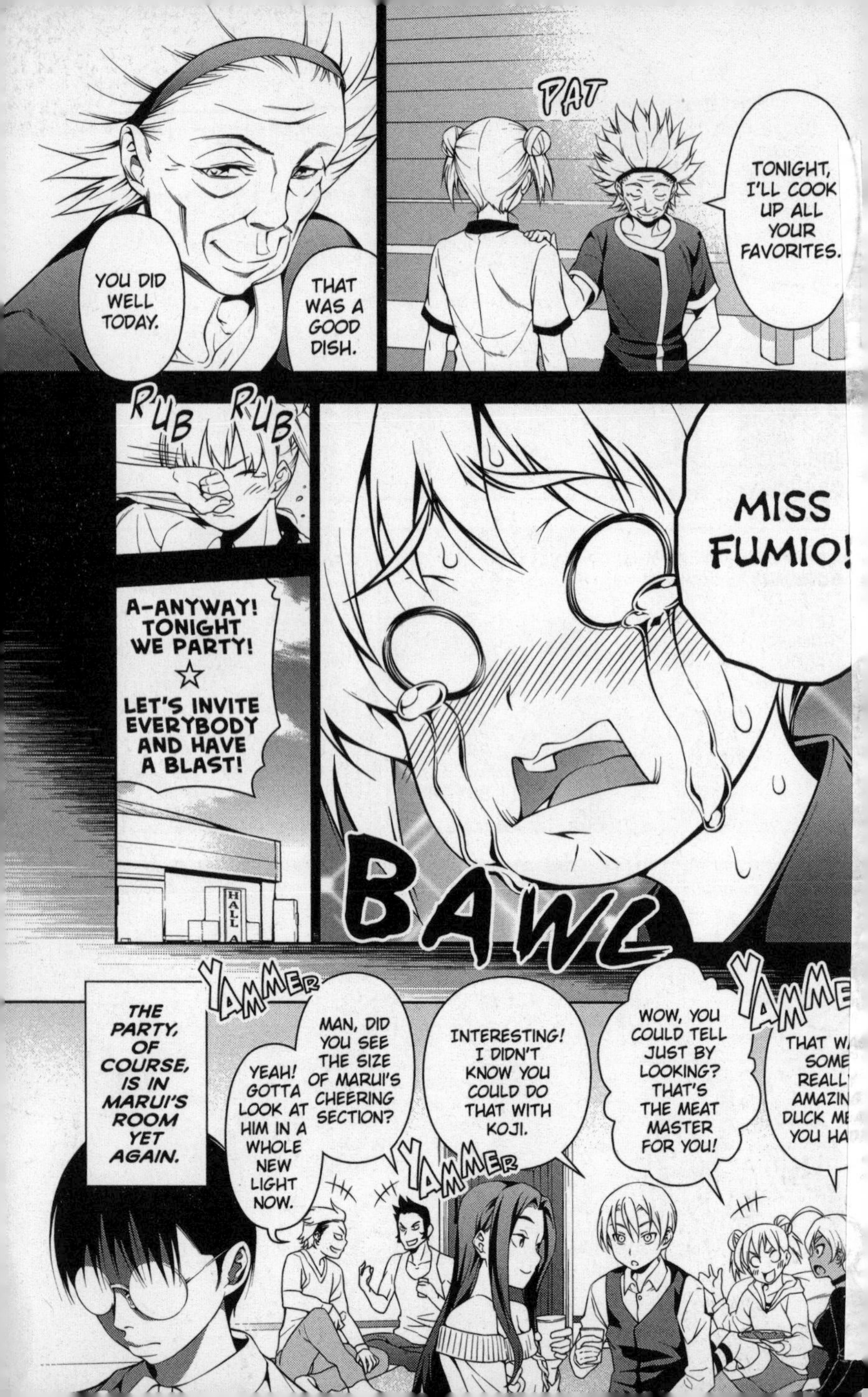
PAT
TONIGHT, I'LL COOK UP ALL YOUR FAVORITES.
THAT WAS A GOOD DISH.
YOU DID WELL TODAY.
MISS FUMIO!
BAWL
RUB RUB
A-ANYWAY! TONIGHT WE PARTY! ☆ LET'S INVITE EVERYBODY AND HAVE A BLAST!
HALL A
YAMME
THAT WA SOME REALL AMAZIN DUCK ME YOU HA
WOW, YOU COULD TELL JUST BY LOOKING? THAT'S THE MEAT MASTER FOR YOU!
INTERESTING! I DIDN'T KNOW YOU COULD DO THAT WITH KOJI.
YAMMER
MAN, DID YOU SEE THE SIZE OF MARUI'S CHEERING SECTION?
YEAH! GOTTA LOOK AT HIM IN A WHOLE NEW LIGHT NOW.
YAMMER
THE PARTY, OF COURSE, IS IN MARUI'S ROOM YET AGAIN.

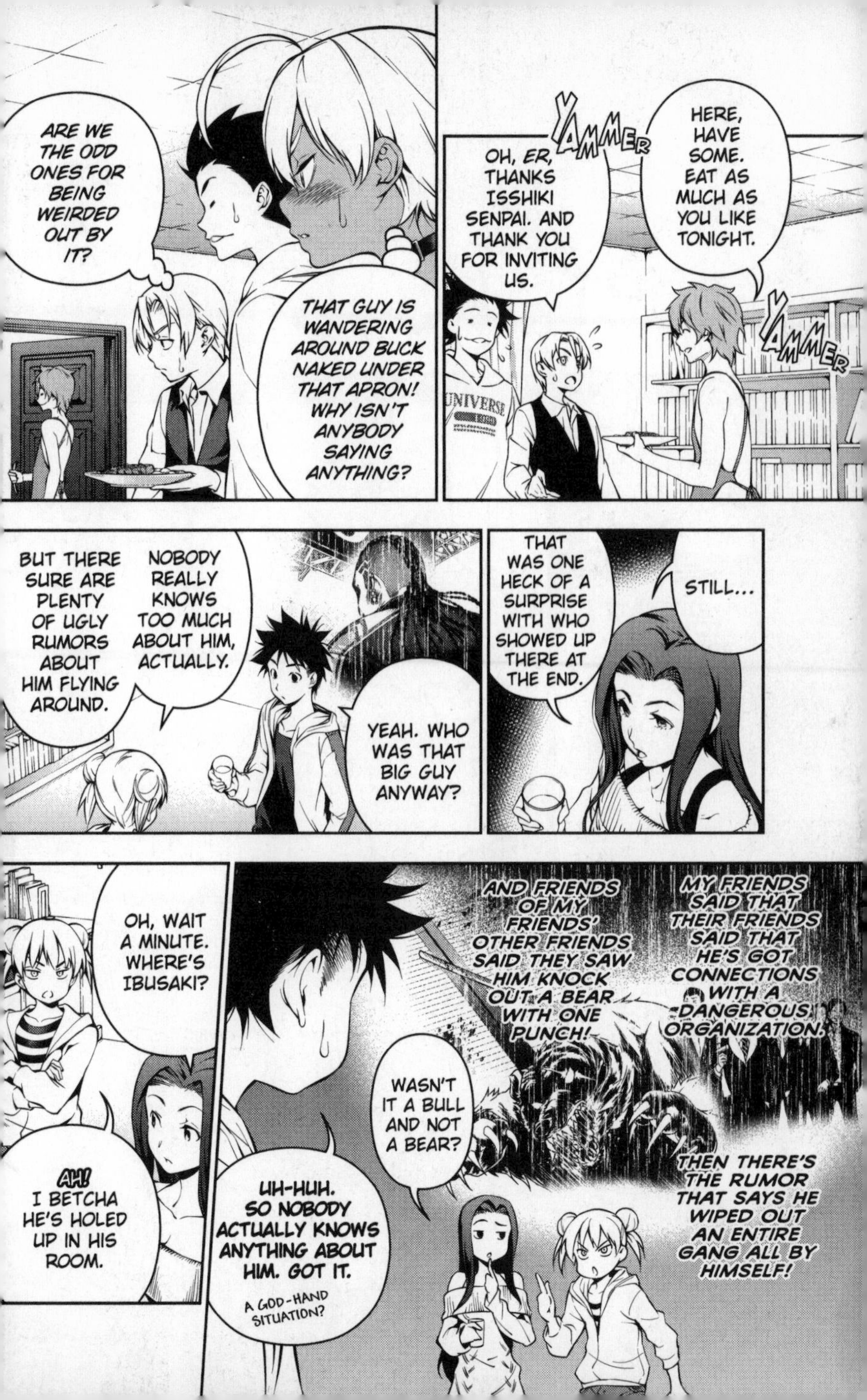
HERE, HAVE SOME. EAT AS MUCH AS YOU LIKE TONIGHT.
YAMMER
OH, ER, THANKS ISSHIKI SENPAI. AND THANK YOU FOR INVITING US.
YAMMER
THAT GUY IS WANDERING AROUND BUCK NAKED UNDER THAT APRON! WHY ISN'T ANYBODY SAYING ANYTHING?
ARE WE THE ODD ONES FOR BEING WEIRDED OUT BY IT?
STILL...
THAT WAS ONE HECK OF A SURPRISE WITH WHO SHOWED UP THERE AT THE END.
YEAH. WHO WAS THAT BIG GUY ANYWAY?
NOBODY REALLY KNOWS TOO MUCH ABOUT HIM, ACTUALLY.
BUT THERE SURE ARE PLENTY OF UGLY RUMORS ABOUT HIM FLYING AROUND.
MY FRIENDS SAID THAT THEIR FRIENDS SAID THAT HE'S GOT CONNECTIONS WITH A DANGEROUS ORGANIZATION.
AND FRIENDS OF MY FRIENDS' OTHER FRIENDS SAID THEY SAW HIM KNOCK OUT A BEAR WITH ONE PUNCH!
WASN'T IT A BULL AND NOT A BEAR?
THEN THERE'S THE RUMOR THAT SAYS HE WIPED OUT AN ENTIRE GANG ALL BY HIMSELF!
UH-HUH. SO NOBODY ACTUALLY KNOWS ANYTHING ABOUT HIM. GOT IT.
A GOD-HAND SITUATION?
OH, WAIT A MINUTE. WHERE'S IBUSAKI?
AH! I BETCHA HE'S HOLED UP IN HIS ROOM.

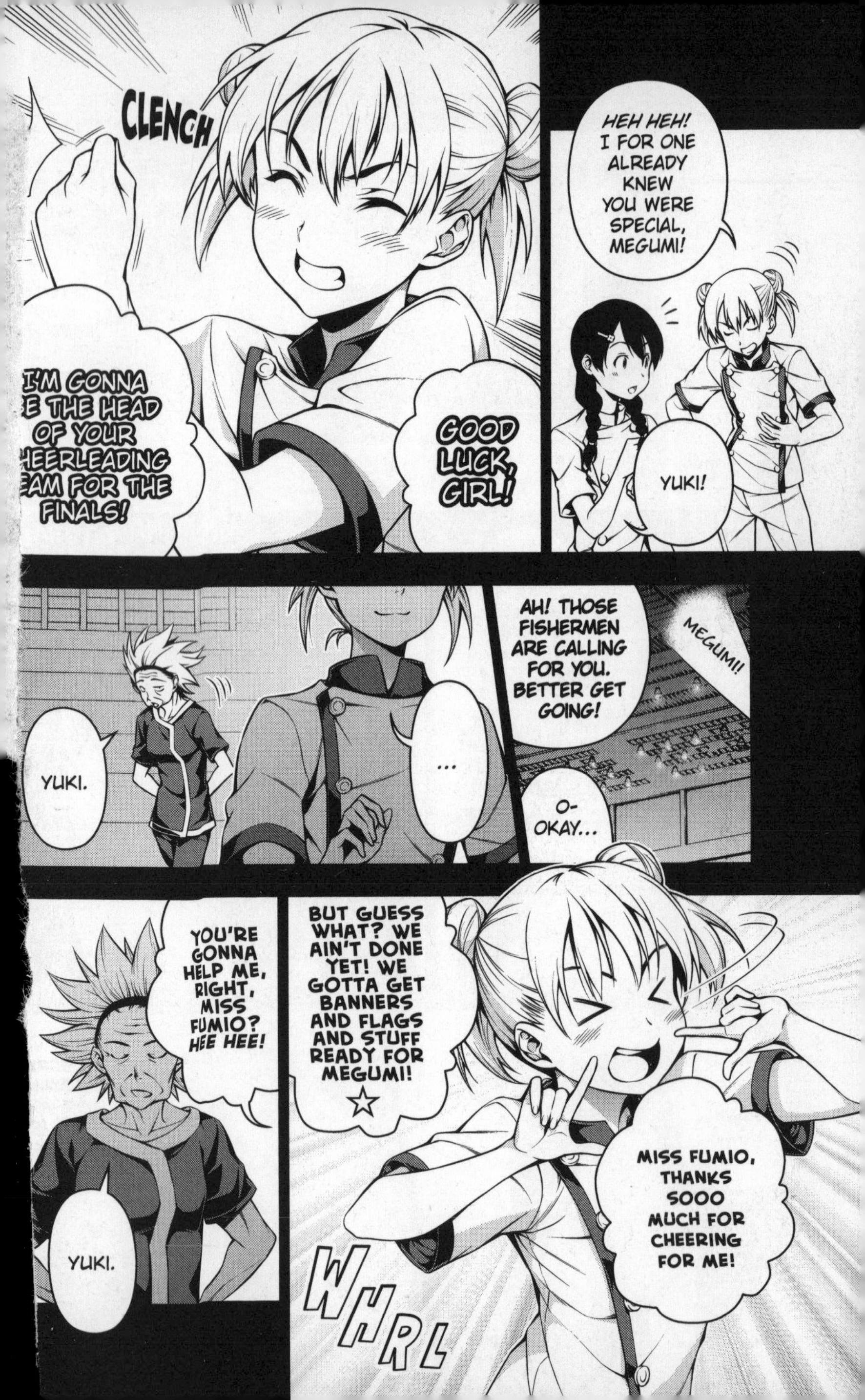
HEH HEH! I FOR ONE ALREADY KNEW YOU WERE SPECIAL, MEGUMI!
YUKI!
CLENCH
GOOD LUCK, GIRL!
I'M GONNA E THE HEAD OF YOUR HEERLEADING EAM FOR THE FINALS!
MEGUMI!
AH! THOSE FISHERMEN ARE CALLING FOR YOU. BETTER GET GOING!
O- OKAY...
...
YUKI.
MISS FUMIO, THANKS SOOO MUCH FOR CHEERING FOR ME!
WHRL
BUT GUESS WHAT? WE AIN'T DONE YET! WE GOTTA GET BANNERS AND FLAGS AND STUFF READY FOR MEGUMI! ☆
YOU'RE GONNA HELP ME, RIGHT, MISS FUMIO? HEE HEE!
YUKI.

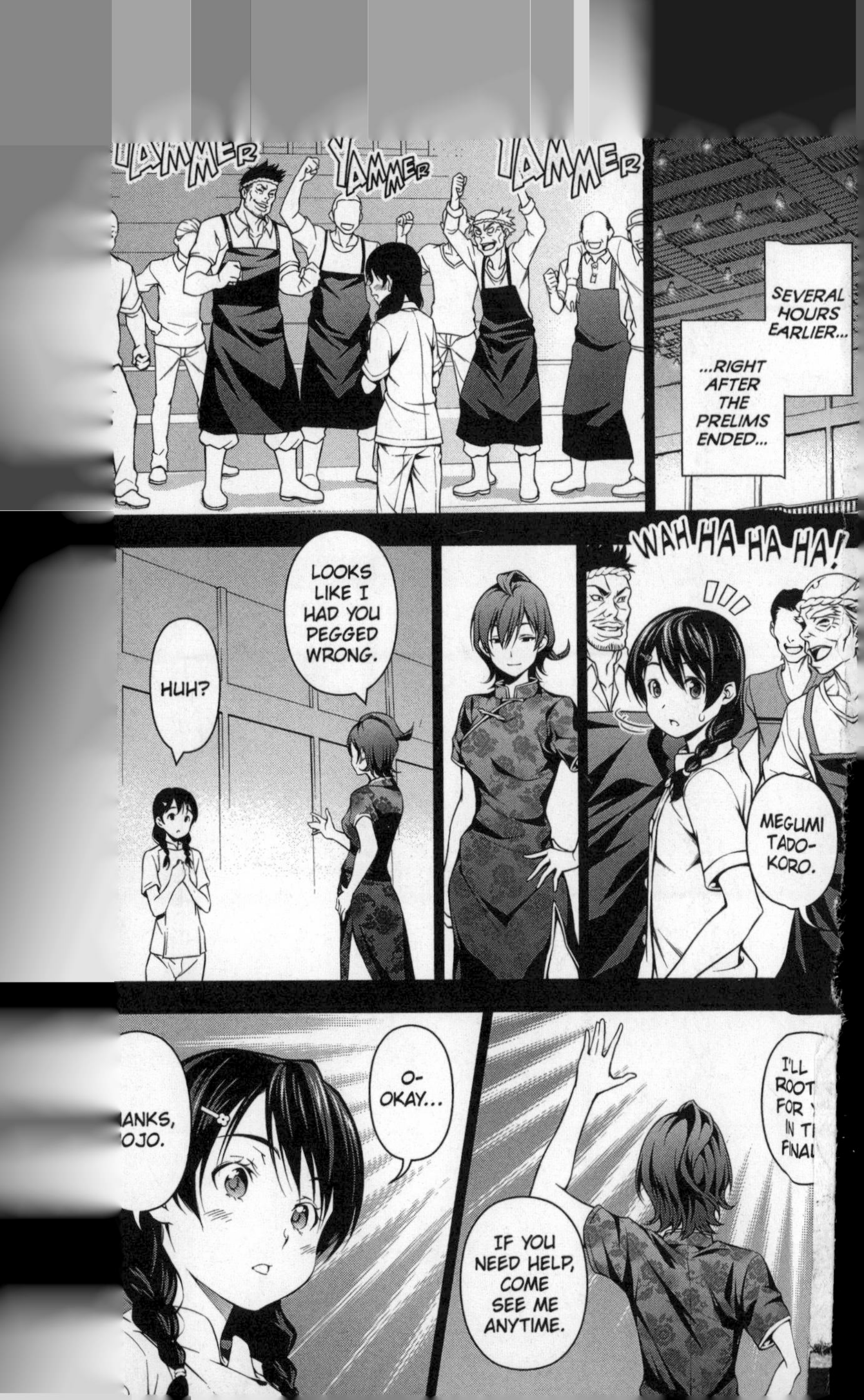
SEVERAL HOURS EARLIER...
...RIGHT AFTER THE PRELIMS ENDED...
YAMMER
YAMMER
YAMMER
WAH HA HA HA!
MEGUMI TADOKORO.
LOOKS LIKE I HAD YOU PEGGED WRONG.
HUH?
I'LL ROOT FOR IN T FINA
IF YOU NEED HELP, COME SEE ME ANYTIME.
O- OKAY...
ANKS, OJO.

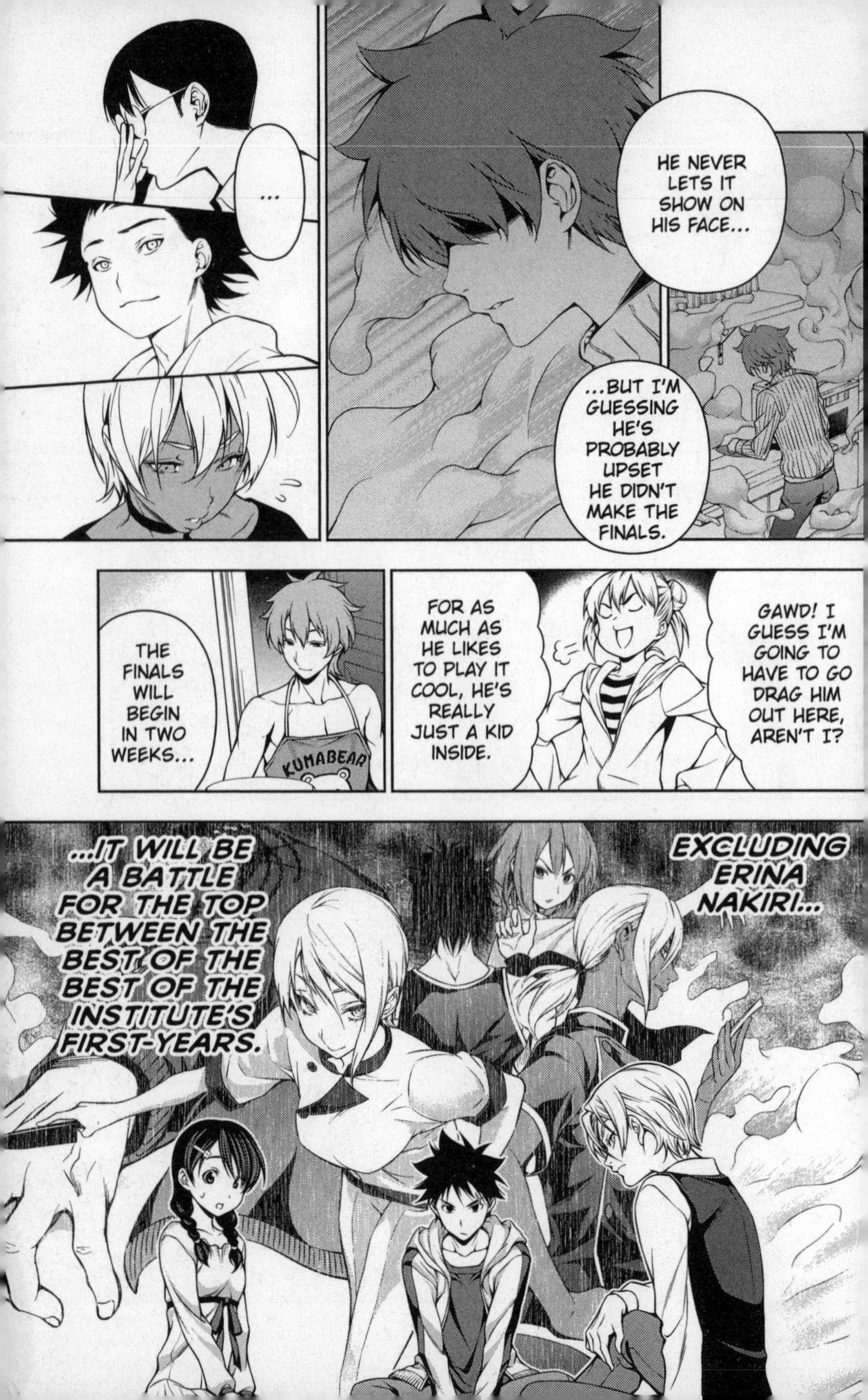
HE NEVER LETS IT SHOW ON HIS FACE...
...BUT I'M GUESSING HE'S PROBABLY UPSET HE DIDN'T MAKE THE FINALS.
...
GAWD! I GUESS I'M GOING TO HAVE TO GO DRAG HIM OUT HERE, AREN'T I?
FOR AS MUCH AS HE LIKES TO PLAY IT COOL, HE'S REALLY JUST A KID INSIDE.
THE FINALS WILL BEGIN IN TWO WEEKS...
KUMABEAR
EXCLUDING ERINA NAKIRI...
...IT WILL BE A BATTLE FOR THE TOP BETWEEN THE BEST OF THE BEST OF THE INSTITUTE'S FIRST-YEARS.

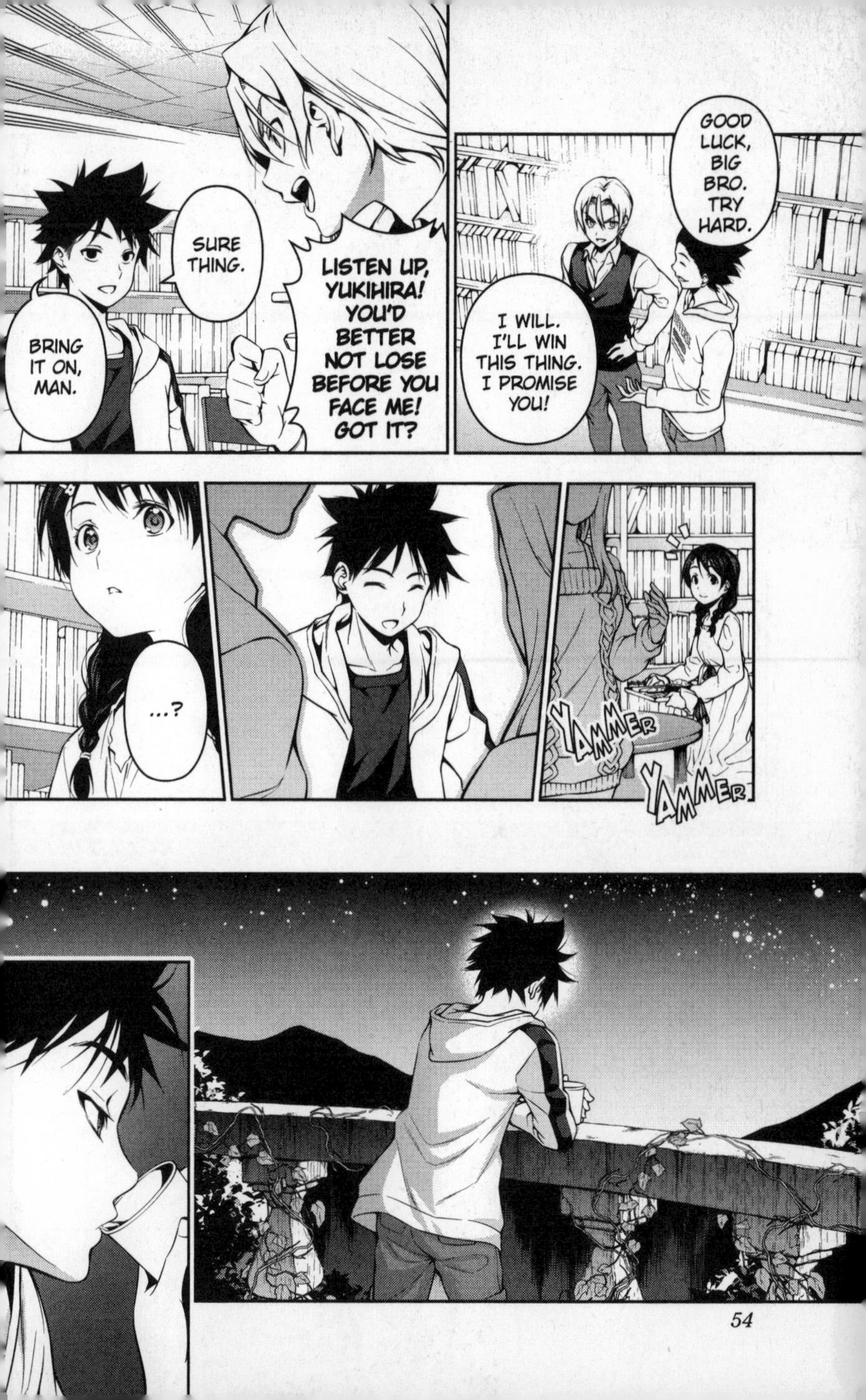
GOOD LUCK, BIG BRO. TRY HARD.
I WILL. I'LL WIN THIS THING. I PROMISE YOU!
LISTEN UP, YUKIHIRA! YOU'D BETTER NOT LOSE BEFORE YOU FACE ME! GOT IT?
SURE THING.
BRING IT ON, MAN.
YAMMER
YAMMER
...?

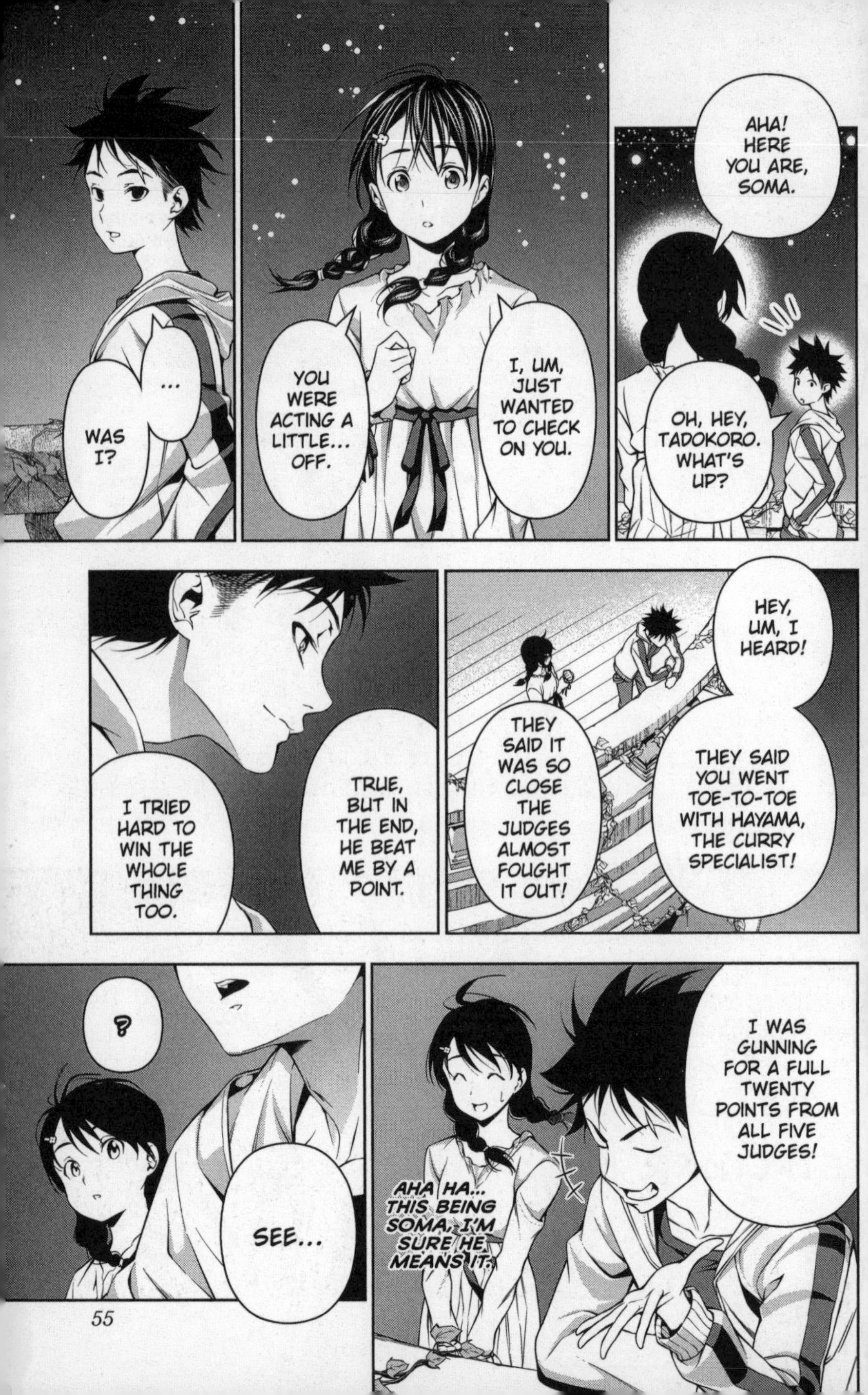
AHA! HERE YOU ARE, SOMA.
OH, HEY, TADOKORO. WHAT'S UP?
I, UM, JUST WANTED TO CHECK ON YOU.
YOU WERE ACTING A LITTLE... OFF.
...
WAS I?
HEY, UM, I HEARD!
THEY SAID YOU WENT TOE-TO-TOE WITH HAYAMA, THE CURRY SPECIALIST!
THEY SAID IT WAS SO CLOSE THE JUDGES ALMOST FOUGHT IT OUT!
TRUE, BUT IN THE END, HE BEAT ME BY A POINT.
I TRIED HARD TO WIN THE WHOLE THING TOO.
I WAS GUNNING FOR A FULL TWENTY POINTS FROM ALL FIVE JUDGES!
AHA HA... THIS BEING SOMA, I'M SURE HE MEANS IT.
?
SEE...

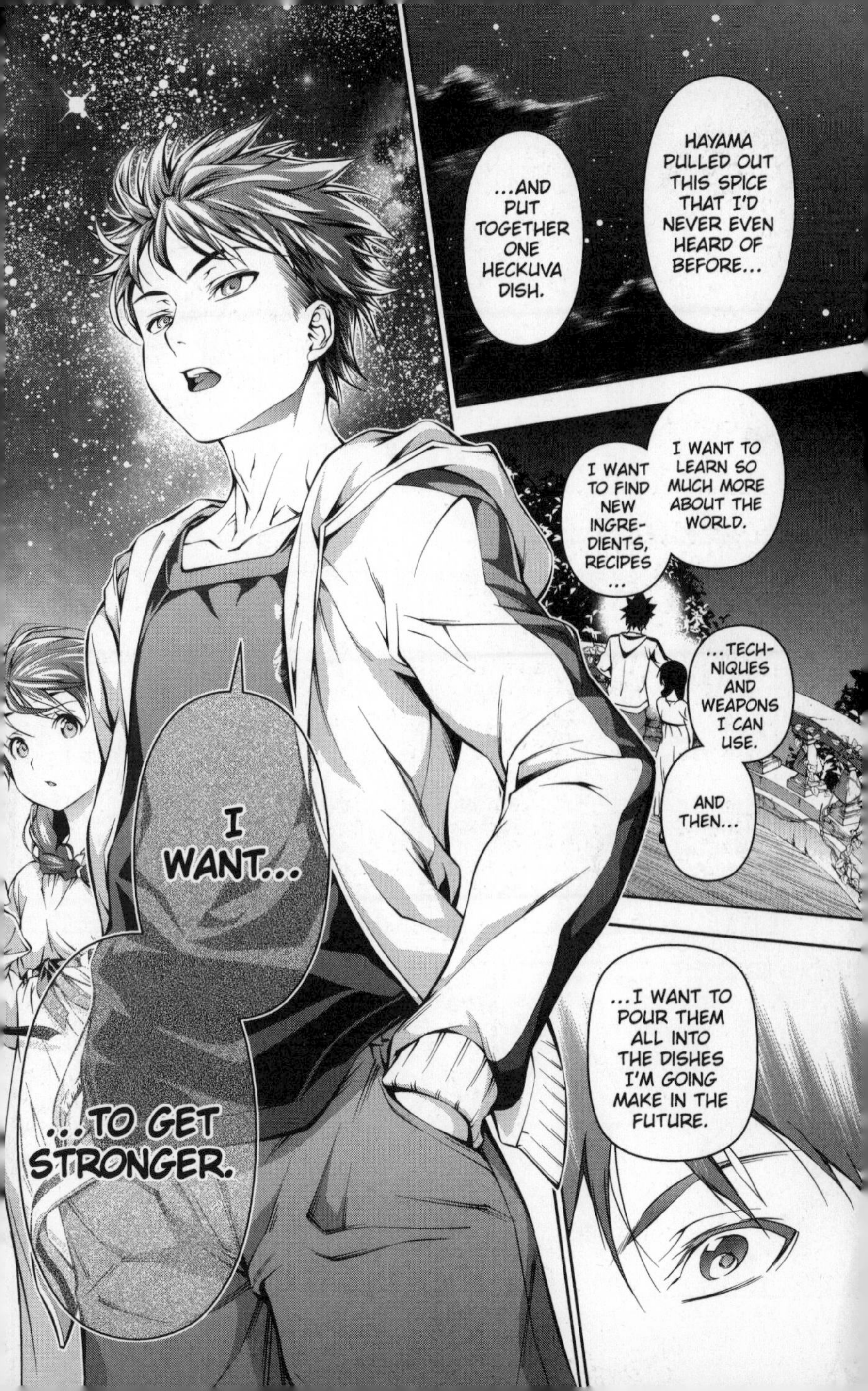
HAYAMA PULLED OUT THIS SPICE THAT I'D NEVER EVEN HEARD OF BEFORE...
...AND PUT TOGETHER ONE HECKUVA DISH.
I WANT TO LEARN SO MUCH MORE ABOUT THE WORLD.
I WANT TO FIND NEW INGRE-DIENTS, RECIPES...
...TECH-NIQUES AND WEAPONS I CAN USE.
AND THEN...
...I WANT TO POUR THEM ALL INTO THE DISHES I'M GOING MAKE IN THE FUTURE.
I WANT...
...TO GET STRONGER.

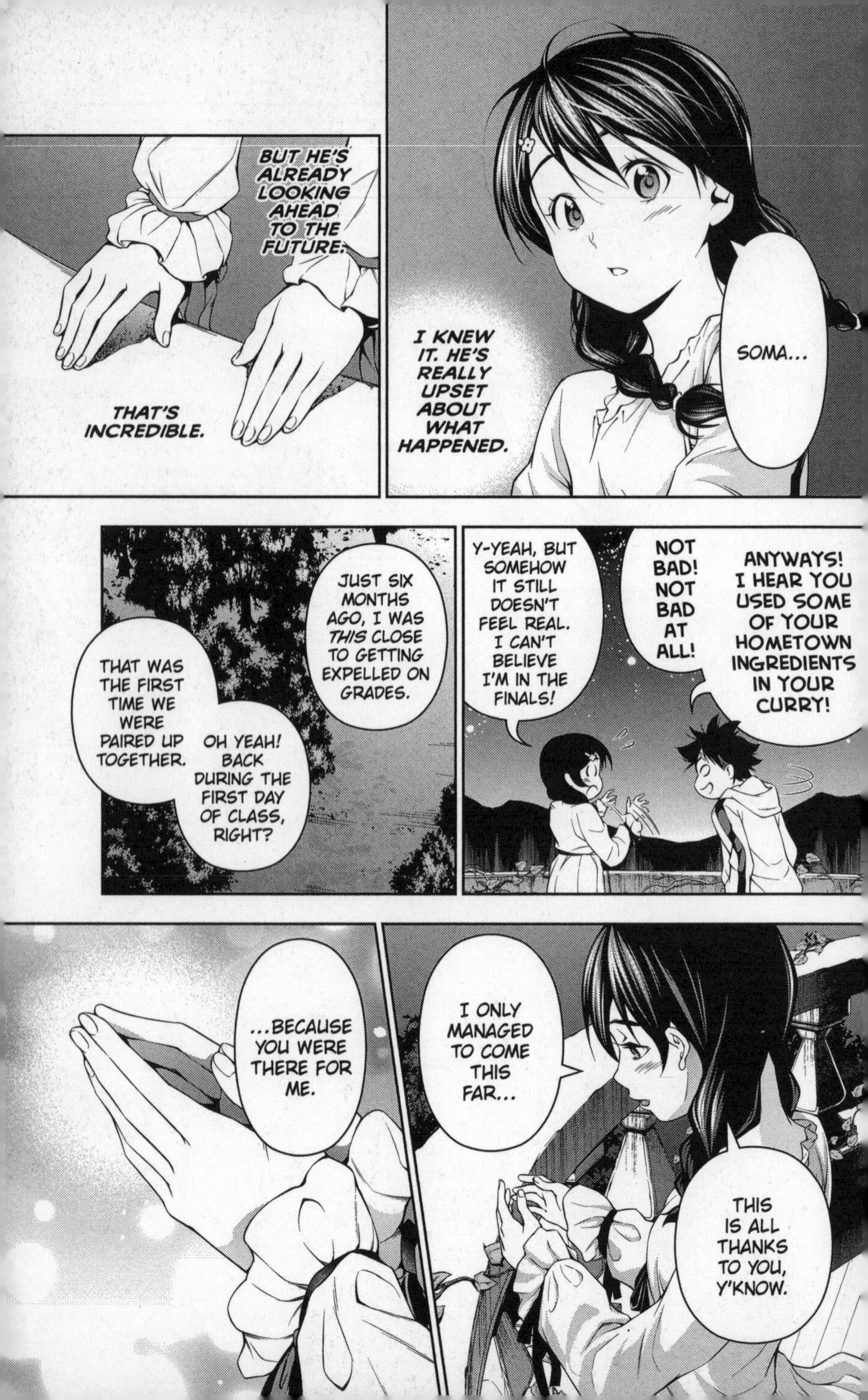
SOMA...
I KNEW IT. HE'S REALLY UPSET ABOUT WHAT HAPPENED.
BUT HE'S ALREADY LOOKING AHEAD TO THE FUTURE.
THAT'S INCREDIBLE.
ANYWAYS! I HEAR YOU USED SOME OF YOUR HOMETOWN INGREDIENTS IN YOUR CURRY!
NOT BAD! NOT BAD AT ALL!
Y-YEAH, BUT SOMEHOW IT STILL DOESN'T FEEL REAL. I CAN'T BELIEVE I'M IN THE FINALS!
JUST SIX MONTHS AGO, I WAS *THIS* CLOSE TO GETTING EXPELLED ON GRADES.
OH YEAH! BACK DURING THE FIRST DAY OF CLASS, RIGHT?
THAT WAS THE FIRST TIME WE WERE PAIRED UP TOGETHER.
THIS IS ALL THANKS TO YOU, Y'KNOW.
I ONLY MANAGED TO COME THIS FAR...
...BECAUSE YOU WERE THERE FOR ME.

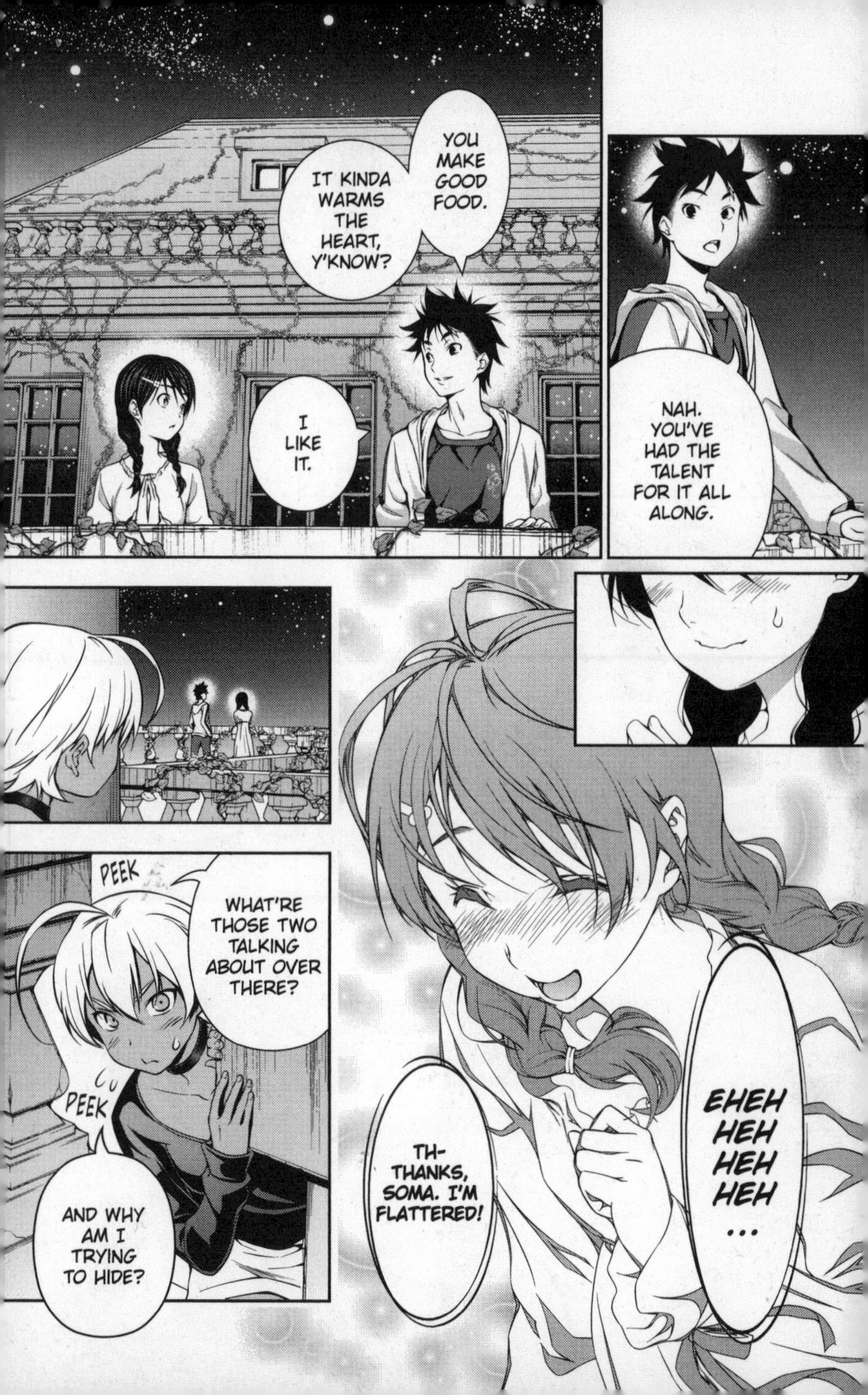
NAH. YOU'VE HAD THE TALENT FOR IT ALL ALONG.
YOU MAKE GOOD FOOD.
IT KINDA WARMS THE HEART, Y'KNOW?
I LIKE IT.
EHEH HEH HEH HEH ...
TH-THANKS, SOMA. I'M FLATTERED!
PEEK
WHAT'RE THOSE TWO TALKING ABOUT OVER THERE?
PEEK
AND WHY AM I TRYING TO HIDE?

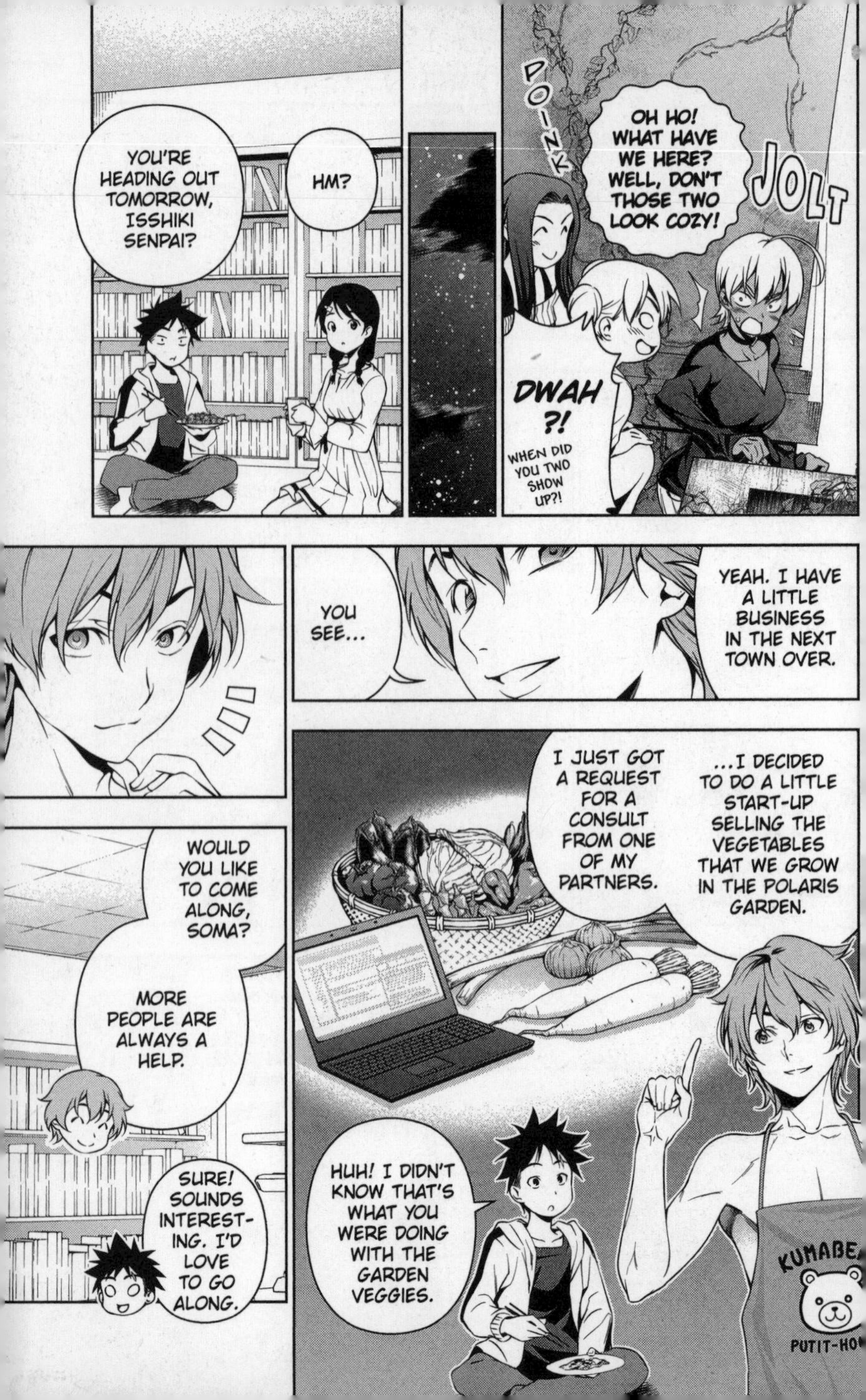
POINK
OH HO! WHAT HAVE WE HERE? WELL, DON'T THOSE TWO LOOK COZY!
JOLT
DWAH ?!
WHEN DID YOU TWO SHOW UP?!
HM?
YOU'RE HEADING OUT TOMORROW, ISSHIKI SENPAI?
YEAH. I HAVE A LITTLE BUSINESS IN THE NEXT TOWN OVER.
YOU SEE...
...I DECIDED TO DO A LITTLE START-UP SELLING THE VEGETABLES THAT WE GROW IN THE POLARIS GARDEN.
I JUST GOT A REQUEST FOR A CONSULT FROM ONE OF MY PARTNERS.
KUMABE
PUTIT-HO
HUH! I DIDN'T KNOW THAT'S WHAT YOU WERE DOING WITH THE GARDEN VEGGIES.
WOULD YOU LIKE TO COME ALONG, SOMA?
MORE PEOPLE ARE ALWAYS A HELP.
SURE! SOUNDS INTEREST-ING. I'D LOVE TO GO ALONG.

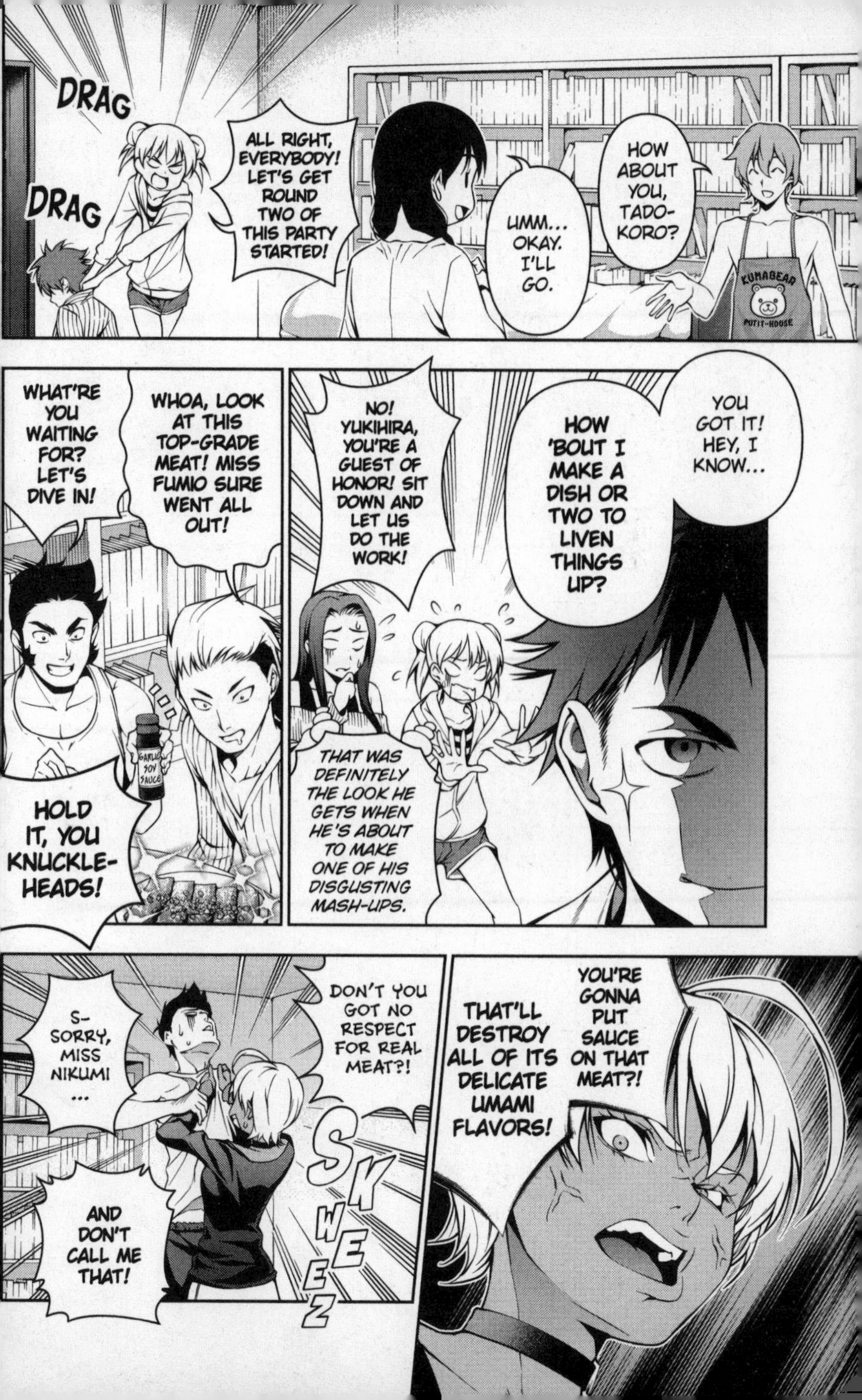
HOW ABOUT YOU, TADOKORO?
KUMABEAR
PUTIT-HOUSE
UMM... OKAY. I'LL GO.
ALL RIGHT, EVERYBODY! LET'S GET ROUND TWO OF THIS PARTY STARTED!
DRAG
DRAG
YOU GOT IT! HEY, I KNOW...
HOW 'BOUT I MAKE A DISH OR TWO TO LIVEN THINGS UP?
NO! YUKIHIRA, YOU'RE A GUEST OF HONOR! SIT DOWN AND LET US DO THE WORK!
THAT WAS DEFINITELY THE LOOK HE GETS WHEN HE'S ABOUT TO MAKE ONE OF HIS DISGUSTING MASH-UPS.
WHOA, LOOK AT THIS TOP-GRADE MEAT! MISS FUMIO SURE WENT ALL OUT!
WHAT'RE YOU WAITING FOR? LET'S DIVE IN!
GARLIC SOY SAUCE
HOLD IT, YOU KNUCKLEHEADS!
YOU'RE GONNA PUT SAUCE ON THAT MEAT?!
THAT'LL DESTROY ALL OF ITS DELICATE UMAMI FLAVORS!
DON'T YOU GOT NO RESPECT FOR REAL MEAT?!
SKWEEZ
S-SORRY, MISS NIKUMI...
AND DON'T CALL ME THAT!

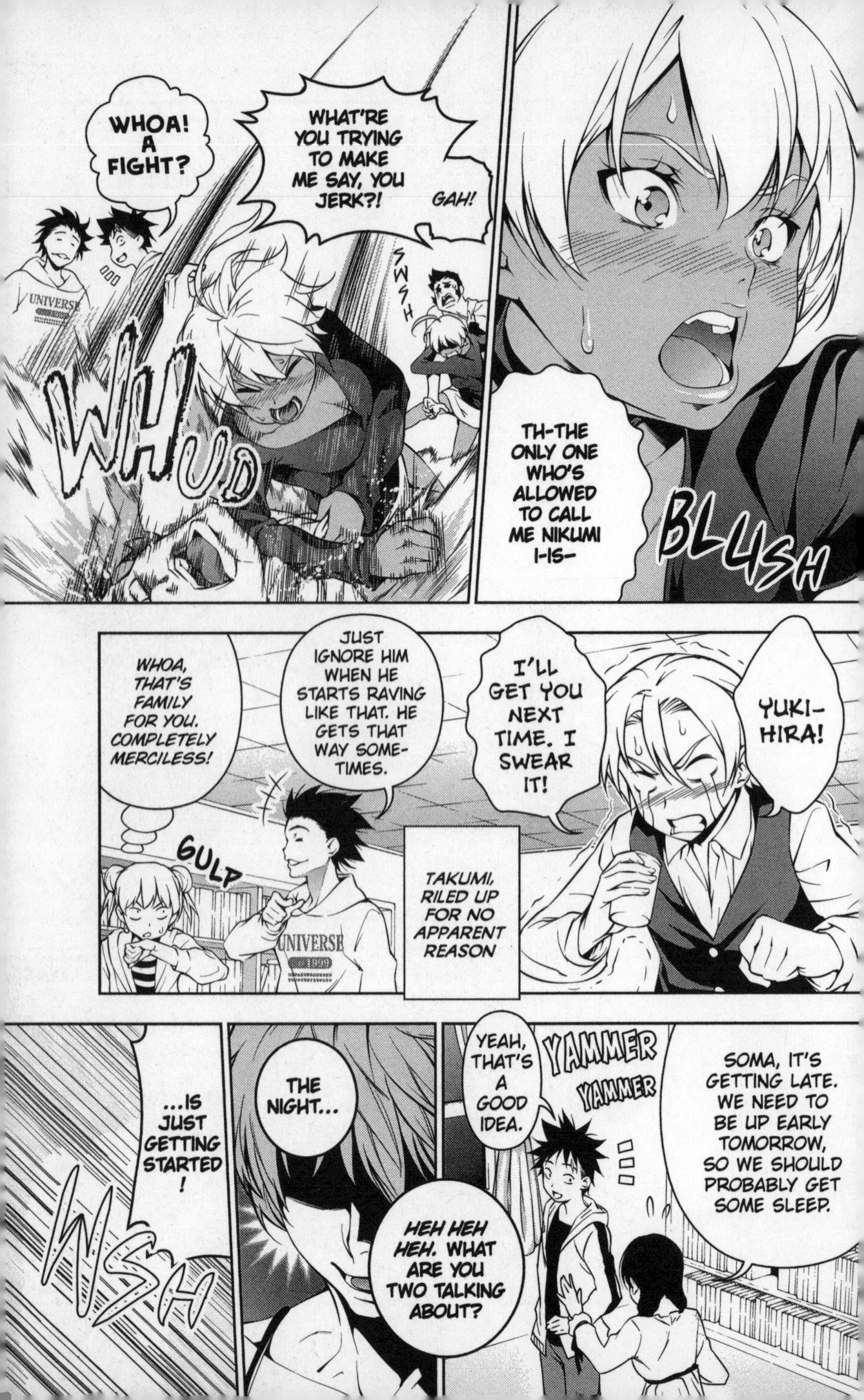
TH-THE ONLY ONE WHO'S ALLOWED TO CALL ME NIKUMI I-IS-
BLUSH
WHAT'RE YOU TRYING TO MAKE ME SAY, YOU JERK?!
GAH!
SWSH
WHOA! A FIGHT?
WHUD
YUKI-HIRA!
I'LL GET YOU NEXT TIME. I SWEAR IT!
TAKUMI, RILED UP FOR NO APPARENT REASON
JUST IGNORE HIM WHEN HE STARTS RAVING LIKE THAT. HE GETS THAT WAY SOME-TIMES.
WHOA, THAT'S FAMILY FOR YOU. COMPLETELY MERCILESS!
GULP
SOMA, IT'S GETTING LATE. WE NEED TO BE UP EARLY TOMORROW, SO WE SHOULD PROBABLY GET SOME SLEEP.
YAMMER
YAMMER
YEAH, THAT'S A GOOD IDEA.
THE NIGHT...
HEH HEH HEH. WHAT ARE YOU TWO TALKING ABOUT?
...IS JUST GETTING STARTED!
WSH

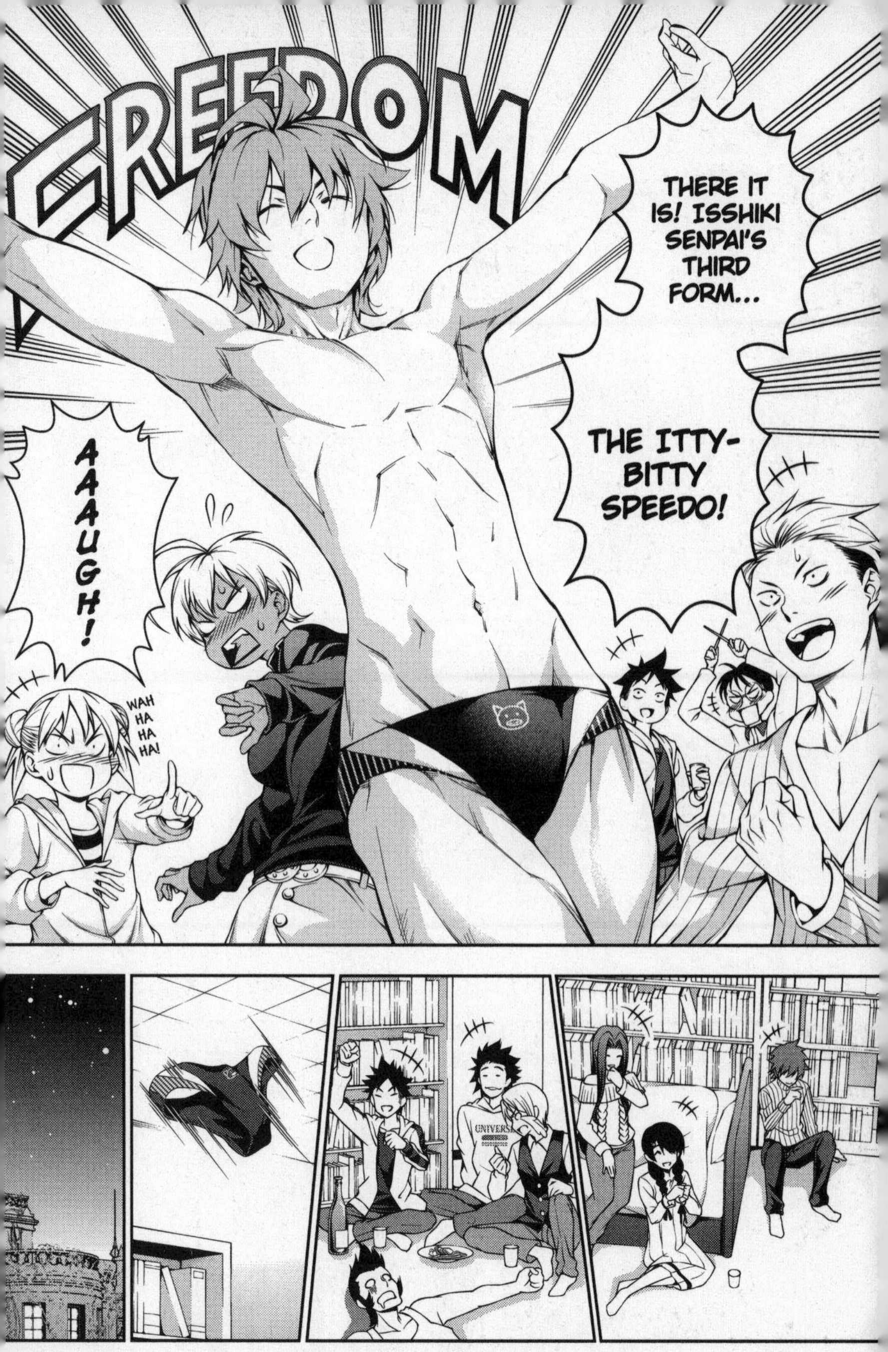
THERE IT IS! ISSHIKI SENPAI'S THIRD FORM...
THE ITTY-BITTY SPEEDO!
GREEDOM
AAAAUGH!
WAH HA HA HA!

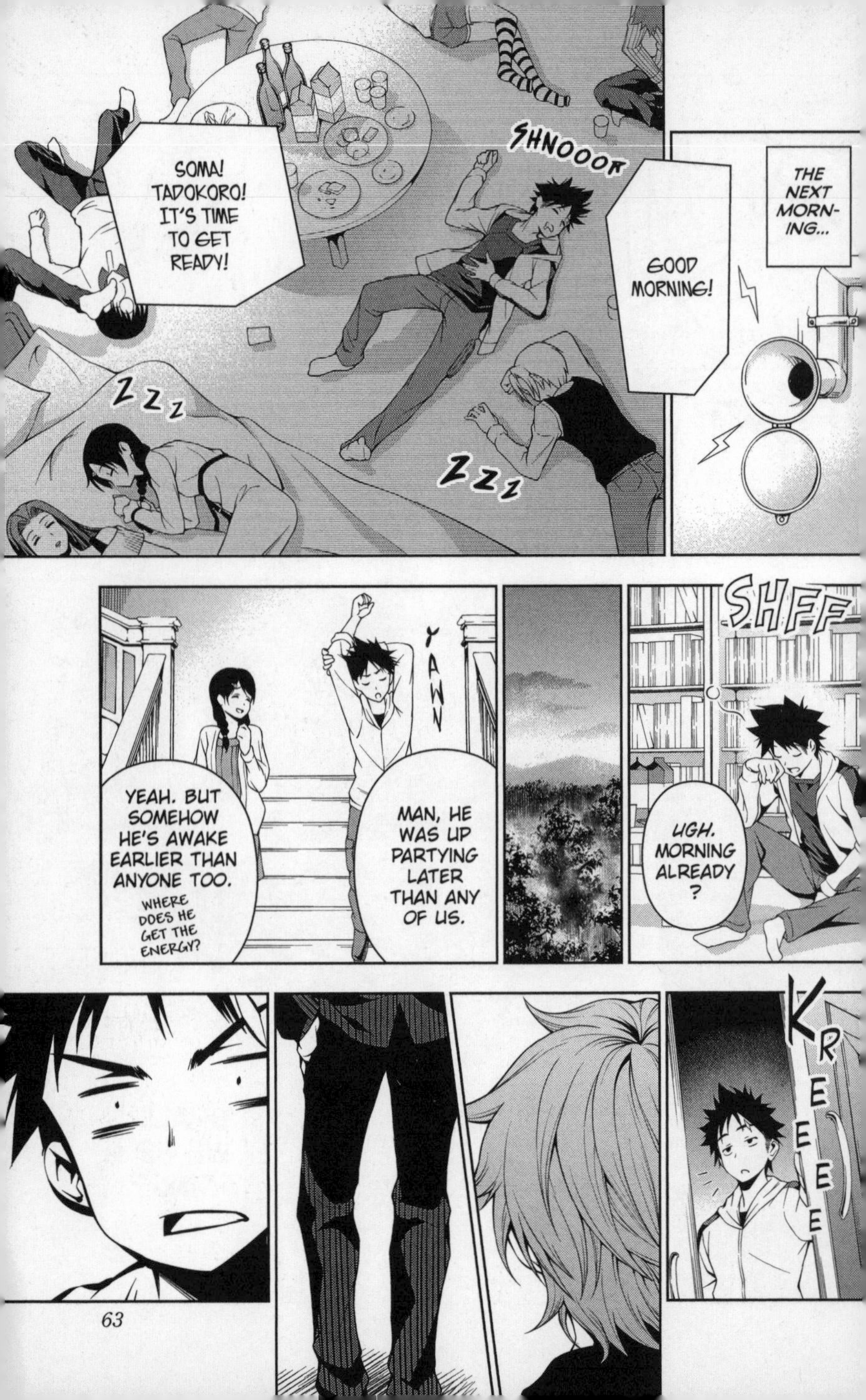

THE NEXT MORNING...
GOOD MORNING!
SHNOOOR
SOMA! TADOKORO! IT'S TIME TO GET READY!
ZZZ
ZZZ
SHFF
UGH. MORNING ALREADY?
YAWN
MAN, HE WAS UP PARTYING LATER THAN ANY OF US.
YEAH. BUT SOMEHOW HE'S AWAKE EARLIER THAN ANYONE TOO.
WHERE DOES HE GET THE ENERGY?
KREEEE

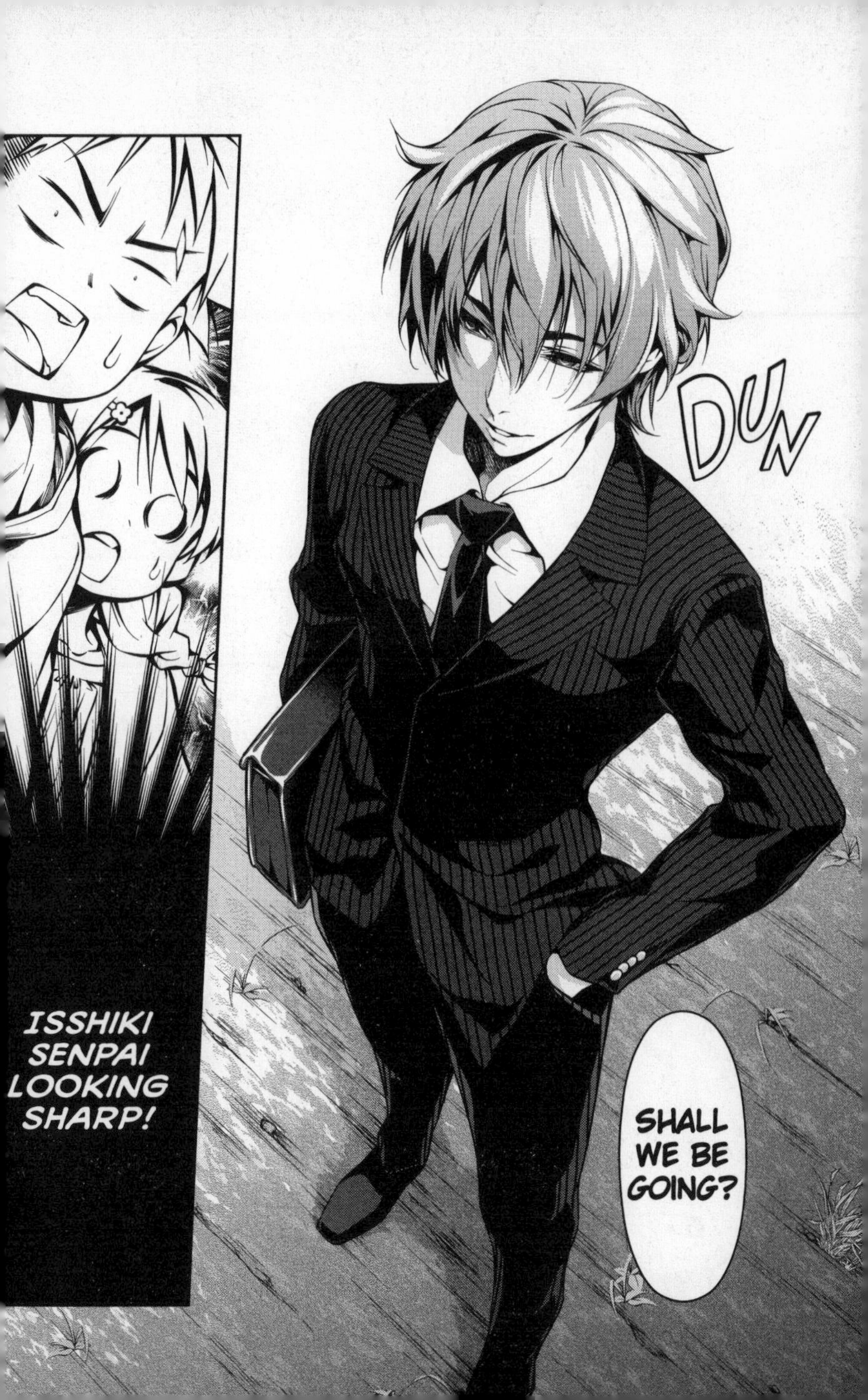
DUN
SHALL WE BE GOING?
ISSHIKI SENPAI LOOKING SHARP!

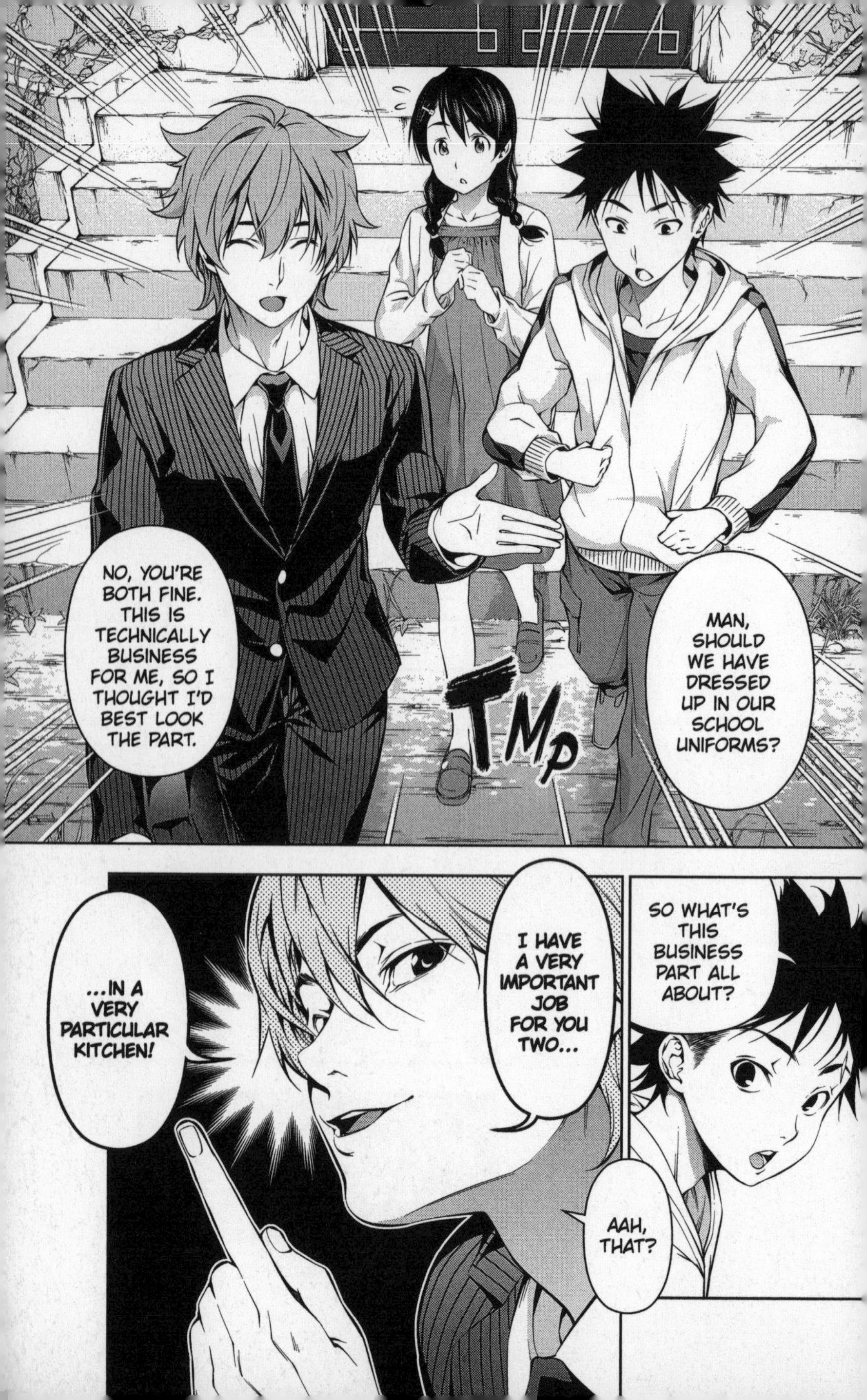
MAN, SHOULD WE HAVE DRESSED UP IN OUR SCHOOL UNIFORMS?
TMP
NO, YOU'RE BOTH FINE. THIS IS TECHNICALLY BUSINESS FOR ME, SO I THOUGHT I'D BEST LOOK THE PART.
SO WHAT'S THIS BUSINESS PART ALL ABOUT?
AAH, THAT?
I HAVE A VERY IMPORTANT JOB FOR YOU TWO...
...IN A VERY PARTICULAR KITCHEN!

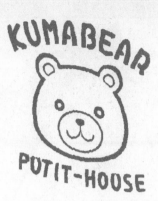

KUMABEAR PUTIT-HOUSE

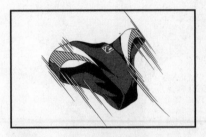

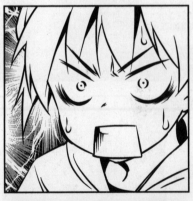

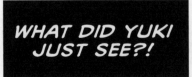

WHAT DID YUKI JUST SEE?!

CONTINUED ON PAGE 110!

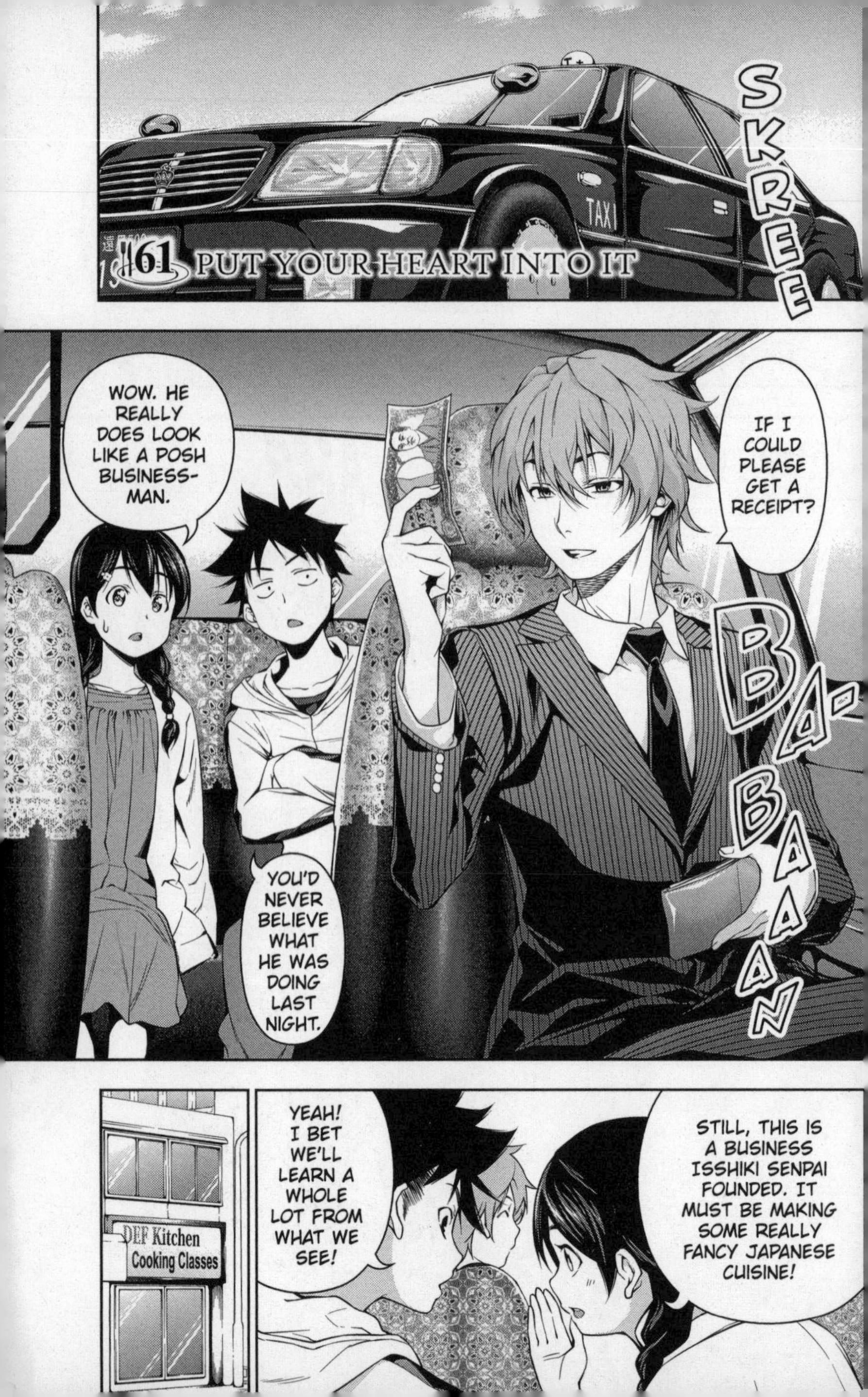
161 PUT YOUR HEART INTO IT
TAXI
SKREEE
IF I COULD PLEASE GET A RECEIPT?
BA-BAAAAN
WOW. HE REALLY DOES LOOK LIKE A POSH BUSINESS-MAN.
YOU'D NEVER BELIEVE WHAT HE WAS DOING LAST NIGHT.
STILL, THIS IS A BUSINESS ISSHIKI SENPAI FOUNDED. IT MUST BE MAKING SOME REALLY FANCY JAPANESE CUISINE!
YEAH! I BET WE'LL LEARN A WHOLE LOT FROM WHAT WE SEE!
DEF Kitchen
Cooking Classes

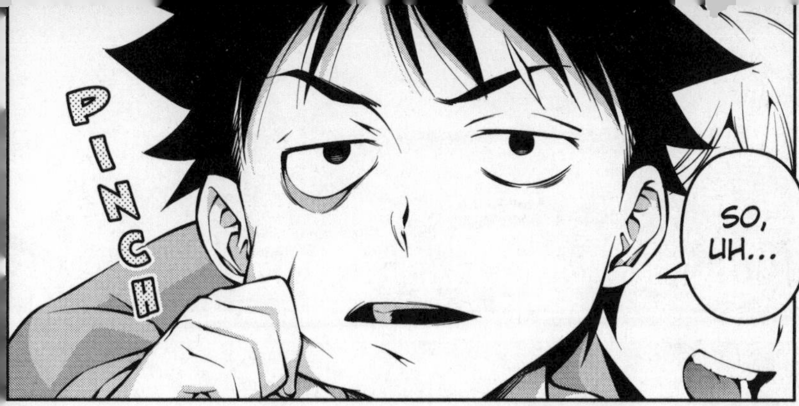
SO, UH...
PINCH

61 PUT YOUR HEART INTO IT

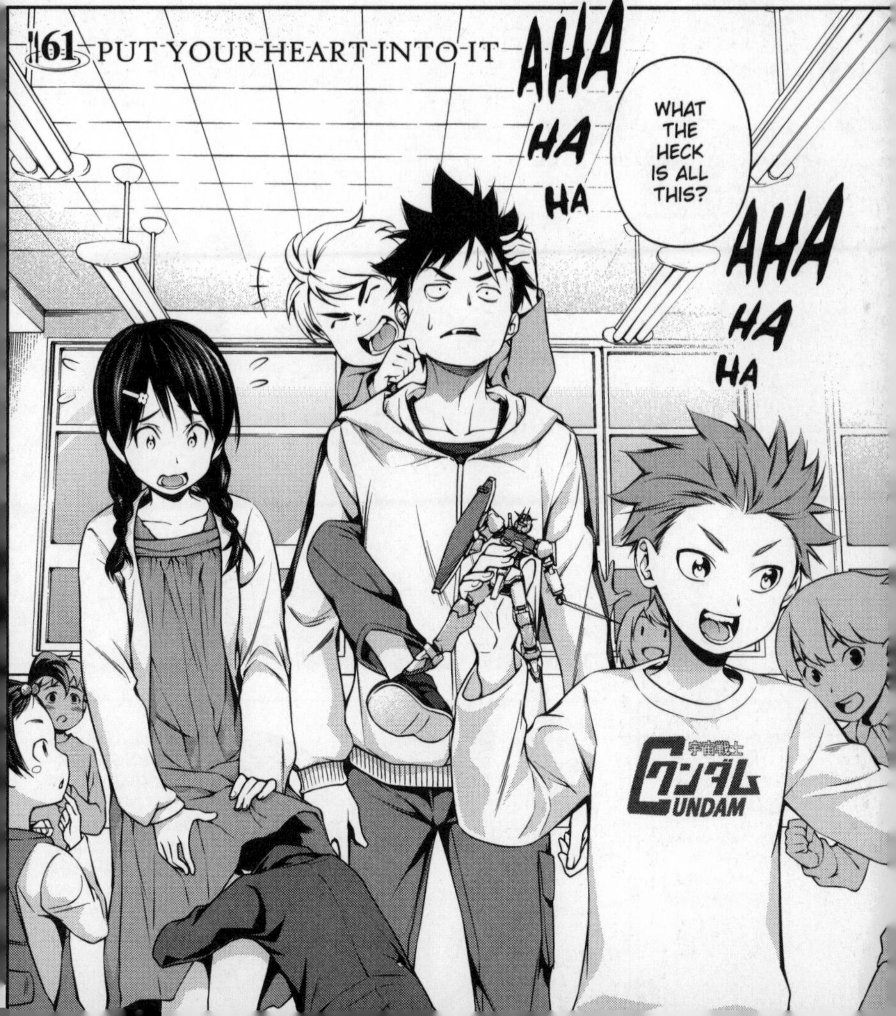
AHA HA HA
WHAT THE HECK IS ALL THIS?
AHA HA HA
GUNDAM

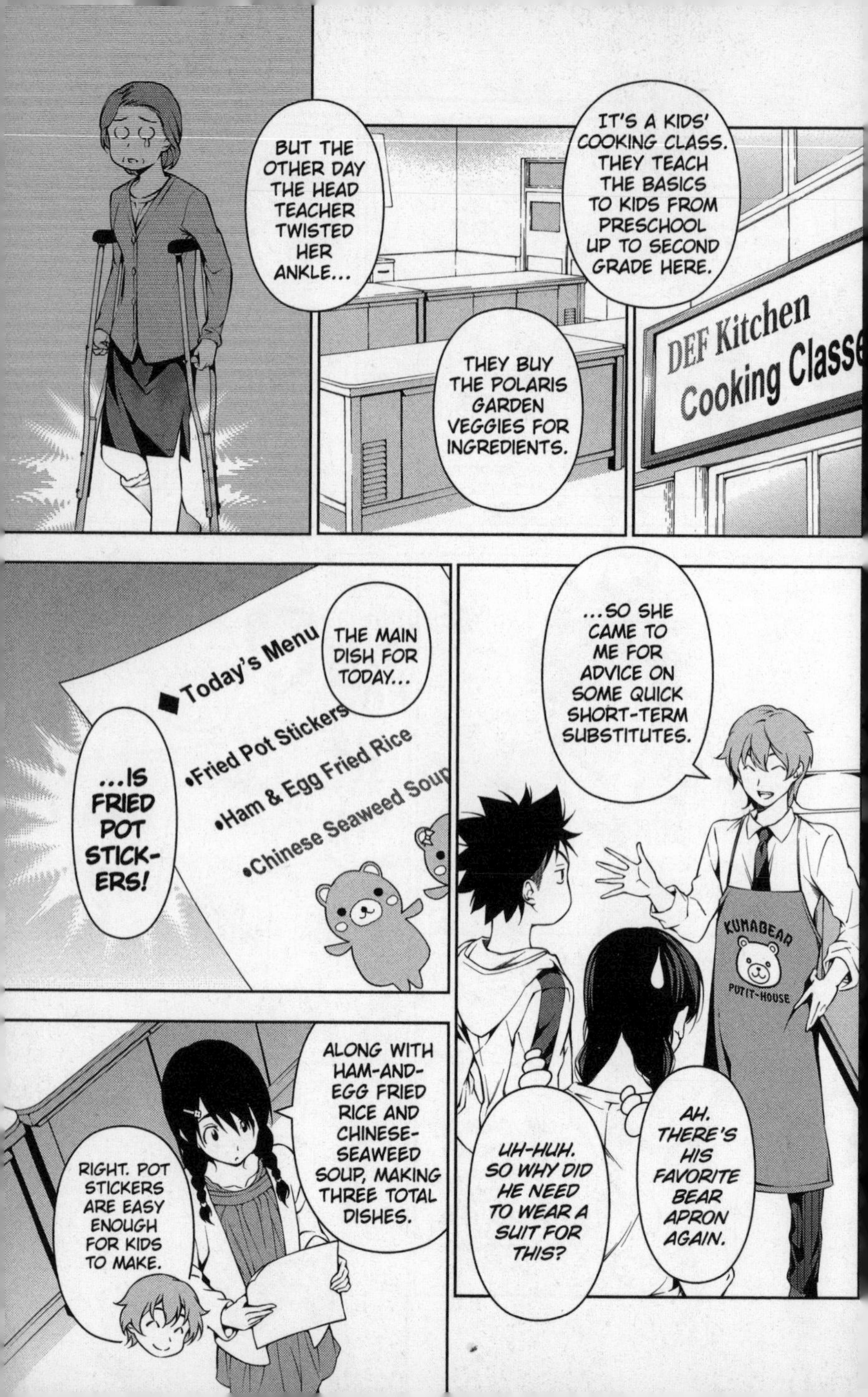
IT'S A KIDS' COOKING CLASS. THEY TEACH THE BASICS TO KIDS FROM PRESCHOOL UP TO SECOND GRADE HERE.
DEF Kitchen
Cooking Classe
THEY BUY THE POLARIS GARDEN VEGGIES FOR INGREDIENTS.
BUT THE OTHER DAY THE HEAD TEACHER TWISTED HER ANKLE...
...SO SHE CAME TO ME FOR ADVICE ON SOME QUICK SHORT-TERM SUBSTITUTES.
KUMABEAR
POTIT-HOUSE
AH. THERE'S HIS FAVORITE BEAR APRON AGAIN.
UH-HUH. SO WHY DID HE NEED TO WEAR A SUIT FOR THIS?
THE MAIN DISH FOR TODAY...
Today's Menu
•Fried Pot Stickers
•Ham & Egg Fried Rice
•Chinese Seaweed Soup
...IS FRIED POT STICK-ERS!
ALONG WITH HAM-AND-EGG FRIED RICE AND CHINESE-SEAWEED SOUP, MAKING THREE TOTAL DISHES.
RIGHT. POT STICKERS ARE EASY ENOUGH FOR KIDS TO MAKE.

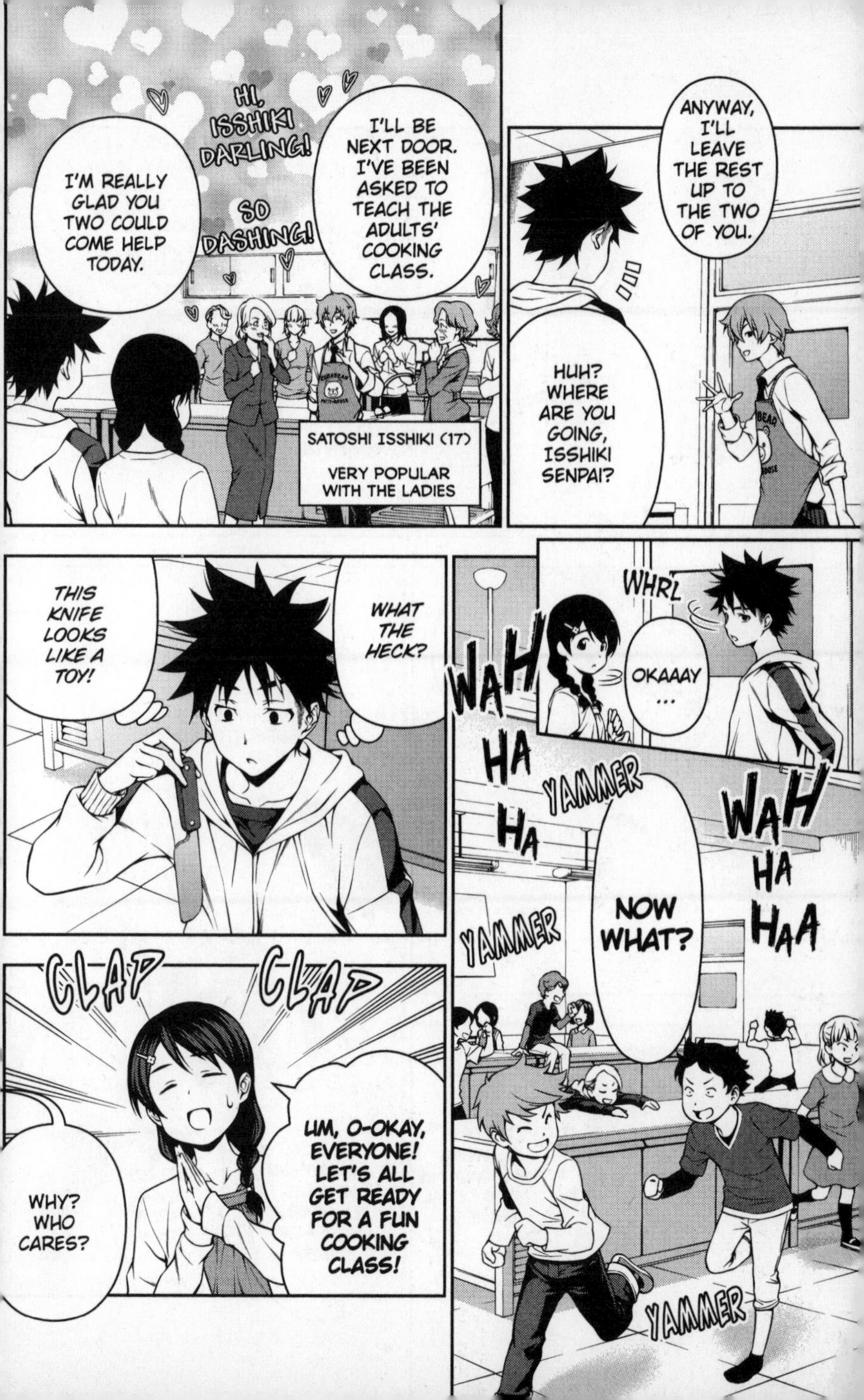
I'M REALLY GLAD YOU TWO COULD COME HELP TODAY.
HI, ISSHIKI DARLING!
SO DASHING!
I'LL BE NEXT DOOR. I'VE BEEN ASKED TO TEACH THE ADULTS' COOKING CLASS.
SATOSHI ISSHIKI (17)
VERY POPULAR WITH THE LADIES
ANYWAY, I'LL LEAVE THE REST UP TO THE TWO OF YOU.
HUH? WHERE ARE YOU GOING, ISSHIKI SENPAI?
WHRL
OKAAAY ...
WAH HA HA
YAMMER
WAH HA HAA
NOW WHAT?
YAMMER
YAMMER
WHAT THE HECK?
THIS KNIFE LOOKS LIKE A TOY!
CLAP CLAP
UM, O-OKAY, EVERYONE! LET'S ALL GET READY FOR A FUN COOKING CLASS!
WHY? WHO CARES?

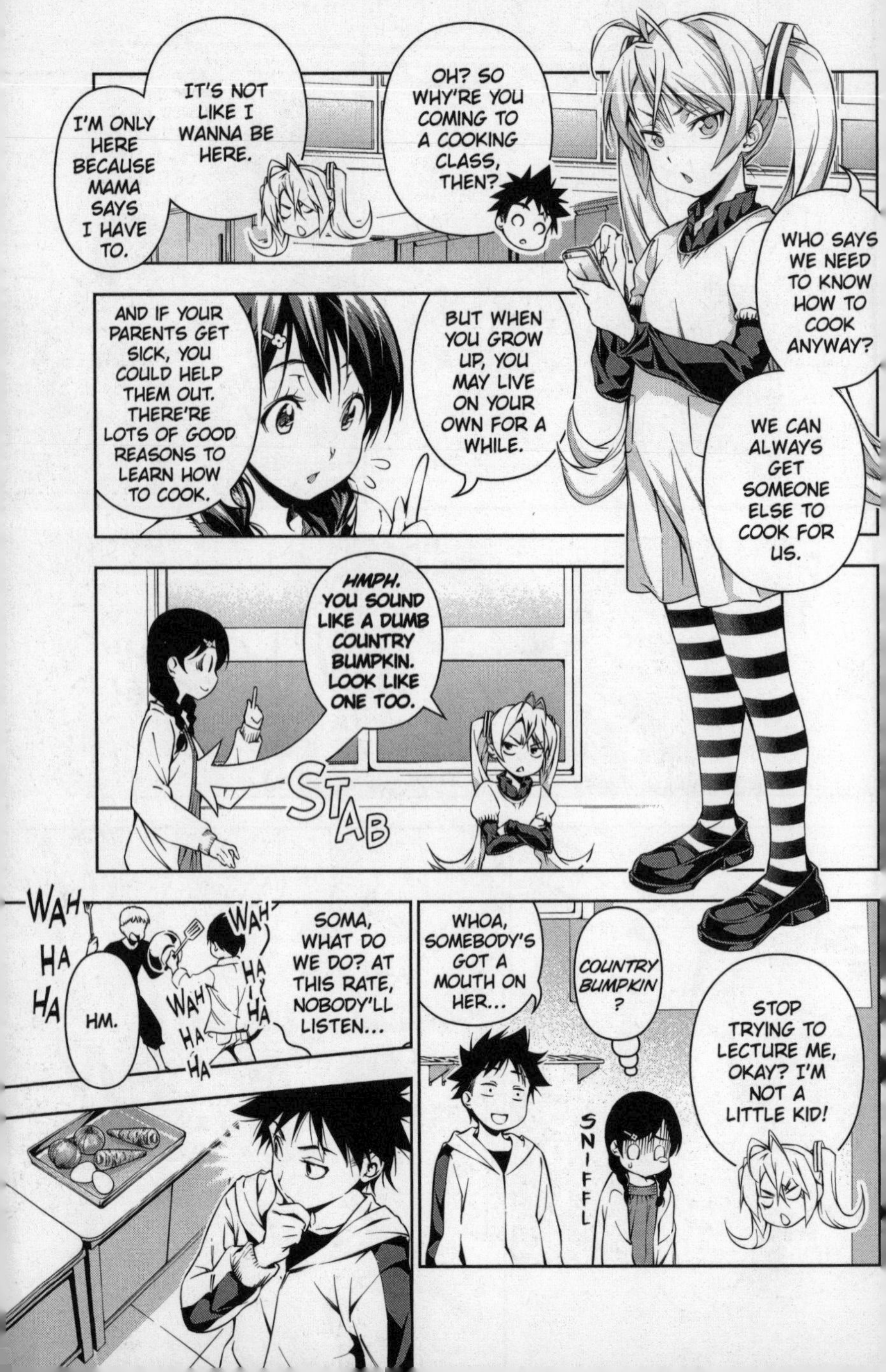
IT'S NOT LIKE I WANNA BE HERE.
OH? SO WHY'RE YOU COMING TO A COOKING CLASS, THEN?
I'M ONLY HERE BECAUSE MAMA SAYS I HAVE TO.
WHO SAYS WE NEED TO KNOW HOW TO COOK ANYWAY?
WE CAN ALWAYS GET SOMEONE ELSE TO COOK FOR US.
BUT WHEN YOU GROW UP, YOU MAY LIVE ON YOUR OWN FOR A WHILE.
AND IF YOUR PARENTS GET SICK, YOU COULD HELP THEM OUT. THERE'RE LOTS OF GOOD REASONS TO LEARN HOW TO COOK.
HMPH. YOU SOUND LIKE A DUMB COUNTRY BUMPKIN. LOOK LIKE ONE TOO.
STAB
STOP TRYING TO LECTURE ME, OKAY? I'M NOT A LITTLE KID!
COUNTRY BUMPKIN?
SNIFFL
WHOA, SOMEBODY'S GOT A MOUTH ON HER...
SOMA, WHAT DO WE DO? AT THIS RATE, NOBODY'LL LISTEN...
WAH HA HA
WAH HA HA
WAH HA HA
HM.

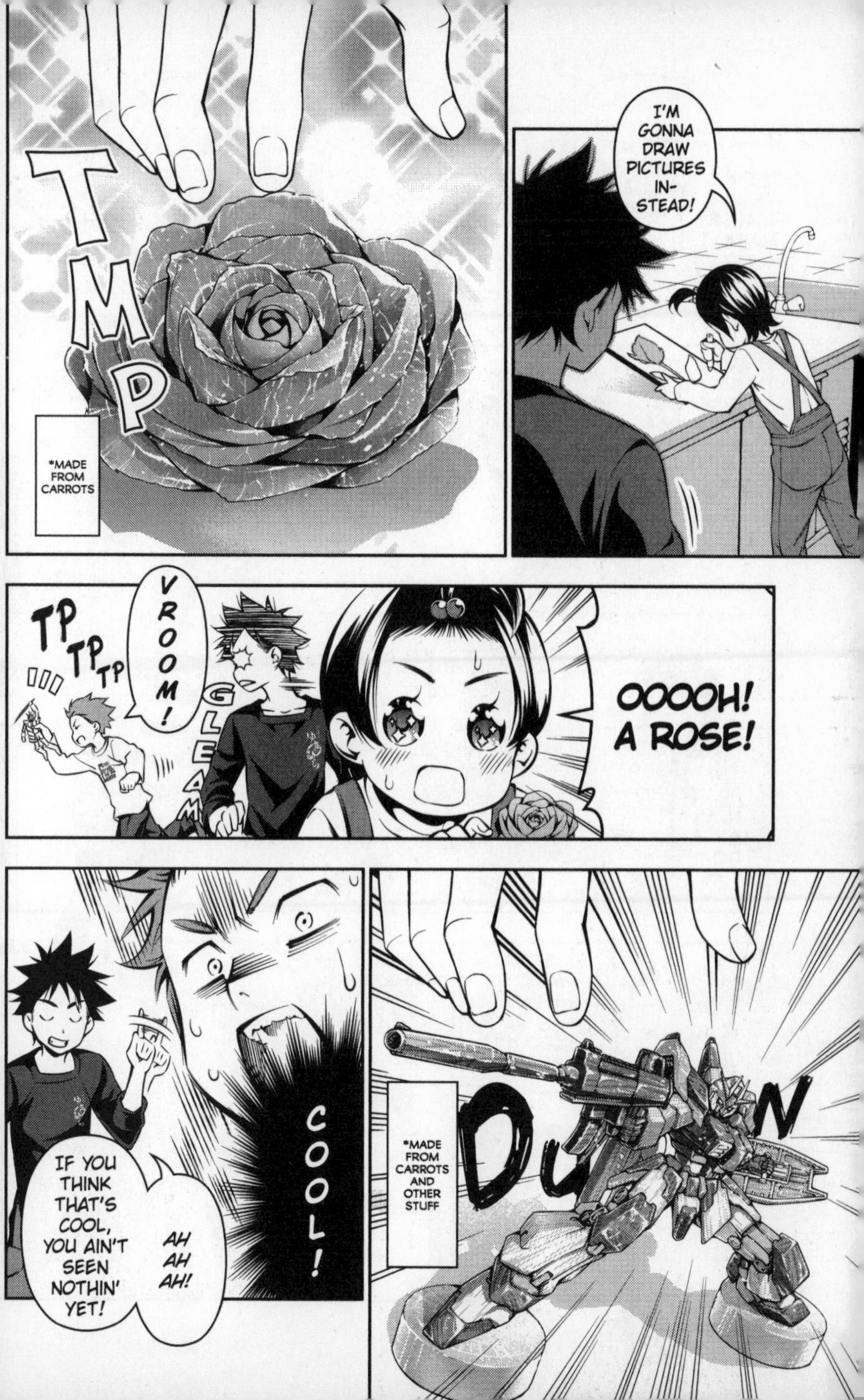
I'M GONNA DRAW PICTURES IN-STEAD!
TMP
*MADE FROM CARROTS
OOOOH! A ROSE!
GLEAM
VROOM!
TP TP TP
*MADE FROM CARROTS AND OTHER STUFF
COOL!
AH AH AH!
IF YOU THINK THAT'S COOL, YOU AIN'T SEEN NOTHIN' YET!

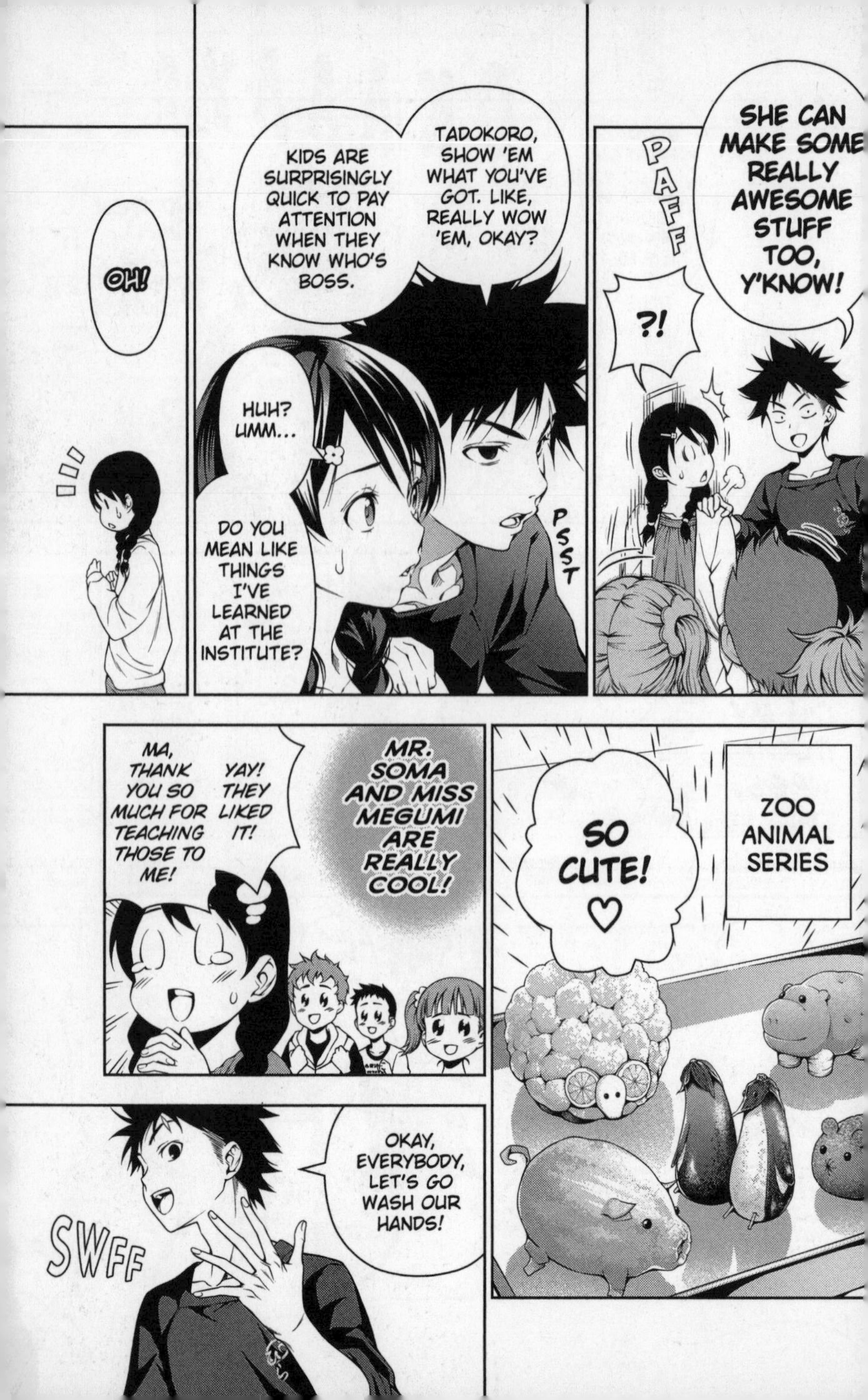
SHE CAN MAKE SOME REALLY AWESOME STUFF TOO, Y'KNOW!
PAFF
?!
TADOKORO, SHOW 'EM WHAT YOU'VE GOT. LIKE, REALLY WOW 'EM, OKAY?
KIDS ARE SURPRISINGLY QUICK TO PAY ATTENTION WHEN THEY KNOW WHO'S BOSS.
PSST
HUH? UMM...
DO YOU MEAN LIKE THINGS I'VE LEARNED AT THE INSTITUTE?
OH!
ZOO ANIMAL SERIES
SO CUTE! ♡
MR. SOMA AND MISS MEGUMI ARE REALLY COOL!
YAY! THEY LIKED IT!
MA, THANK YOU SO MUCH FOR TEACHING THOSE TO ME!
OKAY, EVERYBODY, LET'S GO WASH OUR HANDS!
SWFF

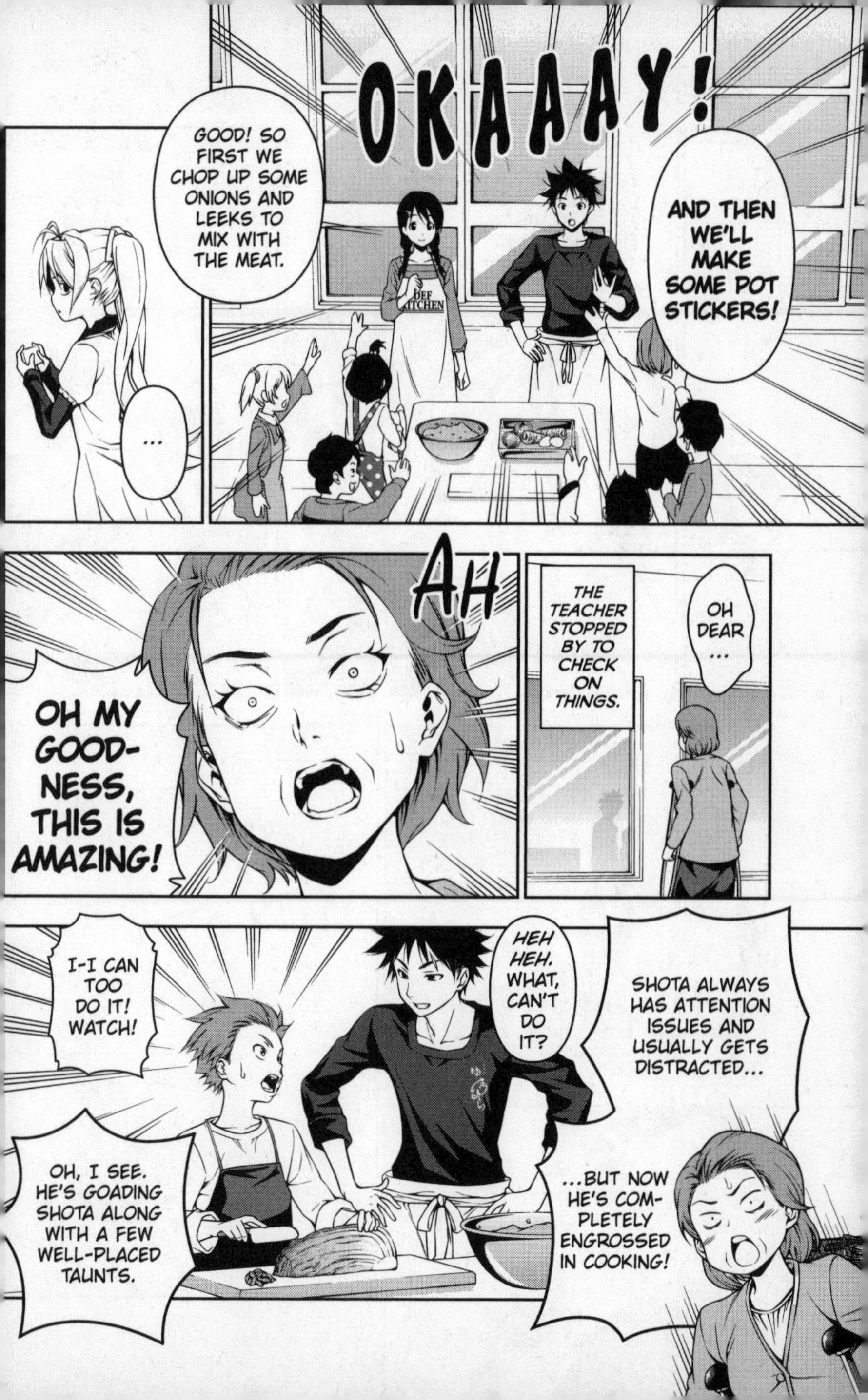
OKAAAY!
AND THEN WE'LL MAKE SOME POT STICKERS!
GOOD! SO FIRST WE CHOP UP SOME ONIONS AND LEEKS TO MIX WITH THE MEAT.
DEF KITCHEN
...
OH DEAR...
THE TEACHER STOPPED BY TO CHECK ON THINGS.
AH
OH MY GOOD-NESS, THIS IS AMAZING!
SHOTA ALWAYS HAS ATTENTION ISSUES AND USUALLY GETS DISTRACTED...
HEH HEH. WHAT, CAN'T DO IT?
I-I CAN TOO DO IT! WATCH!
...BUT NOW HE'S COM-PLETELY ENGROSSED IN COOKING!
OH, I SEE. HE'S GOADING SHOTA ALONG WITH A FEW WELL-PLACED TAUNTS.

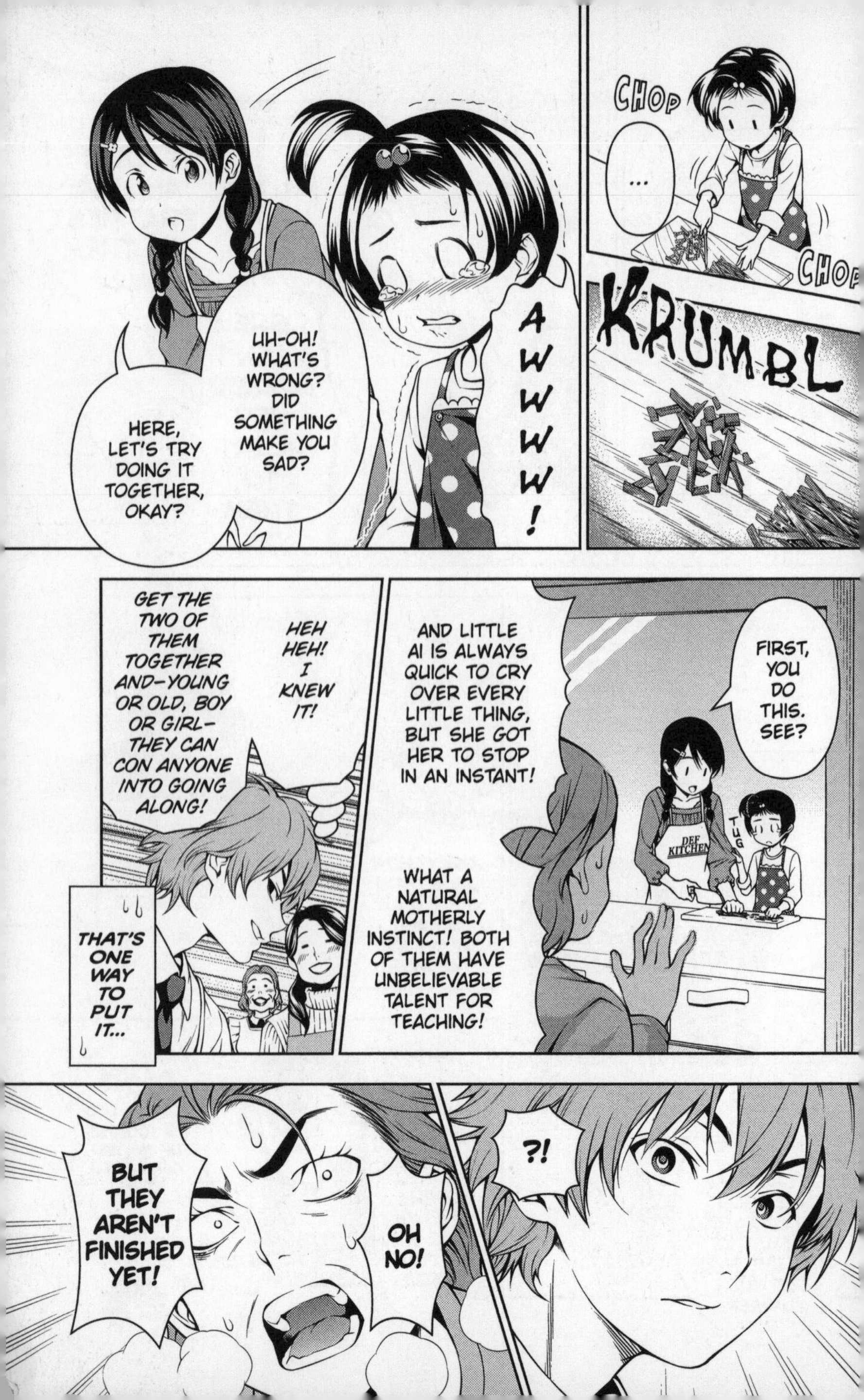
CHOP
...
CHOP
KRUMBL
AWWWWW!
UH-OH! WHAT'S WRONG? DID SOMETHING MAKE YOU SAD?
HERE, LET'S TRY DOING IT TOGETHER, OKAY?
FIRST, YOU DO THIS. SEE?
TUG
DEF KITCHEN
AND LITTLE AI IS ALWAYS QUICK TO CRY OVER EVERY LITTLE THING, BUT SHE GOT HER TO STOP IN AN INSTANT!
WHAT A NATURAL MOTHERLY INSTINCT! BOTH OF THEM HAVE UNBELIEVABLE TALENT FOR TEACHING!
HEH HEH! I KNEW IT!
GET THE TWO OF THEM TOGETHER AND—YOUNG OR OLD, BOY OR GIRL—THEY CAN CON ANYONE INTO GOING ALONG!
THAT'S ONE WAY TO PUT IT...
?!
OH NO!
BUT THEY AREN'T FINISHED YET!

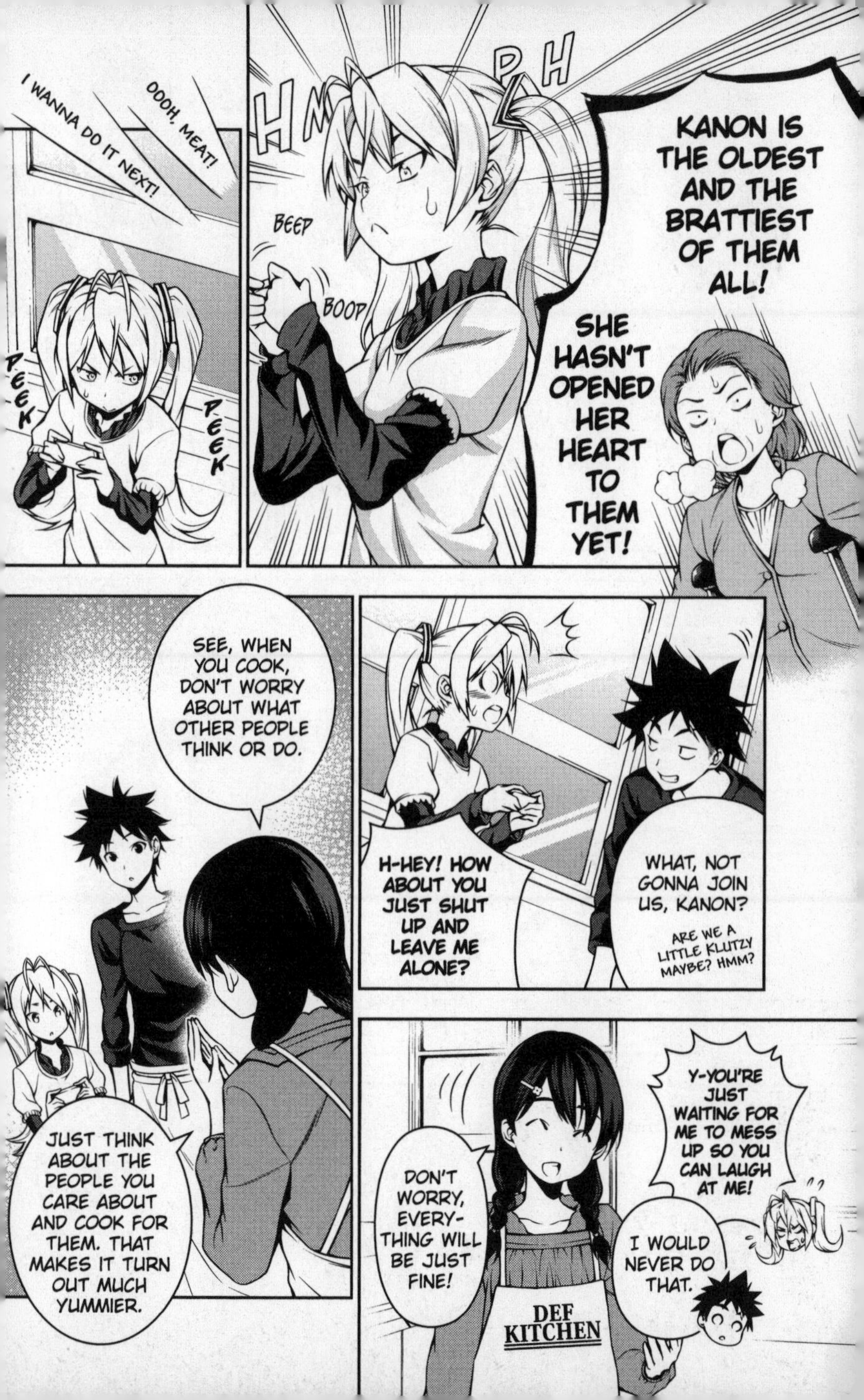
KANON IS THE OLDEST AND THE BRATTIEST OF THEM ALL!
SHE HASN'T OPENED HER HEART TO THEM YET!
HMPH
BEEP
BOOP
OOOH, MEAT!
I WANNA DO IT NEXT!
PEEK
PEEK
WHAT, NOT GONNA JOIN US, KANON?
ARE WE A LITTLE KLUTZY MAYBE? HMM?
H-HEY! HOW ABOUT YOU JUST SHUT UP AND LEAVE ME ALONE?
Y-YOU'RE JUST WAITING FOR ME TO MESS UP SO YOU CAN LAUGH AT ME!
I WOULD NEVER DO THAT.
DON'T WORRY, EVERY-THING WILL BE JUST FINE!
DEF KITCHEN
SEE, WHEN YOU COOK, DON'T WORRY ABOUT WHAT OTHER PEOPLE THINK OR DO.
JUST THINK ABOUT THE PEOPLE YOU CARE ABOUT AND COOK FOR THEM. THAT MAKES IT TURN OUT MUCH YUMMIER.

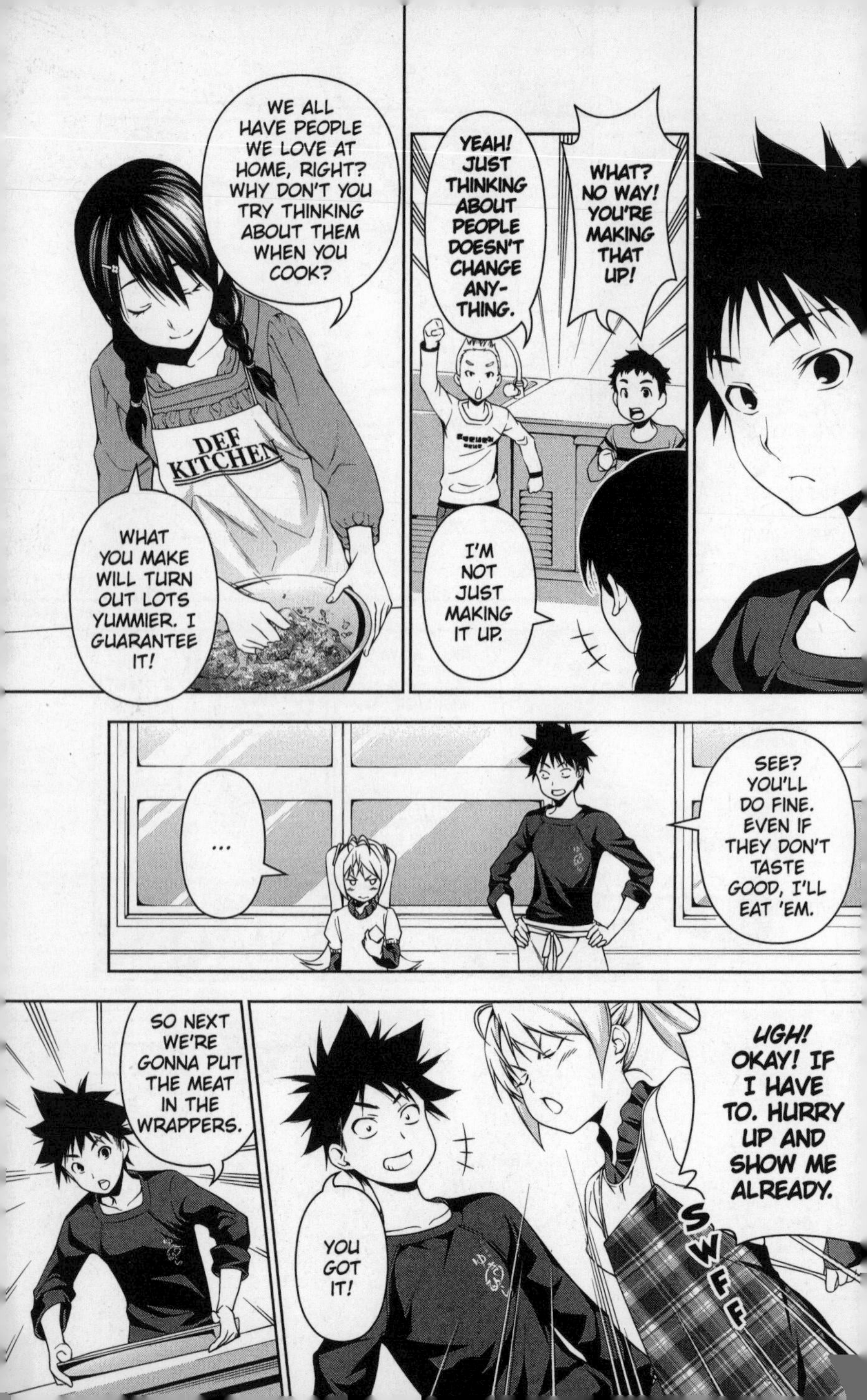
WHAT? NO WAY! YOU'RE MAKING THAT UP!
YEAH! JUST THINKING ABOUT PEOPLE DOESN'T CHANGE ANYTHING.
I'M NOT JUST MAKING IT UP.
WE ALL HAVE PEOPLE WE LOVE AT HOME, RIGHT? WHY DON'T YOU TRY THINKING ABOUT THEM WHEN YOU COOK?
DEF KITCHEN
WHAT YOU MAKE WILL TURN OUT LOTS YUMMIER. I GUARANTEE IT!
SEE? YOU'LL DO FINE. EVEN IF THEY DON'T TASTE GOOD, I'LL EAT 'EM.
...
UGH! OKAY! IF I HAVE TO. HURRY UP AND SHOW ME ALREADY.
SWFF
YOU GOT IT!
SO NEXT WE'RE GONNA PUT THE MEAT IN THE WRAPPERS.

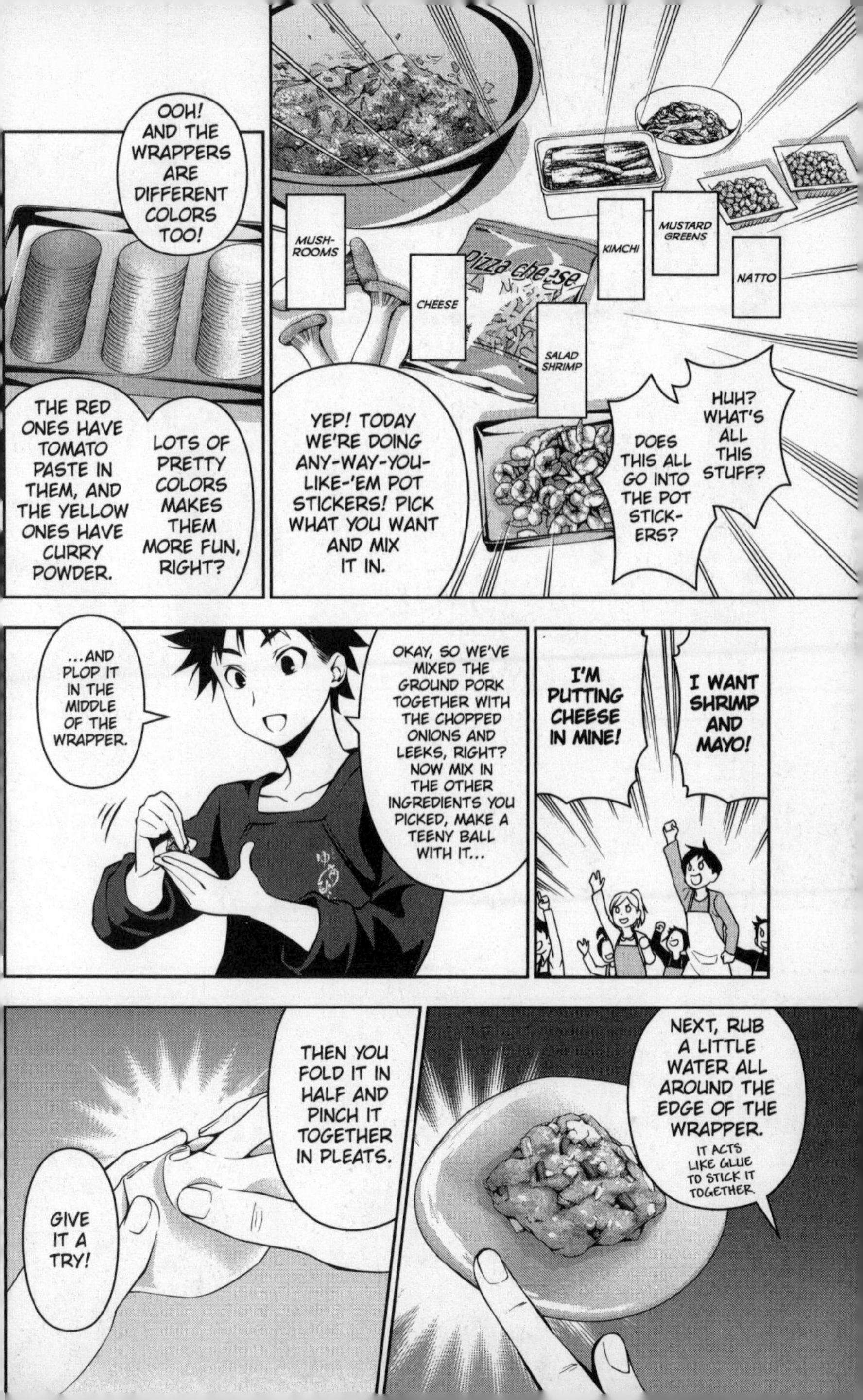
MUSTARD GREENS
KIMCHI
MUSH-ROOMS
NATTO
CHEESE
Pizza cheese
SALAD SHRIMP
HUH? WHAT'S ALL THIS STUFF?
DOES THIS ALL GO INTO THE POT STICK-ERS?
YEP! TODAY WE'RE DOING ANY-WAY-YOU-LIKE-'EM POT STICKERS! PICK WHAT YOU WANT AND MIX IT IN.
OOH! AND THE WRAPPERS ARE DIFFERENT COLORS TOO!
LOTS OF PRETTY COLORS MAKES THEM MORE FUN, RIGHT?
THE RED ONES HAVE TOMATO PASTE IN THEM, AND THE YELLOW ONES HAVE CURRY POWDER.
I WANT SHRIMP AND MAYO!
I'M PUTTING CHEESE IN MINE!
OKAY, SO WE'VE MIXED THE GROUND PORK TOGETHER WITH THE CHOPPED ONIONS AND LEEKS, RIGHT? NOW MIX IN THE OTHER INGREDIENTS YOU PICKED, MAKE A TEENY BALL WITH IT...
...AND PLOP IT IN THE MIDDLE OF THE WRAPPER.
NEXT, RUB A LITTLE WATER ALL AROUND THE EDGE OF THE WRAPPER.
IT ACTS LIKE GLUE TO STICK IT TOGETHER.
THEN YOU FOLD IT IN HALF AND PINCH IT TOGETHER IN PLEATS.
GIVE IT A TRY!

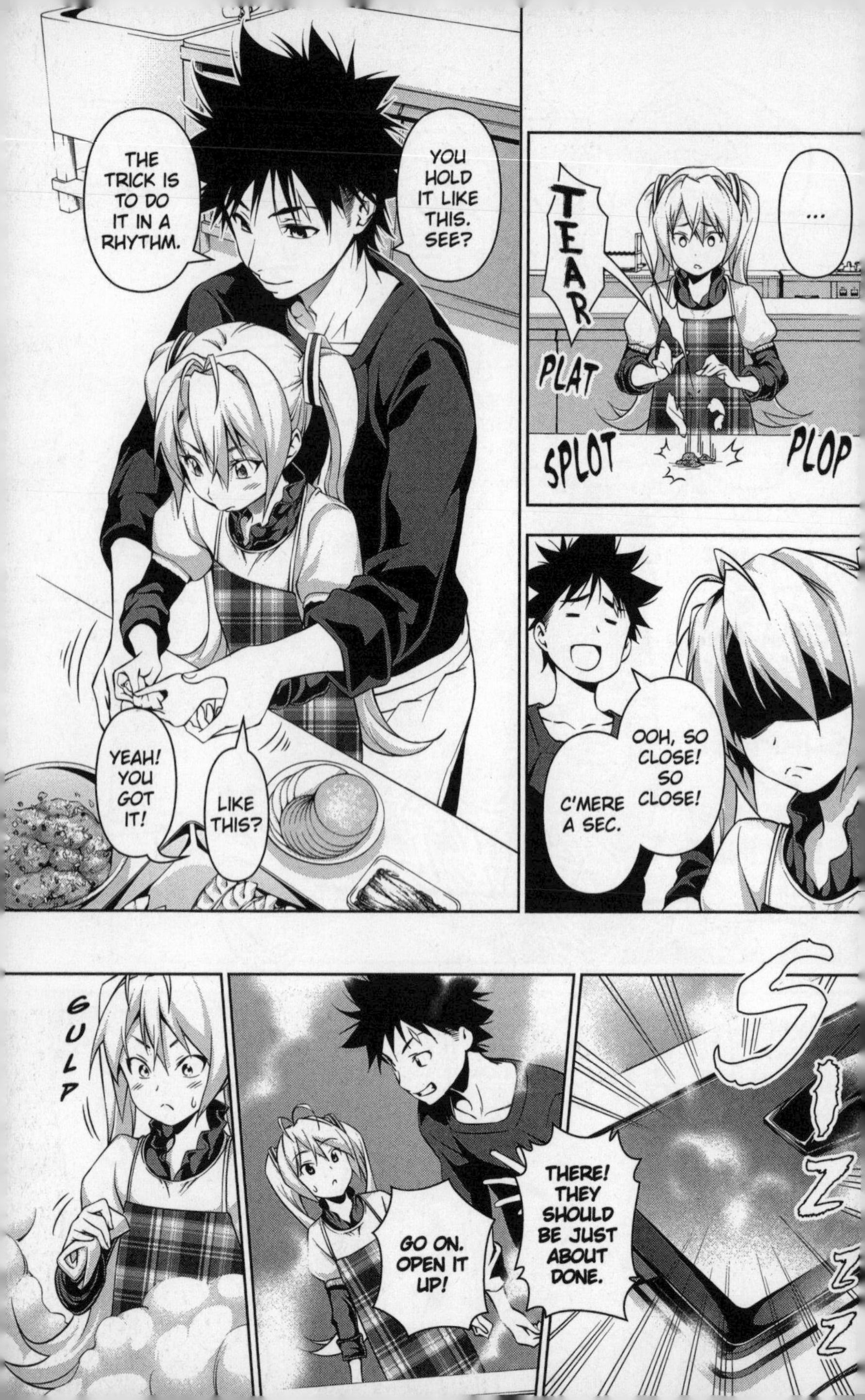
...
TEAR
PLAT
PLOP
SPLOT
OOH, SO CLOSE! SO CLOSE!
C'MERE A SEC.
YOU HOLD IT LIKE THIS. SEE?
THE TRICK IS TO DO IT IN A RHYTHM.
LIKE THIS?
YEAH! YOU GOT IT!
SIZZZ
THERE! THEY SHOULD BE JUST ABOUT DONE.
GO ON. OPEN IT UP!
GULP

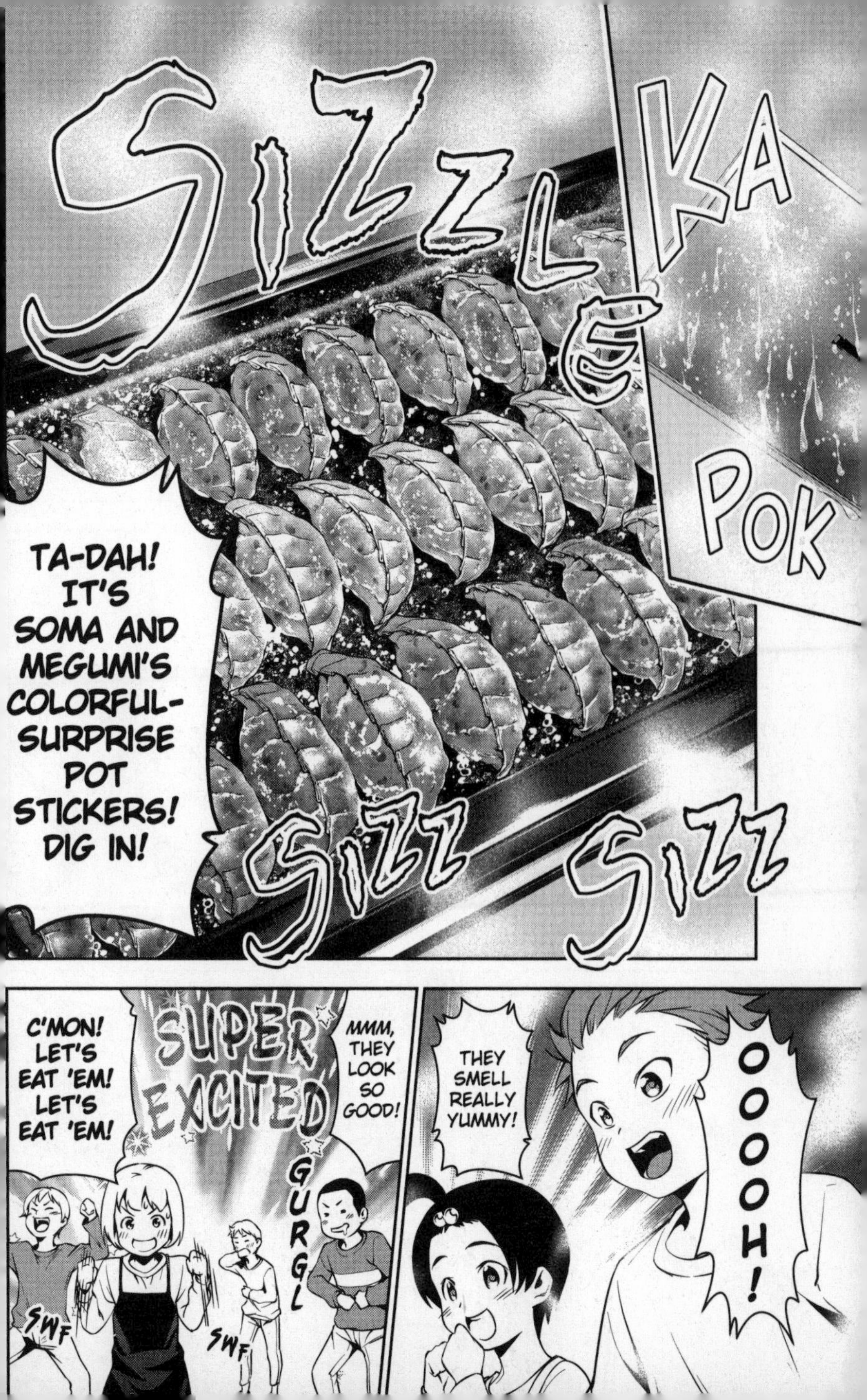
KA
POK
SIZZLE
TA-DAH! IT'S SOMA AND MEGUMI'S COLORFUL-SURPRISE POT STICKERS! DIG IN!
SIZZ
SIZZ
OOOOOH!
THEY SMELL REALLY YUMMY!
MMM, THEY LOOK SO GOOD!
SUPER EXCITED
C'MON! LET'S EAT 'EM! LET'S EAT 'EM!
GURGL
SWF
SWF

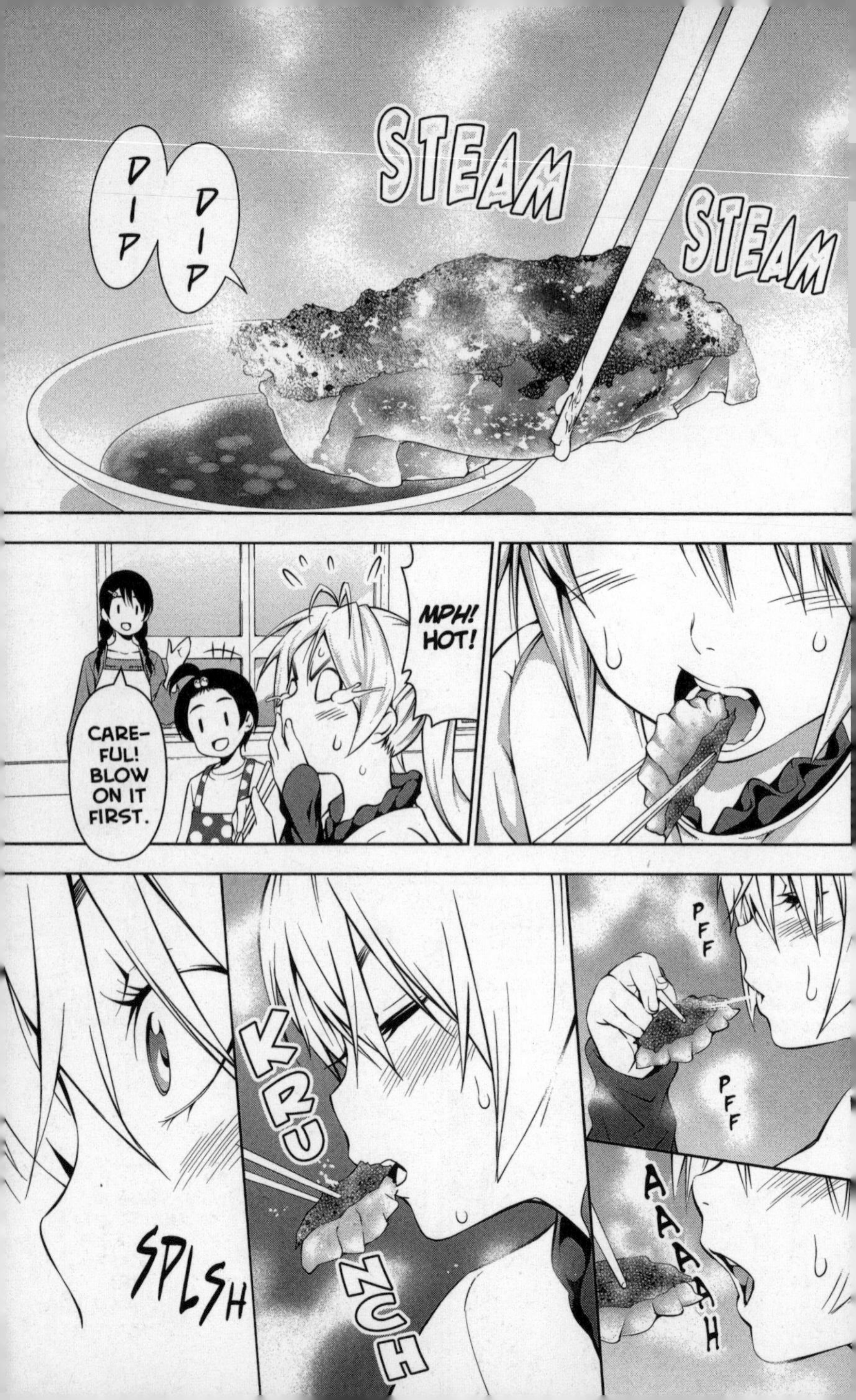
STEAM
STEAM
DIP DIP
MPH! HOT!
CARE-FUL! BLOW ON IT FIRST.
PFF
PFF
AAAAAH
KRUNCH
SPLSH

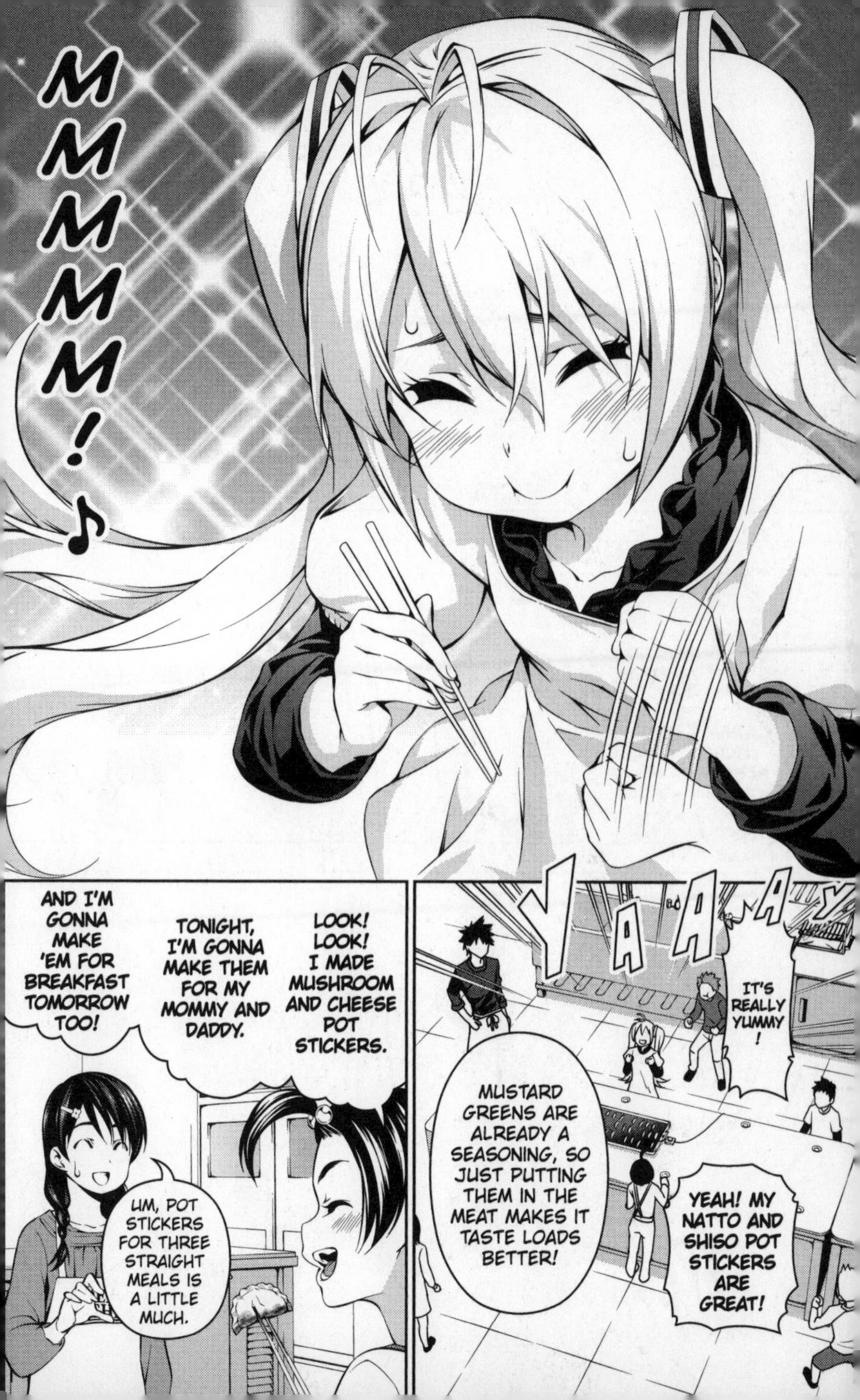
MMMMM!♪
YAAAY
IT'S REALLY YUMMY!
MUSTARD GREENS ARE ALREADY A SEASONING, SO JUST PUTTING THEM IN THE MEAT MAKES IT TASTE LOADS BETTER!
YEAH! MY NATTO AND SHISO POT STICKERS ARE GREAT!
LOOK! LOOK! I MADE MUSHROOM AND CHEESE POT STICKERS.
TONIGHT, I'M GONNA MAKE THEM FOR MY MOMMY AND DADDY.
AND I'M GONNA MAKE 'EM FOR BREAKFAST TOMORROW TOO!
UM, POT STICKERS FOR THREE STRAIGHT MEALS IS A LITTLE MUCH.

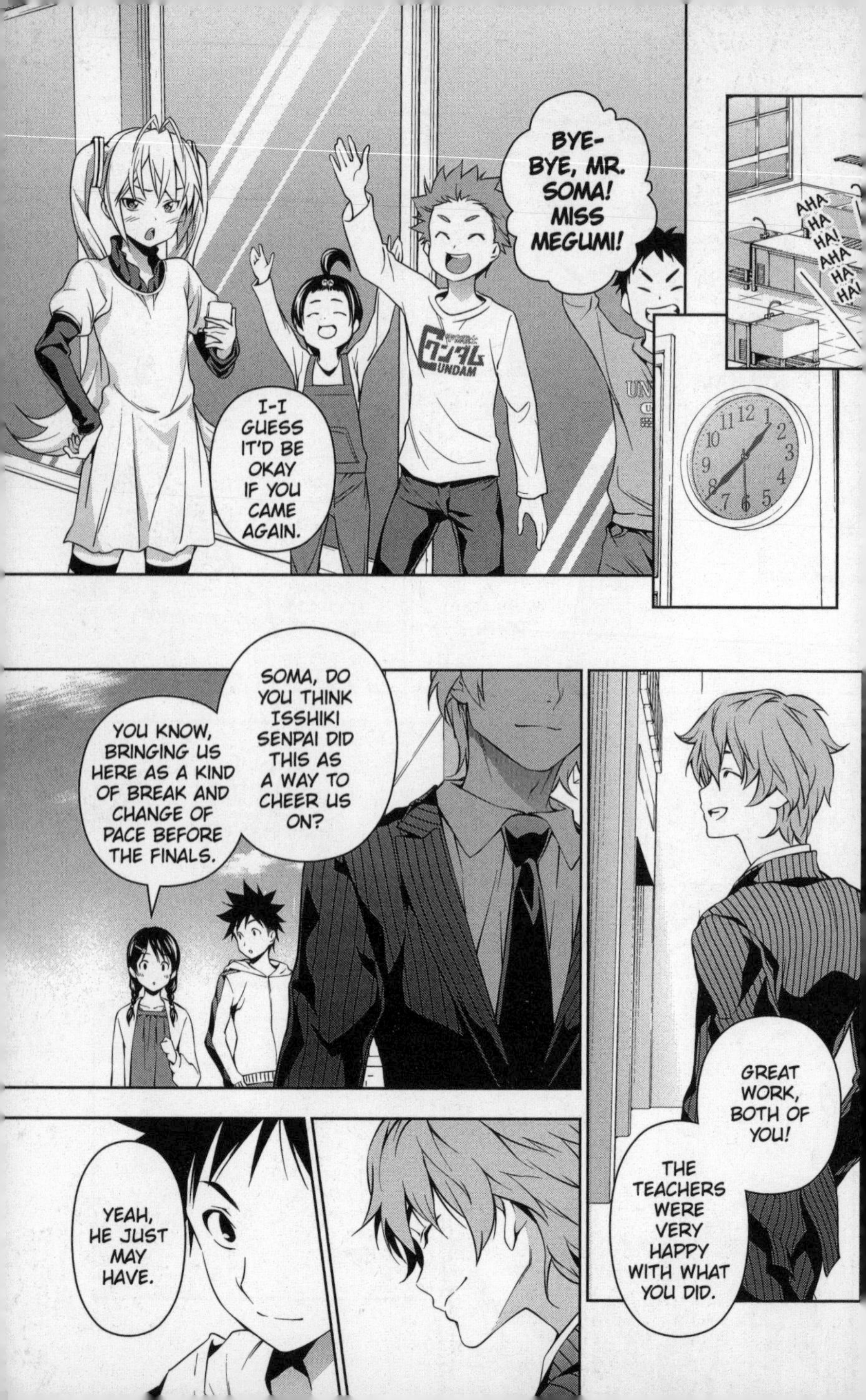
AHA HA HA! AHA HA HA!
BYE-BYE, MR. SOMA! MISS MEGUMI!
I-I GUESS IT'D BE OKAY IF YOU CAME AGAIN.
GREAT WORK, BOTH OF YOU!
THE TEACHERS WERE VERY HAPPY WITH WHAT YOU DID.
SOMA, DO YOU THINK ISSHIKI SENPAI DID THIS AS A WAY TO CHEER US ON?
YOU KNOW, BRINGING US HERE AS A KIND OF BREAK AND CHANGE OF PACE BEFORE THE FINALS.
YEAH, HE JUST MAY HAVE.

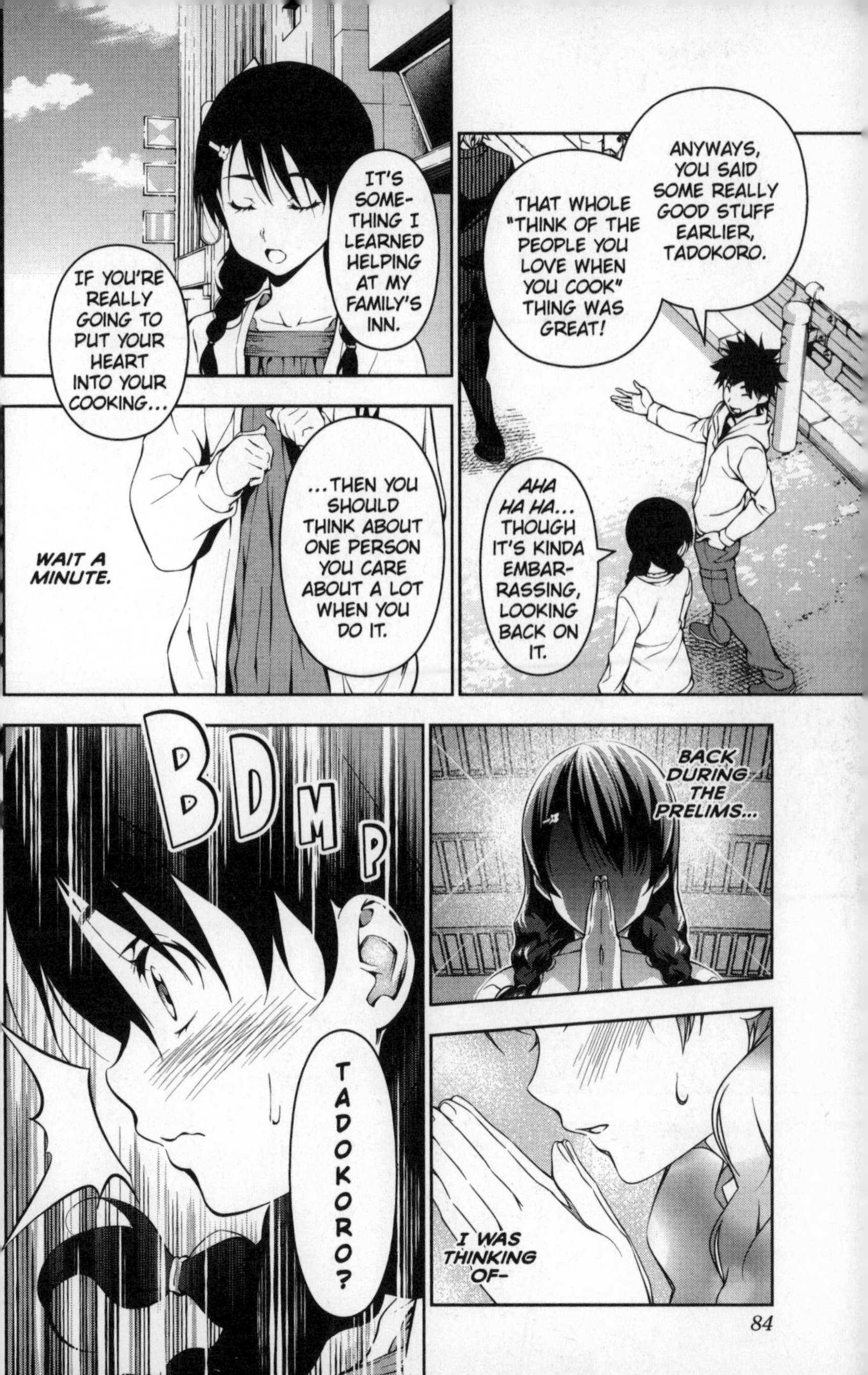
ANYWAYS, YOU SAID SOME REALLY GOOD STUFF EARLIER, TADOKORO.
THAT WHOLE "THINK OF THE PEOPLE YOU LOVE WHEN YOU COOK" THING WAS GREAT!
AHA HA HA... THOUGH IT'S KINDA EMBARRASSING, LOOKING BACK ON IT.
IT'S SOMETHING I LEARNED HELPING AT MY FAMILY'S INN.
IF YOU'RE REALLY GOING TO PUT YOUR HEART INTO YOUR COOKING...
...THEN YOU SHOULD THINK ABOUT ONE PERSON YOU CARE ABOUT A LOT WHEN YOU DO IT.
WAIT A MINUTE.
BACK DURING THE PRELIMS...
I WAS THINKING OF-
BDMP
TADOKORO?

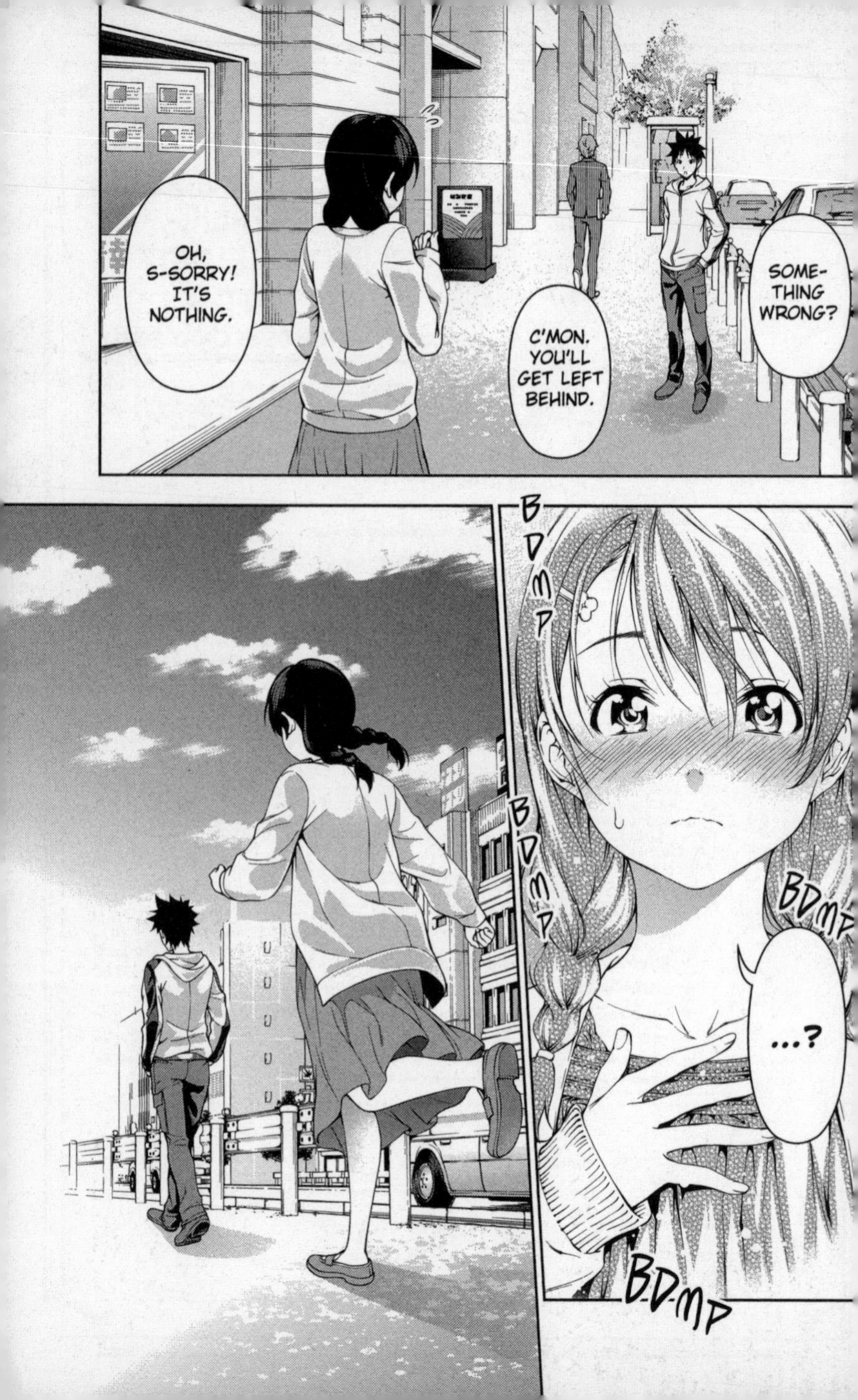
SOME-THING WRONG?
OH, S-SORRY! IT'S NOTHING.
C'MON. YOU'LL GET LEFT BEHIND.
BDMP
BDMP
BDMP
...?
B-D-MP

RECIPE BY: YUKI MORISAKI

PRACTICAL RECIPE #2

VOLUME 8
SPECIAL SUPPLEMENT!

COLORFUL-SURPRISE POT STICKERS
(WHITE WRAPPERS OKAY TOO)

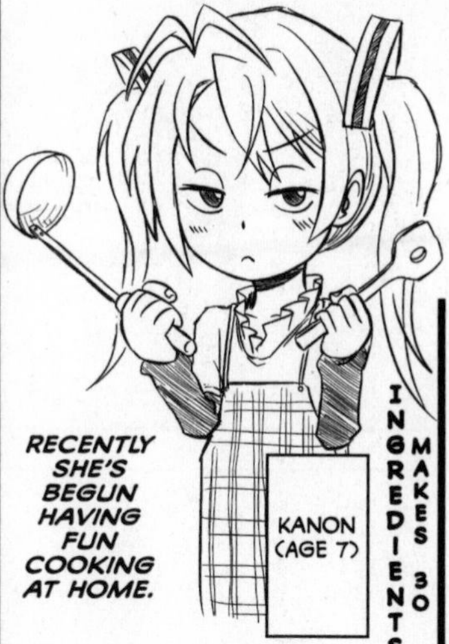
KANON (AGE 7)

RECENTLY SHE'S BEGUN HAVING FUN COOKING AT HOME.

ARTIST: YUTO TSUKUDA

INGREDIENTS MAKES 30

1 PACKAGE COMMERCIAL POTSTICKER WRAPPERS (HOLDS APPROXIMATELY 30)

200 GRAMS SLICED PORK BELLY

1/2 BUNDLE LEEKS

1/2 GREEN ONION

★ **PICK YOUR FAVORITE STUFFINGS**

- MUSTARD GREENS
- KIMCHI
- NATTO
- CHEESE
- SALAD SHRIMP
- MAYONNAISE
- MUSHROOMS
- (OR OTHERS)

[A]
- 2 TEASPOONS EACH GRATED GINGER AND SOY SAUCE
- 1 TABLESPOON OYSTER SAUCE
- 2 PINCHES CHICKEN BOUILLON
- 2 TABLESPOONS WATER

1 TABLESPOON EACH CANOLA OIL AND SESAME OIL

200 ~ 300 CC WATER

★ **SAUCE**

[B] VINEGAR, SOY SAUCE, CHILI OIL

1. MINCE THE SLICED PORK BELLY. (CAN BE SUBSTITUTED WITH GROUND PORK, BUT MINCING IT THIS WAY MAKES IT JUICIER.)

2. FINELY CHOP THE LEEKS AND THE GREEN ONION.

3. PUT (1) IN A BOWL AND MIX IN (A). ONCE THOROUGHLY BLENDED, MIX IN (2).

4. PUT A SMALL BALL OF THE MIXTURE FROM (3) AND THE CHOSEN STUFFING ONTO THE MIDDLE OF A WRAPPER. DAMPEN THE EDGES OF THE WRAPPER WITH A SMEAR OF WATER. FOLD THE EDGES TOGETHER AND PLEAT TO SEAL.

   ★ **MUSTARD GREENS:** FINELY CHOP MUSTARD GREENS AND ADD A PINCH TO THE MEATBALL.

   ★ **KIMCHI:** FINELY CHOP KIMCHI AND ADD A PINCH TO THE MEATBALL.

   ★ **NATTO AND CHEESE:** ADD A DOLLOP OF NATTO AND A PINCH OF SHREDDED CHEESE TO MEATBALL.

   ★ **SHRIMP AND MAYO:** CHOP THE SHRIMP AND MIX WITH A DOLLOP OF MAYONNAISE. ADD TO THE MEATBALL.

   ★ **MUSHROOM AND CHEESE:** CHOP THE MUSHROOMS AND ADD WITH A PINCH OF SHREDDED CHEESE TO THE MEATBALL.

5. POUR THE OIL IN A FRYING PAN AND CAREFULLY LINE (4) IN IT. POUR THE WATER OVER TOP, TURN ON HIGH HEAT AND COVER. COOK UNTIL ALL WATER IS GONE AND THEN POUR THE SESAME OIL INTO THE PAN FROM AROUND THE EDGES TO ADD COLOR. REMOVE FROM HEAT AND PLACE ONTO PLATES.

6. MIX DESIRED AMOUNTS OF (B) TO MAKE THE DIPPING SAUCE, PLACE (5) ON THE SIDE, AND DONE!

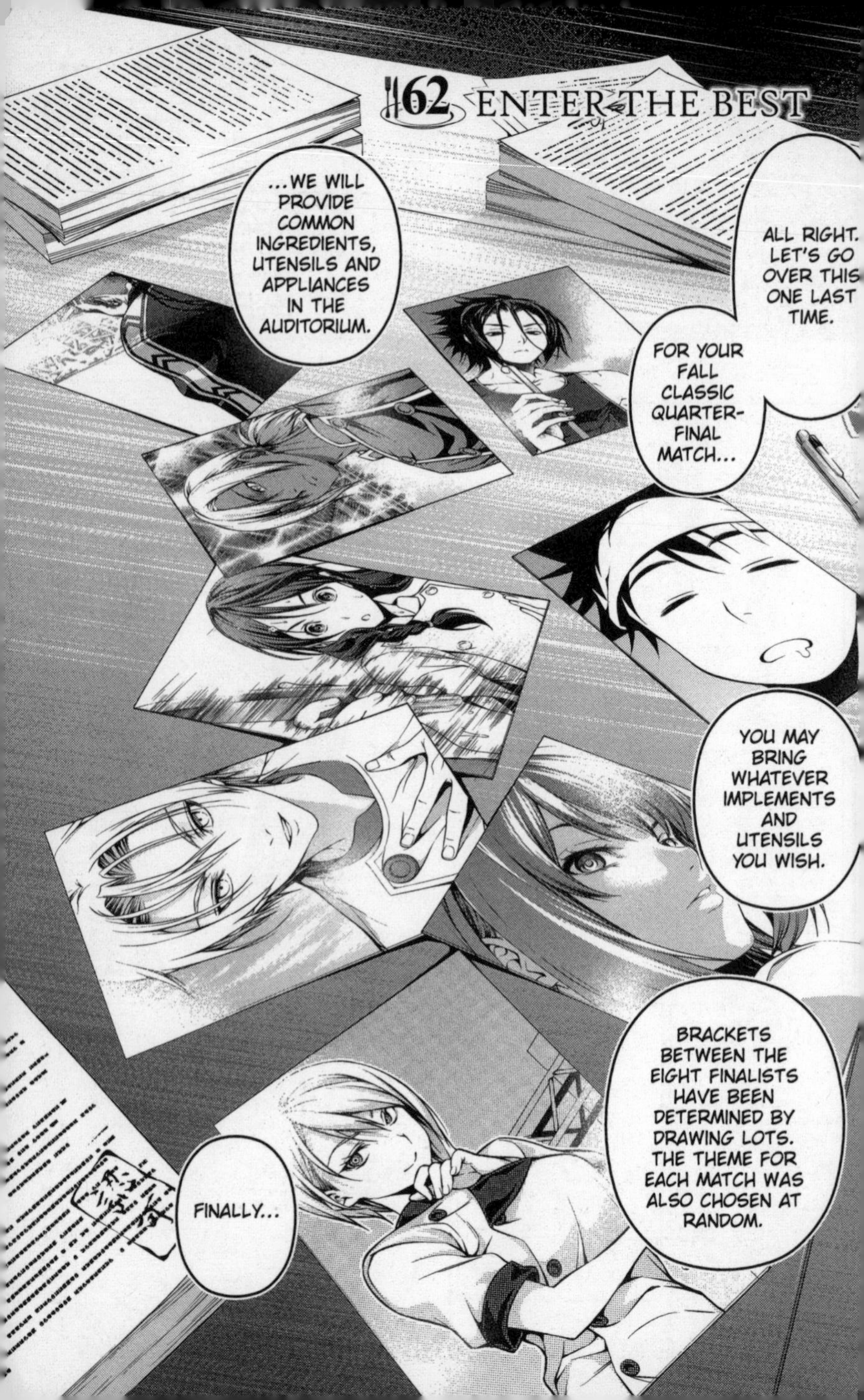
62 ENTER THE BEST
ALL RIGHT. LET'S GO OVER THIS ONE LAST TIME.
FOR YOUR FALL CLASSIC QUARTER-FINAL MATCH...
...WE WILL PROVIDE COMMON INGREDIENTS, UTENSILS AND APPLIANCES IN THE AUDITORIUM.
YOU MAY BRING WHATEVER IMPLEMENTS AND UTENSILS YOU WISH.
BRACKETS BETWEEN THE EIGHT FINALISTS HAVE BEEN DETERMINED BY DRAWING LOTS. THE THEME FOR EACH MATCH WAS ALSO CHOSEN AT RANDOM.
FINALLY...

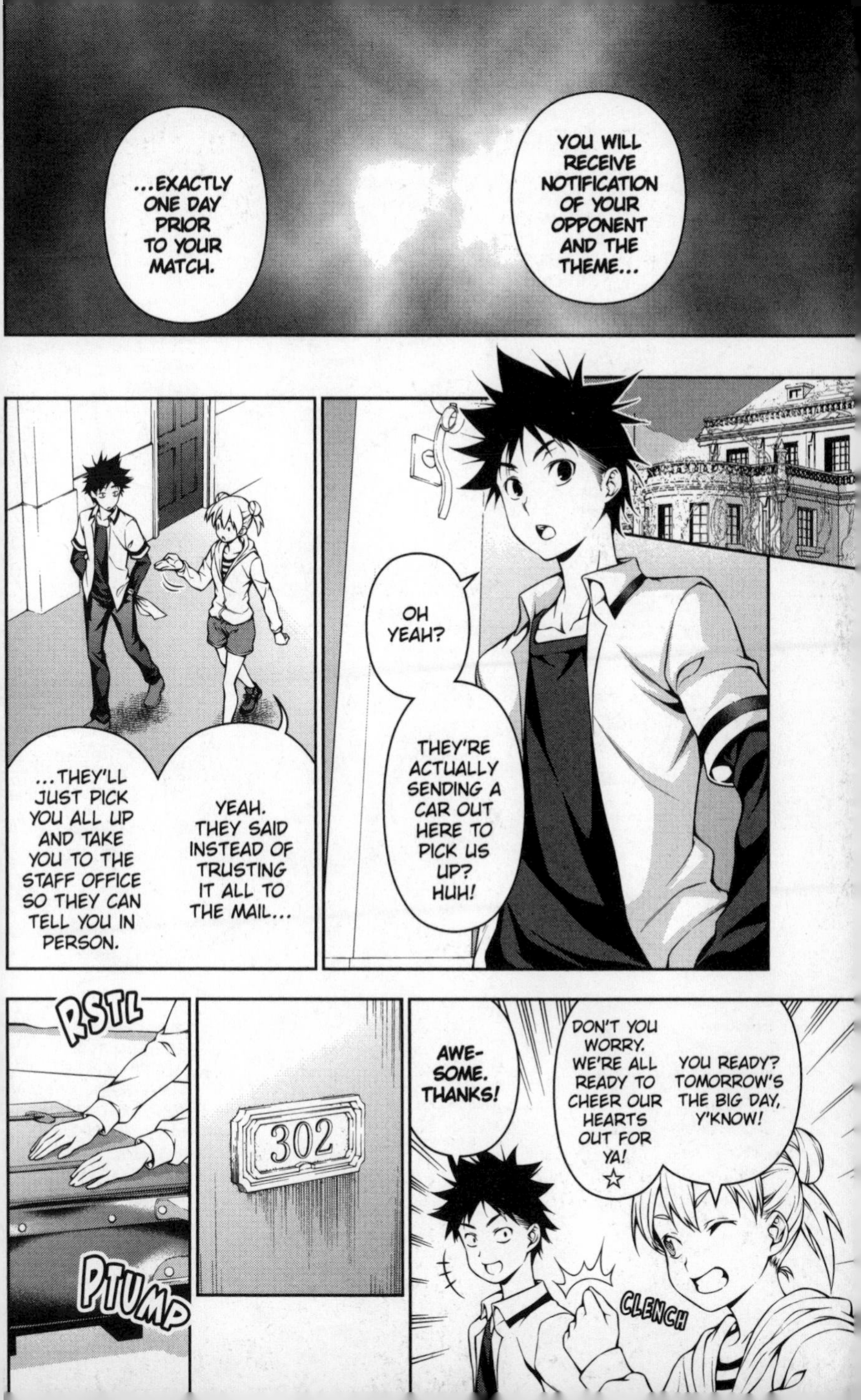
YOU WILL RECEIVE NOTIFICATION OF YOUR OPPONENT AND THE THEME...
...EXACTLY ONE DAY PRIOR TO YOUR MATCH.
OH YEAH?
THEY'RE ACTUALLY SENDING A CAR OUT HERE TO PICK US UP? HUH!
YEAH. THEY SAID INSTEAD OF TRUSTING IT ALL TO THE MAIL...
...THEY'LL JUST PICK YOU ALL UP AND TAKE YOU TO THE STAFF OFFICE SO THEY CAN TELL YOU IN PERSON.
YOU READY? TOMORROW'S THE BIG DAY, Y'KNOW!
DON'T YOU WORRY. WE'RE ALL READY TO CHEER OUR HEARTS OUT FOR YA! ☆
AWE-SOME. THANKS!
CLENCH
302
RSTL
PTUMP

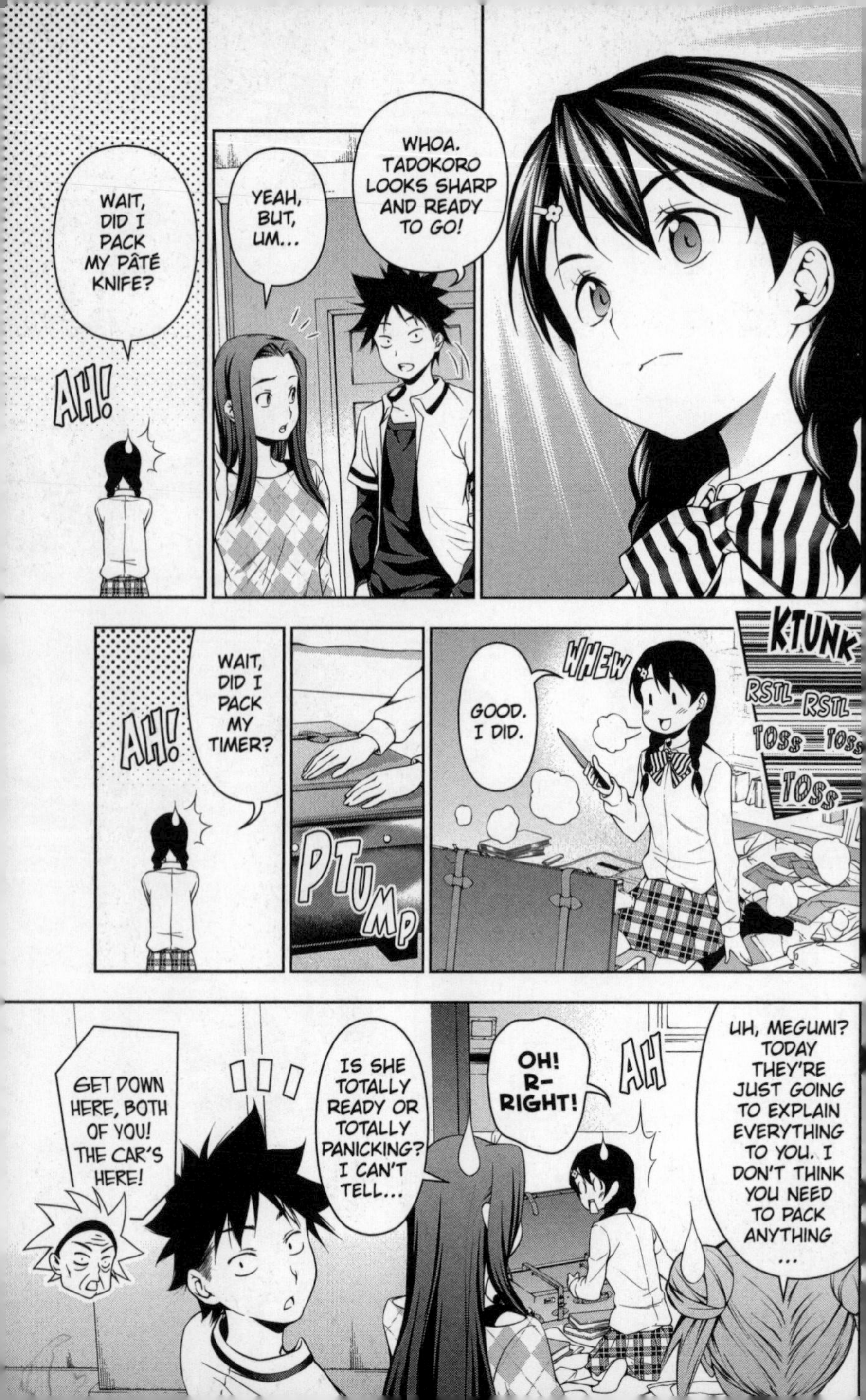
WHOA. TADOKORO LOOKS SHARP AND READY TO GO!
YEAH, BUT, UM...
WAIT, DID I PACK MY PÂTÉ KNIFE?
AH!
KTUNK
RSTL RSTL
TOSS TOSS
TOSS
WHEW
GOOD. I DID.
PTUMP
WAIT, DID I PACK MY TIMER?
AH!
UH, MEGUMI? TODAY THEY'RE JUST GOING TO EXPLAIN EVERYTHING TO YOU. I DON'T THINK YOU NEED TO PACK ANYTHING ...
AH
OH! R-RIGHT!
IS SHE TOTALLY READY OR TOTALLY PANICKING? I CAN'T TELL...
GET DOWN HERE, BOTH OF YOU! THE CAR'S HERE!

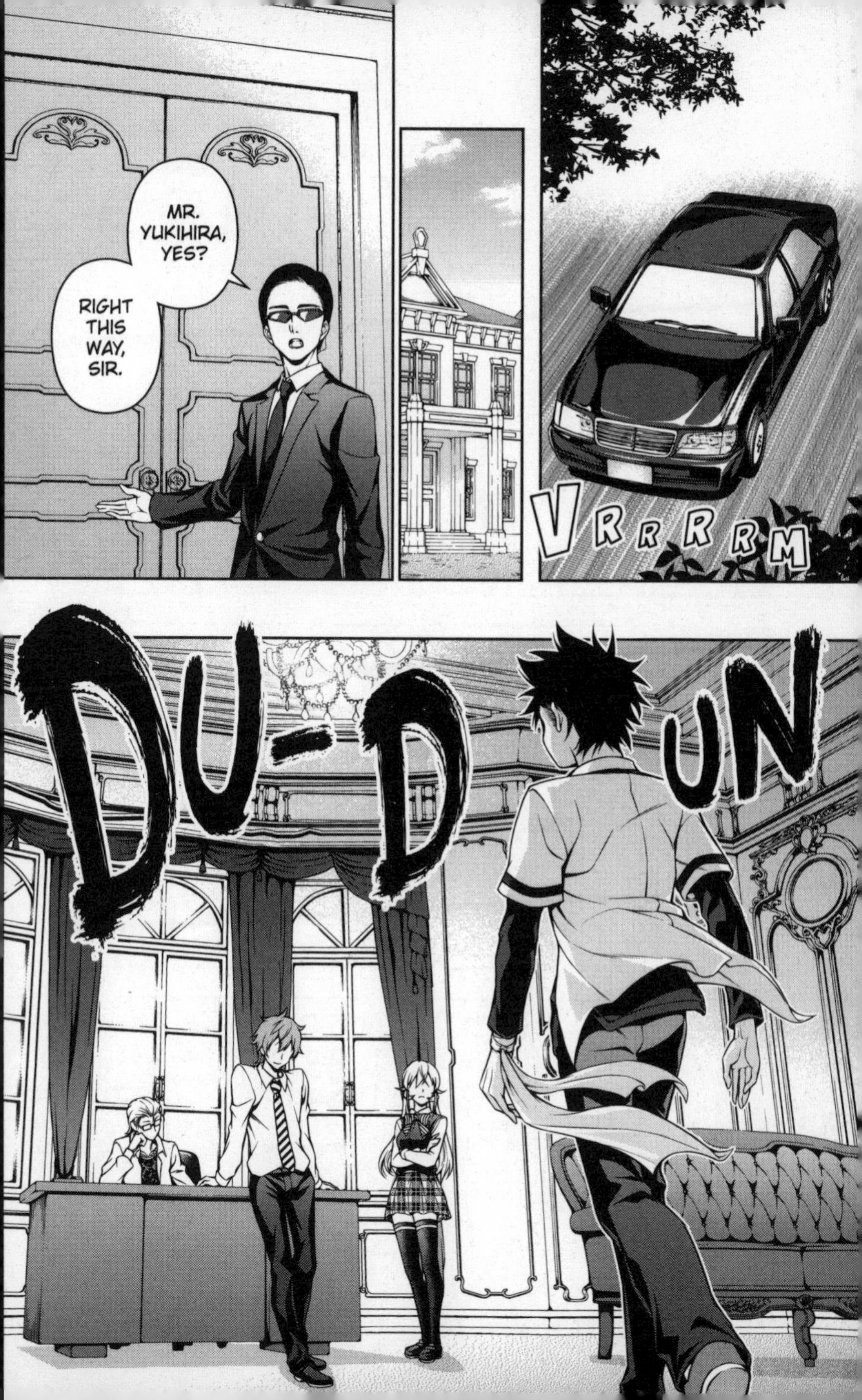
VRRRRM
MR. YUKIHIRA, YES?
RIGHT THIS WAY, SIR.
DU-D-UN

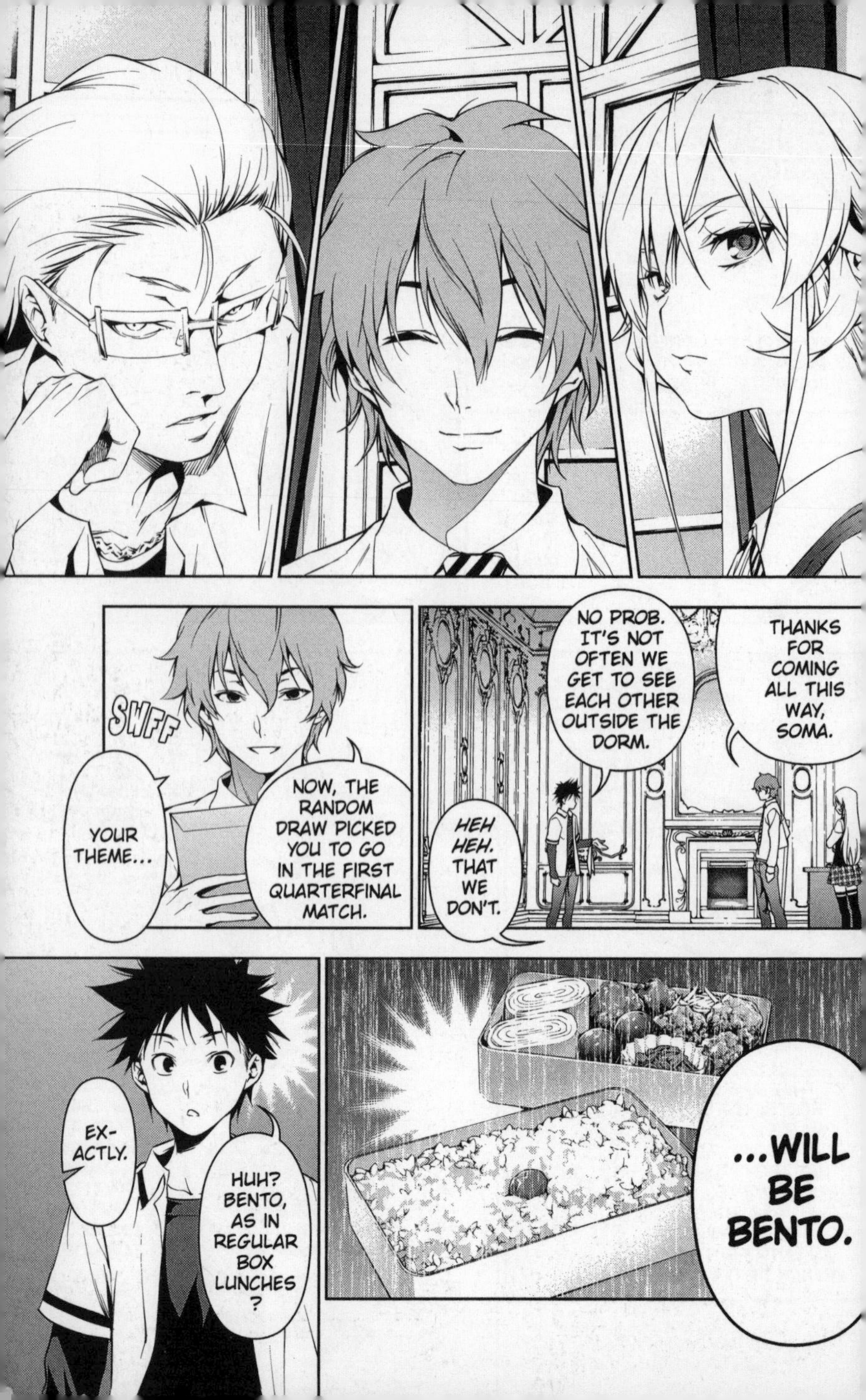
THANKS FOR COMING ALL THIS WAY, SOMA.
NO PROB. IT'S NOT OFTEN WE GET TO SEE EACH OTHER OUTSIDE THE DORM.
HEH HEH. THAT WE DON'T.
SWFF
NOW, THE RANDOM DRAW PICKED YOU TO GO IN THE FIRST QUARTERFINAL MATCH.
YOUR THEME...
...WILL BE BENTO.
HUH? BENTO, AS IN REGULAR BOX LUNCHES?
EX-ACTLY.

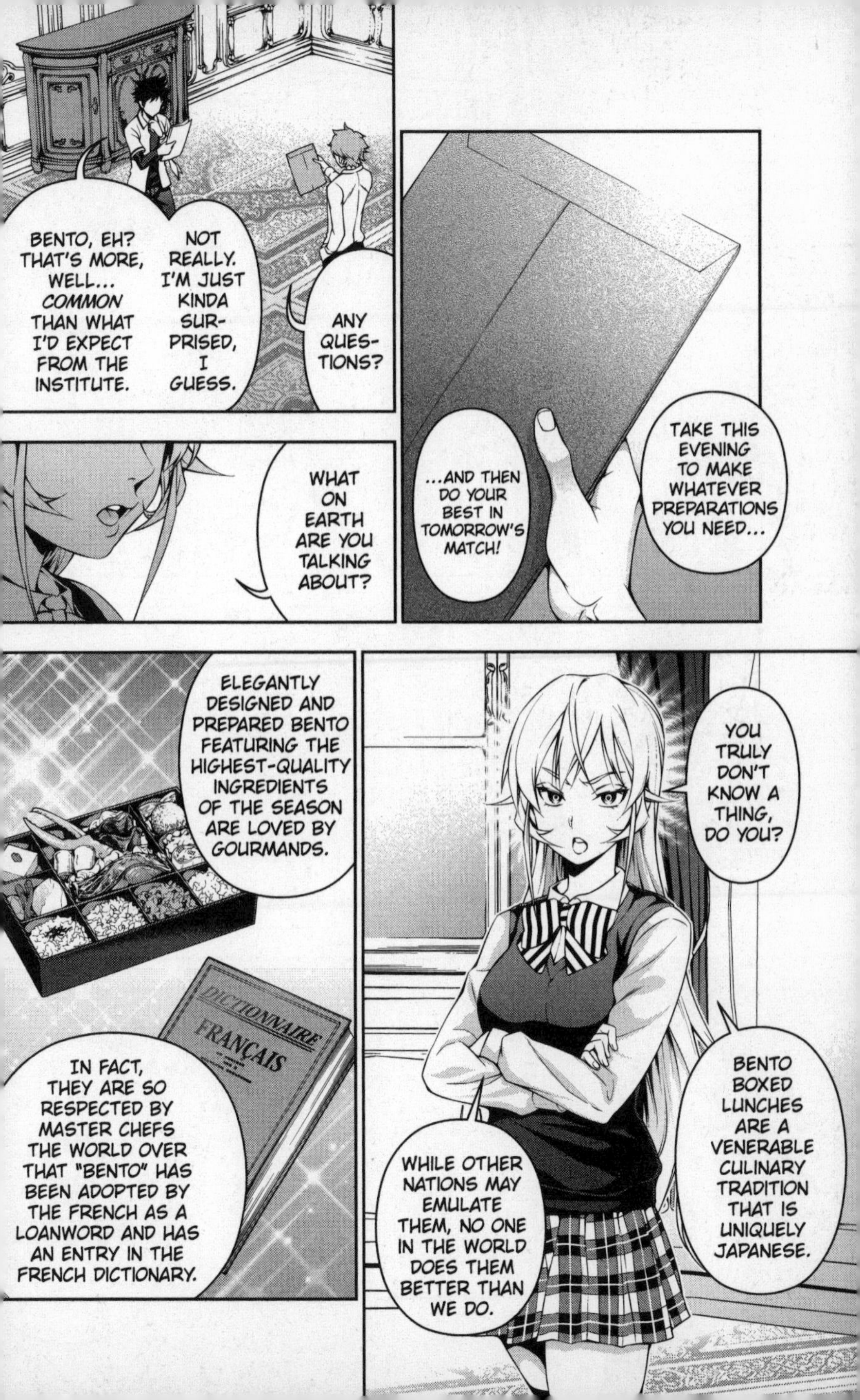
TAKE THIS EVENING TO MAKE WHATEVER PREPARATIONS YOU NEED...
...AND THEN DO YOUR BEST IN TOMORROW'S MATCH!
ANY QUES- TIONS?
NOT REALLY. I'M JUST KINDA SUR- PRISED, I GUESS.
BENTO, EH? THAT'S MORE, WELL... *COMMON* THAN WHAT I'D EXPECT FROM THE INSTITUTE.
WHAT ON EARTH ARE YOU TALKING ABOUT?
YOU TRULY DON'T KNOW A THING, DO YOU?
BENTO BOXED LUNCHES ARE A VENERABLE CULINARY TRADITION THAT IS UNIQUELY JAPANESE.
WHILE OTHER NATIONS MAY EMULATE THEM, NO ONE IN THE WORLD DOES THEM BETTER THAN WE DO.
ELEGANTLY DESIGNED AND PREPARED BENTO FEATURING THE HIGHEST-QUALITY INGREDIENTS OF THE SEASON ARE LOVED BY GOURMANDS.
DICTIONNAIRE FRANÇAIS
IN FACT, THEY ARE SO RESPECTED BY MASTER CHEFS THE WORLD OVER THAT "BENTO" HAS BEEN ADOPTED BY THE FRENCH AS A LOANWORD AND HAS AN ENTRY IN THE FRENCH DICTIONARY.

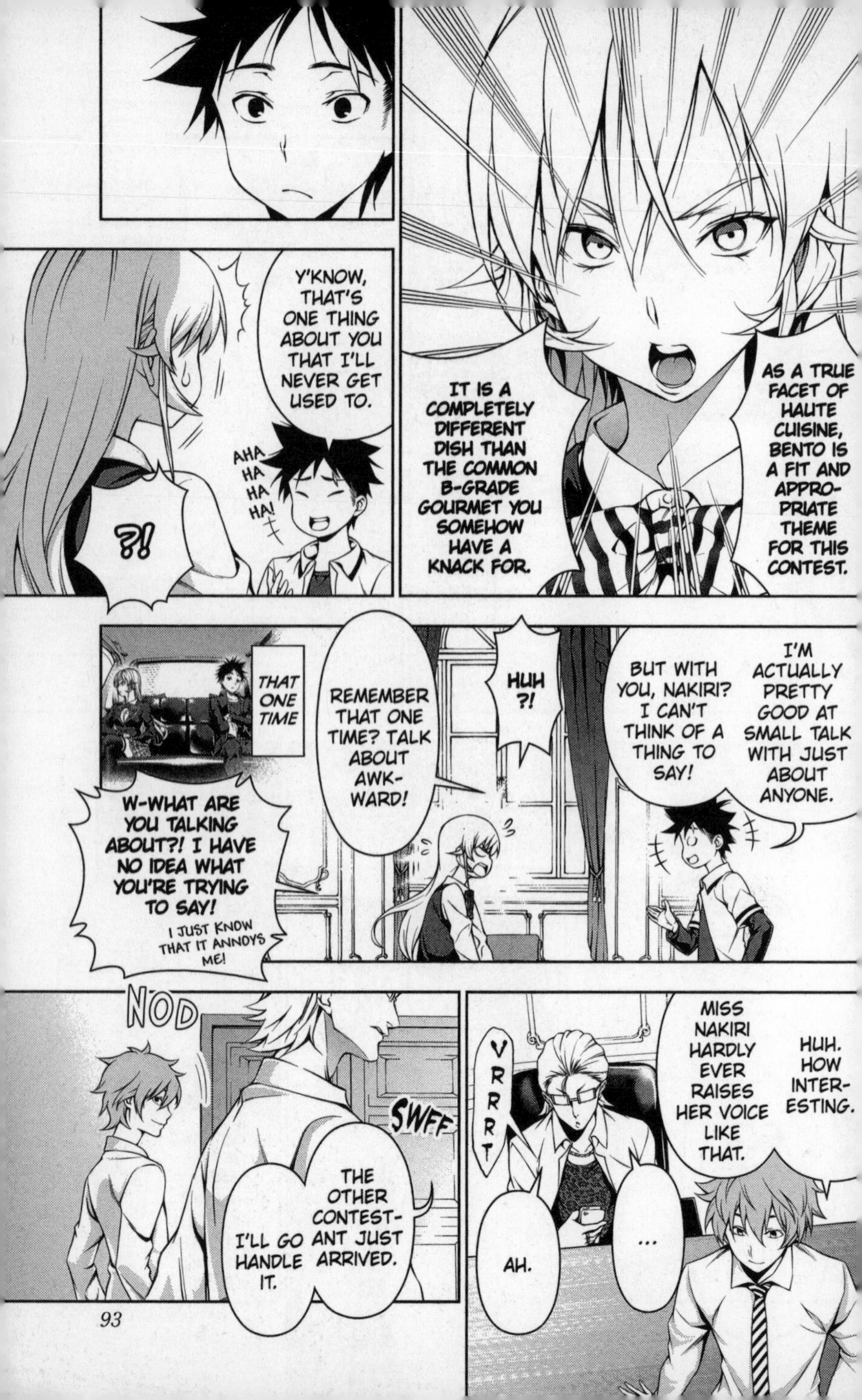
AS A TRUE FACET OF HAUTE CUISINE, BENTO IS A FIT AND APPROPRIATE THEME FOR THIS CONTEST.
IT IS A COMPLETELY DIFFERENT DISH THAN THE COMMON B-GRADE GOURMET YOU SOMEHOW HAVE A KNACK FOR.
Y'KNOW, THAT'S ONE THING ABOUT YOU THAT I'LL NEVER GET USED TO.
AHA HA HA HA!
?!
I'M ACTUALLY PRETTY GOOD AT SMALL TALK WITH JUST ABOUT ANYONE.
BUT WITH YOU, NAKIRI? I CAN'T THINK OF A THING TO SAY!
HUH?!
REMEMBER THAT ONE TIME? TALK ABOUT AWK-WARD!
THAT ONE TIME
W-WHAT ARE YOU TALKING ABOUT?! I HAVE NO IDEA WHAT YOU'RE TRYING TO SAY!
I JUST KNOW THAT IT ANNOYS ME!
HUH. HOW INTER-ESTING.
MISS NAKIRI HARDLY EVER RAISES HER VOICE LIKE THAT.
VRRRT
...
AH.
NOD
SWFF
THE OTHER CONTEST-ANT JUST ARRIVED.
I'LL GO HANDLE IT.

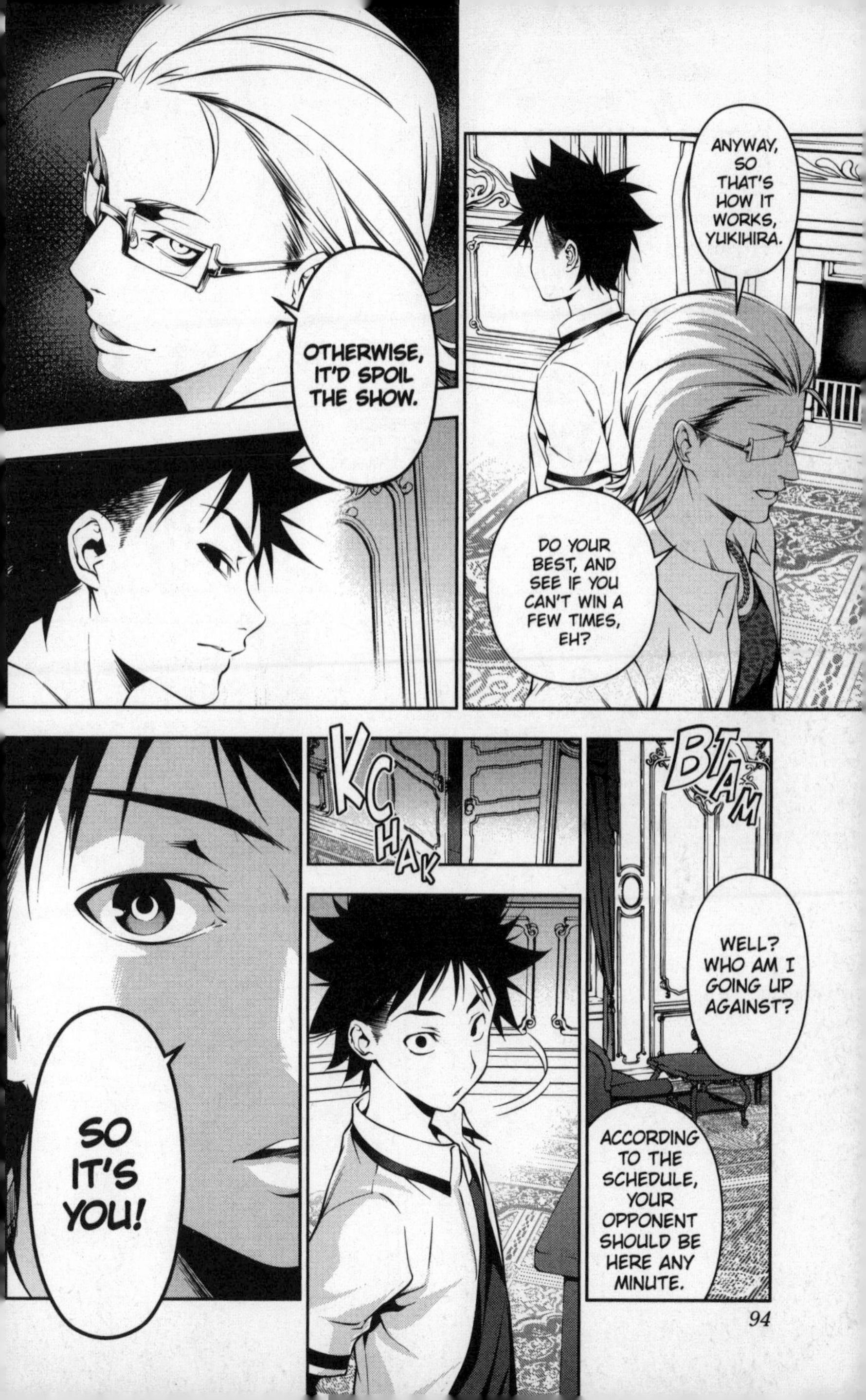

ANYWAY, SO THAT'S HOW IT WORKS, YUKIHIRA.
DO YOUR BEST, AND SEE IF YOU CAN'T WIN A FEW TIMES, EH?
OTHERWISE, IT'D SPOIL THE SHOW.
BTAM
WELL? WHO AM I GOING UP AGAINST?
ACCORDING TO THE SCHEDULE, YOUR OPPONENT SHOULD BE HERE ANY MINUTE.
KCHAK
SO IT'S YOU!

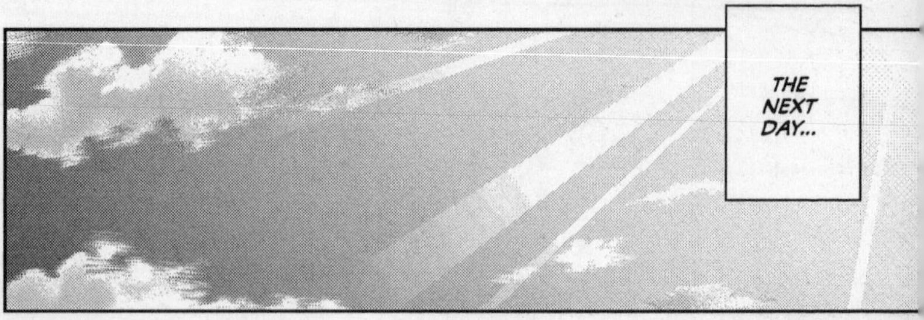
THE NEXT DAY...

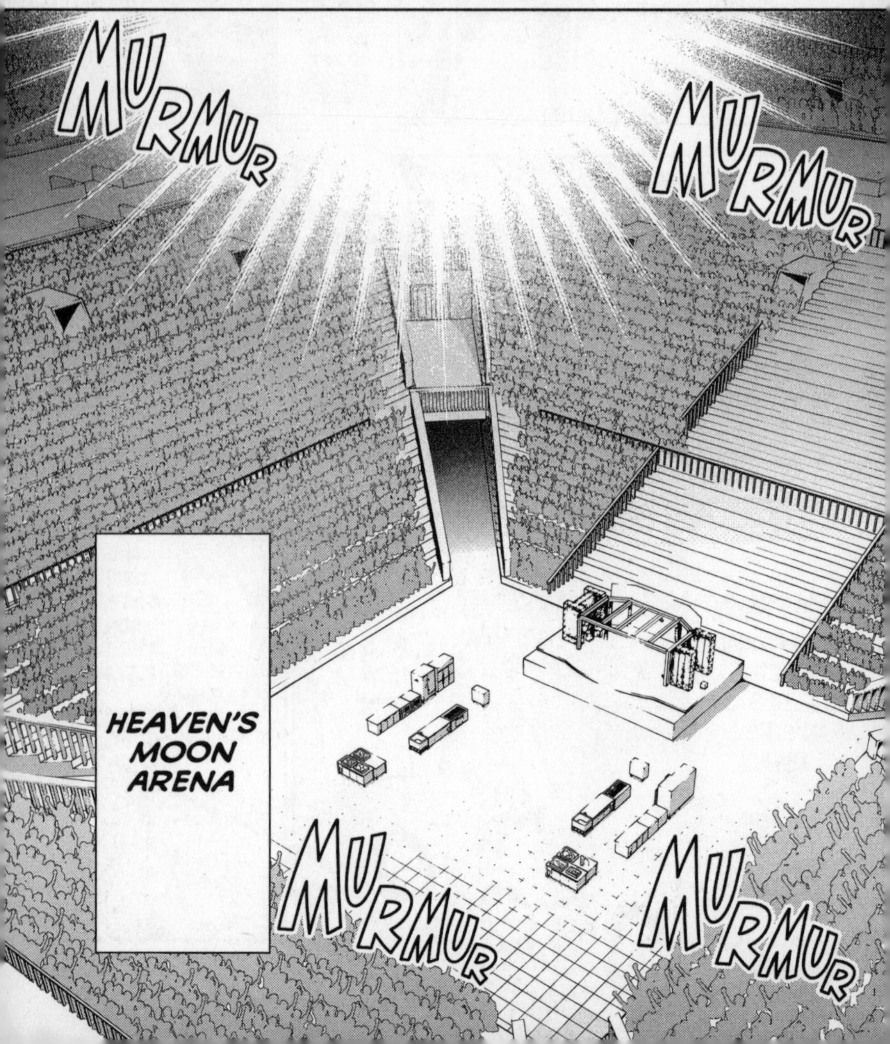
MURMUR
MURMUR
HEAVEN'S MOON ARENA
MURMUR
MURMUR

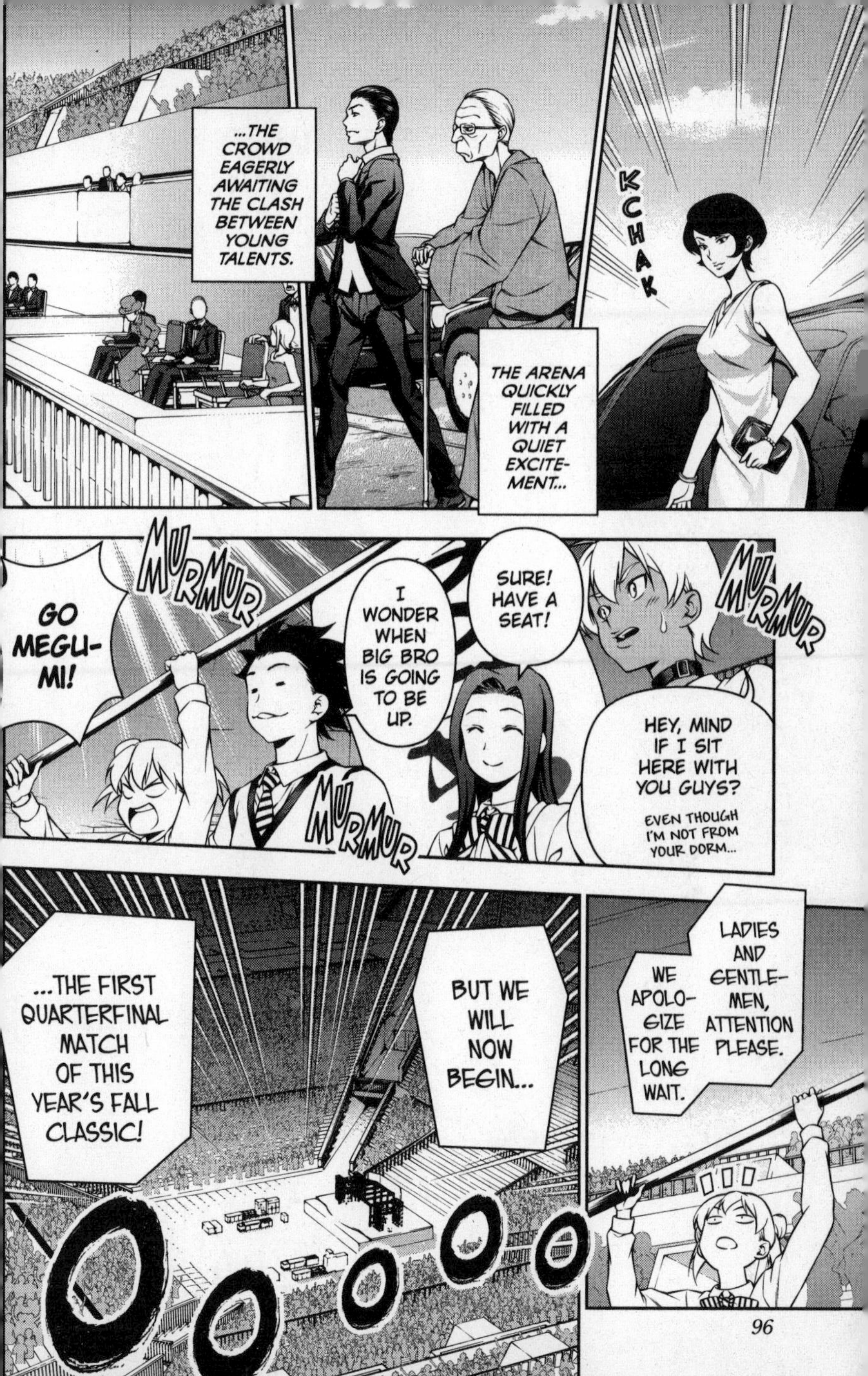
KCHAK
THE ARENA QUICKLY FILLED WITH A QUIET EXCITE-MENT...
...THE CROWD EAGERLY AWAITING THE CLASH BETWEEN YOUNG TALENTS.
HEY, MIND IF I SIT HERE WITH YOU GUYS?
EVEN THOUGH I'M NOT FROM YOUR DORM...
MURMUR
SURE! HAVE A SEAT!
I WONDER WHEN BIG BRO IS GOING TO BE UP.
MURMUR
GO MEGU-MI!
MURMUR
LADIES AND GENTLE-MEN, ATTENTION PLEASE.
WE APOLO-GIZE FOR THE LONG WAIT.
BUT WE WILL NOW BEGIN...
...THE FIRST QUARTERFINAL MATCH OF THIS YEAR'S FALL CLASSIC!
OOOOOO

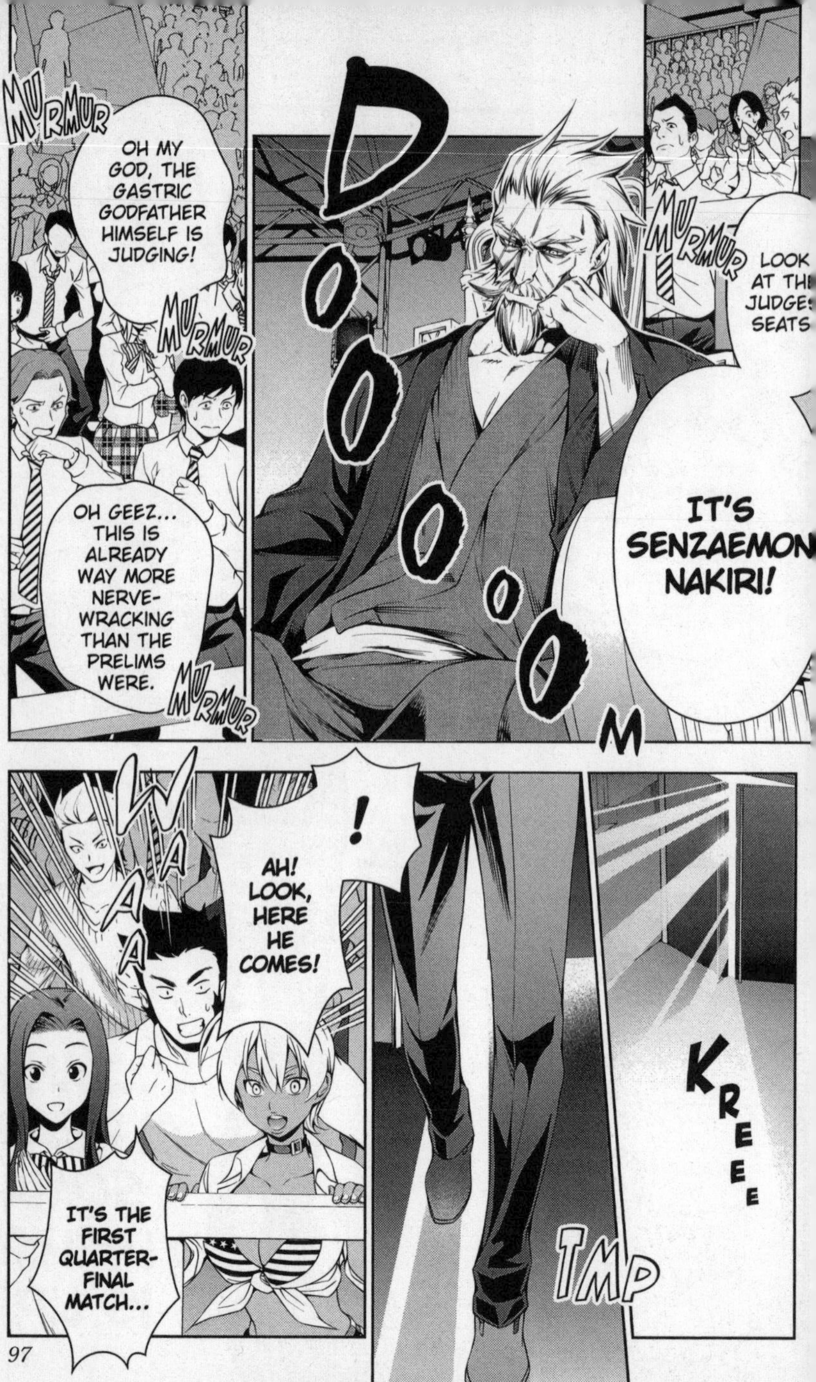
MURMUR
LOOK AT THE JUDGES SEATS
DOOOOOOM
IT'S SENZAEMON NAKIRI!
MURMUR
OH MY GOD, THE GASTRIC GODFATHER HIMSELF IS JUDGING!
MURMUR
OH GEEZ... THIS IS ALREADY WAY MORE NERVE-WRACKING THAN THE PRELIMS WERE.
MURMUR
KREEE
TMP
!
WAAAA
AH! LOOK, HERE HE COMES!
IT'S THE FIRST QUARTER-FINAL MATCH...

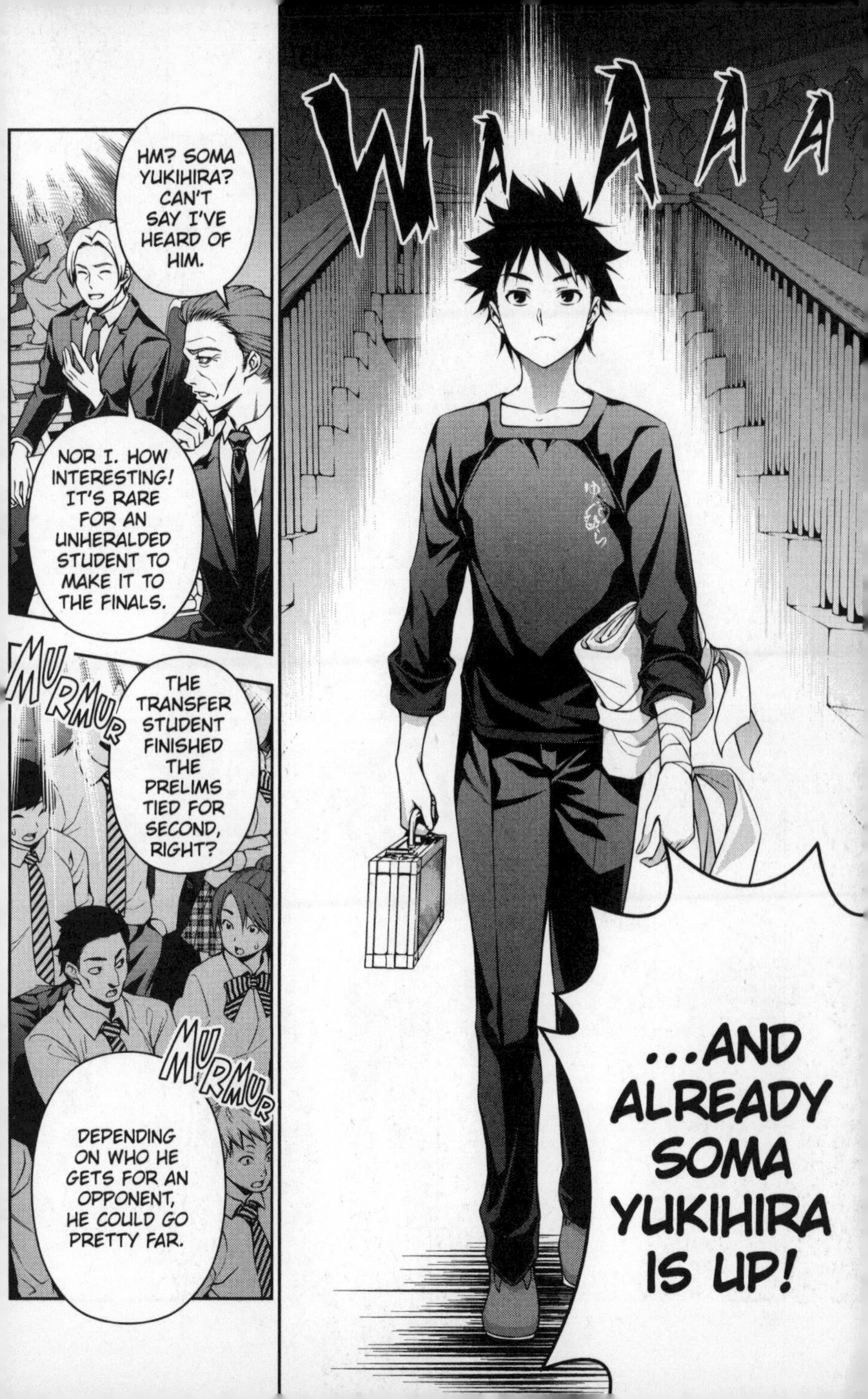
WAAAAA
...AND ALREADY SOMA YUKIHIRA IS UP!
HM? SOMA YUKIHIRA? CAN'T SAY I'VE HEARD OF HIM.
NOR I. HOW INTERESTING! IT'S RARE FOR AN UNHERALDED STUDENT TO MAKE IT TO THE FINALS.
MURMUR
THE TRANSFER STUDENT FINISHED THE PRELIMS TIED FOR SECOND, RIGHT?
MURMUR
DEPENDING ON WHO HE GETS FOR AN OPPONENT, HE COULD GO PRETTY FAR.

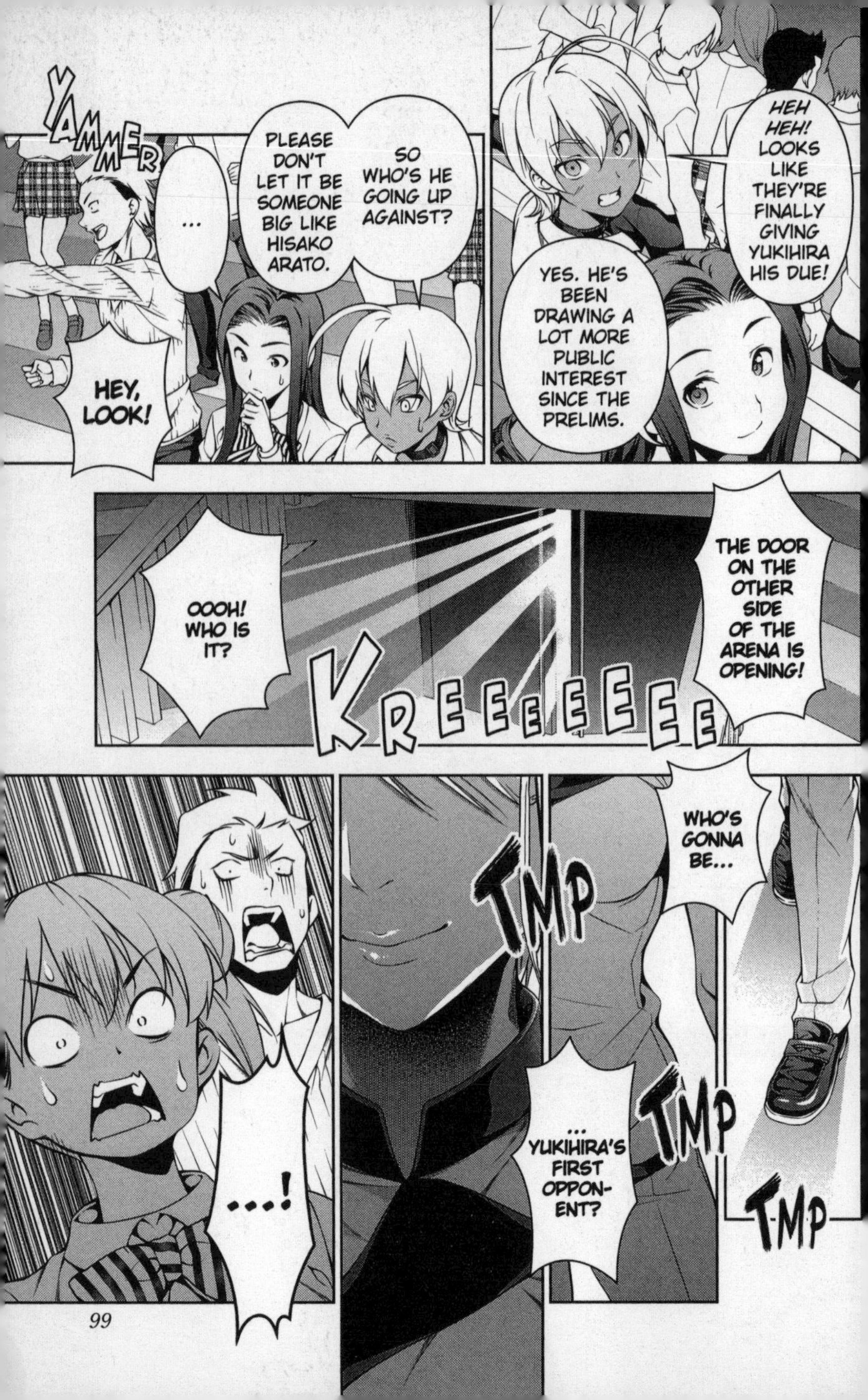
HEH HEH! LOOKS LIKE THEY'RE FINALLY GIVING YUKIHIRA HIS DUE!
YES. HE'S BEEN DRAWING A LOT MORE PUBLIC INTEREST SINCE THE PRELIMS.
SO WHO'S HE GOING UP AGAINST?
PLEASE DON'T LET IT BE SOMEONE BIG LIKE HISAKO ARATO.
...
YAMMER
HEY, LOOK!
THE DOOR ON THE OTHER SIDE OF THE ARENA IS OPENING!
KREEEEEEEE
OOOH! WHO IS IT?
WHO'S GONNA BE...
TMP
TMP
T-MP
... YUKIHIRA'S FIRST OPPONENT?
TMP
...!

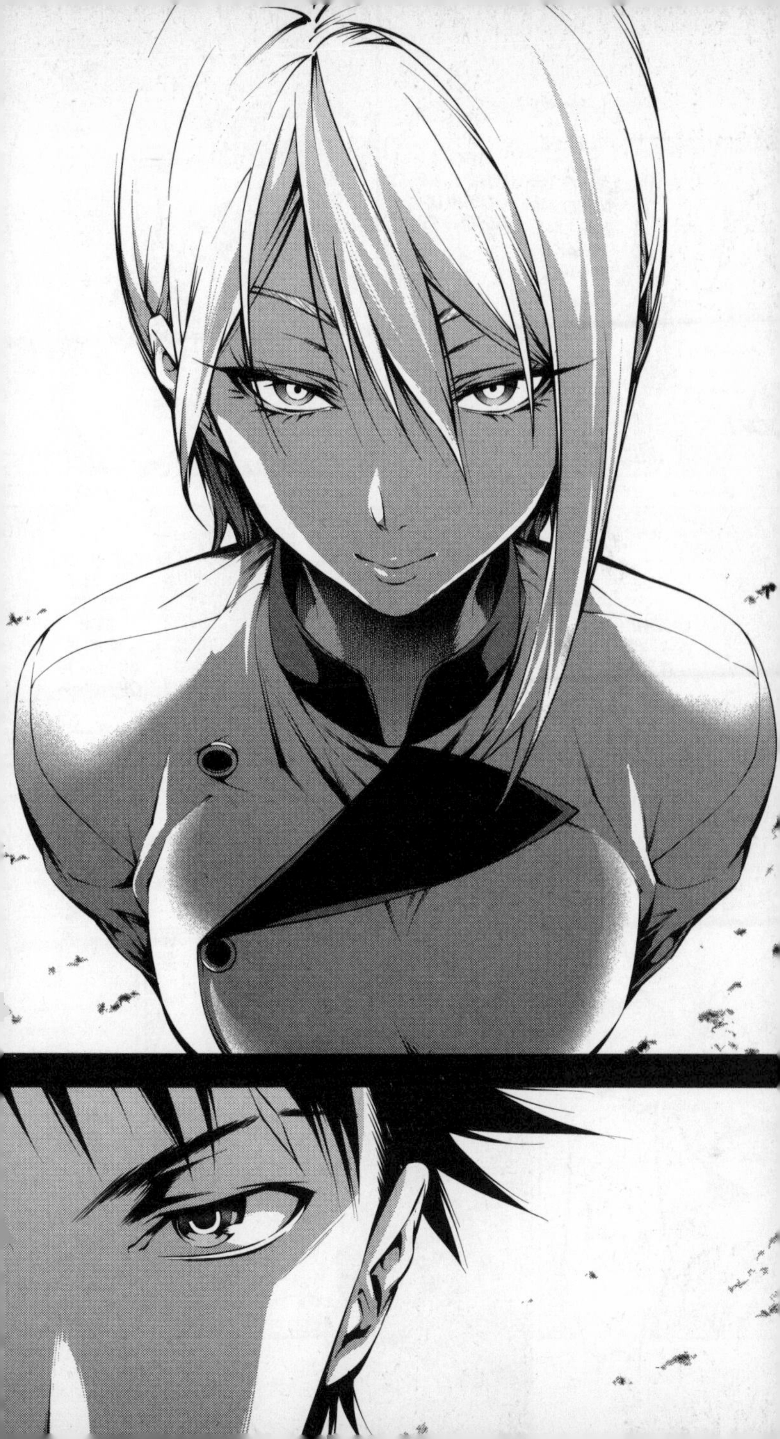

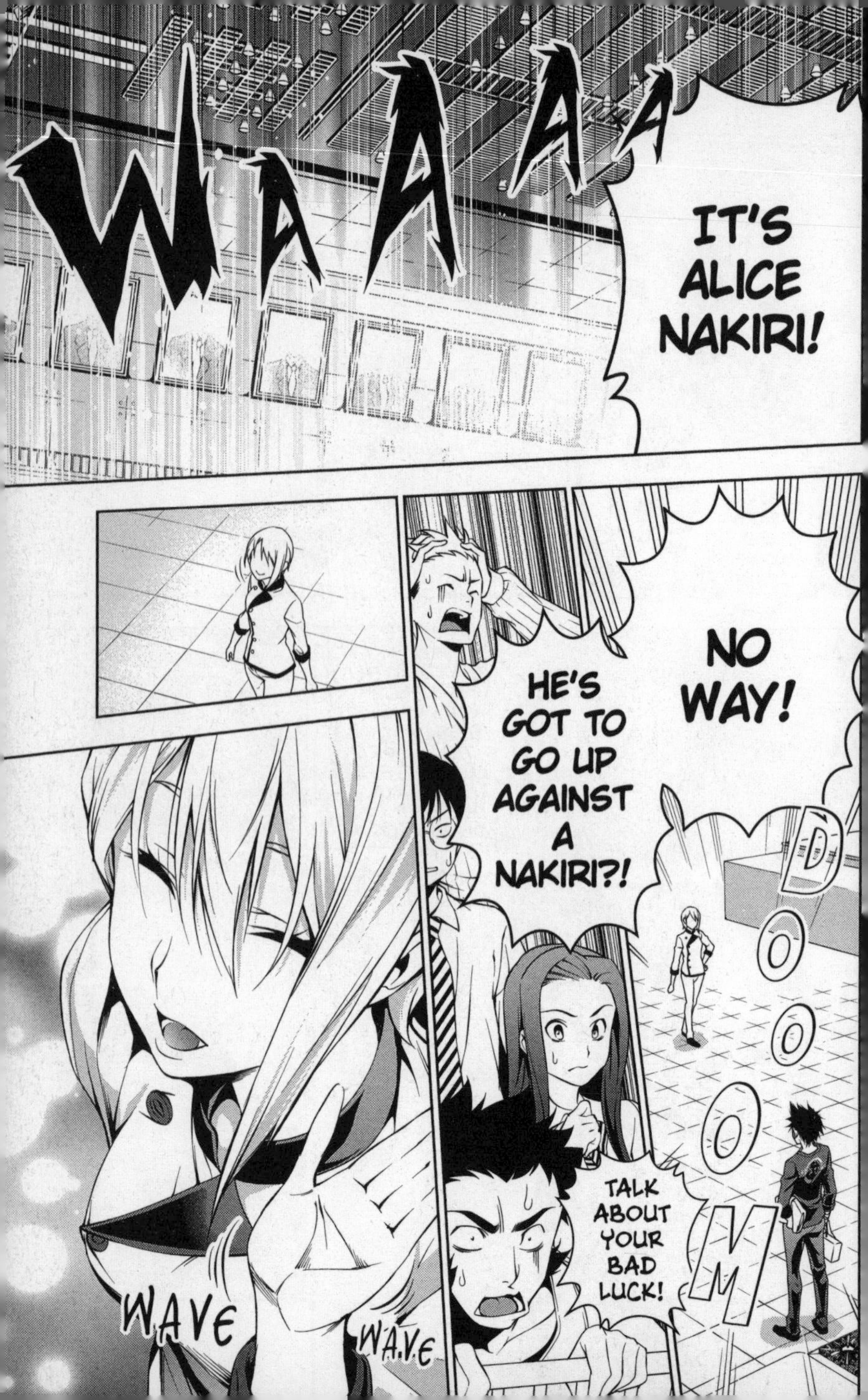
WAAAA
IT'S ALICE NAKIRI!
NO WAY!
HE'S GOT TO GO UP AGAINST A NAKIRI?!
DOOOOM
TALK ABOUT YOUR BAD LUCK!
WAVE
WAVE

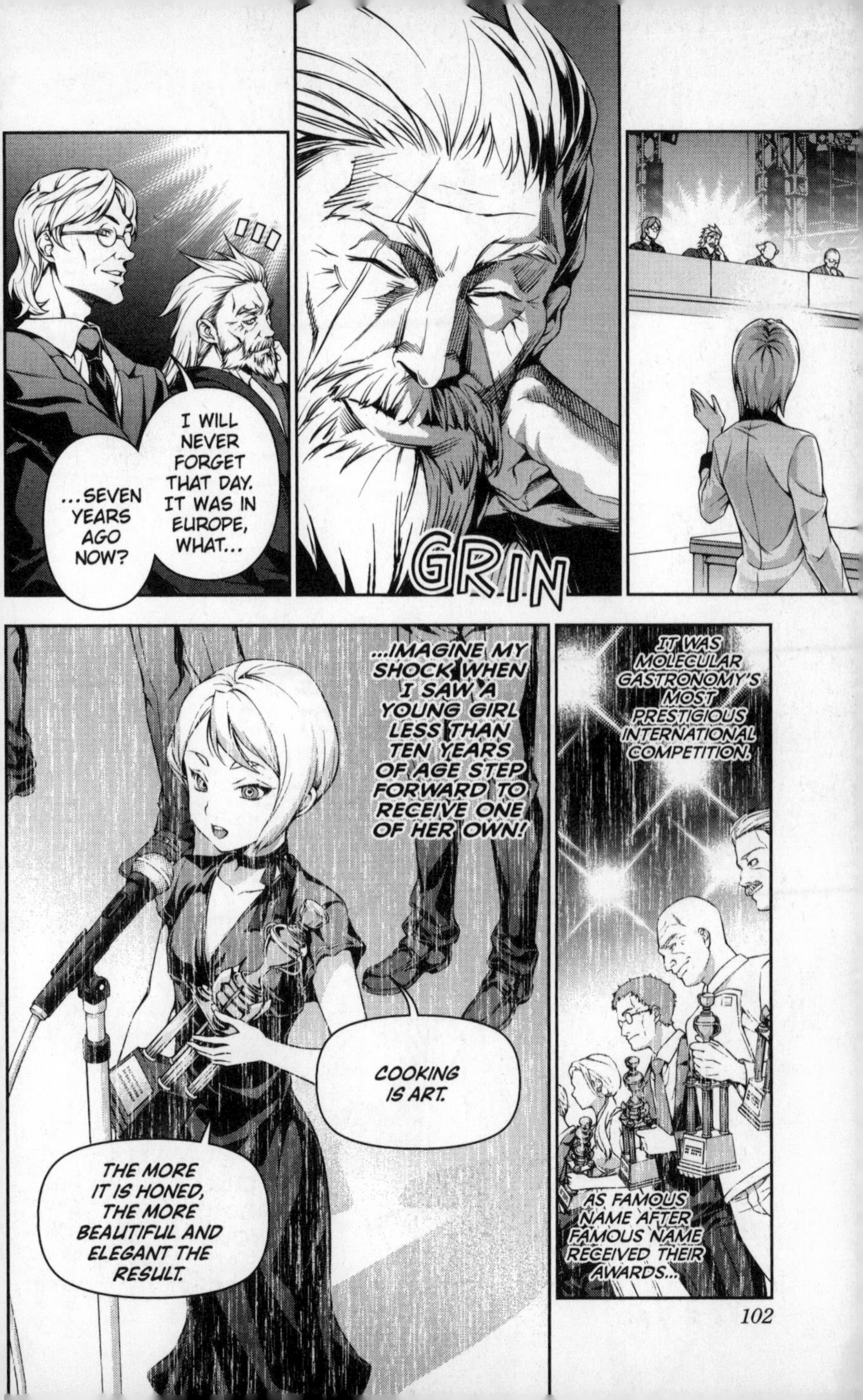
GRIN
I WILL NEVER FORGET THAT DAY. IT WAS IN EUROPE, WHAT...
...SEVEN YEARS AGO NOW?
IT WAS MOLECULAR GASTRONOMY'S MOST PRESTIGIOUS INTERNATIONAL COMPETITION.
AS FAMOUS NAME AFTER FAMOUS NAME RECEIVED THEIR AWARDS...
...IMAGINE MY SHOCK WHEN I SAW A YOUNG GIRL LESS THAN TEN YEARS OF AGE STEP FORWARD TO RECEIVE ONE OF HER OWN!
COOKING IS ART.
THE MORE IT IS HONED, THE MORE BEAUTIFUL AND ELEGANT THE RESULT.

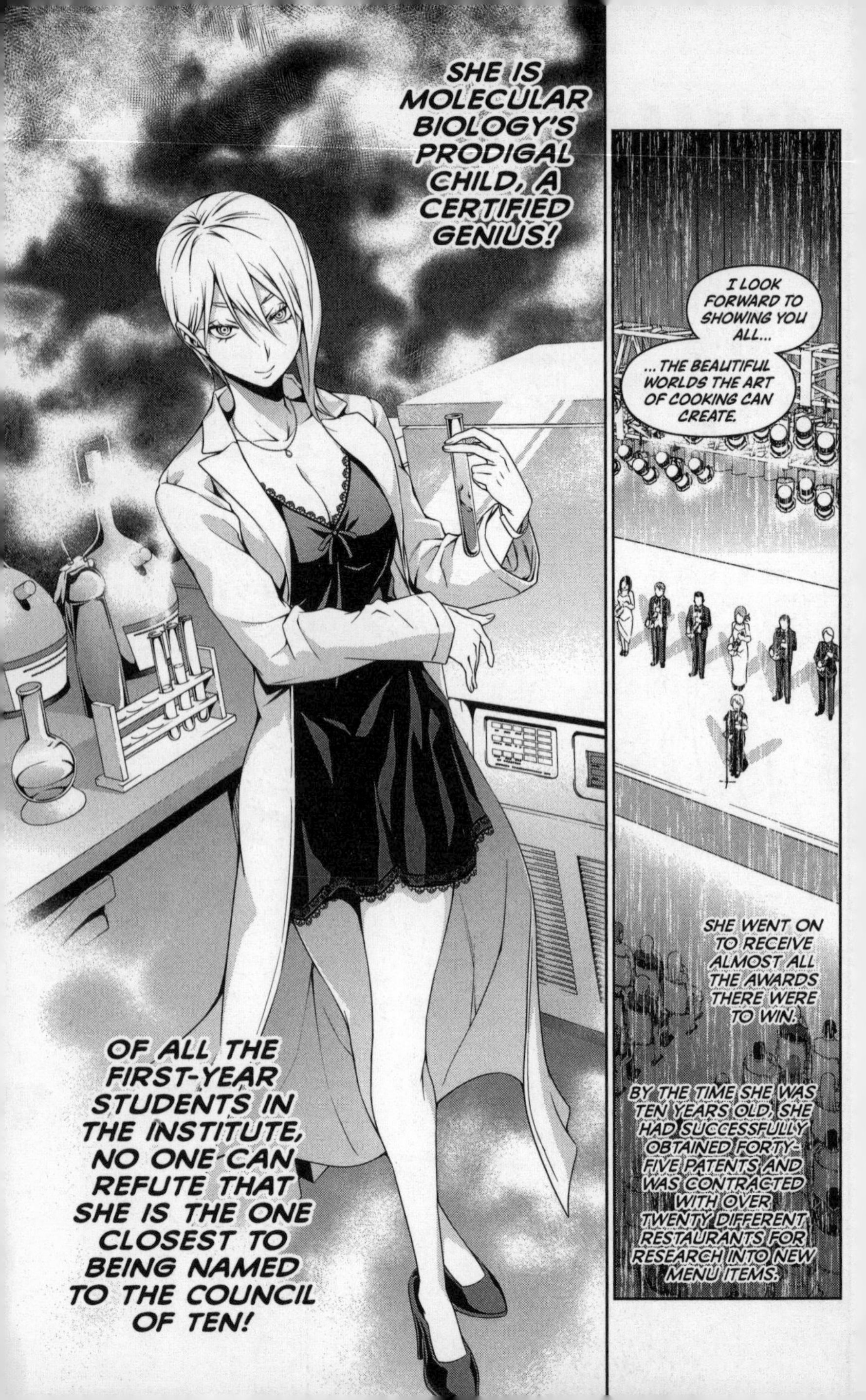
I LOOK FORWARD TO SHOWING YOU ALL...
...THE BEAUTIFUL WORLDS THE ART OF COOKING CAN CREATE.
SHE WENT ON TO RECEIVE ALMOST ALL THE AWARDS THERE WERE TO WIN.
BY THE TIME SHE WAS TEN YEARS OLD, SHE HAD SUCCESSFULLY OBTAINED FORTY-FIVE PATENTS AND WAS CONTRACTED WITH OVER TWENTY DIFFERENT RESTAURANTS FOR RESEARCH INTO NEW MENU ITEMS.
SHE IS MOLECULAR BIOLOGY'S PRODIGAL CHILD, A CERTIFIED GENIUS!
OF ALL THE FIRST-YEAR STUDENTS IN THE INSTITUTE, NO ONE CAN REFUTE THAT SHE IS THE ONE CLOSEST TO BEING NAMED TO THE COUNCIL OF TEN!

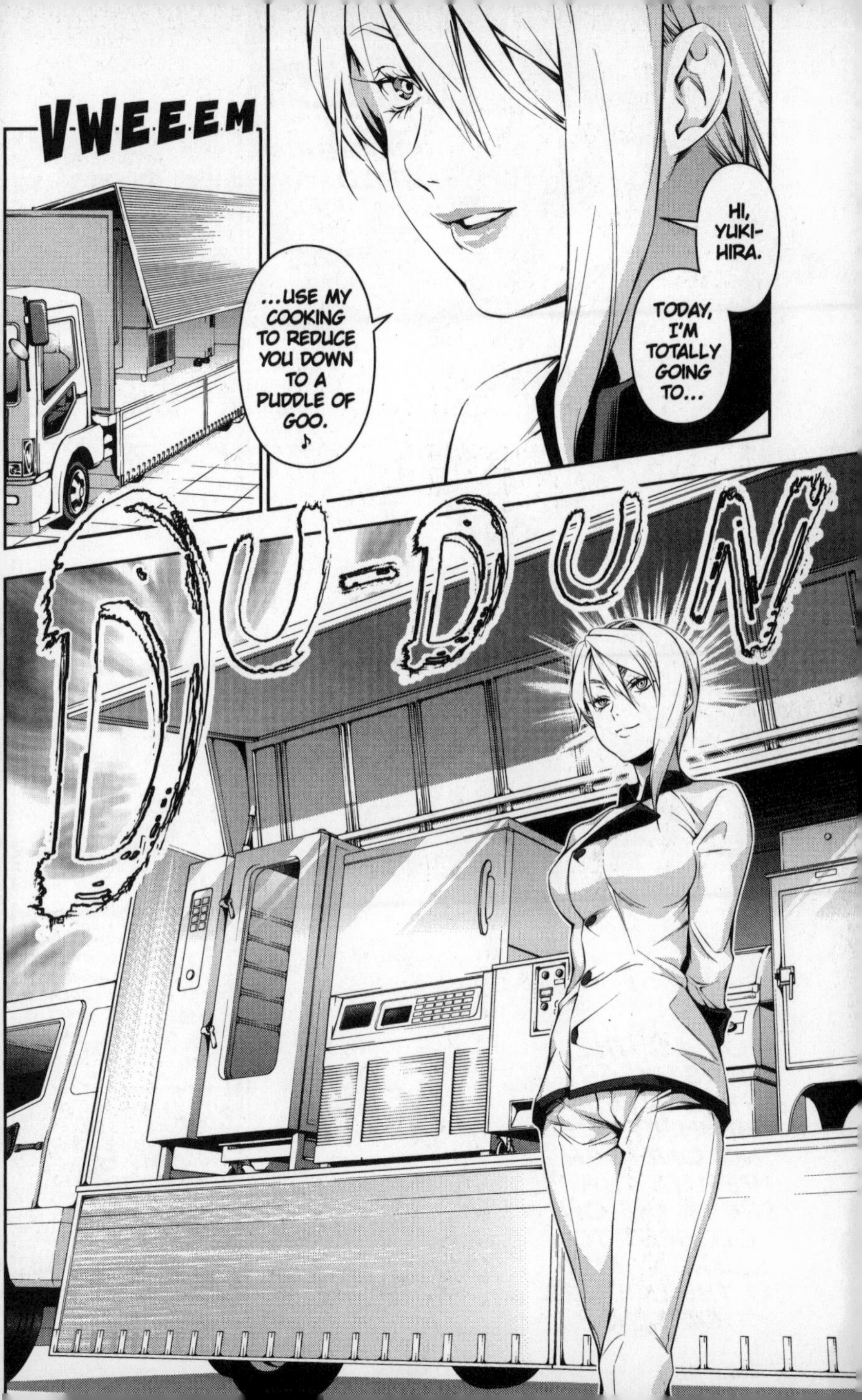
HI, YUKI-HIRA.
TODAY, I'M TOTALLY GOING TO...
...USE MY COOKING TO REDUCE YOU DOWN TO A PUDDLE OF GOO. ♪
V-W-E-E-E-M
DU-DUN

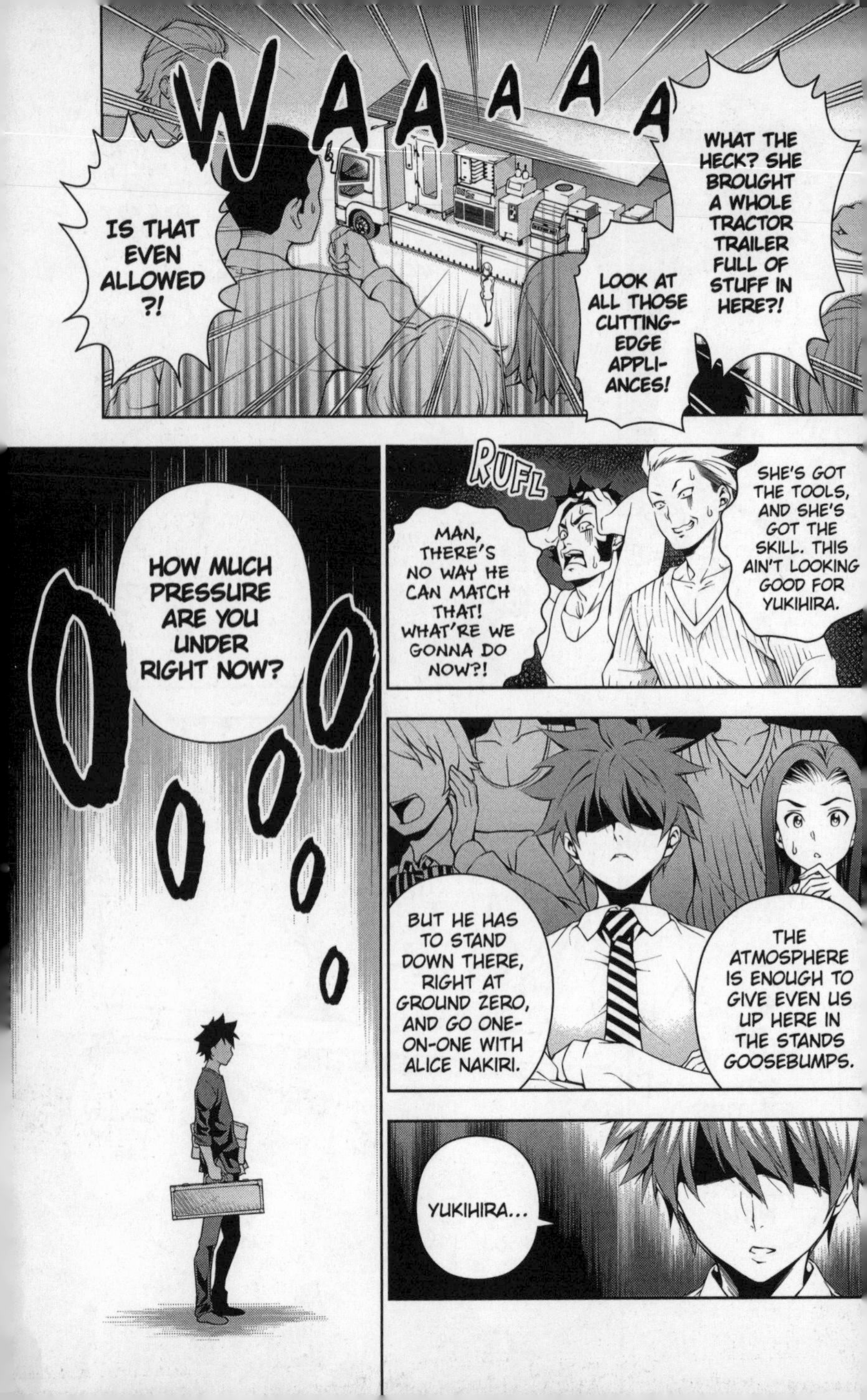
WAAAAA
WHAT THE HECK? SHE BROUGHT A WHOLE TRACTOR TRAILER FULL OF STUFF IN HERE?!
LOOK AT ALL THOSE CUTTING-EDGE APPLIANCES!
IS THAT EVEN ALLOWED?!
RUFL
SHE'S GOT THE TOOLS, AND SHE'S GOT THE SKILL. THIS AIN'T LOOKING GOOD FOR YUKIHIRA.
MAN, THERE'S NO WAY HE CAN MATCH THAT! WHAT'RE WE GONNA DO NOW?!
THE ATMOSPHERE IS ENOUGH TO GIVE EVEN US UP HERE IN THE STANDS GOOSEBUMPS.
BUT HE HAS TO STAND DOWN THERE, RIGHT AT GROUND ZERO, AND GO ONE-ON-ONE WITH ALICE NAKIRI.
YUKIHIRA...
OOOOOOO
HOW MUCH PRESSURE ARE YOU UNDER RIGHT NOW?

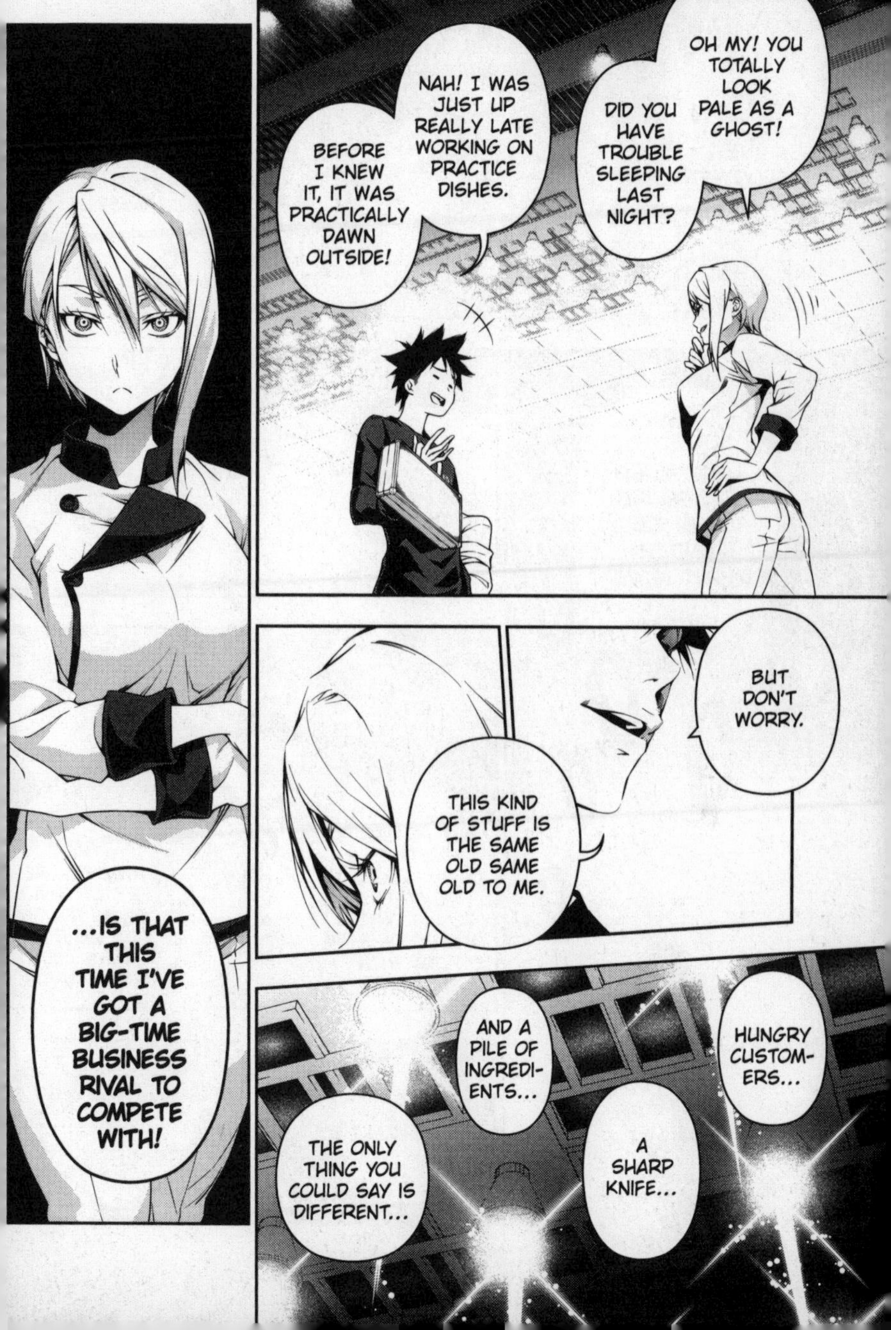
OH MY! YOU TOTALLY LOOK PALE AS A GHOST!
DID YOU HAVE TROUBLE SLEEPING LAST NIGHT?
NAH! I WAS JUST UP REALLY LATE WORKING ON PRACTICE DISHES.
BEFORE I KNEW IT, IT WAS PRACTICALLY DAWN OUTSIDE!
BUT DON'T WORRY.
THIS KIND OF STUFF IS THE SAME OLD SAME OLD TO ME.
HUNGRY CUSTOM-ERS...
AND A PILE OF INGREDI-ENTS...
A SHARP KNIFE...
THE ONLY THING YOU COULD SAY IS DIFFERENT...
...IS THAT THIS TIME I'VE GOT A BIG-TIME BUSINESS RIVAL TO COMPETE WITH!

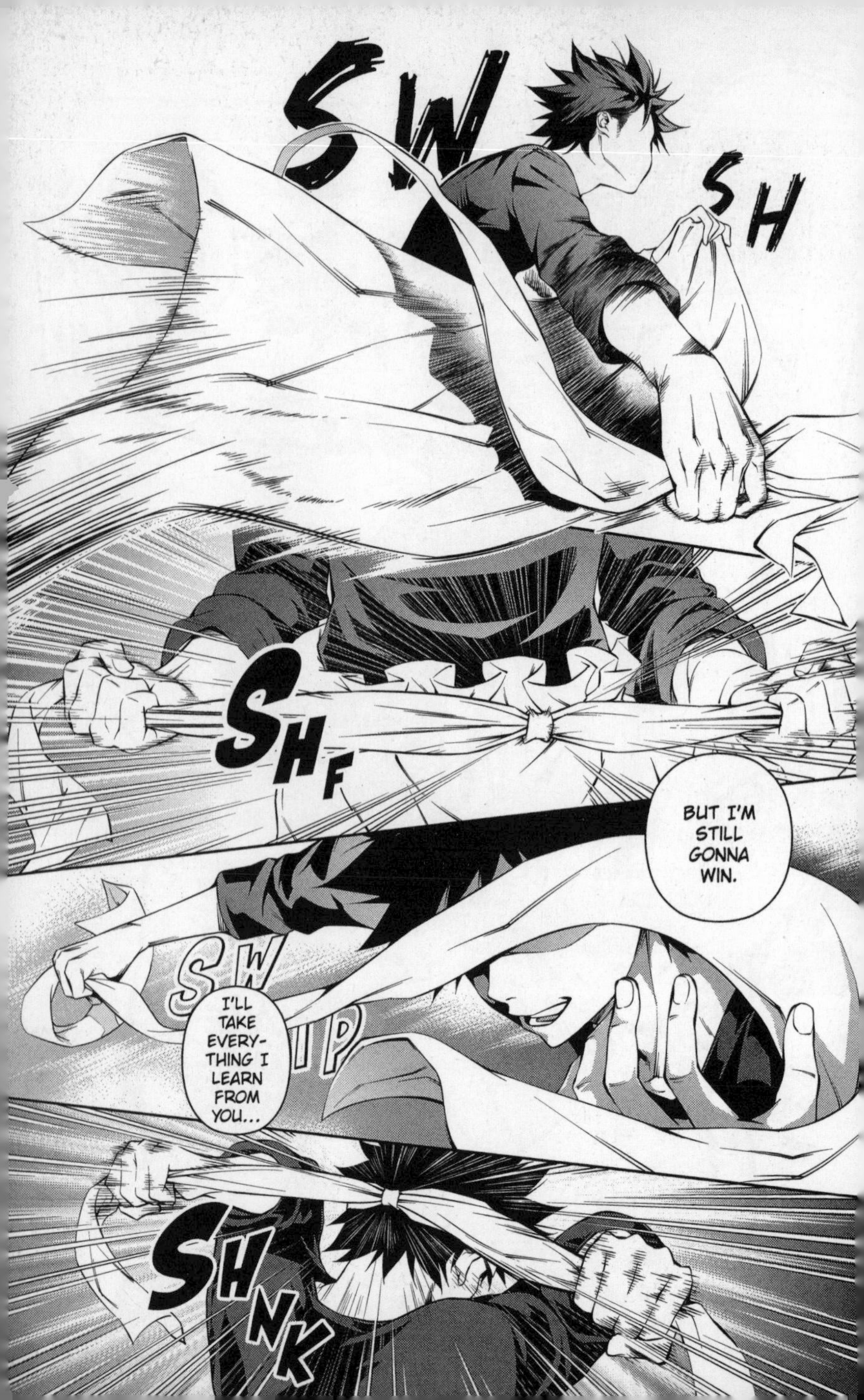
SWSH
SHF
BUT I'M STILL GONNA WIN.
SWIP
I'LL TAKE EVERYTHING I LEARN FROM YOU...
SHNK

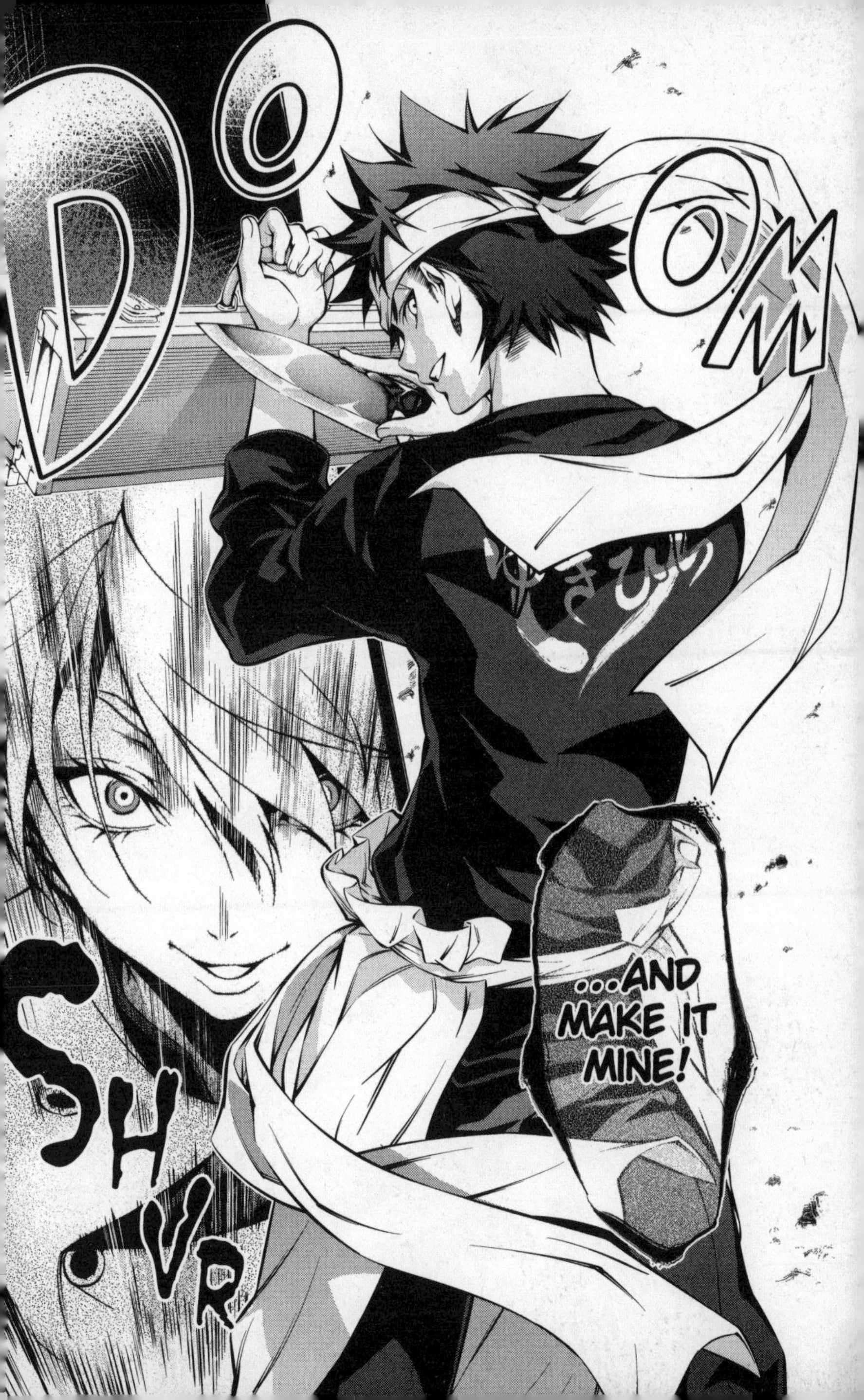
DOOM
...AND MAKE IT MINE!
SHVR

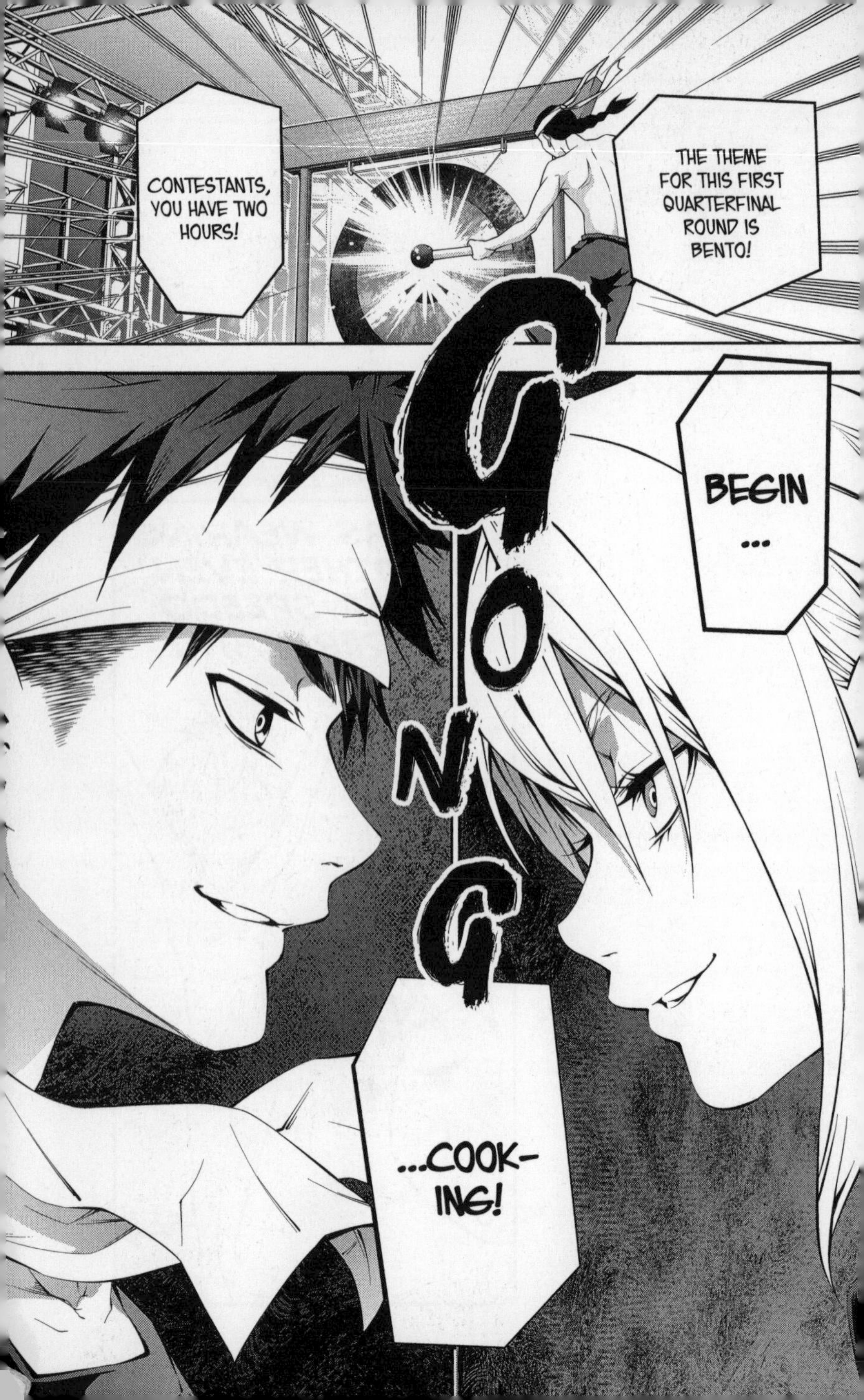
THE THEME FOR THIS FIRST QUARTERFINAL ROUND IS BENTO!
CONTESTANTS, YOU HAVE TWO HOURS!
GONG
BEGIN ...
...COOK-ING!

KUMABEAR

POTIT-HOOSE

CONTINUED FROM PAGE 66!

HE WAS WEARING ANOTHER EVEN TINIER SPEEDO UNDERNEATH!
GOD, DON'T SCARE ME LIKE THAT!

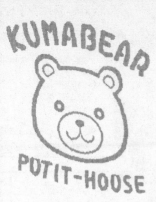

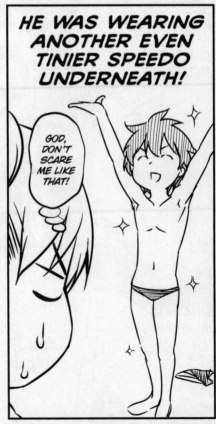

63 PLOTS

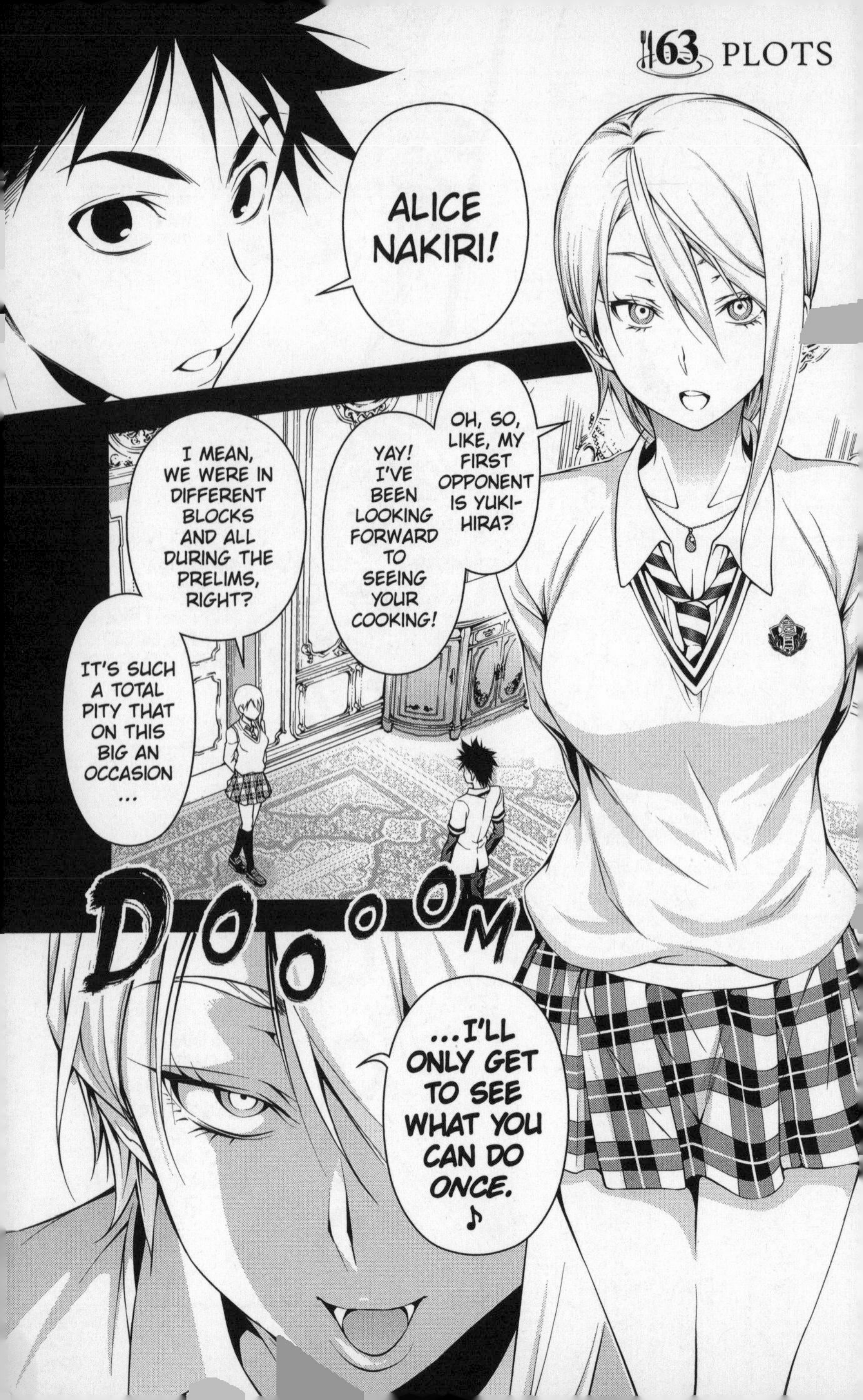
ALICE NAKIRI!
OH, SO, LIKE, MY FIRST OPPONENT IS YUKI-HIRA?
YAY! I'VE BEEN LOOKING FORWARD TO SEEING YOUR COOKING!
I MEAN, WE WERE IN DIFFERENT BLOCKS AND ALL DURING THE PRELIMS, RIGHT?
IT'S SUCH A TOTAL PITY THAT ON THIS BIG AN OCCASION ...
DOOOOM
...I'LL ONLY GET TO SEE WHAT YOU CAN DO ONCE. ♪

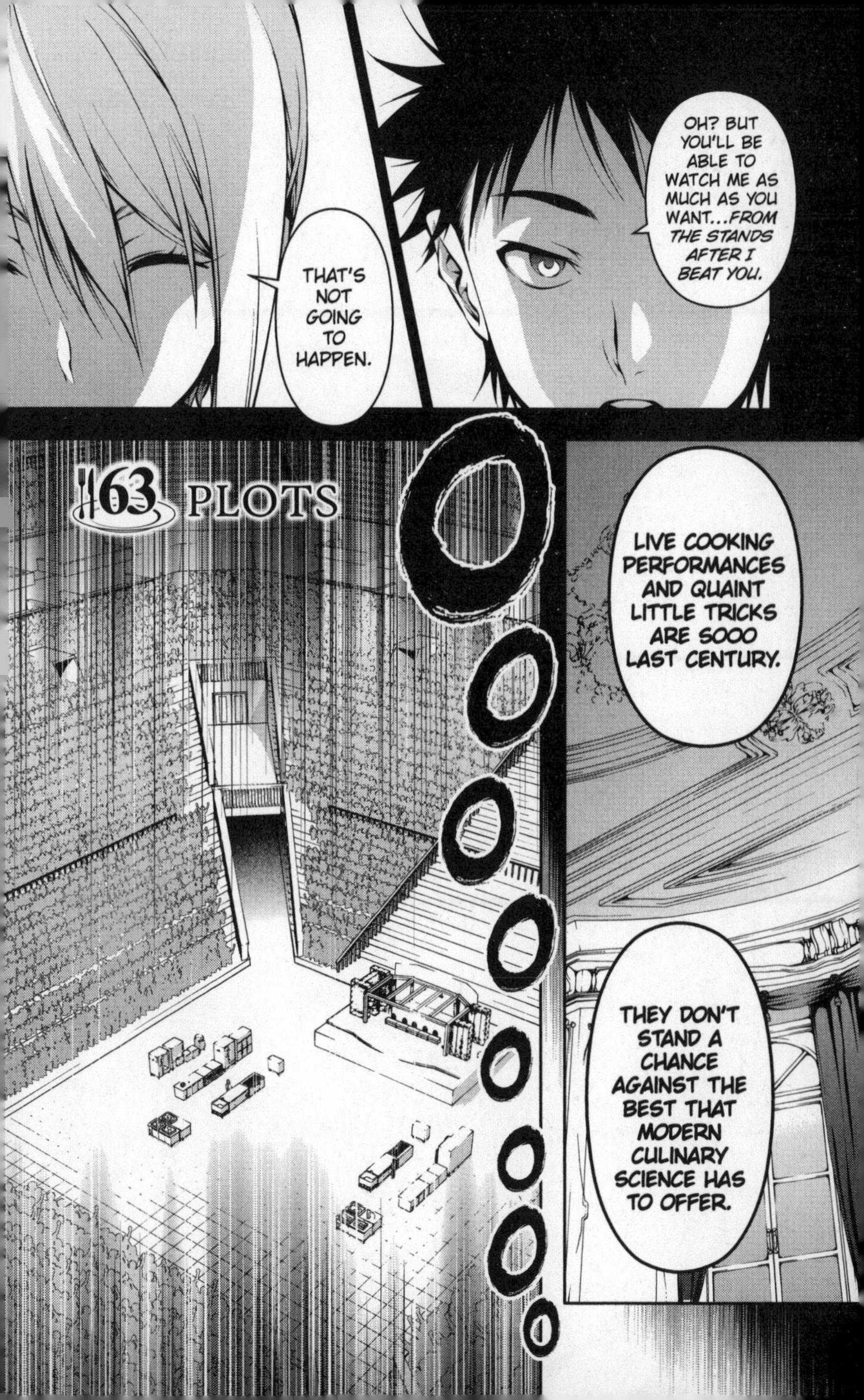
OH? BUT YOU'LL BE ABLE TO WATCH ME AS MUCH AS YOU WANT...FROM THE STANDS AFTER I BEAT YOU.
THAT'S NOT GOING TO HAPPEN.
LIVE COOKING PERFORMANCES AND QUAINT LITTLE TRICKS ARE SOOO LAST CENTURY.
THEY DON'T STAND A CHANCE AGAINST THE BEST THAT MODERN CULINARY SCIENCE HAS TO OFFER.
63 PLOTS

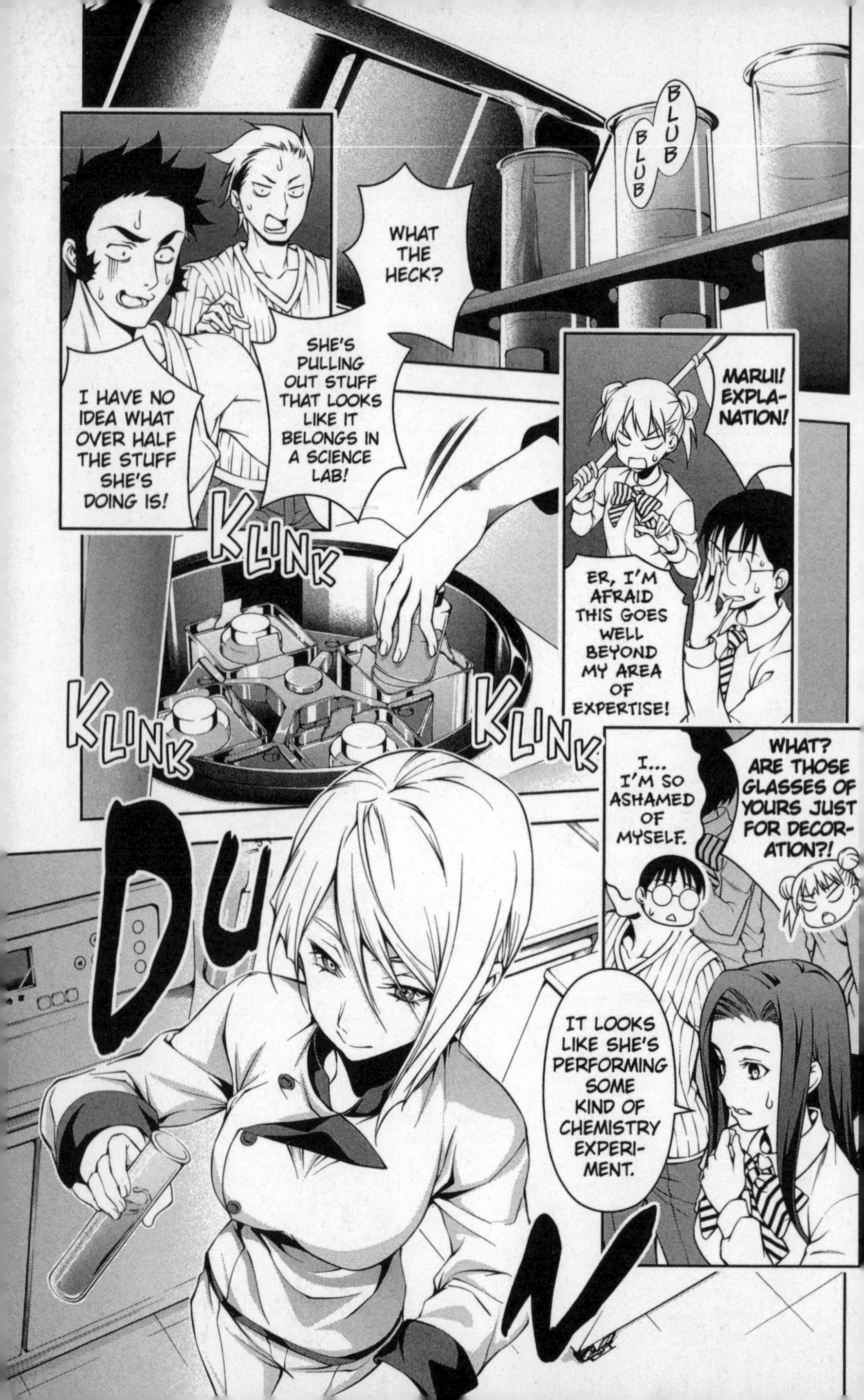
BLUB BLUB
WHAT THE HECK?
SHE'S PULLING OUT STUFF THAT LOOKS LIKE IT BELONGS IN A SCIENCE LAB!
I HAVE NO IDEA WHAT OVER HALF THE STUFF SHE'S DOING IS!
MARUI! EXPLANATION!
ER, I'M AFRAID THIS GOES WELL BEYOND MY AREA OF EXPERTISE!
KLINK
KLINK
KLINK
WHAT? ARE THOSE GLASSES OF YOURS JUST FOR DECORATION?!
I... I'M SO ASHAMED OF MYSELF.
DUN
IT LOOKS LIKE SHE'S PERFORMING SOME KIND OF CHEMISTRY EXPERIMENT.

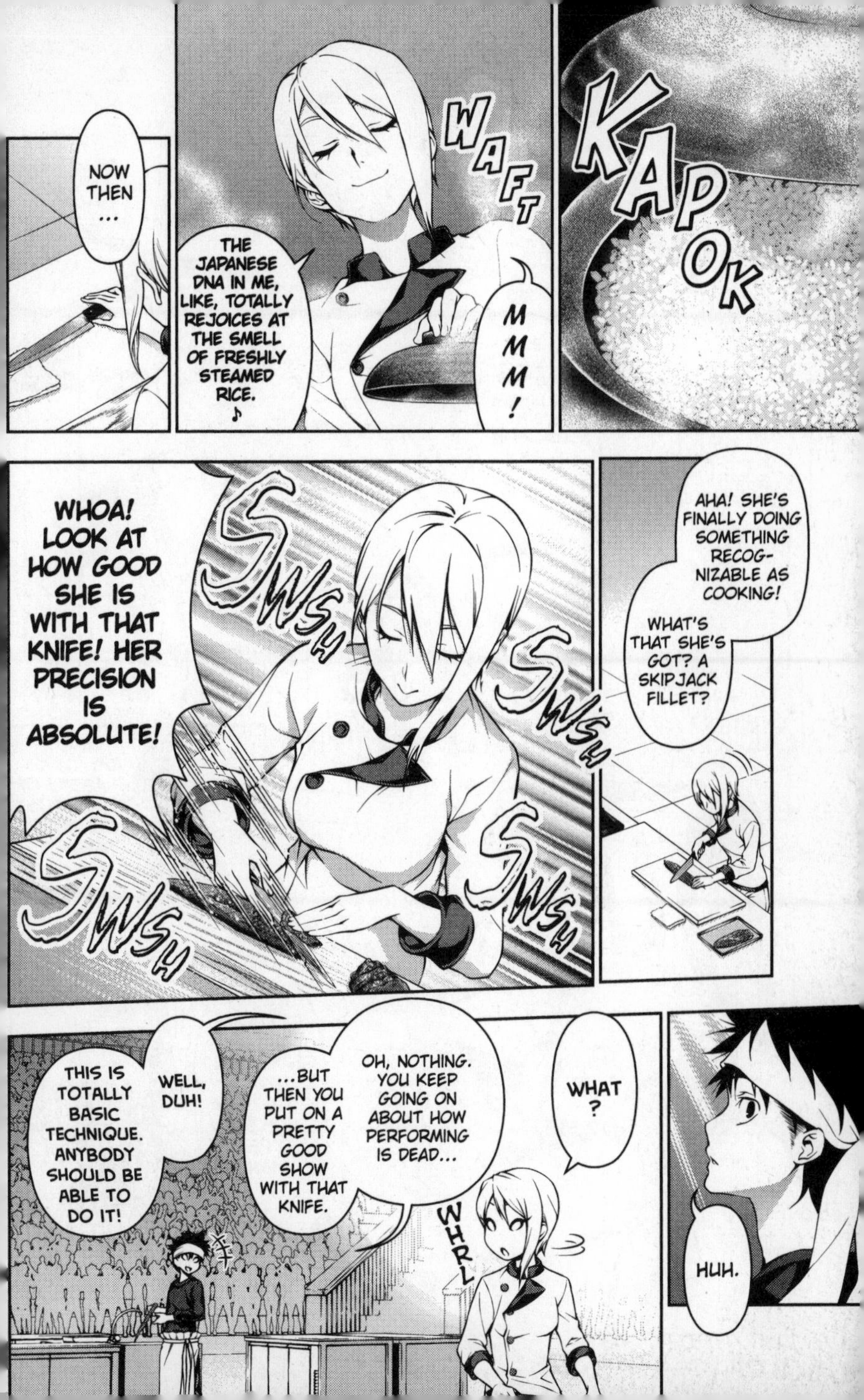
KAPOK
WAFT
MMM!
THE JAPANESE DNA IN ME, LIKE, TOTALLY REJOICES AT THE SMELL OF FRESHLY STEAMED RICE. ♪
NOW THEN...
AHA! SHE'S FINALLY DOING SOMETHING RECOG-NIZABLE AS COOKING!
WHAT'S THAT SHE'S GOT? A SKIPJACK FILLET?
SWSH
SWSH
SWSH
WHOA! LOOK AT HOW GOOD SHE IS WITH THAT KNIFE! HER PRECISION IS ABSOLUTE!
SWSH
HUH.
WHAT?
WHRL
OH, NOTHING. YOU KEEP GOING ON ABOUT HOW PERFORMING IS DEAD...
...BUT THEN YOU PUT ON A PRETTY GOOD SHOW WITH THAT KNIFE.
WELL, DUH!
THIS IS TOTALLY BASIC TECHNIQUE. ANYBODY SHOULD BE ABLE TO DO IT!

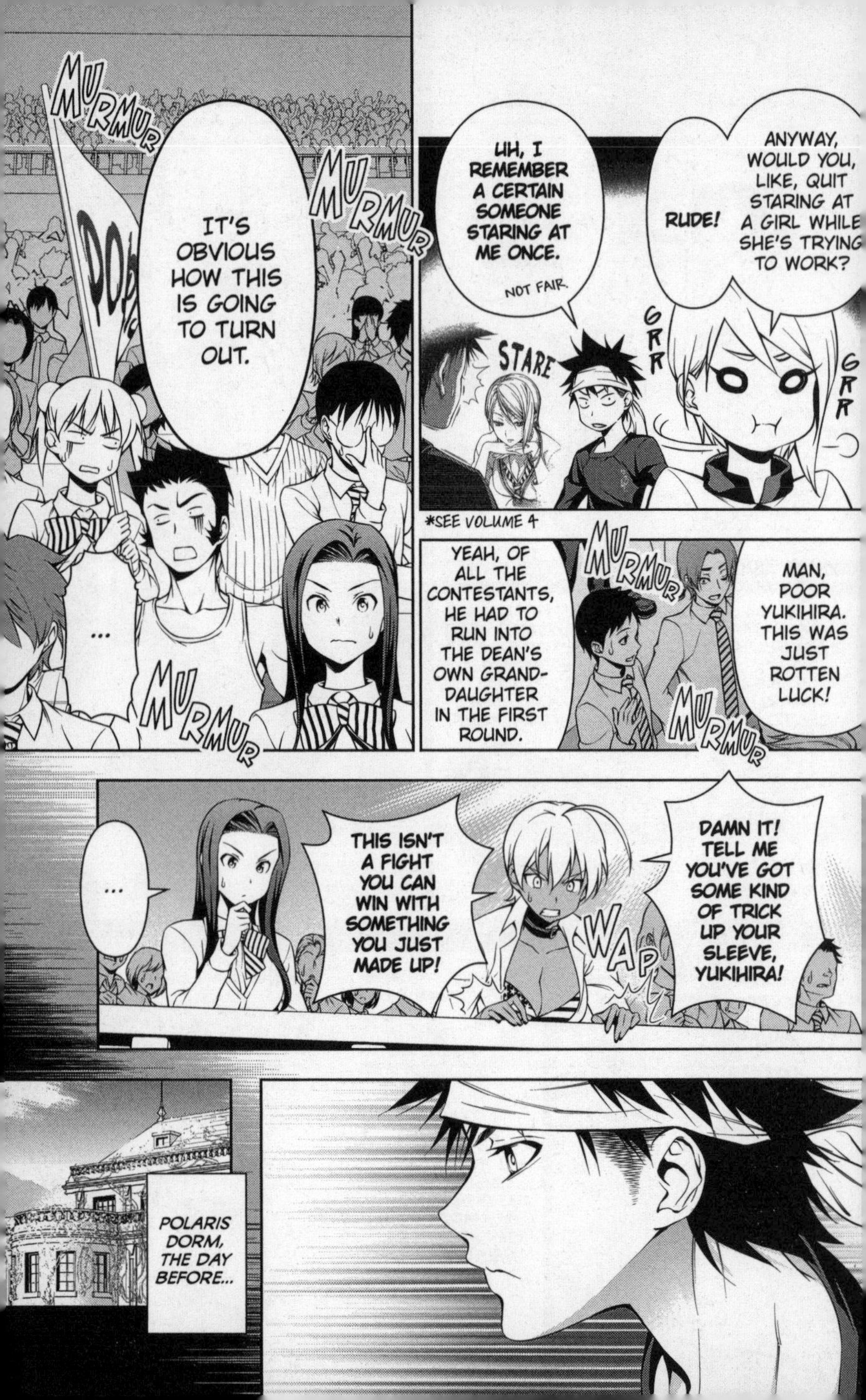
ANYWAY, WOULD YOU, LIKE, QUIT STARING AT A GIRL WHILE SHE'S TRYING TO WORK?
RUDE!
GRR
GRR
UH, I REMEMBER A CERTAIN SOMEONE STARING AT ME ONCE.
NOT FAIR.
STARE
*SEE VOLUME 4
MAN, POOR YUKIHIRA. THIS WAS JUST ROTTEN LUCK!
MURMUR
YEAH, OF ALL THE CONTESTANTS, HE HAD TO RUN INTO THE DEAN'S OWN GRAND-DAUGHTER IN THE FIRST ROUND.
MURMUR
MURMUR
MURMUR
IT'S OBVIOUS HOW THIS IS GOING TO TURN OUT.
...
MURMUR
DAMN IT! TELL ME YOU'VE GOT SOME KIND OF TRICK UP YOUR SLEEVE, YUKIHIRA!
WAP
THIS ISN'T A FIGHT YOU CAN WIN WITH SOMETHING YOU JUST MADE UP!
...
POLARIS DORM, THE DAY BEFORE...

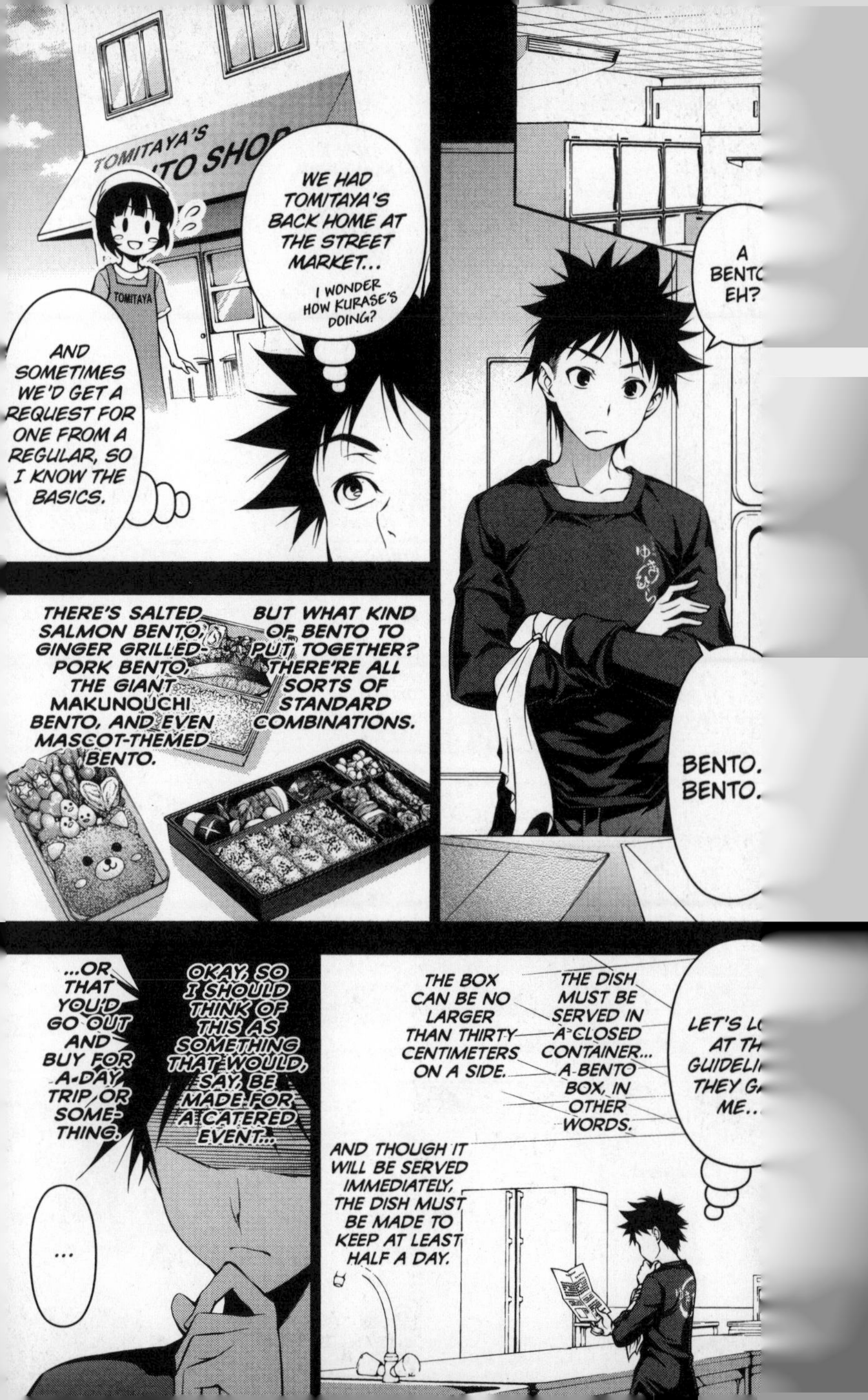
A BENTO EH?
BENTO. BENTO.
TOMITAYA'S
TO SHOP
WE HAD TOMITAYA'S BACK HOME AT THE STREET MARKET...
I WONDER HOW KURASE'S DOING?
TOMITAYA
AND SOMETIMES WE'D GET A REQUEST FOR ONE FROM A REGULAR, SO I KNOW THE BASICS.
BUT WHAT KIND OF BENTO TO PUT TOGETHER? THERE'RE ALL SORTS OF STANDARD COMBINATIONS.
THERE'S SALTED SALMON BENTO, GINGER GRILLED-PORK BENTO, THE GIANT MAKUNOUCHI BENTO, AND EVEN MASCOT-THEMED BENTO.
LET'S L AT TH GUIDELI THEY G ME...
THE DISH MUST BE SERVED IN A CLOSED CONTAINER... A BENTO BOX, IN OTHER WORDS.
THE BOX CAN BE NO LARGER THAN THIRTY CENTIMETERS ON A SIDE.
AND THOUGH IT WILL BE SERVED IMMEDIATELY, THE DISH MUST BE MADE TO KEEP AT LEAST HALF A DAY.
OKAY, SO I SHOULD THINK OF THIS AS SOMETHING THAT WOULD, SAY, BE MADE FOR A CATERED EVENT...
...OR THAT YOU'D GO OUT AND BUY FOR A DAY TRIP OR SOME-THING.
...

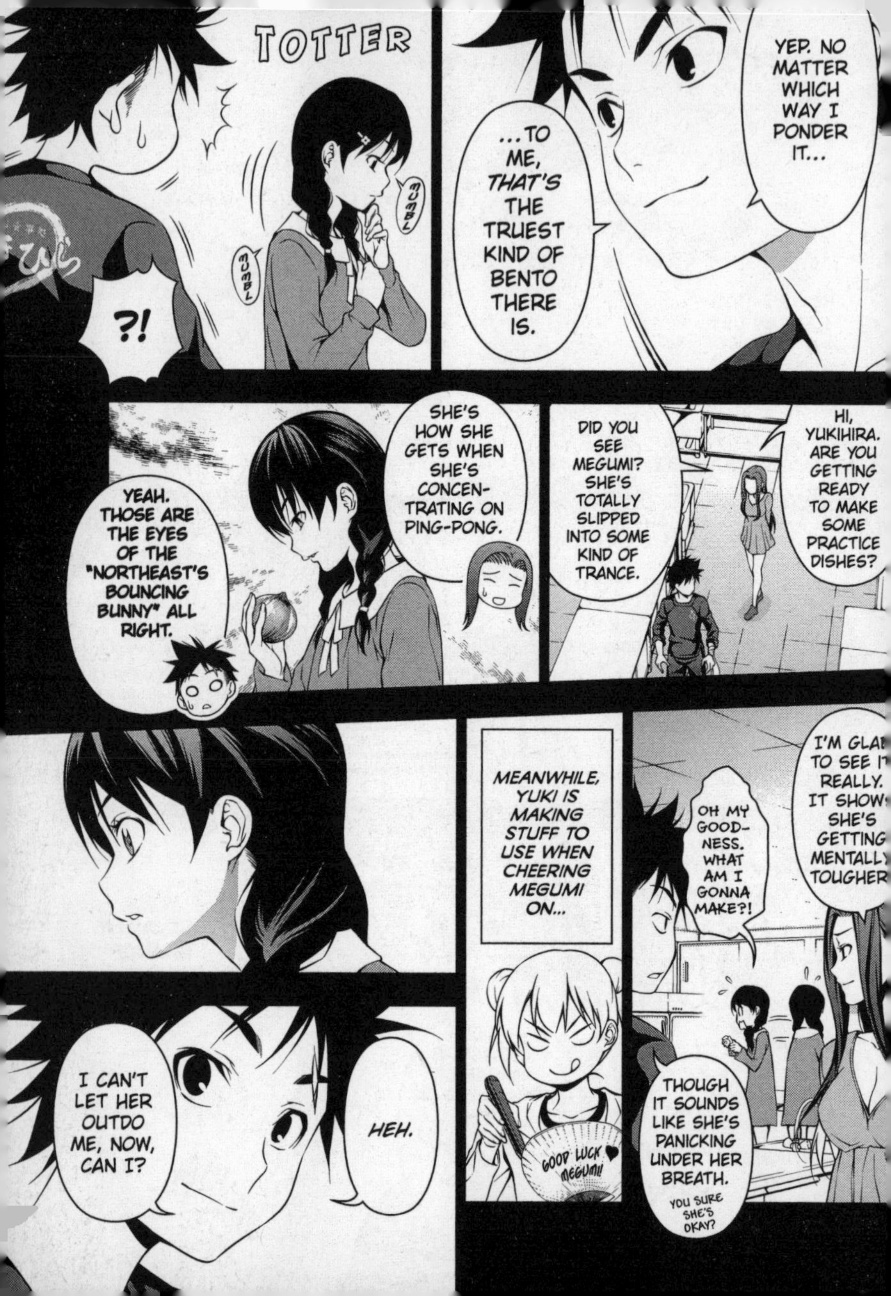
YEP. NO MATTER WHICH WAY I PONDER IT...
...TO ME, THAT'S THE TRUEST KIND OF BENTO THERE IS.
TOTTER
MUMBL
MUMBL
?!
HI, YUKIHIRA. ARE YOU GETTING READY TO MAKE SOME PRACTICE DISHES?
DID YOU SEE MEGUMI? SHE'S TOTALLY SLIPPED INTO SOME KIND OF TRANCE.
SHE'S HOW SHE GETS WHEN SHE'S CONCEN-TRATING ON PING-PONG.
YEAH. THOSE ARE THE EYES OF THE "NORTHEAST'S BOUNCING BUNNY" ALL RIGHT.
I'M GLAD TO SEE IT REALLY. IT SHOWS SHE'S GETTING MENTALLY TOUGHER.
OH MY GOOD-NESS. WHAT AM I GONNA MAKE?!
THOUGH IT SOUNDS LIKE SHE'S PANICKING UNDER HER BREATH.
YOU SURE SHE'S OKAY?
MEANWHILE, YUKI IS MAKING STUFF TO USE WHEN CHEERING MEGUMI ON...
GOOD LUCK MEGUMI!
I CAN'T LET HER OUTDO ME, NOW, CAN I?
HEH.

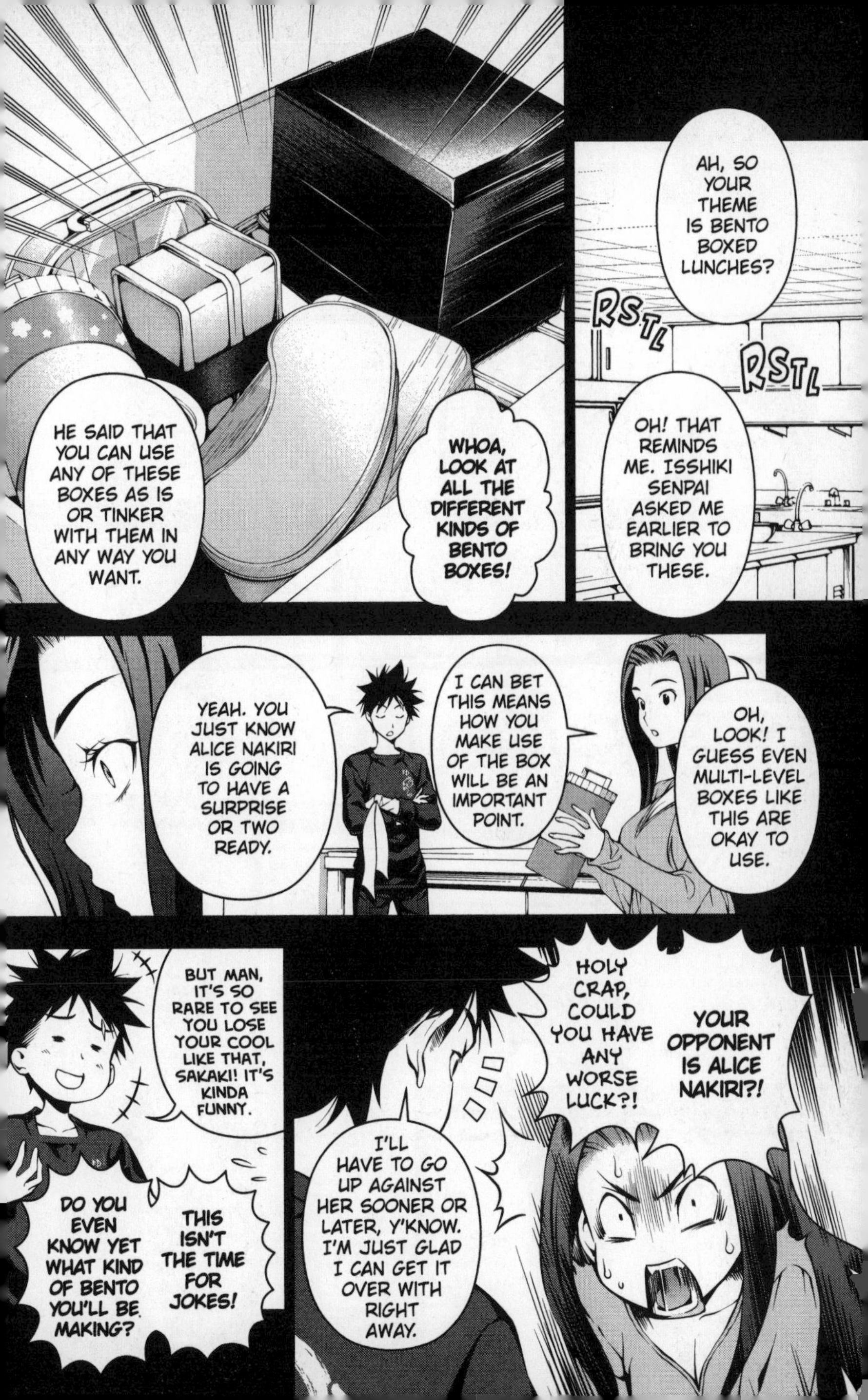
AH, SO YOUR THEME IS BENTO BOXED LUNCHES?
RSTL
RSTL
OH! THAT REMINDS ME. ISSHIKI SENPAI ASKED ME EARLIER TO BRING YOU THESE.
WHOA, LOOK AT ALL THE DIFFERENT KINDS OF BENTO BOXES!
HE SAID THAT YOU CAN USE ANY OF THESE BOXES AS IS OR TINKER WITH THEM IN ANY WAY YOU WANT.
OH, LOOK! I GUESS EVEN MULTI-LEVEL BOXES LIKE THIS ARE OKAY TO USE.
I CAN BET THIS MEANS HOW YOU MAKE USE OF THE BOX WILL BE AN IMPORTANT POINT.
YEAH. YOU JUST KNOW ALICE NAKIRI IS GOING TO HAVE A SURPRISE OR TWO READY.
YOUR OPPONENT IS ALICE NAKIRI?!
HOLY CRAP, COULD YOU HAVE ANY WORSE LUCK?!
I'LL HAVE TO GO UP AGAINST HER SOONER OR LATER, Y'KNOW. I'M JUST GLAD I CAN GET IT OVER WITH RIGHT AWAY.
BUT MAN, IT'S SO RARE TO SEE YOU LOSE YOUR COOL LIKE THAT, SAKAKI! IT'S KINDA FUNNY.
THIS ISN'T THE TIME FOR JOKES!
DO YOU EVEN KNOW YET WHAT KIND OF BENTO YOU'LL BE MAKING?

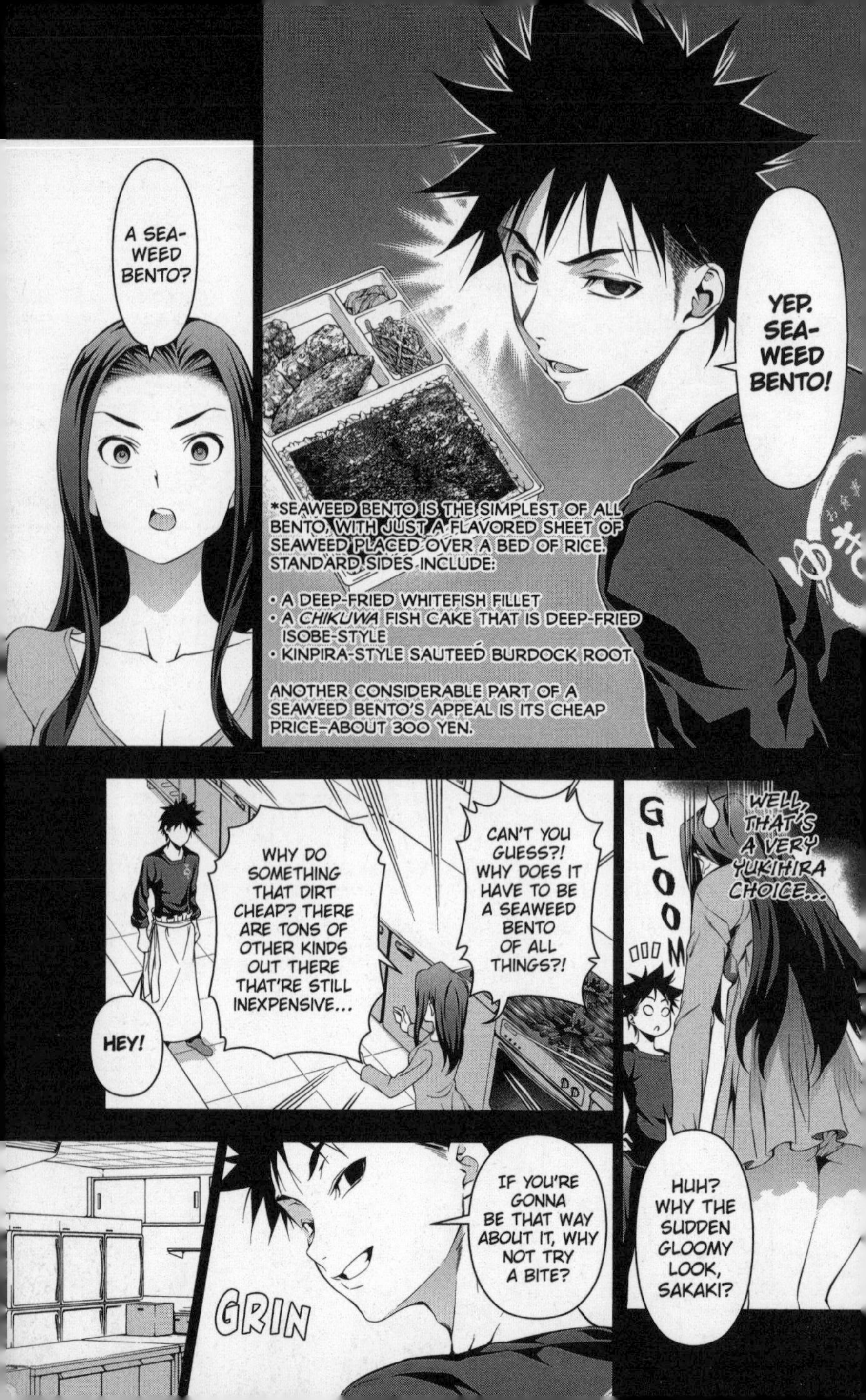
YEP. SEA-WEED BENTO!
*SEAWEED BENTO IS THE SIMPLEST OF ALL BENTO, WITH JUST A FLAVORED SHEET OF SEAWEED PLACED OVER A BED OF RICE. STANDARD SIDES INCLUDE:
• A DEEP-FRIED WHITEFISH FILLET
• A *CHIKUWA* FISH CAKE THAT IS DEEP-FRIED ISOBE-STYLE
• KINPIRA-STYLE SAUTEED BURDOCK ROOT
ANOTHER CONSIDERABLE PART OF A SEAWEED BENTO'S APPEAL IS ITS CHEAP PRICE–ABOUT 300 YEN.
A SEA-WEED BENTO?
WELL, THAT'S A VERY YUKIHIRA CHOICE...
GLOOM
HUH? WHY THE SUDDEN GLOOMY LOOK, SAKAKI?
CAN'T YOU GUESS?! WHY DOES IT HAVE TO BE A SEAWEED BENTO OF ALL THINGS?!
WHY DO SOMETHING THAT DIRT CHEAP? THERE ARE TONS OF OTHER KINDS OUT THERE THAT'RE STILL INEXPENSIVE...
HEY!
IF YOU'RE GONNA BE THAT WAY ABOUT IT, WHY NOT TRY A BITE?
GRIN

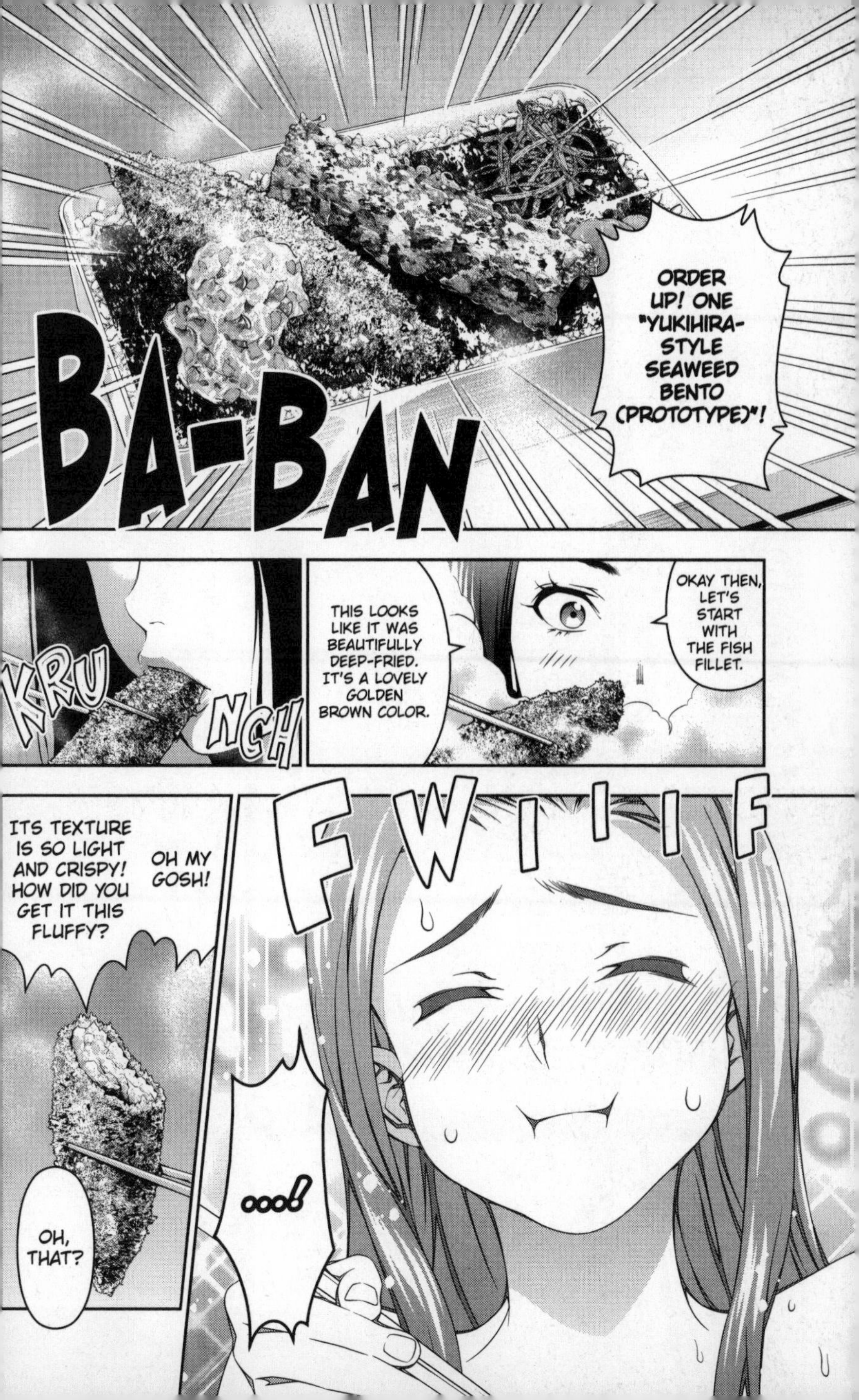
ORDER UP! ONE "YUKIHIRA-STYLE SEAWEED BENTO (PROTOTYPE)"!
BA-BAN
OKAY THEN, LET'S START WITH THE FISH FILLET.
THIS LOOKS LIKE IT WAS BEAUTIFULLY DEEP-FRIED. IT'S A LOVELY GOLDEN BROWN COLOR.
KRUNCH
FWIIIF
ooo!
OH MY GOSH!
ITS TEXTURE IS SO LIGHT AND CRISPY! HOW DID YOU GET IT THIS FLUFFY?
OH, THAT?

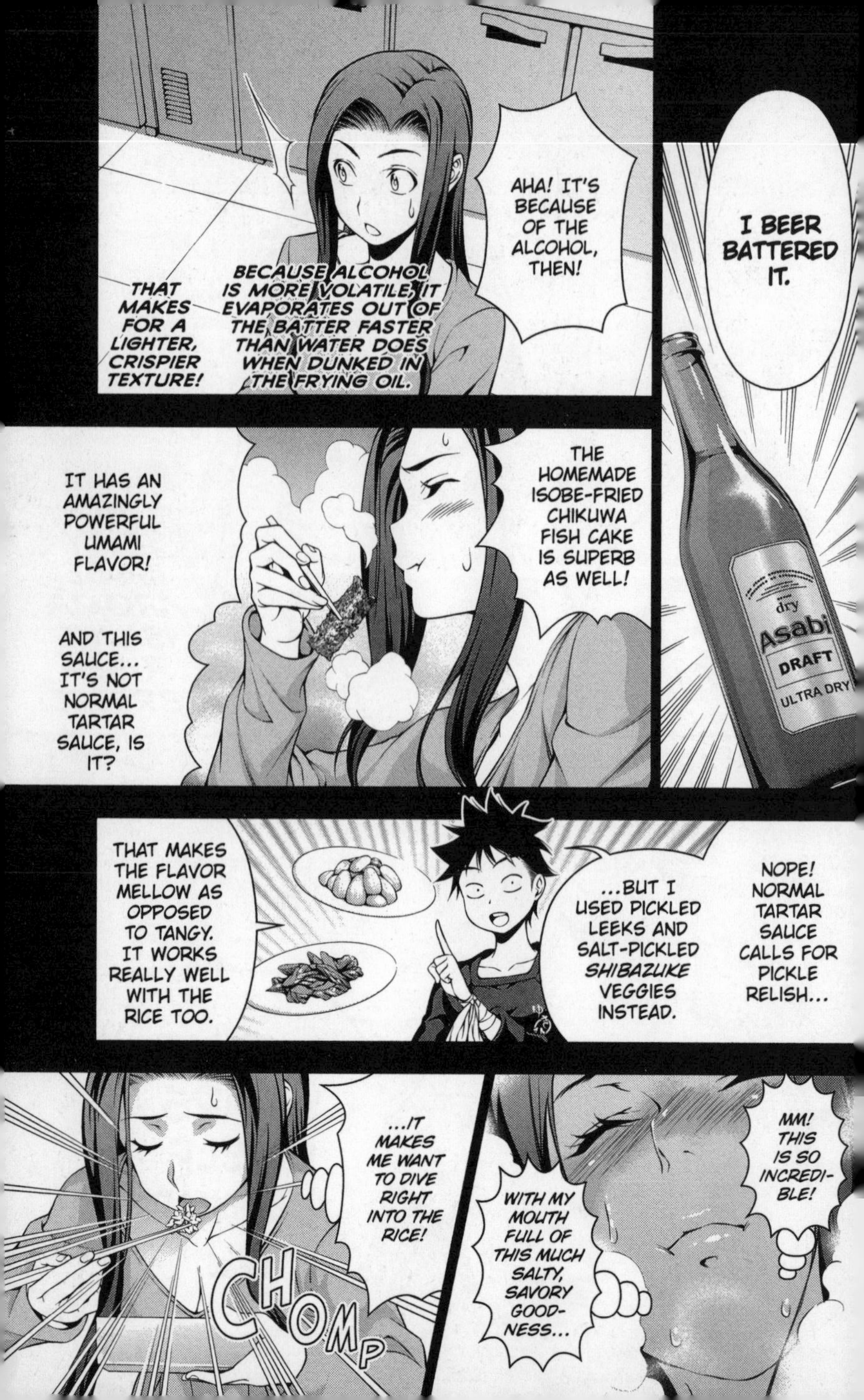
I BEER BATTERED IT.
dry
Asabi
DRAFT
ULTRA DRY
AHA! IT'S BECAUSE OF THE ALCOHOL, THEN!
BECAUSE ALCOHOL IS MORE VOLATILE, IT EVAPORATES OUT OF THE BATTER FASTER THAN WATER DOES WHEN DUNKED IN THE FRYING OIL.
THAT MAKES FOR A LIGHTER, CRISPIER TEXTURE!
THE HOMEMADE ISOBE-FRIED CHIKUWA FISH CAKE IS SUPERB AS WELL!
IT HAS AN AMAZINGLY POWERFUL UMAMI FLAVOR!
AND THIS SAUCE... IT'S NOT NORMAL TARTAR SAUCE, IS IT?
NOPE! NORMAL TARTAR SAUCE CALLS FOR PICKLE RELISH...
...BUT I USED PICKLED LEEKS AND SALT-PICKLED SHIBAZUKE VEGGIES INSTEAD.
THAT MAKES THE FLAVOR MELLOW AS OPPOSED TO TANGY. IT WORKS REALLY WELL WITH THE RICE TOO.
MM! THIS IS SO INCREDI-BLE!
WITH MY MOUTH FULL OF THIS MUCH SALTY, SAVORY GOOD-NESS...
...IT MAKES ME WANT TO DIVE RIGHT INTO THE RICE!
CHOMP

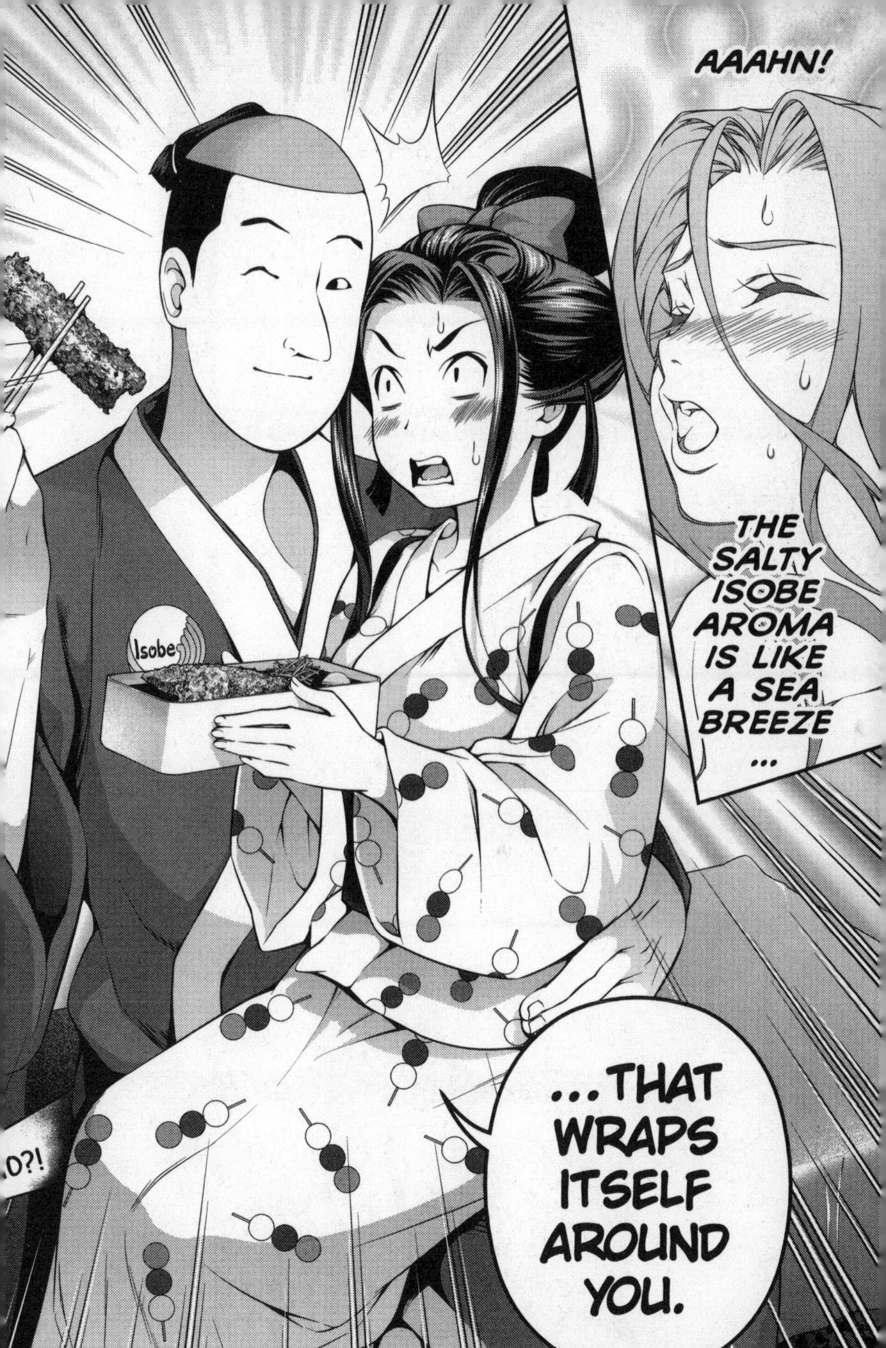
AAAHN!
THE SALTY ISOBE AROMA IS LIKE A SEA BREEZE ...
...THAT WRAPS ITSELF AROUND YOU.
Isobe

*"ISOBEI ISOBE", SHOWN ABOVE, IS A POPULAR CHARACTER IN A MANGA OF THE SAME NAME. HE'S BEING USED HERE AS A PUN ON ISOBE FRYING. ISOBE CAN ALSO MEAN SEACOAST.

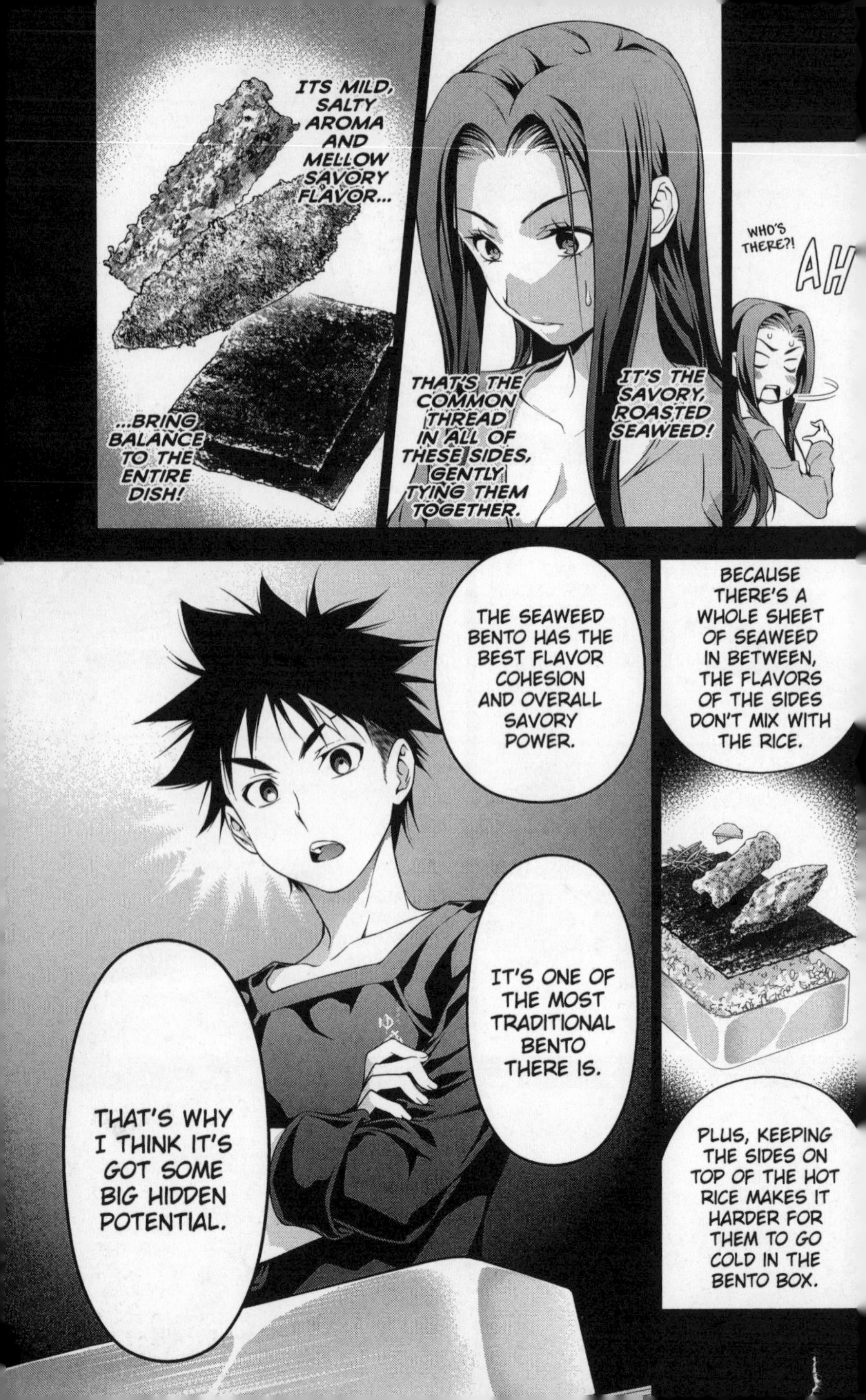
AH
WHO'S THERE?!
IT'S THE SAVORY, ROASTED SEAWEED!
THAT'S THE COMMON THREAD IN ALL OF THESE SIDES, GENTLY TYING THEM TOGETHER.
ITS MILD, SALTY AROMA AND MELLOW SAVORY FLAVOR...
...BRING BALANCE TO THE ENTIRE DISH!
BECAUSE THERE'S A WHOLE SHEET OF SEAWEED IN BETWEEN, THE FLAVORS OF THE SIDES DON'T MIX WITH THE RICE.
PLUS, KEEPING THE SIDES ON TOP OF THE HOT RICE MAKES IT HARDER FOR THEM TO GO COLD IN THE BENTO BOX.
THE SEAWEED BENTO HAS THE BEST FLAVOR COHESION AND OVERALL SAVORY POWER.
IT'S ONE OF THE MOST TRADITIONAL BENTO THERE IS.
THAT'S WHY I THINK IT'S GOT SOME BIG HIDDEN POTENTIAL.

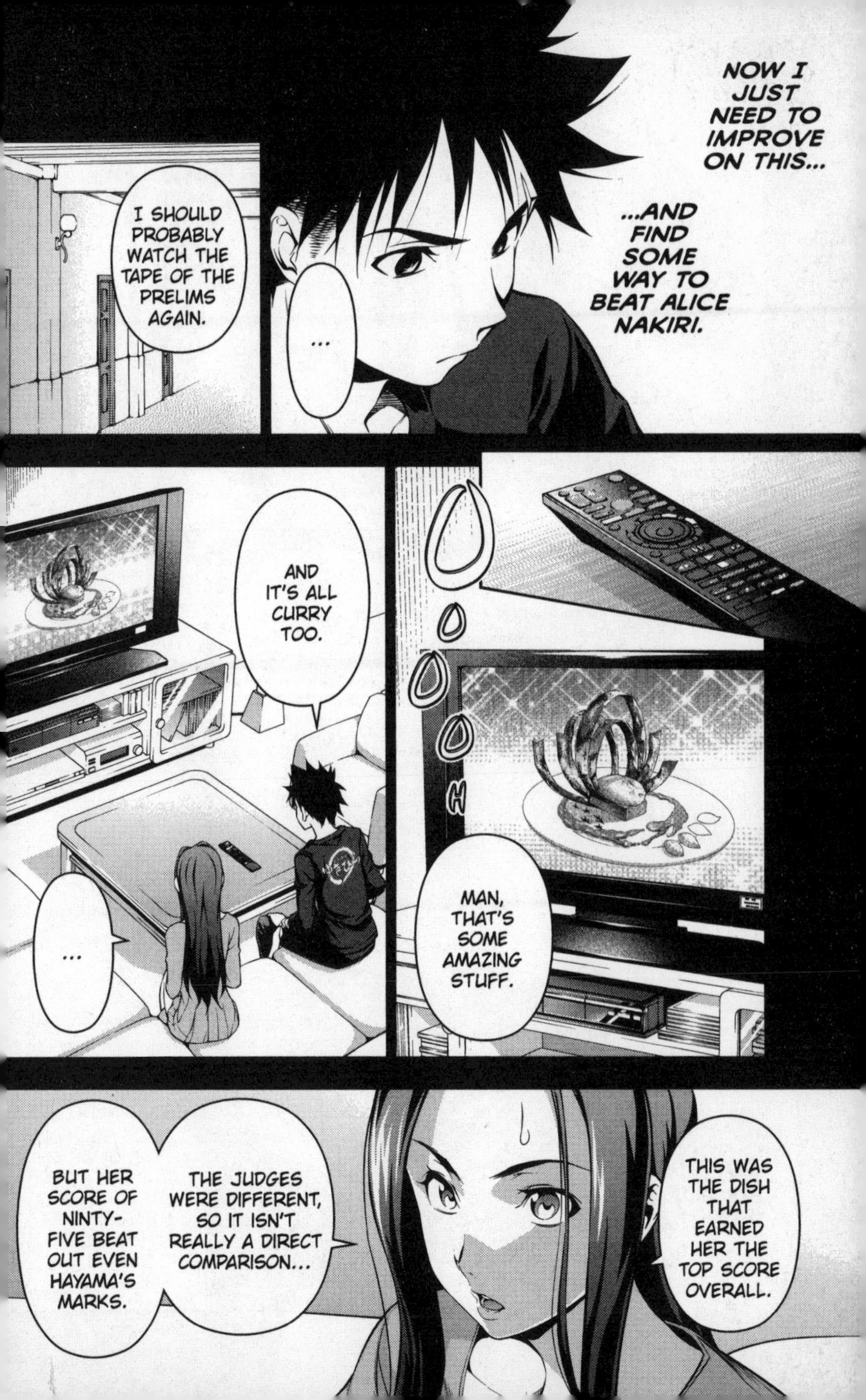
NOW I JUST NEED TO IMPROVE ON THIS...
...AND FIND SOME WAY TO BEAT ALICE NAKIRI.
...
I SHOULD PROBABLY WATCH THE TAPE OF THE PRELIMS AGAIN.
MAN, THAT'S SOME AMAZING STUFF.
AND IT'S ALL CURRY TOO.
...
THIS WAS THE DISH THAT EARNED HER THE TOP SCORE OVERALL.
THE JUDGES WERE DIFFERENT, SO IT ISN'T REALLY A DIRECT COMPARISON...
BUT HER SCORE OF NINTY-FIVE BEAT OUT EVEN HAYAMA'S MARKS.

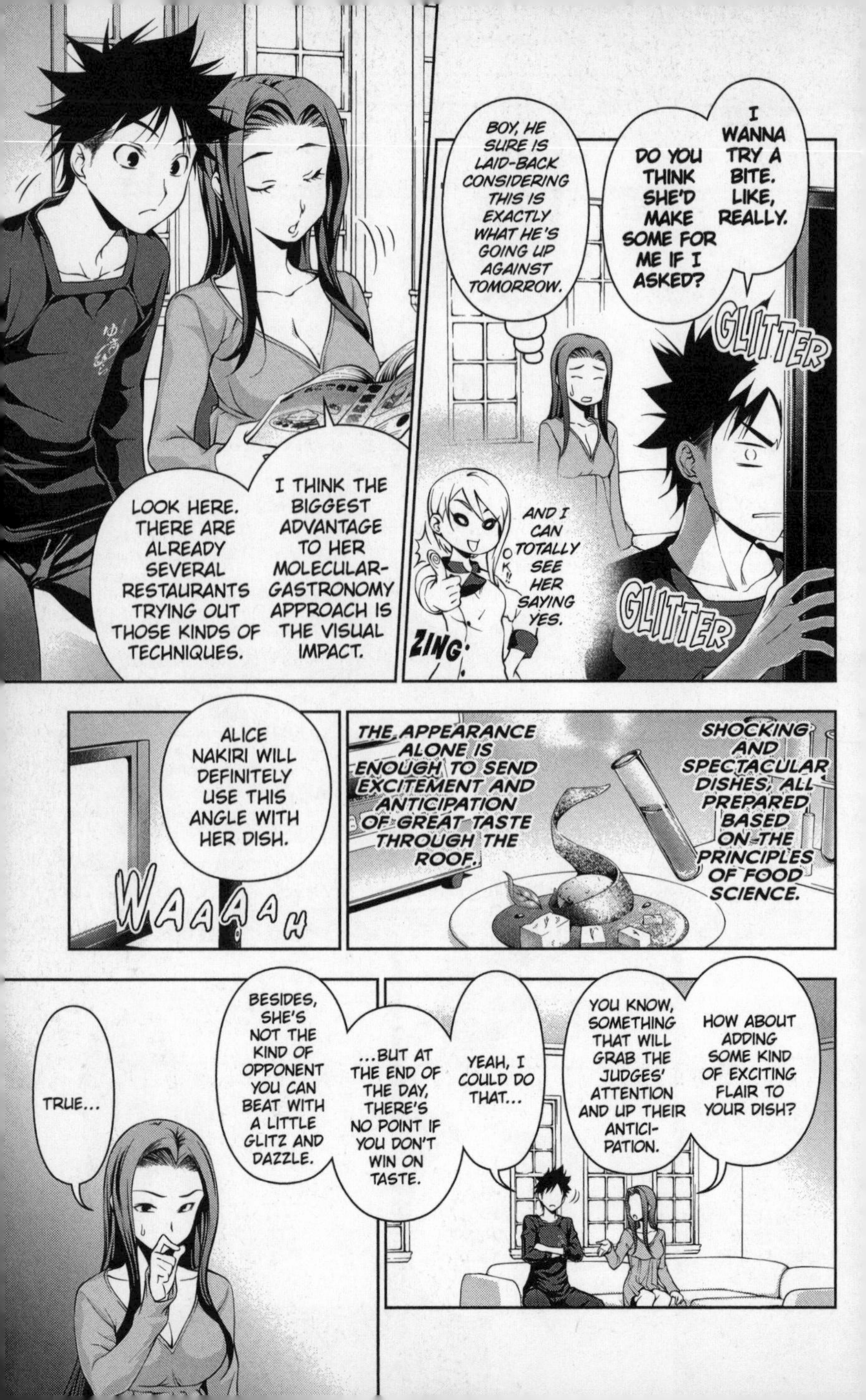

I WANNA TRY A BITE. LIKE, REALLY.
DO YOU THINK SHE'D MAKE SOME FOR ME IF I ASKED?
BOY, HE SURE IS LAID-BACK CONSIDERING THIS IS EXACTLY WHAT HE'S GOING UP AGAINST TOMORROW.
GLITTER
AND I CAN TOTALLY SEE HER SAYING YES.
OK!!
ZING
GLITTER
I THINK THE BIGGEST ADVANTAGE TO HER MOLECULAR-GASTRONOMY APPROACH IS THE VISUAL IMPACT.
LOOK HERE. THERE ARE ALREADY SEVERAL RESTAURANTS TRYING OUT THOSE KINDS OF TECHNIQUES.
SHOCKING AND SPECTACULAR DISHES, ALL PREPARED BASED ON THE PRINCIPLES OF FOOD SCIENCE.
THE APPEARANCE ALONE IS ENOUGH TO SEND EXCITEMENT AND ANTICIPATION OF GREAT TASTE THROUGH THE ROOF.
ALICE NAKIRI WILL DEFINITELY USE THIS ANGLE WITH HER DISH.
WAAAAH
HOW ABOUT ADDING SOME KIND OF EXCITING FLAIR TO YOUR DISH?
YOU KNOW, SOMETHING THAT WILL GRAB THE JUDGES' ATTENTION AND UP THEIR ANTICI-PATION.
YEAH, I COULD DO THAT...
...BUT AT THE END OF THE DAY, THERE'S NO POINT IF YOU DON'T WIN ON TASTE.
BESIDES, SHE'S NOT THE KIND OF OPPONENT YOU CAN BEAT WITH A LITTLE GLITZ AND DAZZLE.
TRUE...

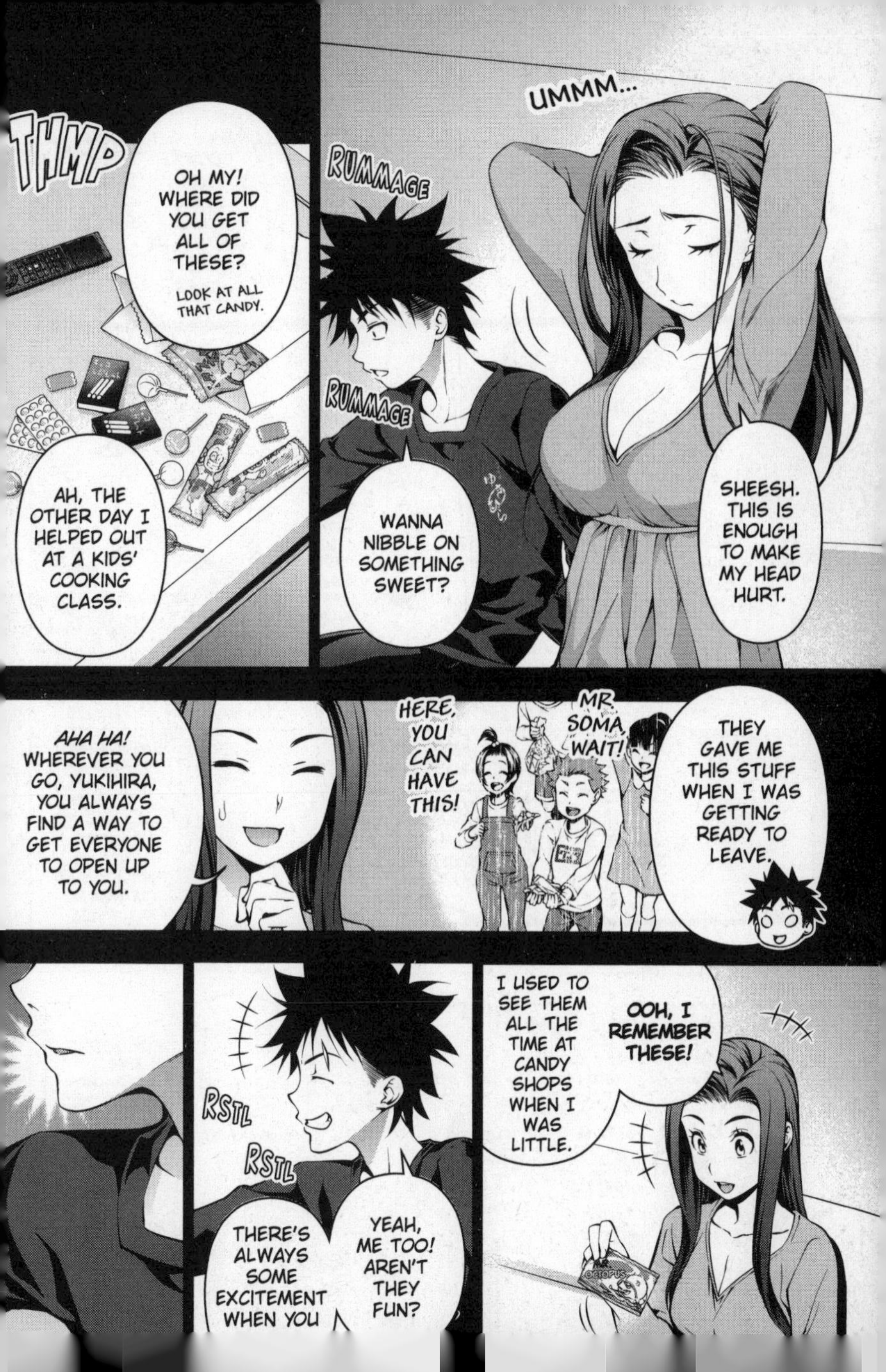
UMMM...
RUMMAGE
RUMMAGE
SHEESH. THIS IS ENOUGH TO MAKE MY HEAD HURT.
WANNA NIBBLE ON SOMETHING SWEET?
THMP
OH MY! WHERE DID YOU GET ALL OF THESE?
LOOK AT ALL THAT CANDY.
AH, THE OTHER DAY I HELPED OUT AT A KIDS' COOKING CLASS.
THEY GAVE ME THIS STUFF WHEN I WAS GETTING READY TO LEAVE.
MR. SOMA, WAIT!
HERE, YOU CAN HAVE THIS!
AHA HA! WHEREVER YOU GO, YUKIHIRA, YOU ALWAYS FIND A WAY TO GET EVERYONE TO OPEN UP TO YOU.
OOH, I REMEMBER THESE!
I USED TO SEE THEM ALL THE TIME AT CANDY SHOPS WHEN I WAS LITTLE.
OCTOPUS
RSTL
RSTL
YEAH, ME TOO! AREN'T THEY FUN?
THERE'S ALWAYS SOME EXCITEMENT WHEN YOU

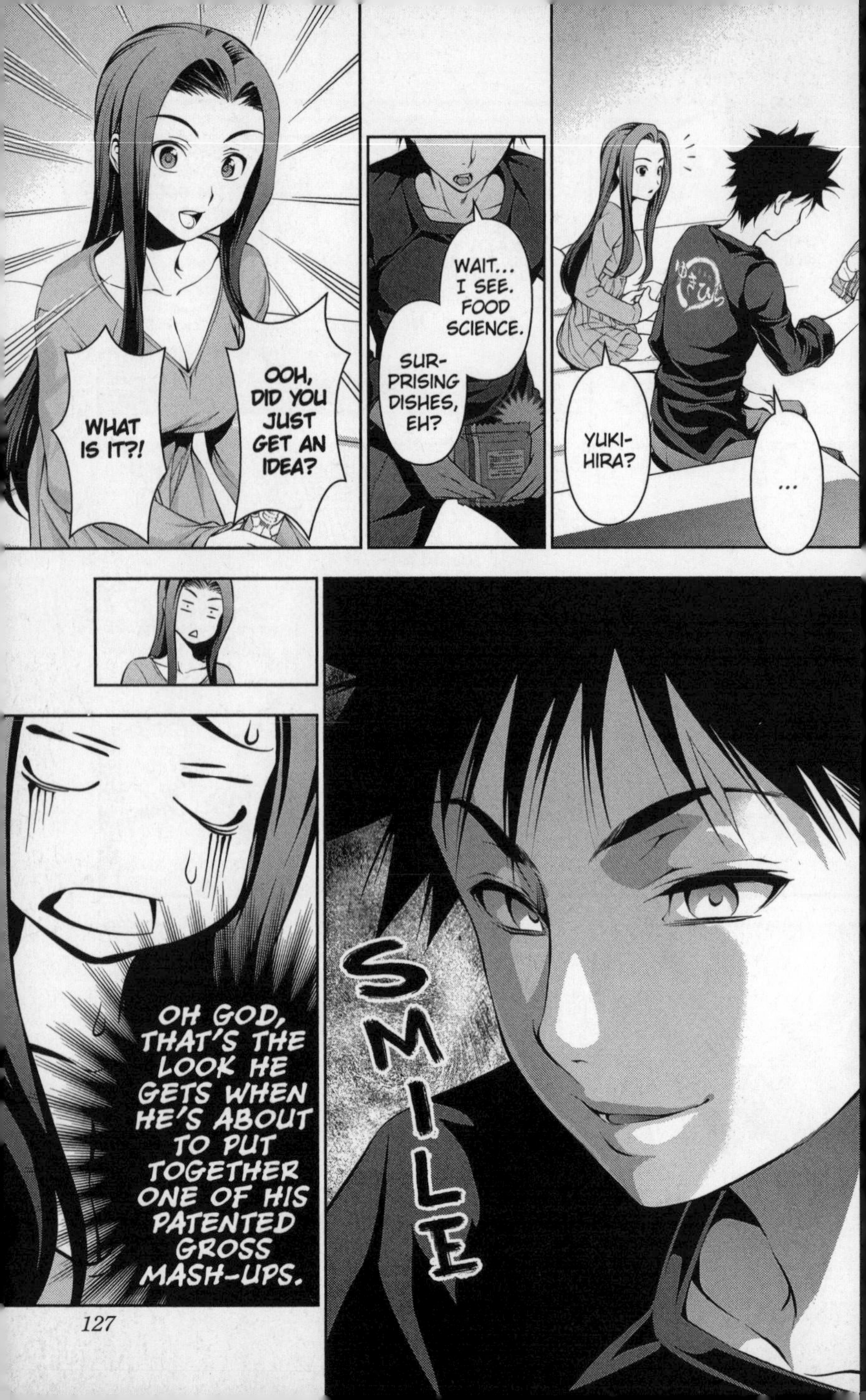
YUKI-HIRA?
...
WAIT... I SEE. FOOD SCIENCE.
SUR-PRISING DISHES, EH?
OOH, DID YOU JUST GET AN IDEA?
WHAT IS IT?!
SMILE
OH GOD, THAT'S THE LOOK HE GETS WHEN HE'S ABOUT TO PUT TOGETHER ONE OF HIS PATENTED GROSS MASH-UPS.

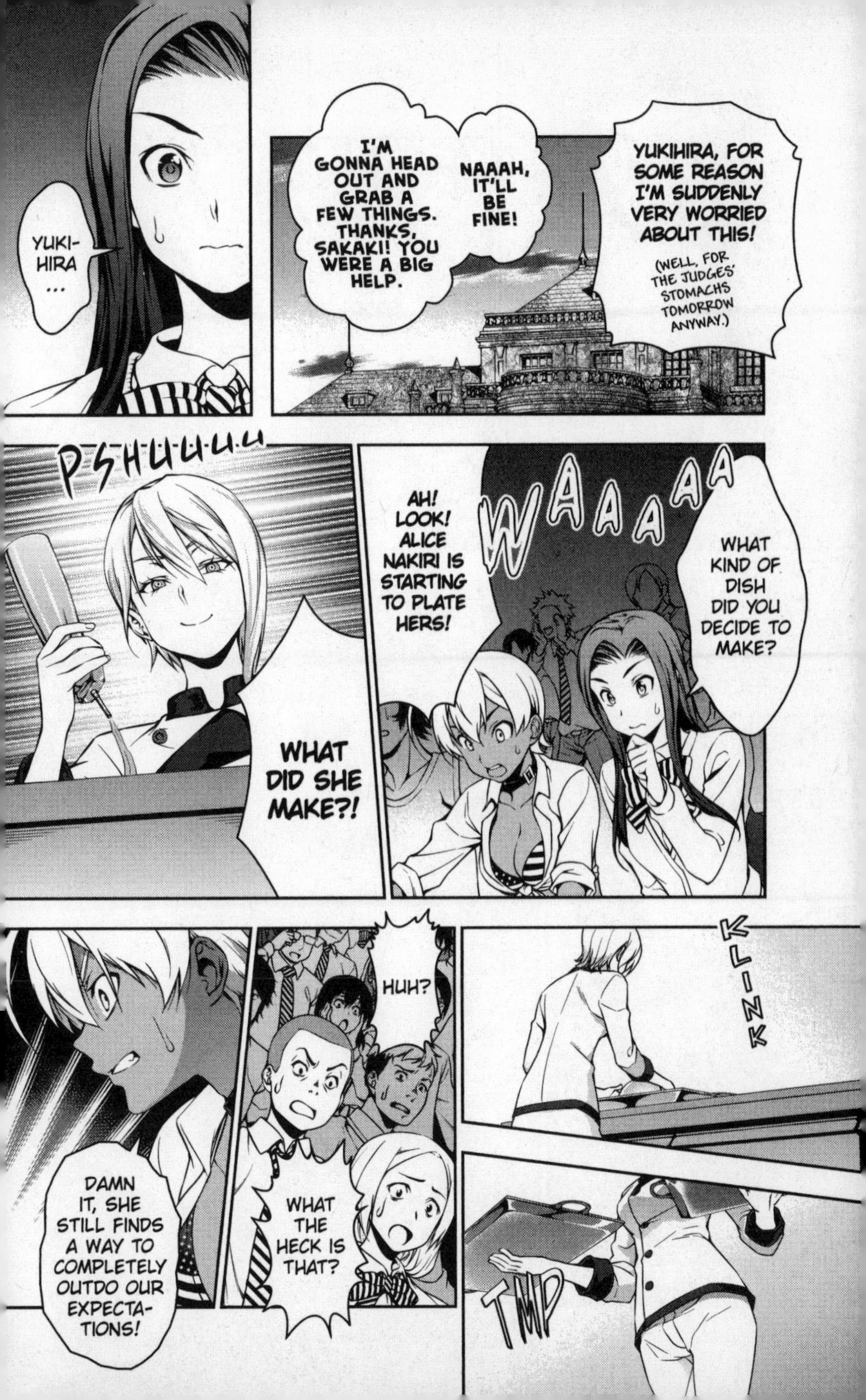
YUKIHIRA, FOR SOME REASON I'M SUDDENLY VERY WORRIED ABOUT THIS!
(WELL, FOR THE JUDGES' STOMACHS TOMORROW ANYWAY.)
NAAAH, IT'LL BE FINE!
I'M GONNA HEAD OUT AND GRAB A FEW THINGS. THANKS, SAKAKI! YOU WERE A BIG HELP.
YUKI-HIRA ...
WAAAAAA
AH! LOOK! ALICE NAKIRI IS STARTING TO PLATE HERS!
WHAT KIND OF DISH DID YOU DECIDE TO MAKE?
PSHUUUUU
WHAT DID SHE MAKE?!
KLINK
TMP
HUH?
WHAT THE HECK IS THAT?
DAMN IT, SHE STILL FINDS A WAY TO COMPLETELY OUTDO OUR EXPECTA-TIONS!

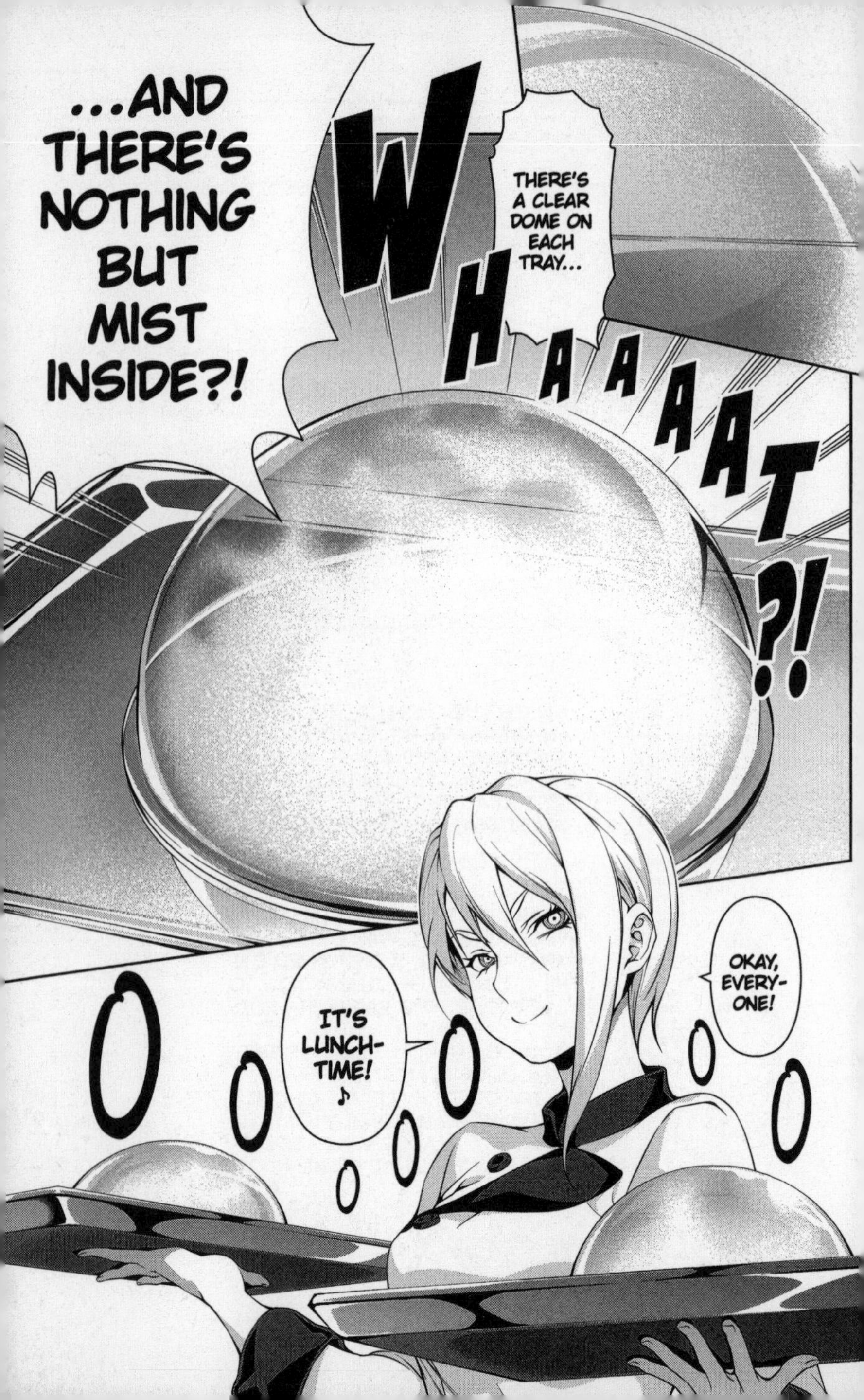
THERE'S A CLEAR DOME ON EACH TRAY...
WHAAAAAT?!
...AND THERE'S NOTHING BUT MIST INSIDE?!
OKAY, EVERYONE!
IT'S LUNCHTIME! ♪

IN CELEBRATION OF THE FIRST ANNIVERSARY OF *FOOD WARS!: SHOKUGEKI NO SOMA*, *WEEKLY SHONEN JUMP* CONDUCTED THE FIRST READER-SUBMITTED RECIPE CONTEST*!* THE THEME OF THE CONTEST WAS DONBURI RICE BOWLS.

AS PART OF THE GRAND PRIZE, THE WINNING RECIPE WAS DRAWN BY MR. SAEKI AND IS DISPLAYED ON THE FACING PAGE. THANK YOU TO EVERYONE WHO PARTICIPATED*!*

ADDITIONALLY, THE END OF THE VOLUME FEATURES A MASS INTRODUCTION OF ALL OF THE TOP-PLACING RECIPES FROM THE CONTEST. READERS, PLEASE *DO* TRY THESE AT HOME*!*

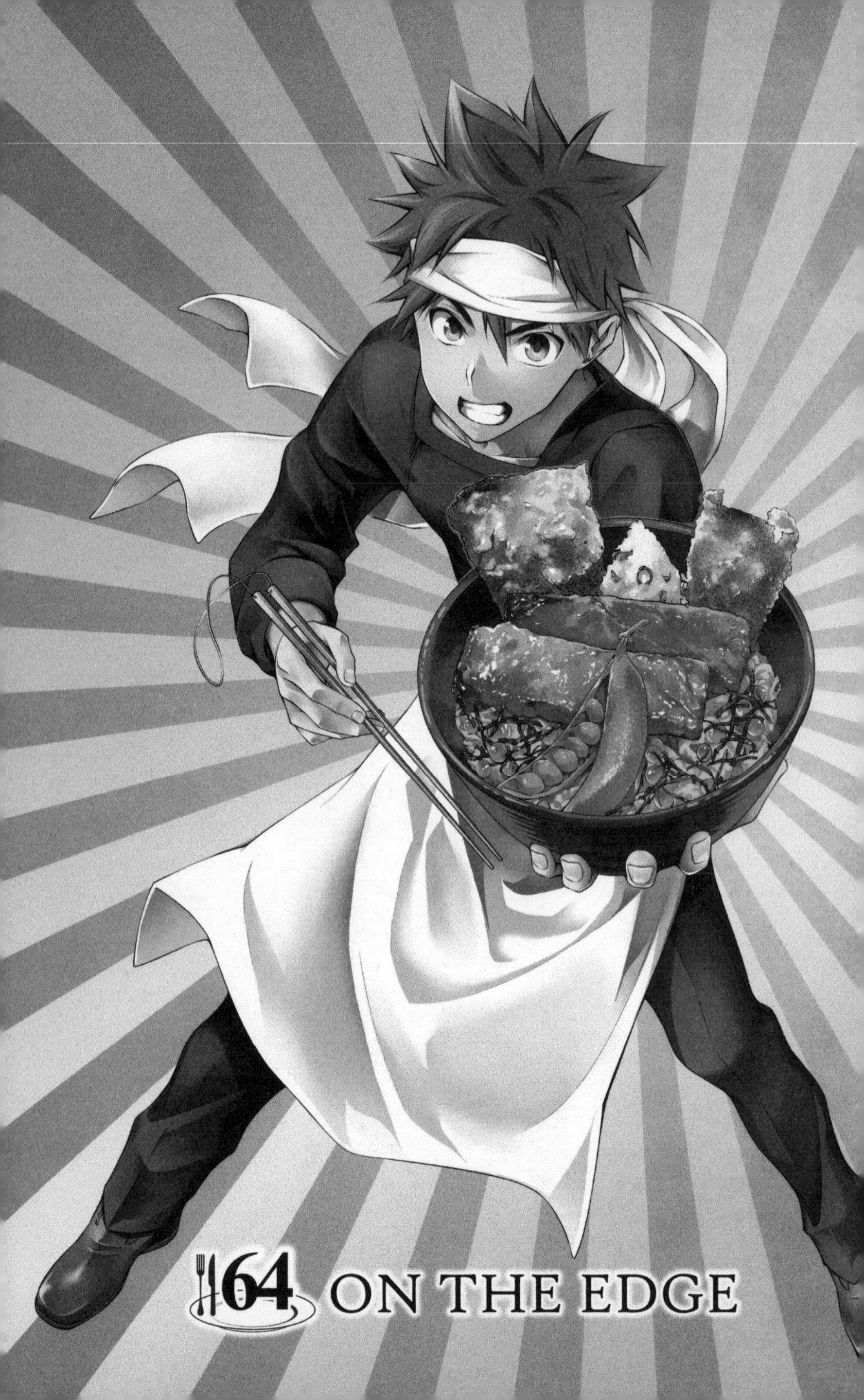
64 ON THE EDGE

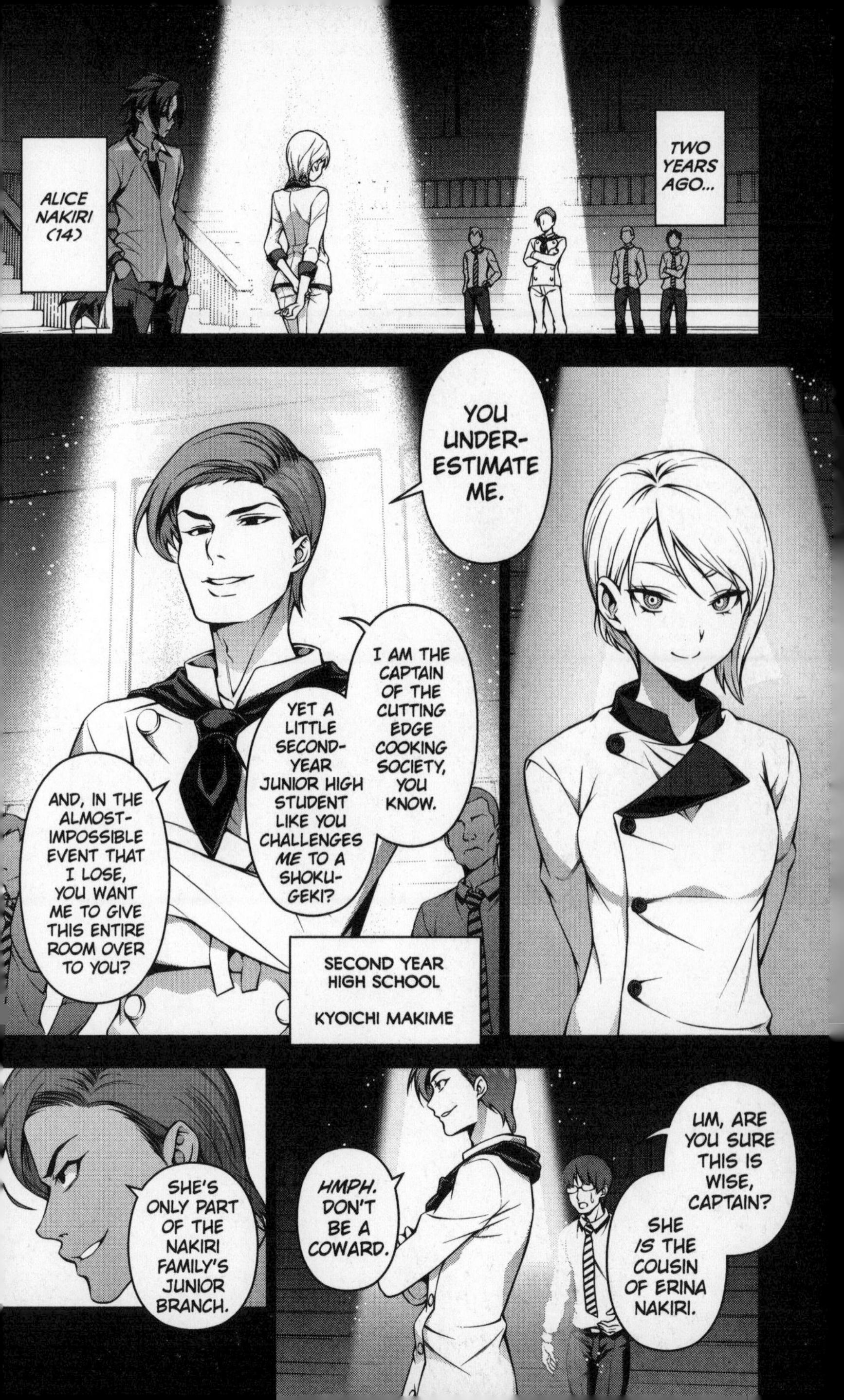

TWO YEARS AGO...
ALICE NAKIRI (14)
YOU UNDERESTIMATE ME.
I AM THE CAPTAIN OF THE CUTTING EDGE COOKING SOCIETY, YOU KNOW.
YET A LITTLE SECOND-YEAR JUNIOR HIGH STUDENT LIKE YOU CHALLENGES *ME* TO A SHOKUGEKI?
AND, IN THE ALMOST-IMPOSSIBLE EVENT THAT I LOSE, YOU WANT ME TO GIVE THIS ENTIRE ROOM OVER TO YOU?
SECOND YEAR HIGH SCHOOL
KYOICHI MAKIME
UM, ARE YOU SURE THIS IS WISE, CAPTAIN?
SHE *IS* THE COUSIN OF ERINA NAKIRI.
HMPH. DON'T BE A COWARD.
SHE'S ONLY PART OF THE NAKIRI FAMILY'S JUNIOR BRANCH.

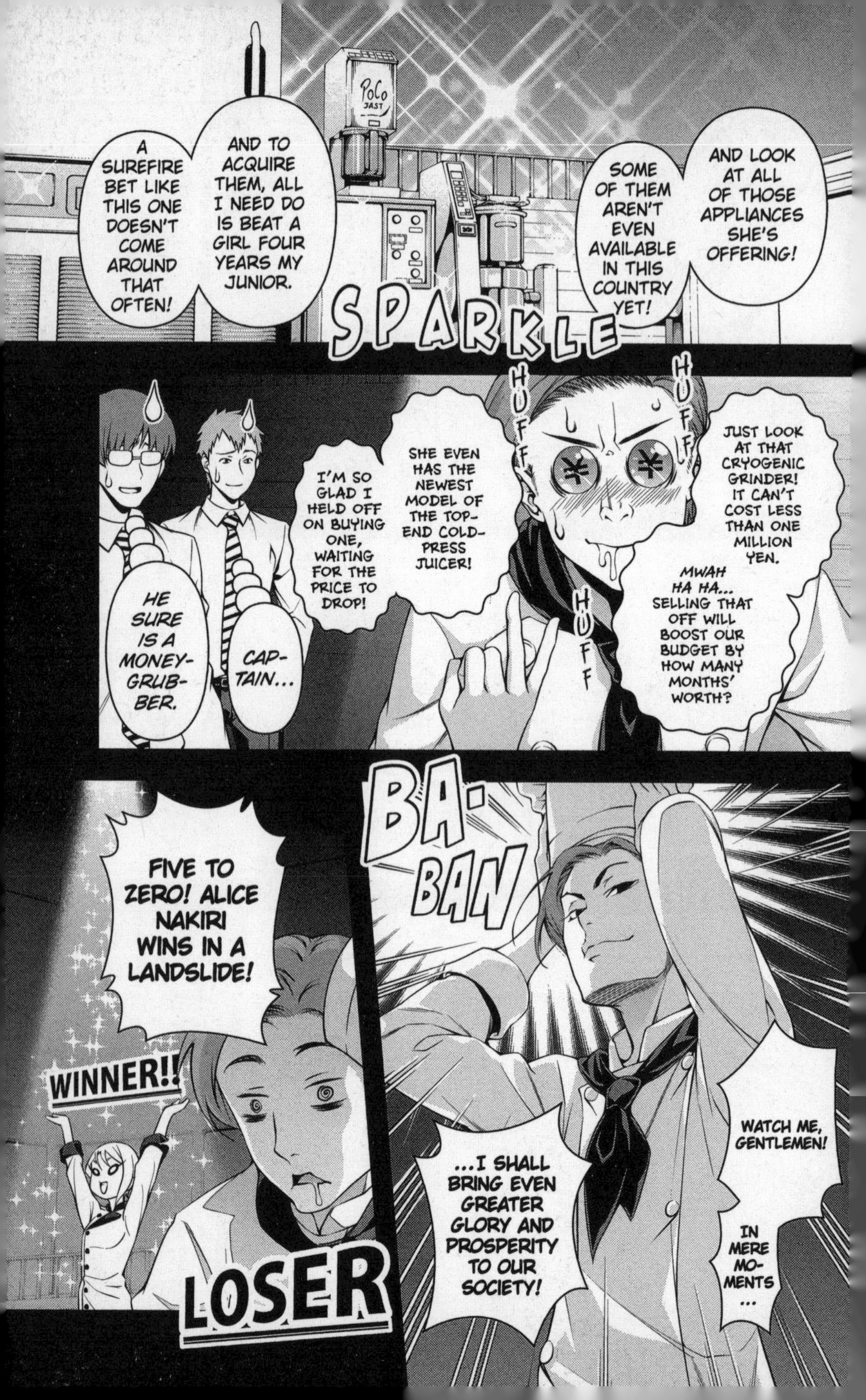
AND LOOK AT ALL OF THOSE APPLIANCES SHE'S OFFERING!
SOME OF THEM AREN'T EVEN AVAILABLE IN THIS COUNTRY YET!
AND TO ACQUIRE THEM, ALL I NEED DO IS BEAT A GIRL FOUR YEARS MY JUNIOR.
A SUREFIRE BET LIKE THIS ONE DOESN'T COME AROUND THAT OFTEN!
SPARKLE
HUFF
HUFF
JUST LOOK AT THAT CRYOGENIC GRINDER! IT CAN'T COST LESS THAN ONE MILLION YEN.
MWAH HA HA... SELLING THAT OFF WILL BOOST OUR BUDGET BY HOW MANY MONTHS' WORTH?
SHE EVEN HAS THE NEWEST MODEL OF THE TOP-END COLD-PRESS JUICER!
I'M SO GLAD I HELD OFF ON BUYING ONE, WAITING FOR THE PRICE TO DROP!
HUFF
CAPTAIN...
HE SURE IS A MONEY-GRUBBER.
BA-BAN
WATCH ME, GENTLEMEN!
IN MERE MOMENTS...
...I SHALL BRING EVEN GREATER GLORY AND PROSPERITY TO OUR SOCIETY!
FIVE TO ZERO! ALICE NAKIRI WINS IN A LANDSLIDE!
WINNER!!
LOSER

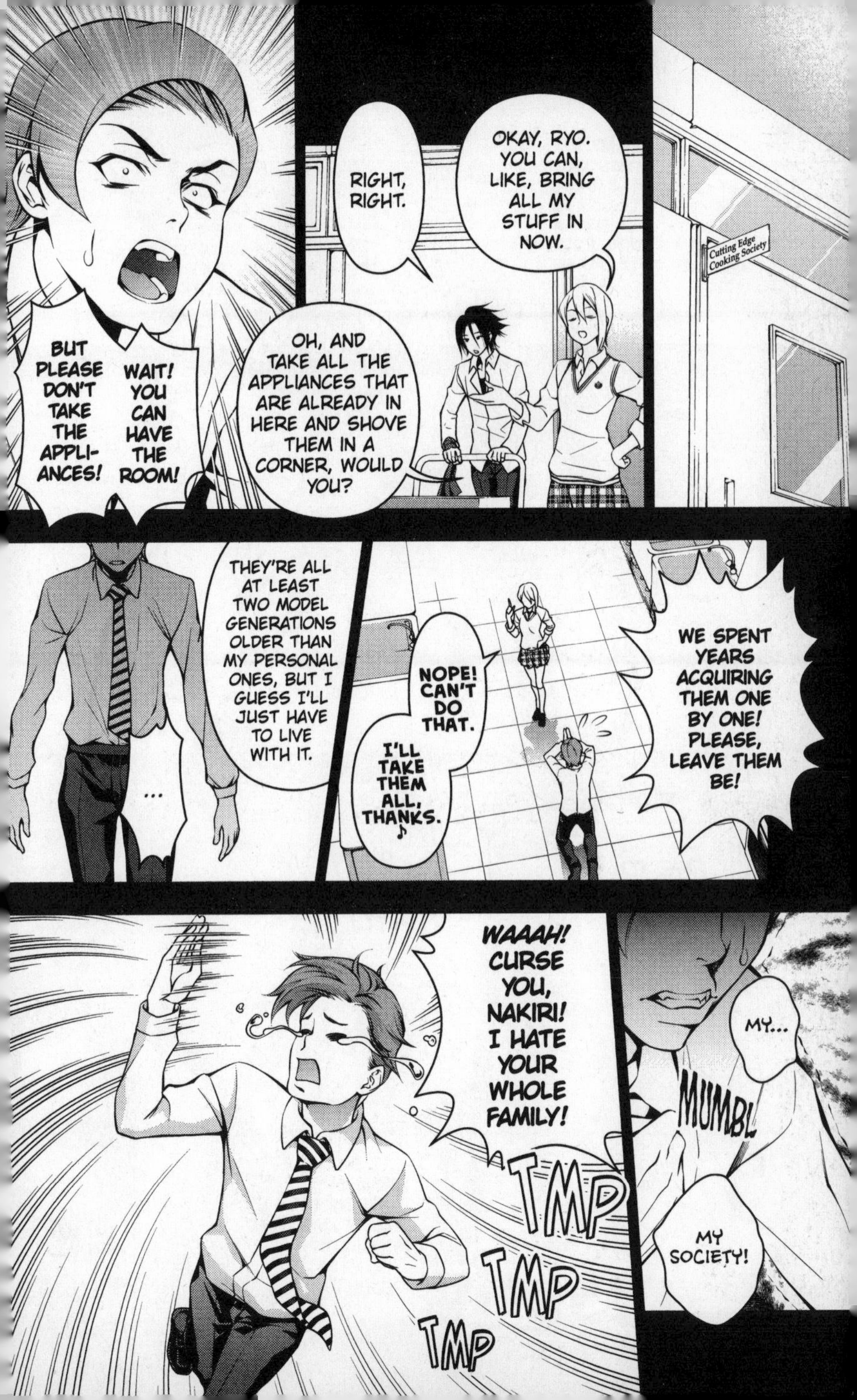

Cutting Edge Cooking Society
OKAY, RYO. YOU CAN, LIKE, BRING ALL MY STUFF IN NOW.
RIGHT, RIGHT.
OH, AND TAKE ALL THE APPLIANCES THAT ARE ALREADY IN HERE AND SHOVE THEM IN A CORNER, WOULD YOU?
WAIT! YOU CAN HAVE THE ROOM!
BUT PLEASE DON'T TAKE THE APPLIANCES!
WE SPENT YEARS ACQUIRING THEM ONE BY ONE! PLEASE, LEAVE THEM BE!
NOPE! CAN'T DO THAT.
I'LL TAKE THEM ALL, THANKS. ♪
THEY'RE ALL AT LEAST TWO MODEL GENERATIONS OLDER THAN MY PERSONAL ONES, BUT I GUESS I'LL JUST HAVE TO LIVE WITH IT.
...
MY...
MUMBL
MY SOCIETY!
WAAAH! CURSE YOU, NAKIRI! I HATE YOUR WHOLE FAMILY!
TMP
TMP
TMP

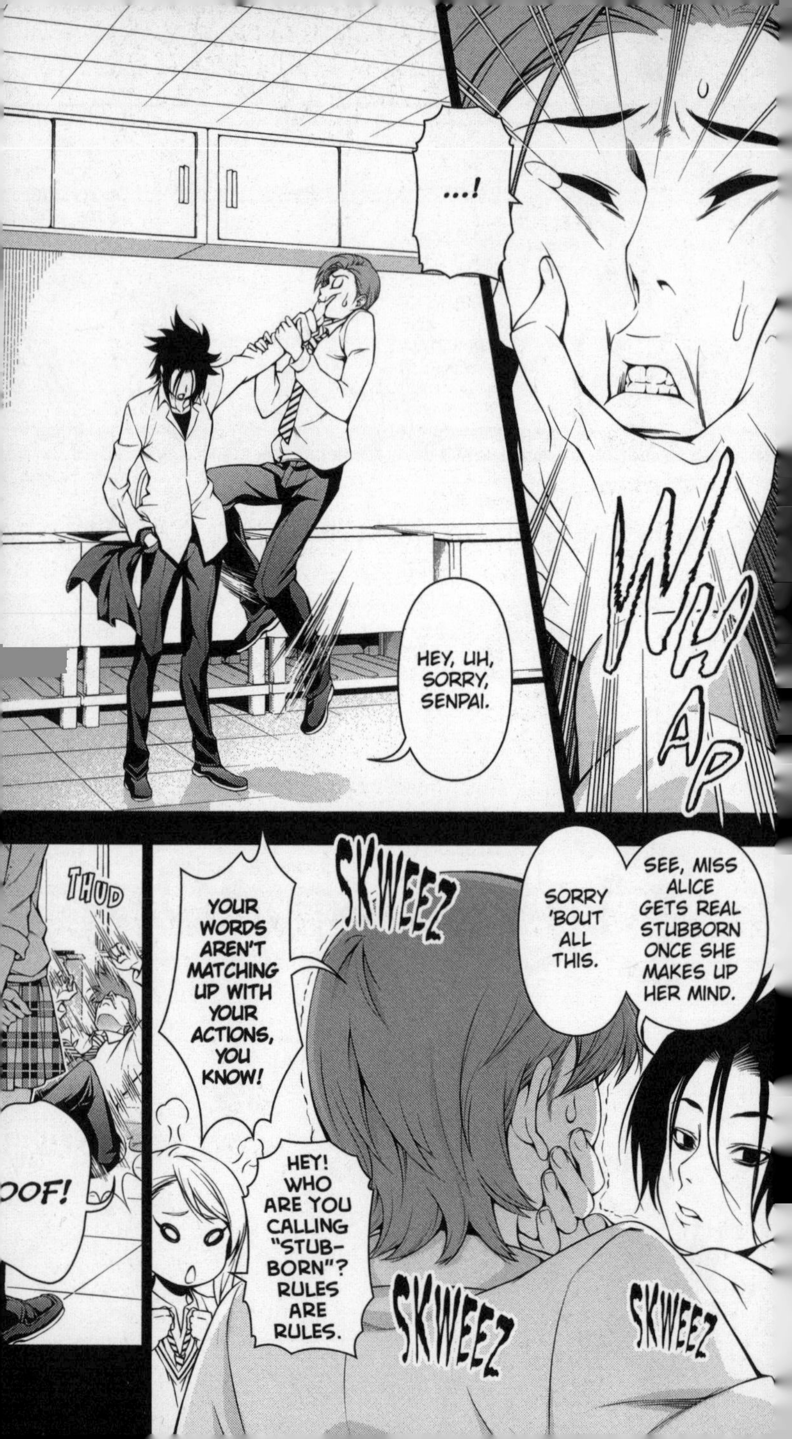
WHAP
...!
HEY, UH, SORRY, SENPAI.
SKWEEZ
SEE, MISS ALICE GETS REAL STUBBORN ONCE SHE MAKES UP HER MIND.
SORRY 'BOUT ALL THIS.
YOUR WORDS AREN'T MATCHING UP WITH YOUR ACTIONS, YOU KNOW!
HEY! WHO ARE YOU CALLING "STUB-BORN"? RULES ARE RULES.
SKWEEZ
SKWEEZ
THUD
OOF!

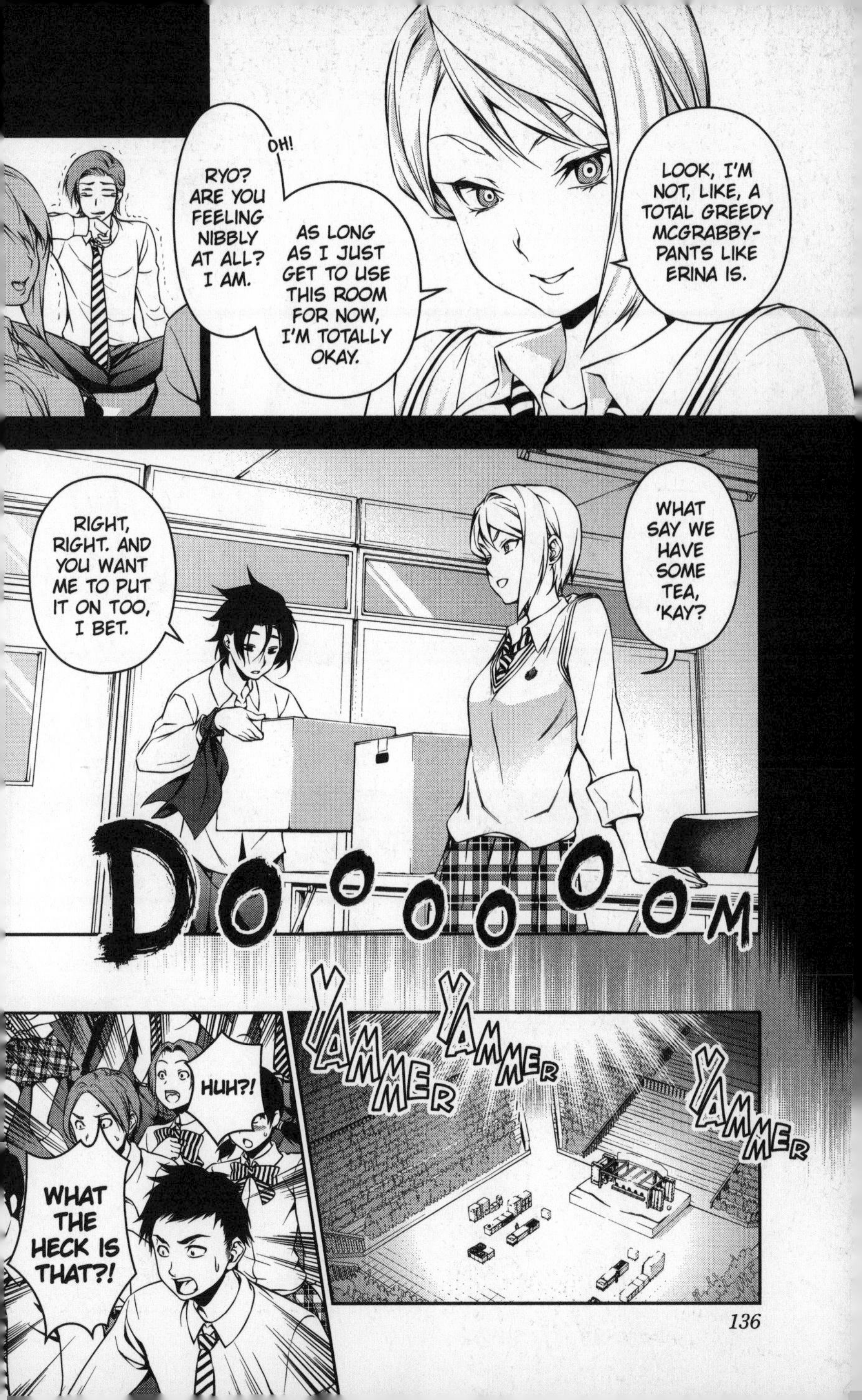
LOOK, I'M NOT, LIKE, A TOTAL GREEDY MCGRABBY-PANTS LIKE ERINA IS.
AS LONG AS I JUST GET TO USE THIS ROOM FOR NOW, I'M TOTALLY OKAY.
OH!
RYO? ARE YOU FEELING NIBBLY AT ALL? I AM.
WHAT SAY WE HAVE SOME TEA, 'KAY?
RIGHT, RIGHT. AND YOU WANT ME TO PUT IT ON TOO, I BET.
DOOOOOOOOM
YAMMER
YAMMER
YAMMER
YAMMER
YAMMER
HUH?!
WHAT THE HECK IS THAT?!

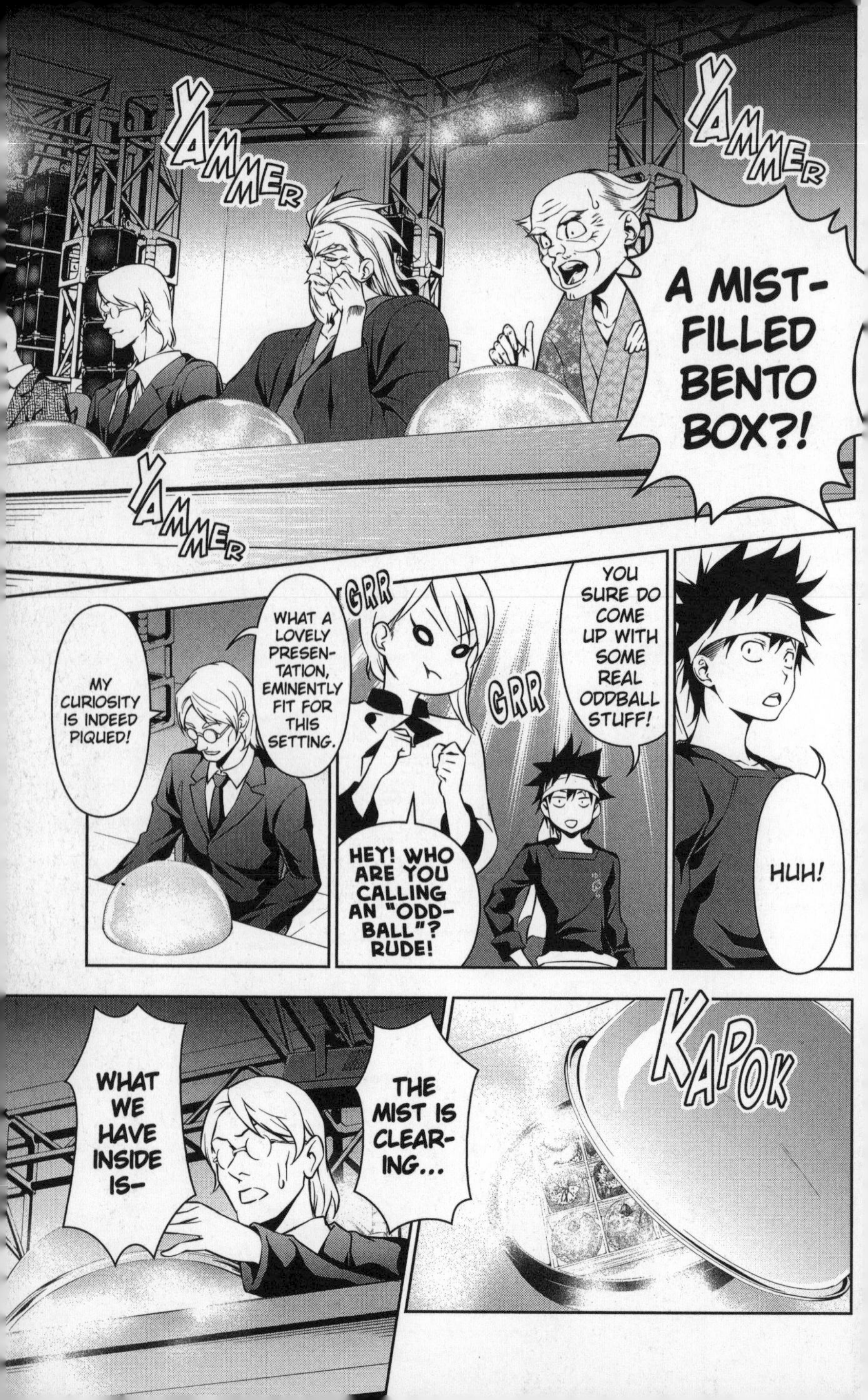
YAMMER
A MIST-FILLED BENTO BOX?!
YAMMER
YAMMER
HUH!
YOU SURE DO COME UP WITH SOME REAL ODDBALL STUFF!
GRR
GRR
WHAT A LOVELY PRESENTATION, EMINENTLY FIT FOR THIS SETTING.
HEY! WHO ARE YOU CALLING AN "ODD-BALL"? RUDE!
MY CURIOSITY IS INDEED PIQUED!
KAPOK
THE MIST IS CLEARING...
WHAT WE HAVE INSIDE IS-

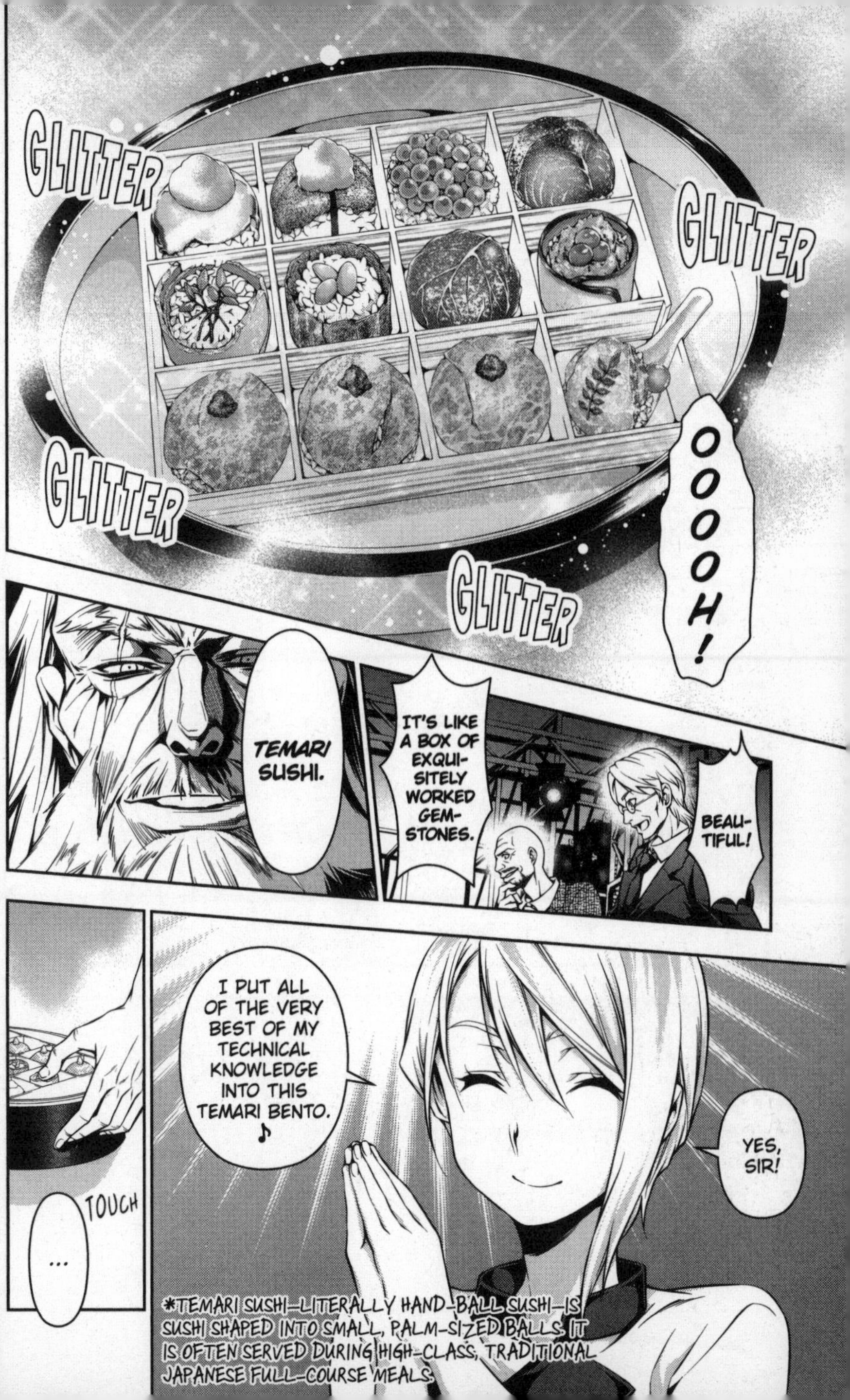
GLITTER
GLITTER
GLITTER
GLITTER
OOOOOH!
BEAU-TIFUL!
IT'S LIKE A BOX OF EXQUI-SITELY WORKED GEM-STONES.
TEMARI SUSHI.
YES, SIR!
I PUT ALL OF THE VERY BEST OF MY TECHNICAL KNOWLEDGE INTO THIS TEMARI BENTO. ♪
TOUCH
...
*TEMARI SUSHI—LITERALLY HAND-BALL SUSHI—IS SUSHI SHAPED INTO SMALL, PALM-SIZED BALLS. IT IS OFTEN SERVED DURING HIGH-CLASS, TRADITIONAL JAPANESE FULL-COURSE MEALS.

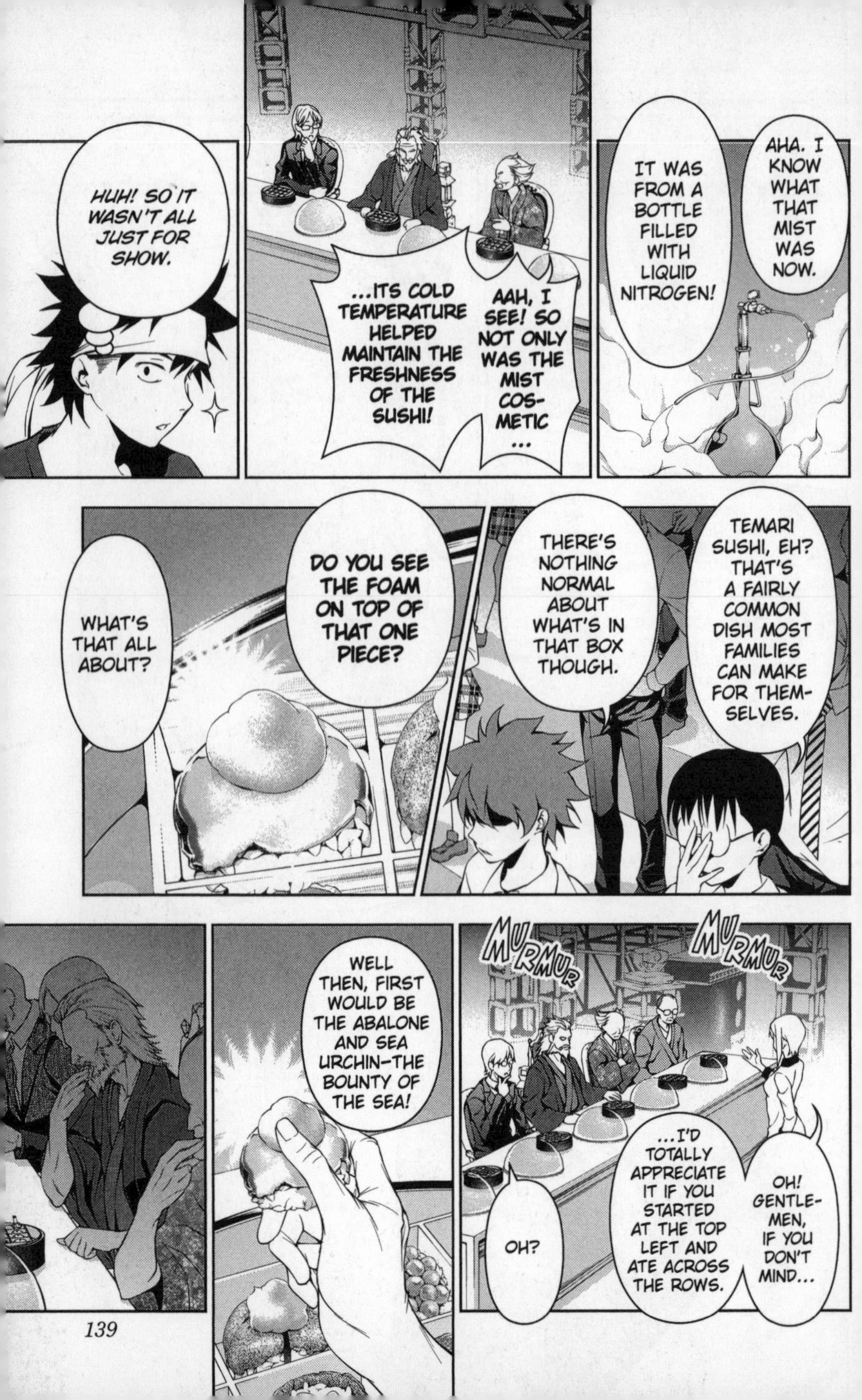
AHA. I KNOW WHAT THAT MIST WAS NOW.
IT WAS FROM A BOTTLE FILLED WITH LIQUID NITROGEN!
AAH, I SEE! SO NOT ONLY WAS THE MIST COSMETIC...
...ITS COLD TEMPERATURE HELPED MAINTAIN THE FRESHNESS OF THE SUSHI!
HUH! SO IT WASN'T ALL JUST FOR SHOW.
TEMARI SUSHI, EH? THAT'S A FAIRLY COMMON DISH MOST FAMILIES CAN MAKE FOR THEMSELVES.
THERE'S NOTHING NORMAL ABOUT WHAT'S IN THAT BOX THOUGH.
DO YOU SEE THE FOAM ON TOP OF THAT ONE PIECE?
WHAT'S THAT ALL ABOUT?
MURMUR
MURMUR
OH! GENTLEMEN, IF YOU DON'T MIND...
...I'D TOTALLY APPRECIATE IT IF YOU STARTED AT THE TOP LEFT AND ATE ACROSS THE ROWS.
OH?
WELL THEN, FIRST WOULD BE THE ABALONE AND SEA URCHIN—THE BOUNTY OF THE SEA!

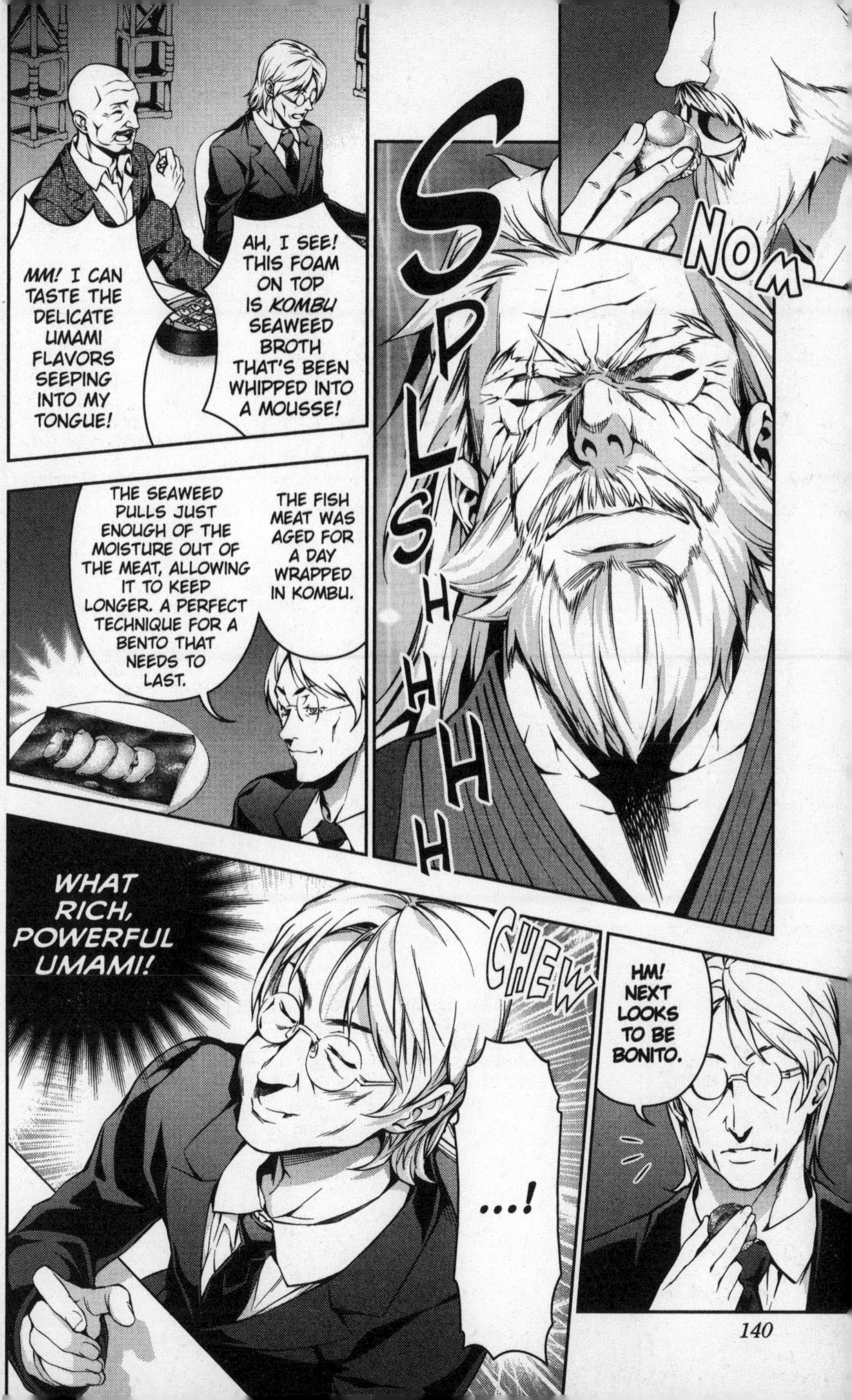
NOM
SPLSHHHHH
AH, I SEE! THIS FOAM ON TOP IS *KOMBU* SEAWEED BROTH THAT'S BEEN WHIPPED INTO A MOUSSE!
MM! I CAN TASTE THE DELICATE UMAMI FLAVORS SEEPING INTO MY TONGUE!
THE FISH MEAT WAS AGED FOR A DAY WRAPPED IN KOMBU.
THE SEAWEED PULLS JUST ENOUGH OF THE MOISTURE OUT OF THE MEAT, ALLOWING IT TO KEEP LONGER. A PERFECT TECHNIQUE FOR A BENTO THAT NEEDS TO LAST.
HM! NEXT LOOKS TO BE BONITO.
CHEW
...!
WHAT RICH, POWERFUL UMAMI!

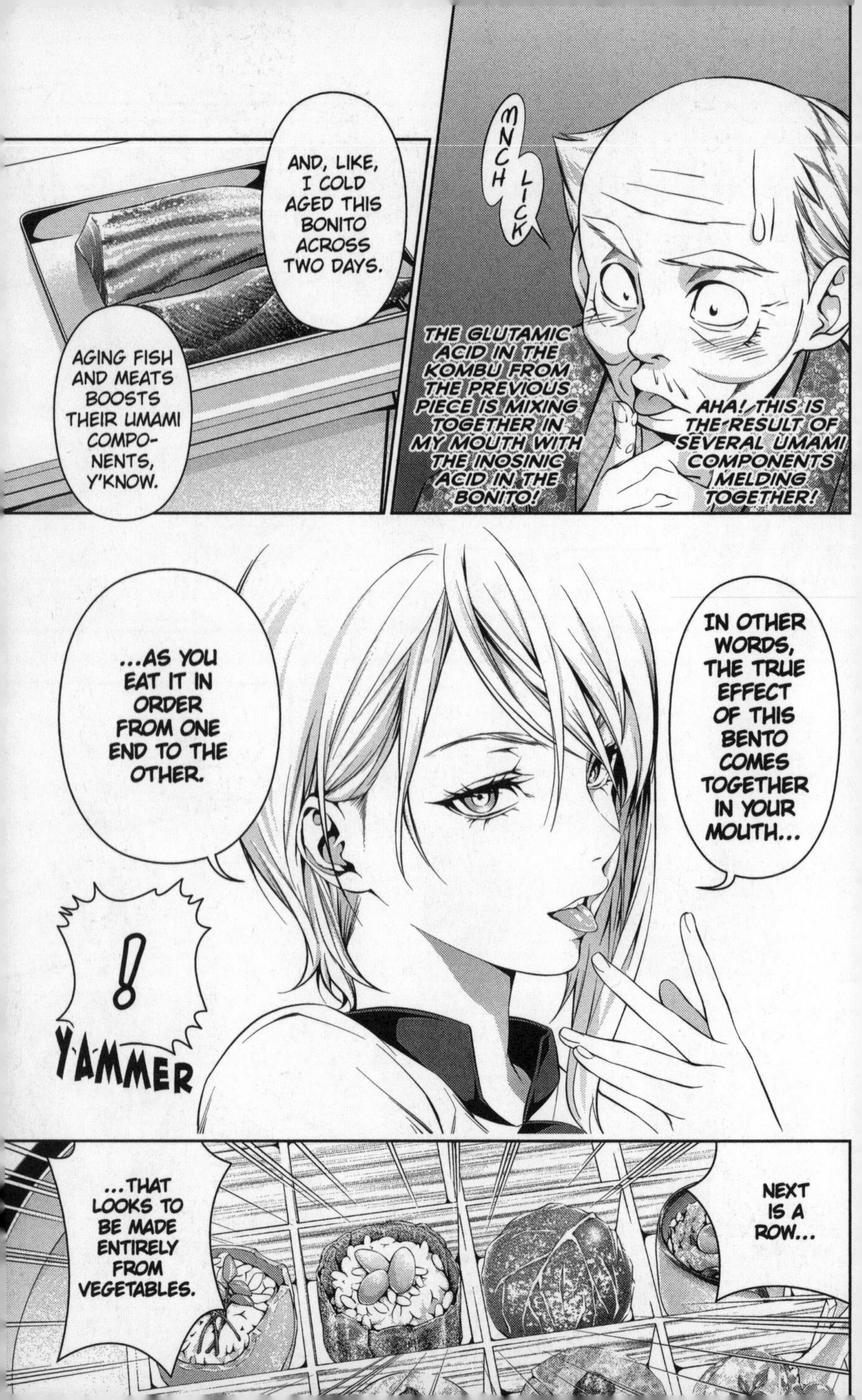
MNCH
LICK
AHA! THIS IS THE RESULT OF SEVERAL UMAMI COMPONENTS MELDING TOGETHER!
THE GLUTAMIC ACID IN THE KOMBU FROM THE PREVIOUS PIECE IS MIXING TOGETHER IN MY MOUTH WITH THE INOSINIC ACID IN THE BONITO!
AND, LIKE, I COLD AGED THIS BONITO ACROSS TWO DAYS.
AGING FISH AND MEATS BOOSTS THEIR UMAMI COMPO-NENTS, Y'KNOW.
IN OTHER WORDS, THE TRUE EFFECT OF THIS BENTO COMES TOGETHER IN YOUR MOUTH...
...AS YOU EAT IT IN ORDER FROM ONE END TO THE OTHER.
!
Y'AMMER
NEXT IS A ROW...
...THAT LOOKS TO BE MADE ENTIRELY FROM VEGETABLES.

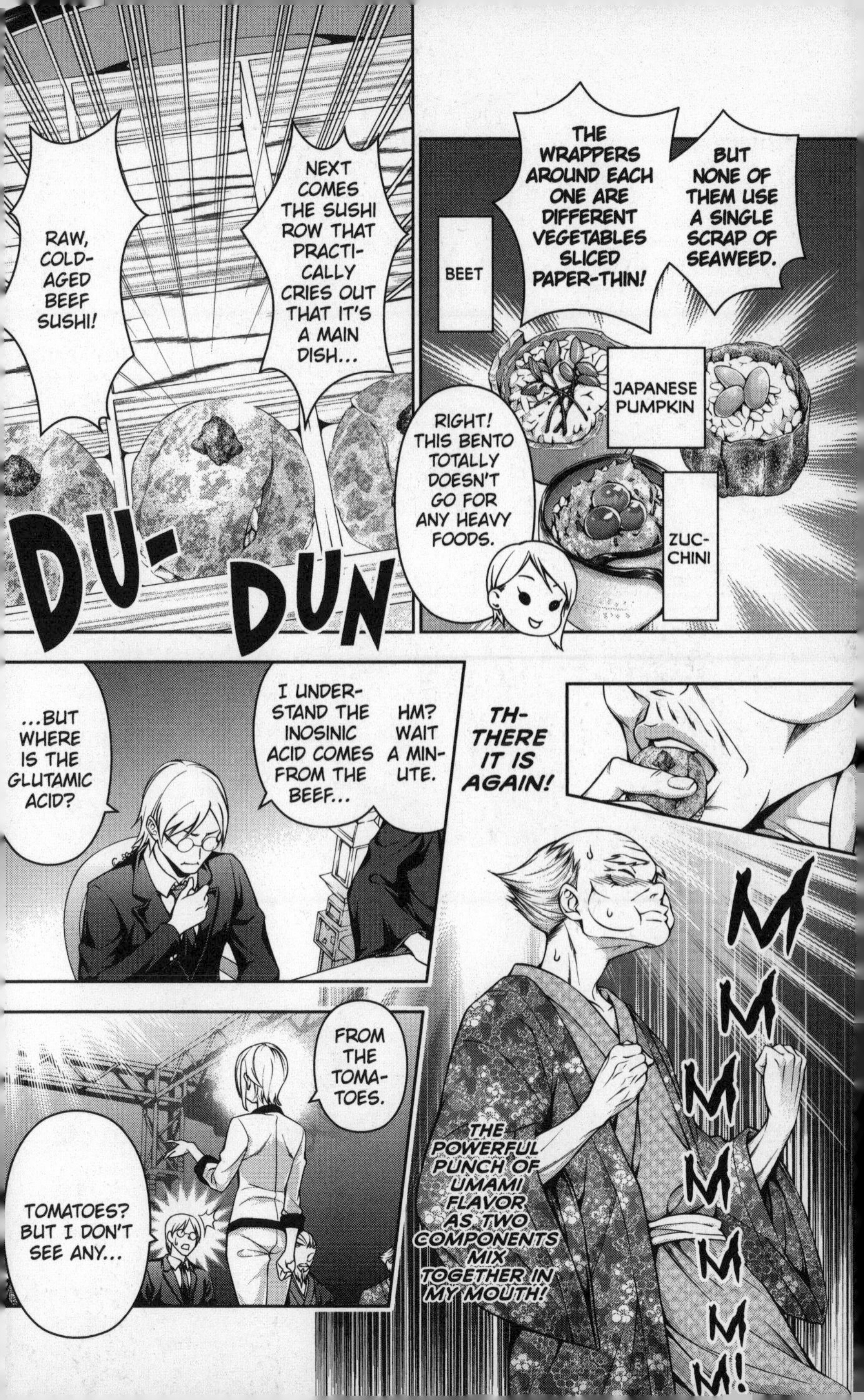
THE WRAPPERS AROUND EACH ONE ARE DIFFERENT VEGETABLES SLICED PAPER-THIN!
BUT NONE OF THEM USE A SINGLE SCRAP OF SEAWEED.
BEET
JAPANESE PUMPKIN
ZUC-CHINI
RIGHT! THIS BENTO TOTALLY DOESN'T GO FOR ANY HEAVY FOODS.
NEXT COMES THE SUSHI ROW THAT PRACTI-CALLY CRIES OUT THAT IT'S A MAIN DISH...
RAW, COLD-AGED BEEF SUSHI!
DU-DUN
TH-THERE IT IS AGAIN!
MMMMMMMMM!
THE POWERFUL PUNCH OF UMAMI FLAVOR AS TWO COMPONENTS MIX TOGETHER IN MY MOUTH!
HM? WAIT A MIN-UTE.
I UNDER-STAND THE INOSINIC ACID COMES FROM THE BEEF...
...BUT WHERE IS THE GLUTAMIC ACID?
FROM THE TOMA-TOES.
TOMATOES? BUT I DON'T SEE ANY...

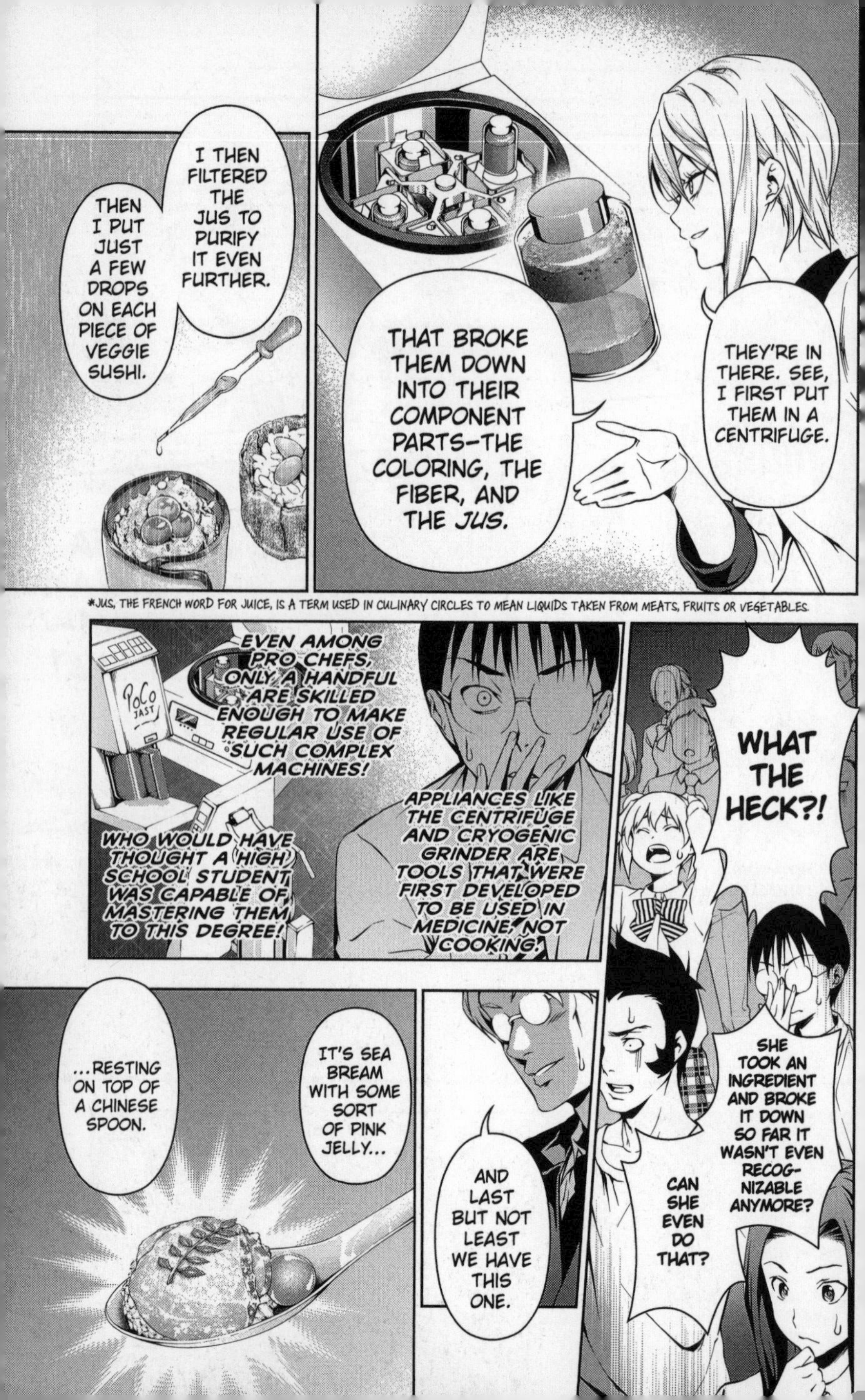
THEY'RE IN THERE. SEE, I FIRST PUT THEM IN A CENTRIFUGE.
THAT BROKE THEM DOWN INTO THEIR COMPONENT PARTS—THE COLORING, THE FIBER, AND THE *JUS*.
I THEN FILTERED THE JUS TO PURIFY IT EVEN FURTHER.
THEN I PUT JUST A FEW DROPS ON EACH PIECE OF VEGGIE SUSHI.
*JUS, THE FRENCH WORD FOR JUICE, IS A TERM USED IN CULINARY CIRCLES TO MEAN LIQUIDS TAKEN FROM MEATS, FRUITS OR VEGETABLES.
WHAT THE HECK?!
EVEN AMONG PRO CHEFS, ONLY A HANDFUL ARE SKILLED ENOUGH TO MAKE REGULAR USE OF SUCH COMPLEX MACHINES!
APPLIANCES LIKE THE CENTRIFUGE AND CRYOGENIC GRINDER ARE TOOLS THAT WERE FIRST DEVELOPED TO BE USED IN MEDICINE, NOT COOKING.
WHO WOULD HAVE THOUGHT A HIGH SCHOOL STUDENT WAS CAPABLE OF MASTERING THEM TO THIS DEGREE!
SHE TOOK AN INGREDIENT AND BROKE IT DOWN SO FAR IT WASN'T EVEN RECOG-NIZABLE ANYMORE?
CAN SHE EVEN DO THAT?
AND LAST BUT NOT LEAST WE HAVE THIS ONE.
IT'S SEA BREAM WITH SOME SORT OF PINK JELLY...
...RESTING ON TOP OF A CHINESE SPOON.

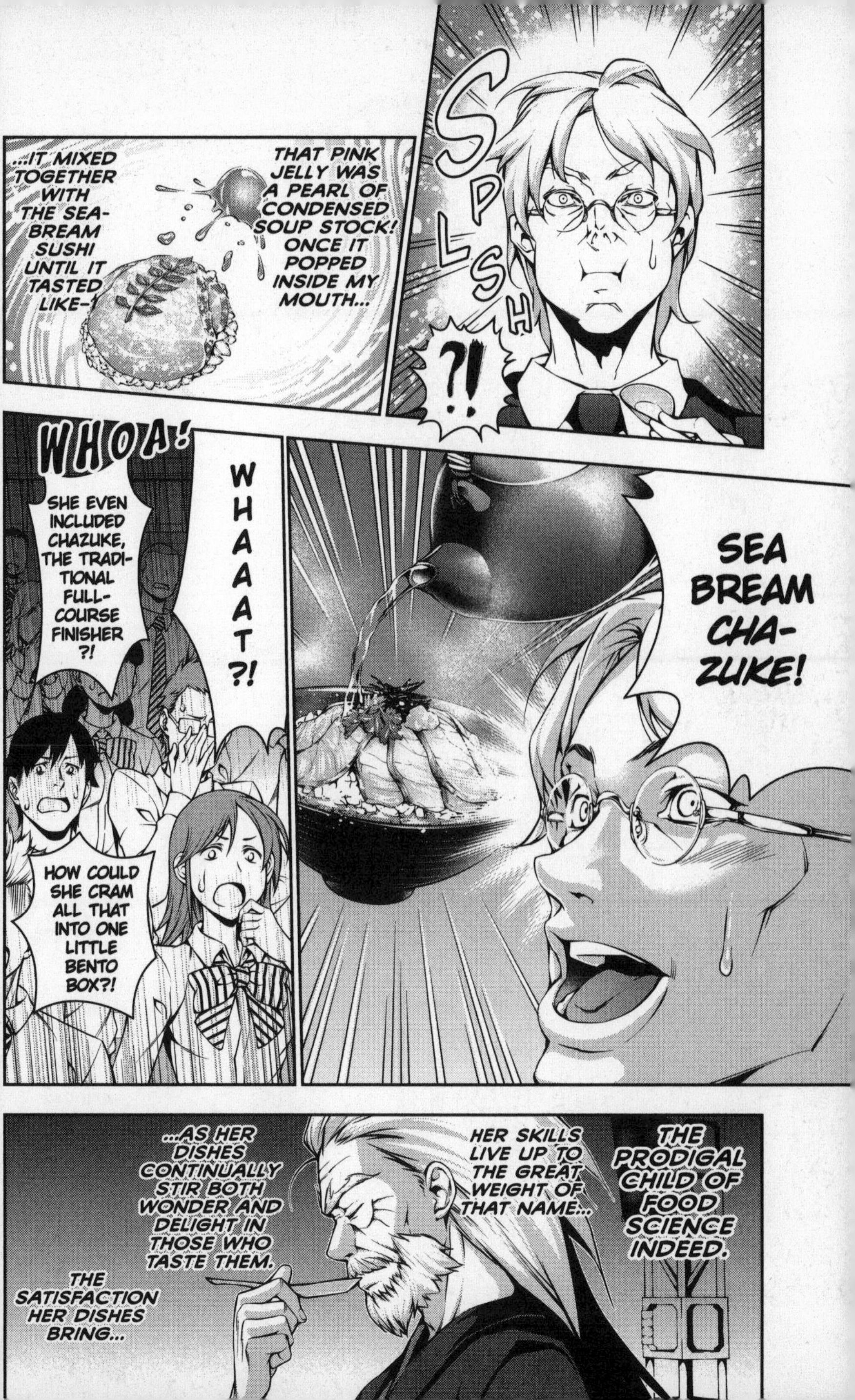
SPLSH
?!
THAT PINK JELLY WAS A PEARL OF CONDENSED SOUP STOCK! ONCE IT POPPED INSIDE MY MOUTH...
...IT MIXED TOGETHER WITH THE SEA-BREAM SUSHI UNTIL IT TASTED LIKE--!
SEA BREAM CHA-ZUKE!
WHOA!
WHAAAAT?!
SHE EVEN INCLUDED CHAZUKE, THE TRADITIONAL FULL-COURSE FINISHER?!
HOW COULD SHE CRAM ALL THAT INTO ONE LITTLE BENTO BOX?!
THE PRODIGAL CHILD OF FOOD SCIENCE INDEED.
HER SKILLS LIVE UP TO THE GREAT WEIGHT OF THAT NAME...
...AS HER DISHES CONTINUALLY STIR BOTH WONDER AND DELIGHT IN THOSE WHO TASTE THEM.
THE SATISFACTION HER DISHES BRING...

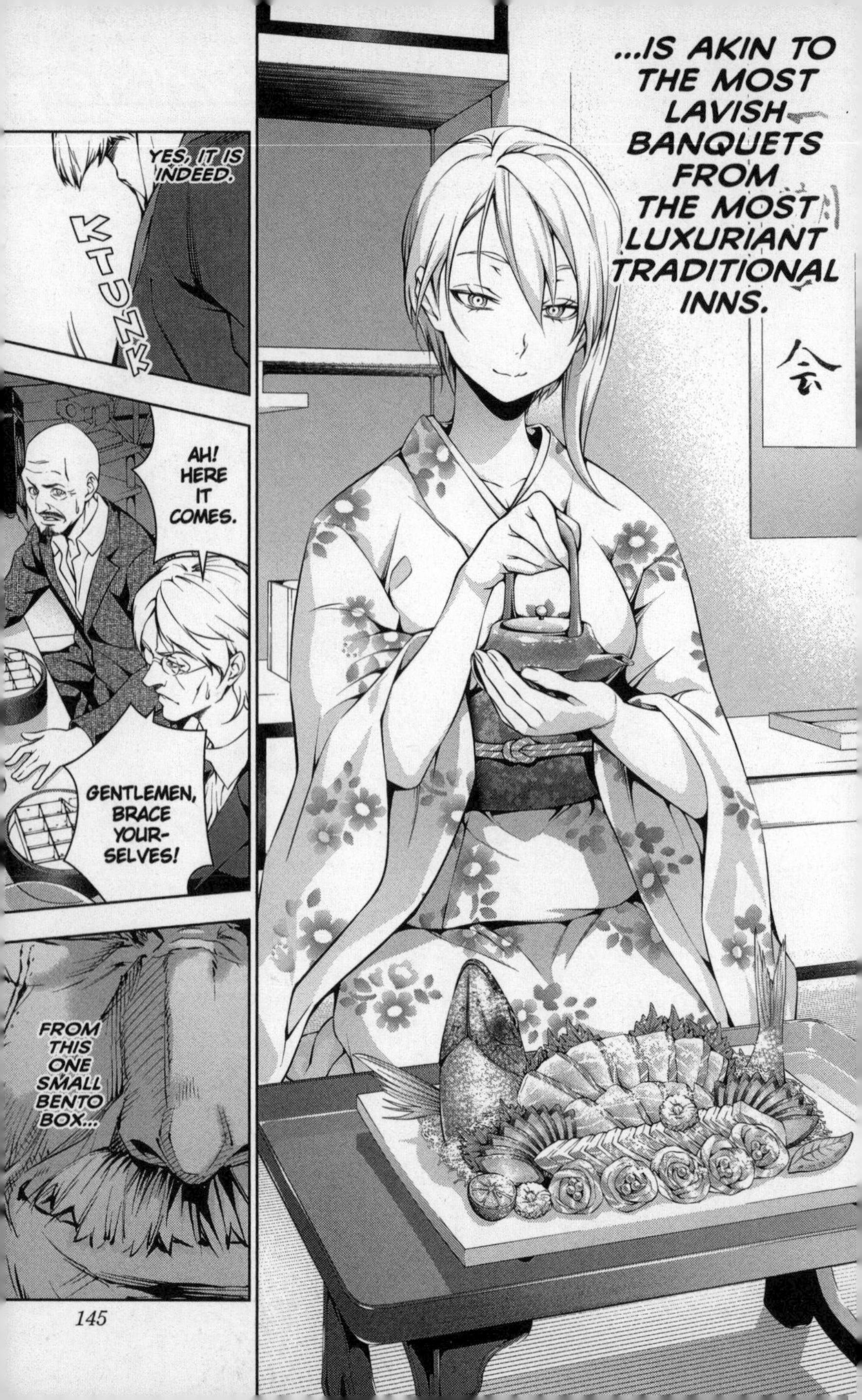
YES, IT IS INDEED.
KTUNK
AH! HERE IT COMES.
GENTLEMEN, BRACE YOUR-SELVES!
FROM THIS ONE SMALL BENTO BOX...
...IS AKIN TO THE MOST LAVISH BANQUETS FROM THE MOST LUXURIANT TRADITIONAL INNS.
会

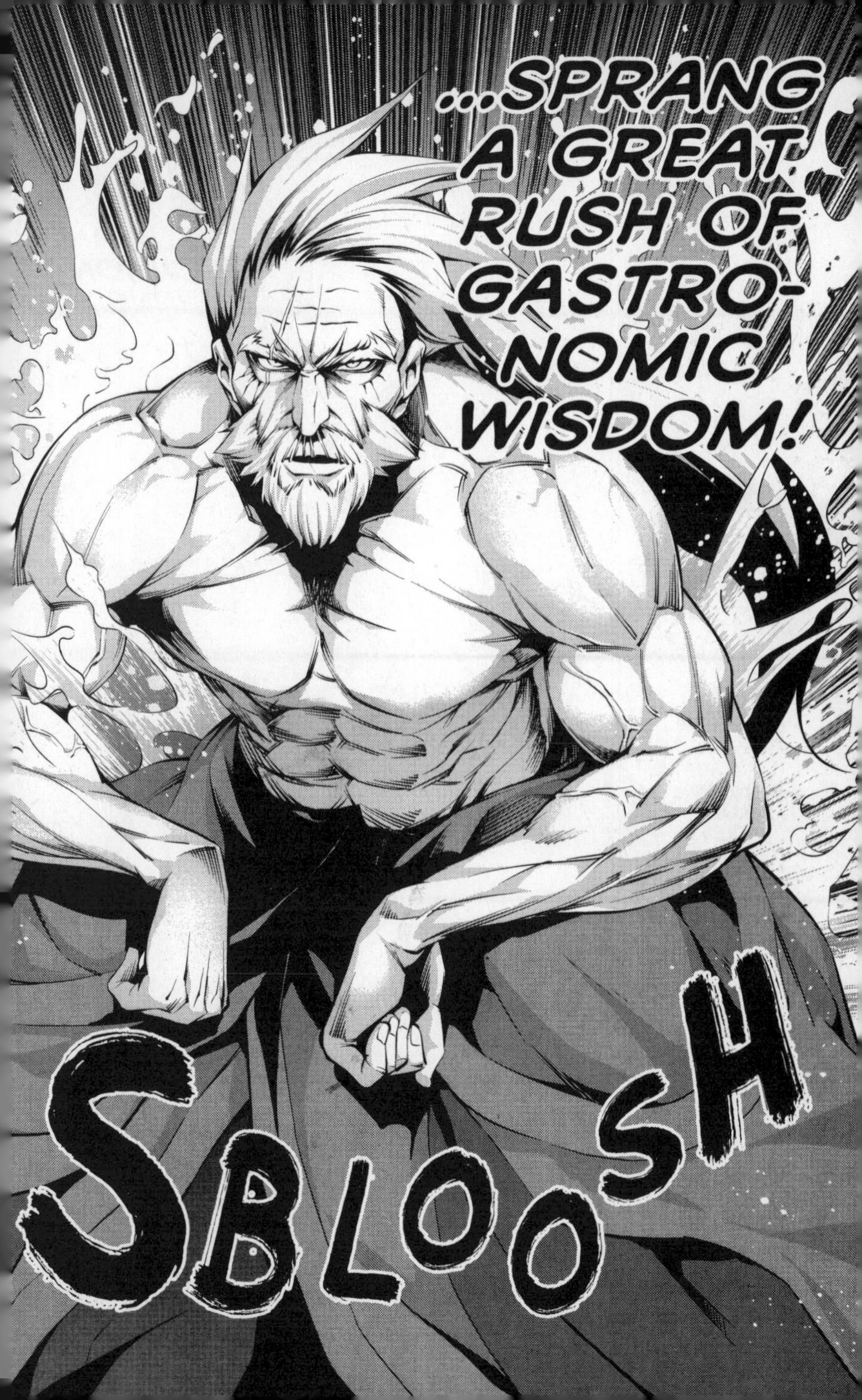
...SPRANG A GREAT RUSH OF GASTRO-NOMIC WISDOM!
SBLOOSH

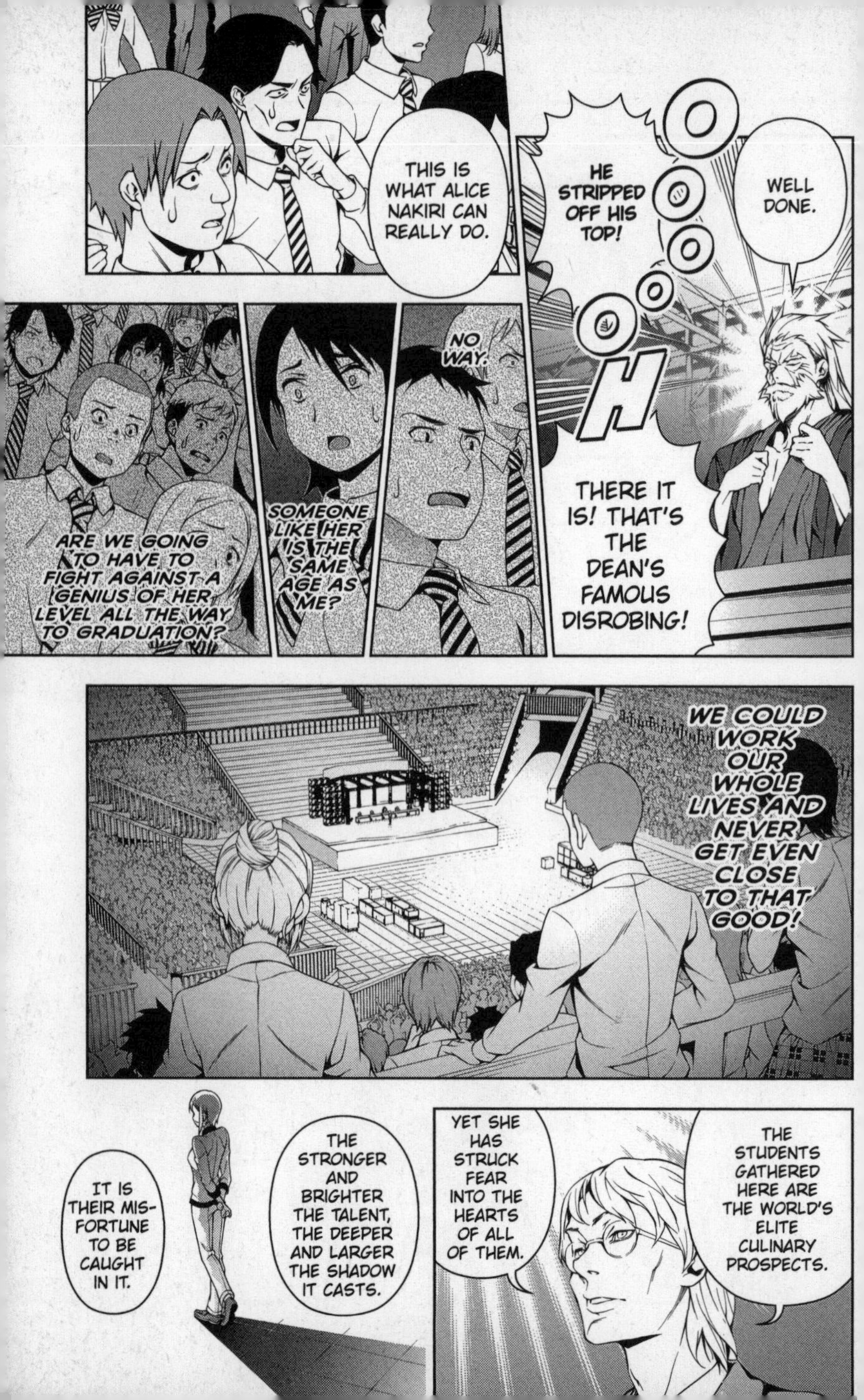
THIS IS WHAT ALICE NAKIRI CAN REALLY DO.
WELL DONE.
OOOOOH
HE STRIPPED OFF HIS TOP!
THERE IT IS! THAT'S THE DEAN'S FAMOUS DISROBING!
NO WAY.
SOMEONE LIKE HER IS THE SAME AGE AS ME?
ARE WE GOING TO HAVE TO FIGHT AGAINST A GENIUS OF HER LEVEL ALL THE WAY TO GRADUATION?
WE COULD WORK OUR WHOLE LIVES AND NEVER GET EVEN CLOSE TO THAT GOOD!
THE STUDENTS GATHERED HERE ARE THE WORLD'S ELITE CULINARY PROSPECTS.
YET SHE HAS STRUCK FEAR INTO THE HEARTS OF ALL OF THEM.
THE STRONGER AND BRIGHTER THE TALENT, THE DEEPER AND LARGER THE SHADOW IT CASTS.
IT IS THEIR MISFORTUNE TO BE CAUGHT IN IT.

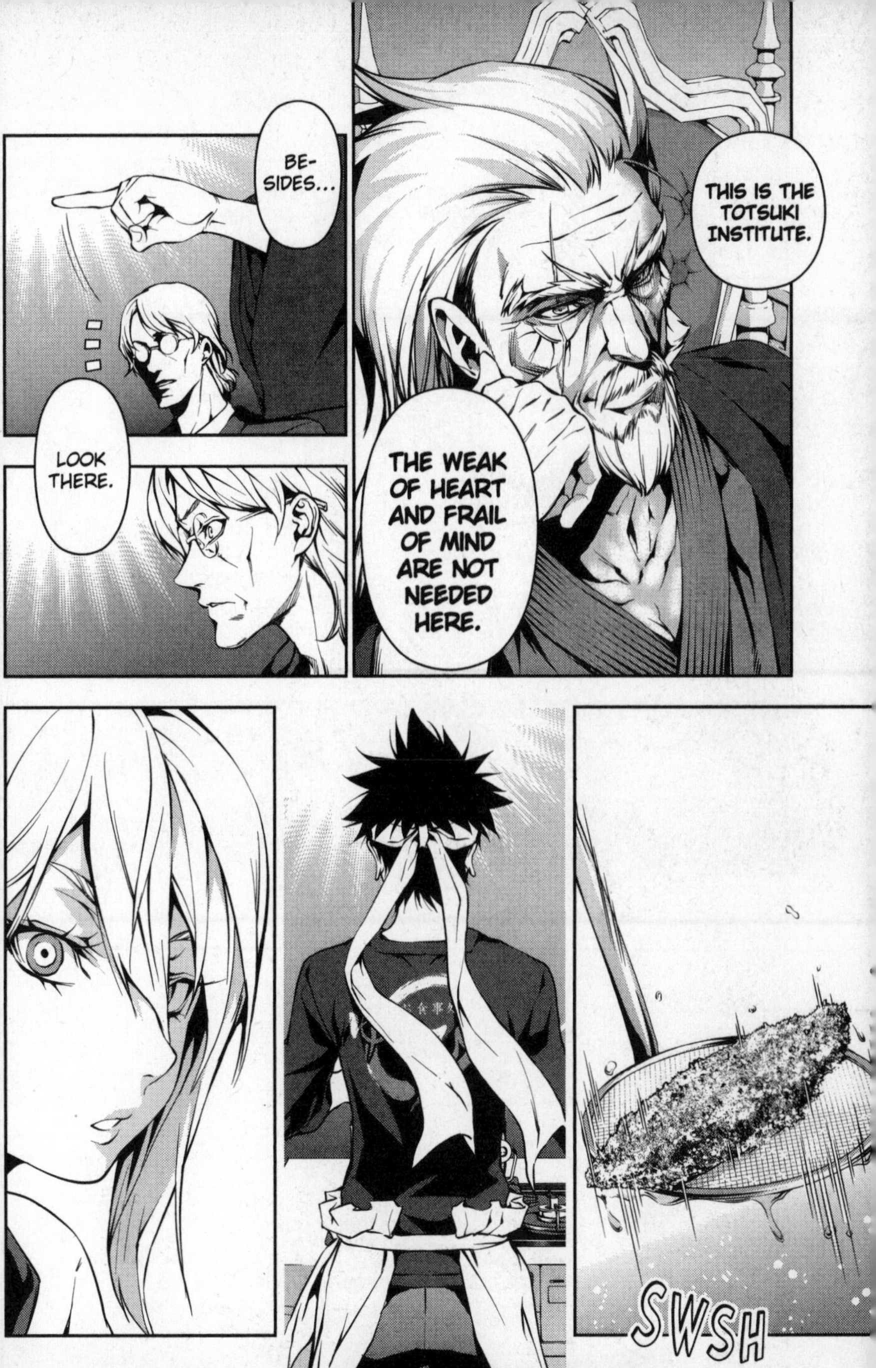
THIS IS THE TOTSUKI INSTITUTE.
THE WEAK OF HEART AND FRAIL OF MIND ARE NOT NEEDED HERE.
BE-SIDES...
LOOK THERE.
SWSH

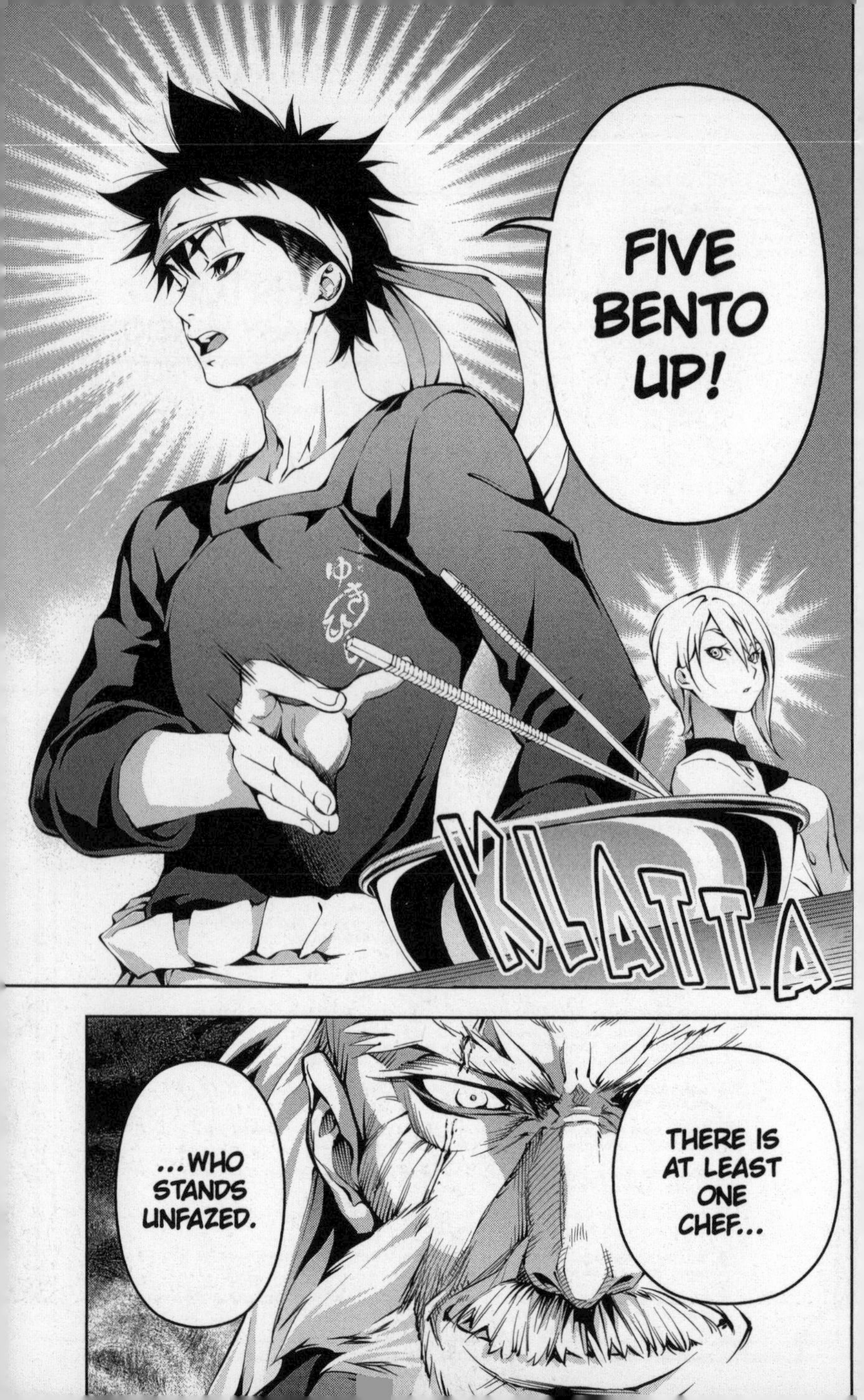
FIVE BENTO UP!
KLATTA
THERE IS AT LEAST ONE CHEF...
...WHO STANDS UNFAZED.

RECIPE BY: YUKI MORISAKI

PRACTICAL RECIPE #3

VOLUME 8 SPECIAL SUPPLEMENT!

ALICE'S TEMARI BENTO (SUPER-EASY VERSION)

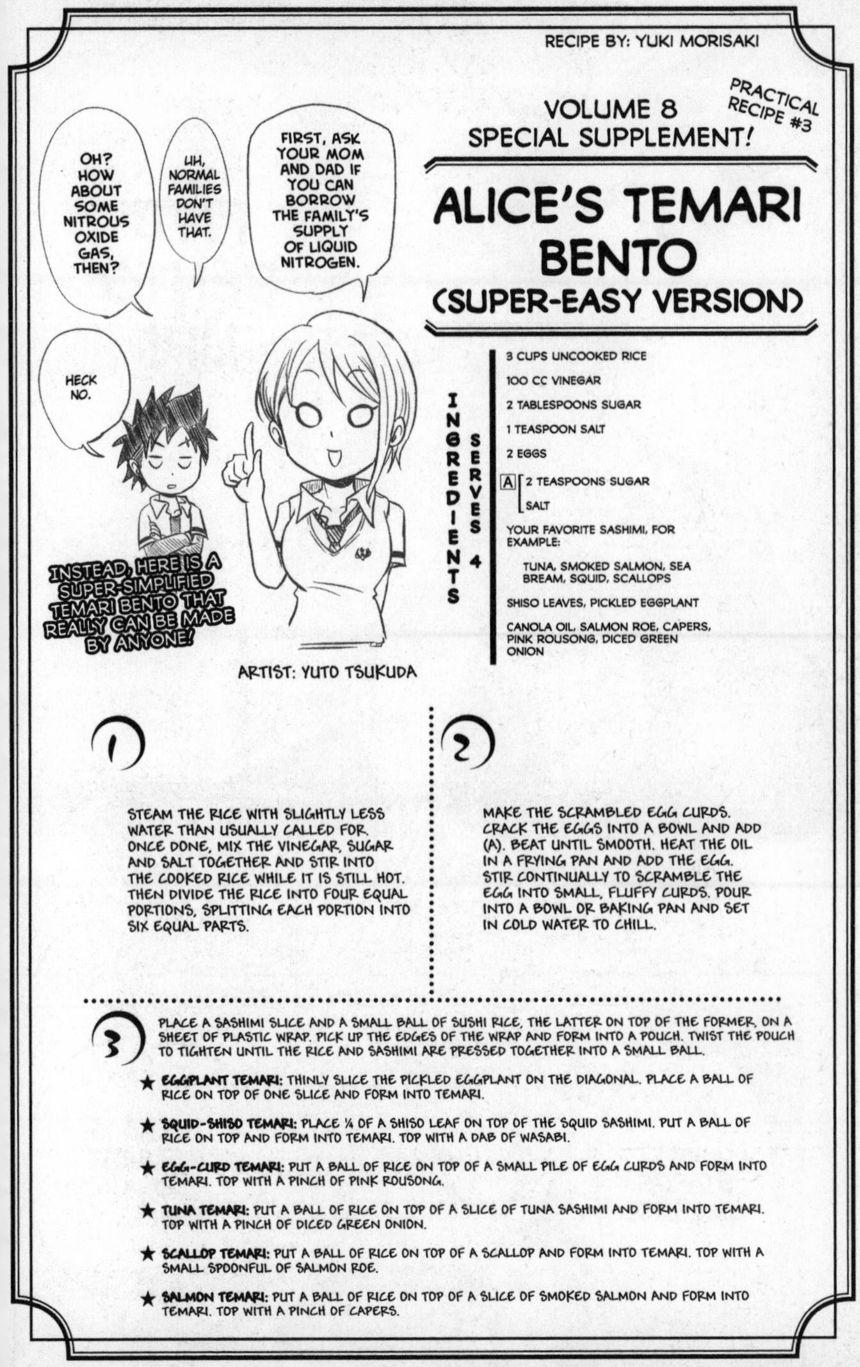
FIRST, ASK YOUR MOM AND DAD IF YOU CAN BORROW THE FAMILY'S SUPPLY OF LIQUID NITROGEN.
UH, NORMAL FAMILIES DON'T HAVE THAT.
OH? HOW ABOUT SOME NITROUS OXIDE GAS, THEN?
HECK NO.
INSTEAD, HERE IS A SUPER-SIMPLIFIED TEMARI BENTO THAT REALLY CAN BE MADE BY ANYONE!

ARTIST: YUTO TSUKUDA

INGREDIENTS SERVES 4

- 3 CUPS UNCOOKED RICE
- 100 CC VINEGAR
- 2 TABLESPOONS SUGAR
- 1 TEASPOON SALT
- 2 EGGS
- [A] 2 TEASPOONS SUGAR
  SALT
- YOUR FAVORITE SASHIMI, FOR EXAMPLE:
  TUNA, SMOKED SALMON, SEA BREAM, SQUID, SCALLOPS
- SHISO LEAVES, PICKLED EGGPLANT
- CANOLA OIL, SALMON ROE, CAPERS, PINK ROUSONG, DICED GREEN ONION

1. STEAM THE RICE WITH SLIGHTLY LESS WATER THAN USUALLY CALLED FOR. ONCE DONE, MIX THE VINEGAR, SUGAR AND SALT TOGETHER AND STIR INTO THE COOKED RICE WHILE IT IS STILL HOT. THEN DIVIDE THE RICE INTO FOUR EQUAL PORTIONS, SPLITTING EACH PORTION INTO SIX EQUAL PARTS.

2. MAKE THE SCRAMBLED EGG CURDS. CRACK THE EGGS INTO A BOWL AND ADD (A). BEAT UNTIL SMOOTH. HEAT THE OIL IN A FRYING PAN AND ADD THE EGG. STIR CONTINUALLY TO SCRAMBLE THE EGG INTO SMALL, FLUFFY CURDS. POUR INTO A BOWL OR BAKING PAN AND SET IN COLD WATER TO CHILL.

3. PLACE A SASHIMI SLICE AND A SMALL BALL OF SUSHI RICE, THE LATTER ON TOP OF THE FORMER, ON A SHEET OF PLASTIC WRAP. PICK UP THE EDGES OF THE WRAP AND FORM INTO A POUCH. TWIST THE POUCH TO TIGHTEN UNTIL THE RICE AND SASHIMI ARE PRESSED TOGETHER INTO A SMALL BALL.

★ **EGGPLANT TEMARI:** THINLY SLICE THE PICKLED EGGPLANT ON THE DIAGONAL. PLACE A BALL OF RICE ON TOP OF ONE SLICE AND FORM INTO TEMARI.

★ **SQUID-SHISO TEMARI:** PLACE ¼ OF A SHISO LEAF ON TOP OF THE SQUID SASHIMI. PUT A BALL OF RICE ON TOP AND FORM INTO TEMARI. TOP WITH A DAB OF WASABI.

★ **EGG-CURD TEMARI:** PUT A BALL OF RICE ON TOP OF A SMALL PILE OF EGG CURDS AND FORM INTO TEMARI. TOP WITH A PINCH OF PINK ROUSONG.

★ **TUNA TEMARI:** PUT A BALL OF RICE ON TOP OF A SLICE OF TUNA SASHIMI AND FORM INTO TEMARI. TOP WITH A PINCH OF DICED GREEN ONION.

★ **SCALLOP TEMARI:** PUT A BALL OF RICE ON TOP OF A SCALLOP AND FORM INTO TEMARI. TOP WITH A SMALL SPOONFUL OF SALMON ROE.

★ **SALMON TEMARI:** PUT A BALL OF RICE ON TOP OF A SLICE OF SMOKED SALMON AND FORM INTO TEMARI. TOP WITH A PINCH OF CAPERS.

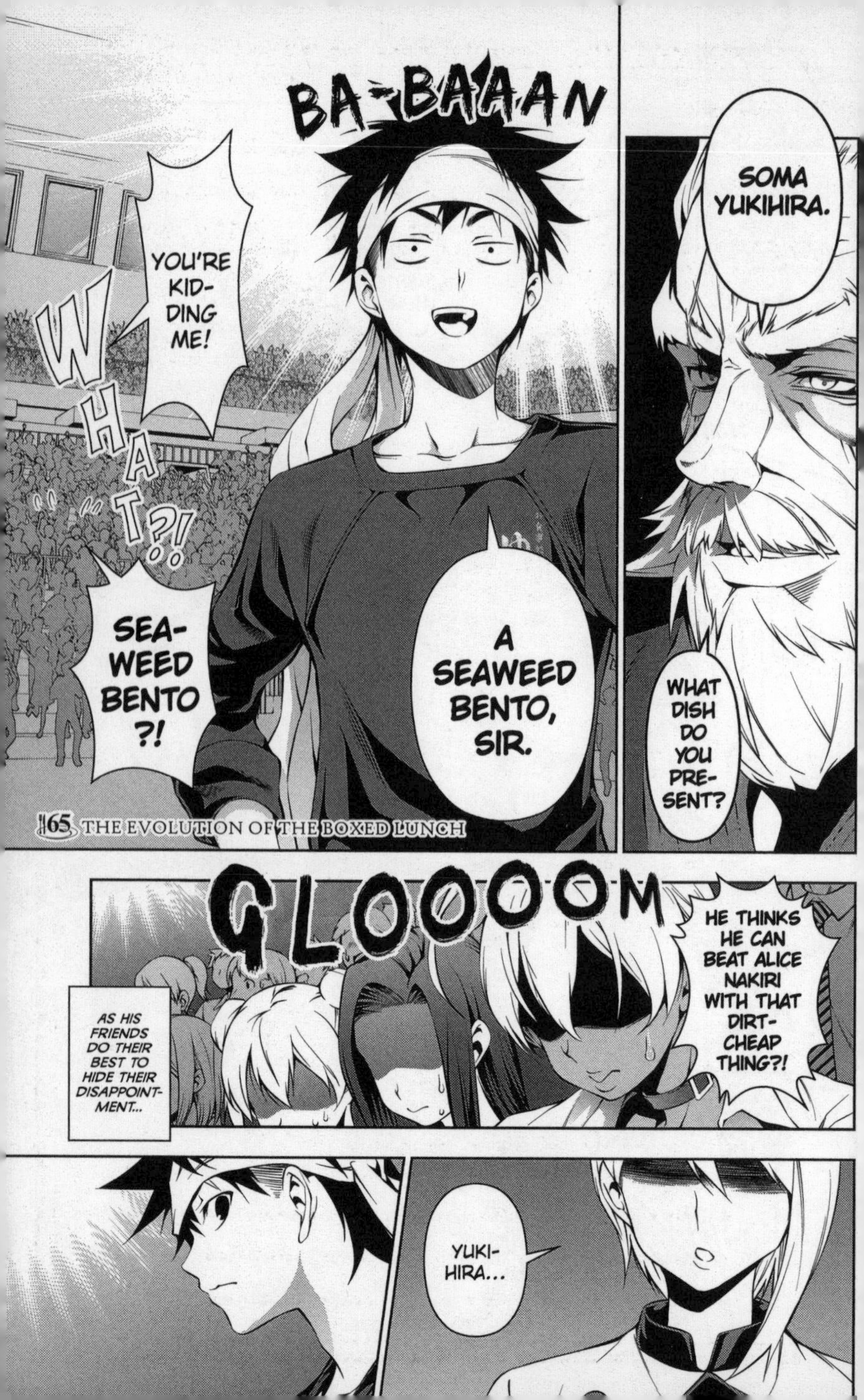
SOMA YUKIHIRA.
WHAT DISH DO YOU PRESENT?
BA-BAAAN
A SEAWEED BENTO, SIR.
YOU'RE KIDDING ME!
WHAT?!
SEAWEED BENTO?!
165 THE EVOLUTION OF THE BOXED LUNCH
HE THINKS HE CAN BEAT ALICE NAKIRI WITH THAT DIRT-CHEAP THING?!
GLOOOOM
AS HIS FRIENDS DO THEIR BEST TO HIDE THEIR DISAPPOINTMENT...
YUKI-HIRA...

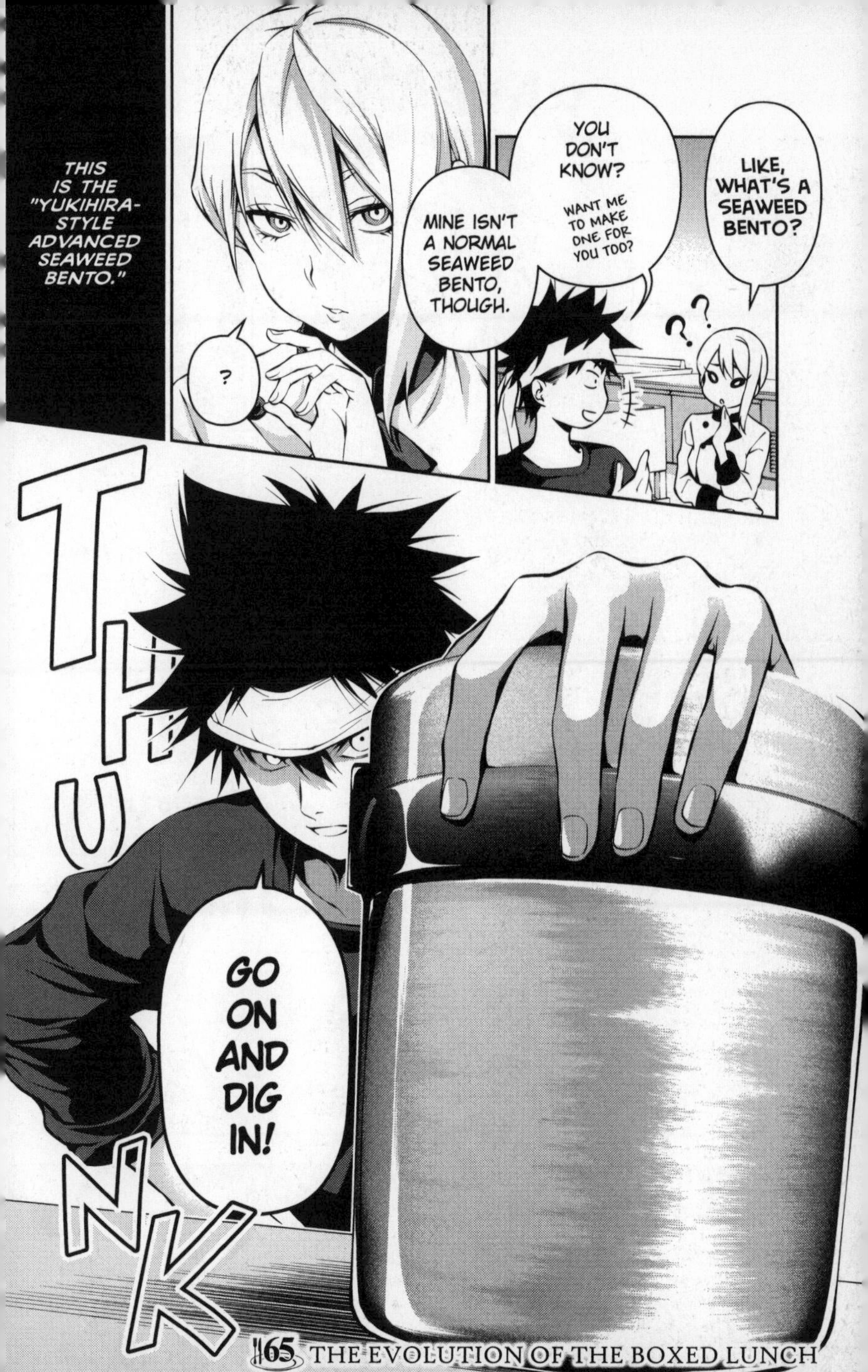
LIKE, WHAT'S A SEAWEED BENTO?
YOU DON'T KNOW?
WANT ME TO MAKE ONE FOR YOU TOO?
MINE ISN'T A NORMAL SEAWEED BENTO, THOUGH.
?
THIS IS THE "YUKIHIRA-STYLE ADVANCED SEAWEED BENTO."
THUNK
GO ON AND DIG IN!

165 THE EVOLUTION OF THE BOXED LUNCH

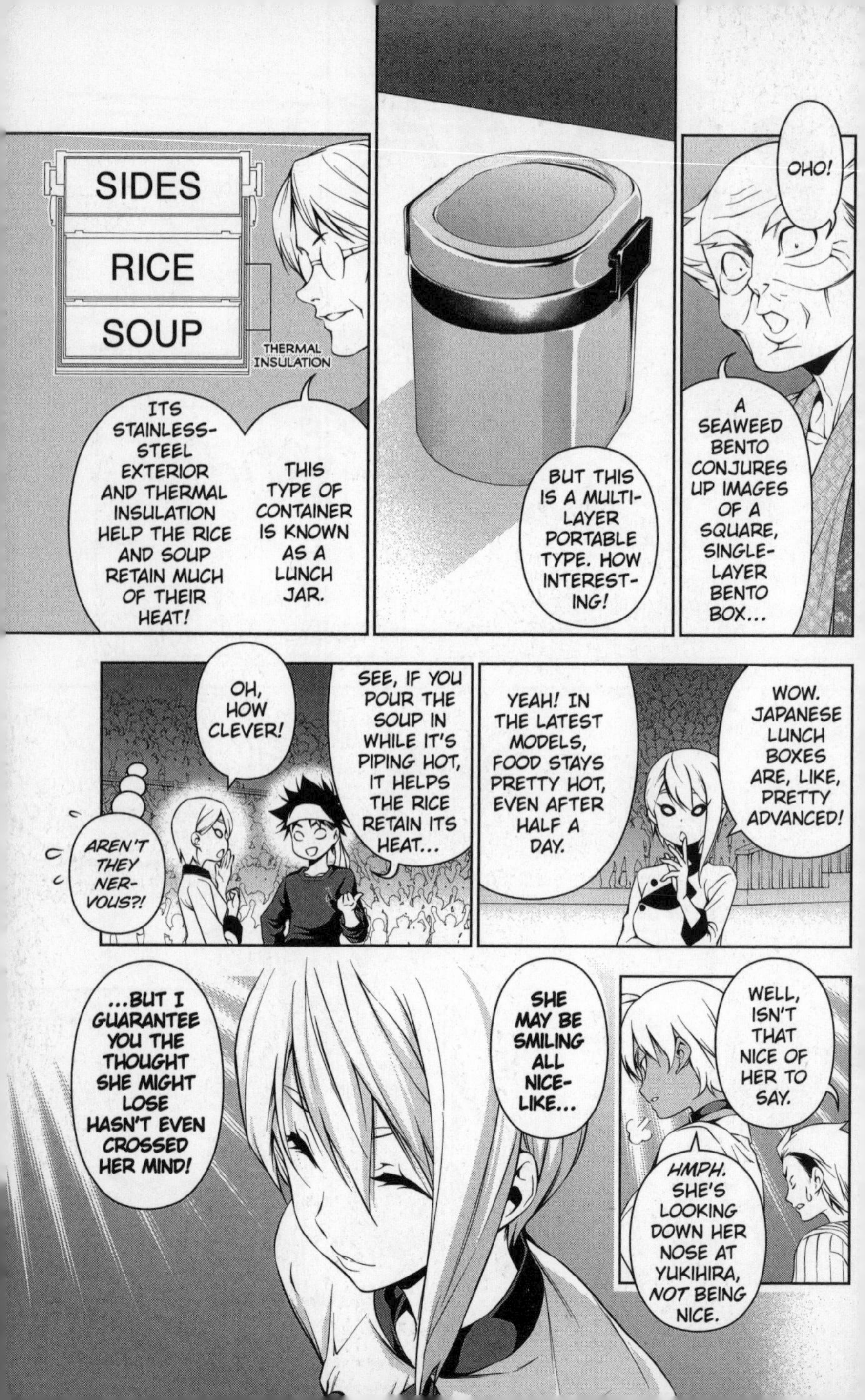
OHO!
A SEAWEED BENTO CONJURES UP IMAGES OF A SQUARE, SINGLE-LAYER BENTO BOX...
BUT THIS IS A MULTI-LAYER PORTABLE TYPE. HOW INTERESTING!
SIDES
RICE
SOUP
THERMAL INSULATION
THIS TYPE OF CONTAINER IS KNOWN AS A LUNCH JAR.
ITS STAINLESS-STEEL EXTERIOR AND THERMAL INSULATION HELP THE RICE AND SOUP RETAIN MUCH OF THEIR HEAT!
WOW. JAPANESE LUNCH BOXES ARE, LIKE, PRETTY ADVANCED!
YEAH! IN THE LATEST MODELS, FOOD STAYS PRETTY HOT, EVEN AFTER HALF A DAY.
SEE, IF YOU POUR THE SOUP IN WHILE IT'S PIPING HOT, IT HELPS THE RICE RETAIN ITS HEAT...
OH, HOW CLEVER!
AREN'T THEY NERVOUS?!
WELL, ISN'T THAT NICE OF HER TO SAY.
HMPH. SHE'S LOOKING DOWN HER NOSE AT YUKIHIRA, NOT BEING NICE.
SHE MAY BE SMILING ALL NICE-LIKE...
...BUT I GUARANTEE YOU THE THOUGHT SHE MIGHT LOSE HASN'T EVEN CROSSED HER MIND!

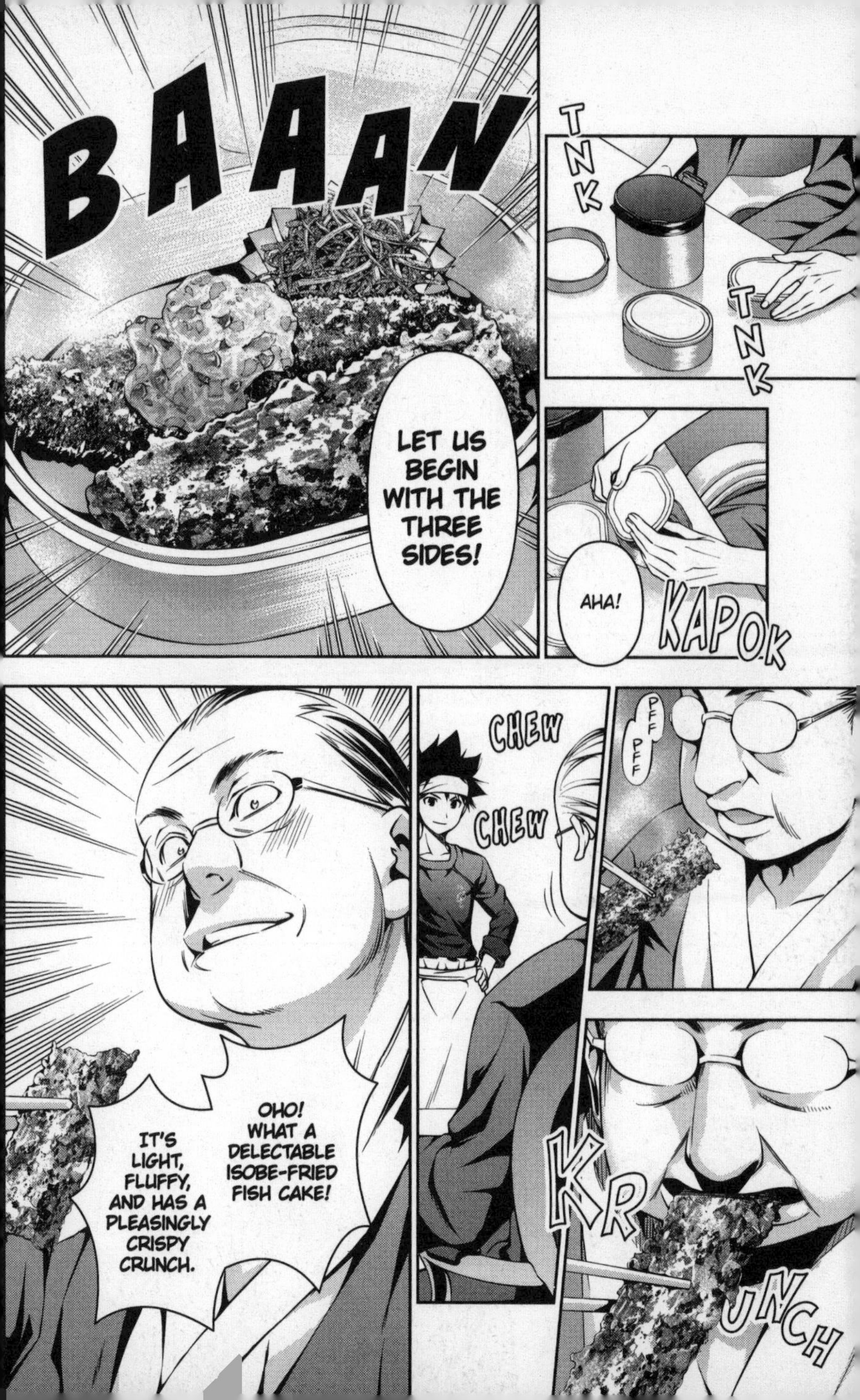
TNK
TNK
AHA!
KAPOK
BAAAN
LET US BEGIN WITH THE THREE SIDES!
PFF PFF
KRUNCH
CHEW
CHEW
OHO! WHAT A DELECTABLE ISOBE-FRIED FISH CAKE!
IT'S LIGHT, FLUFFY, AND HAS A PLEASINGLY CRISPY CRUNCH.

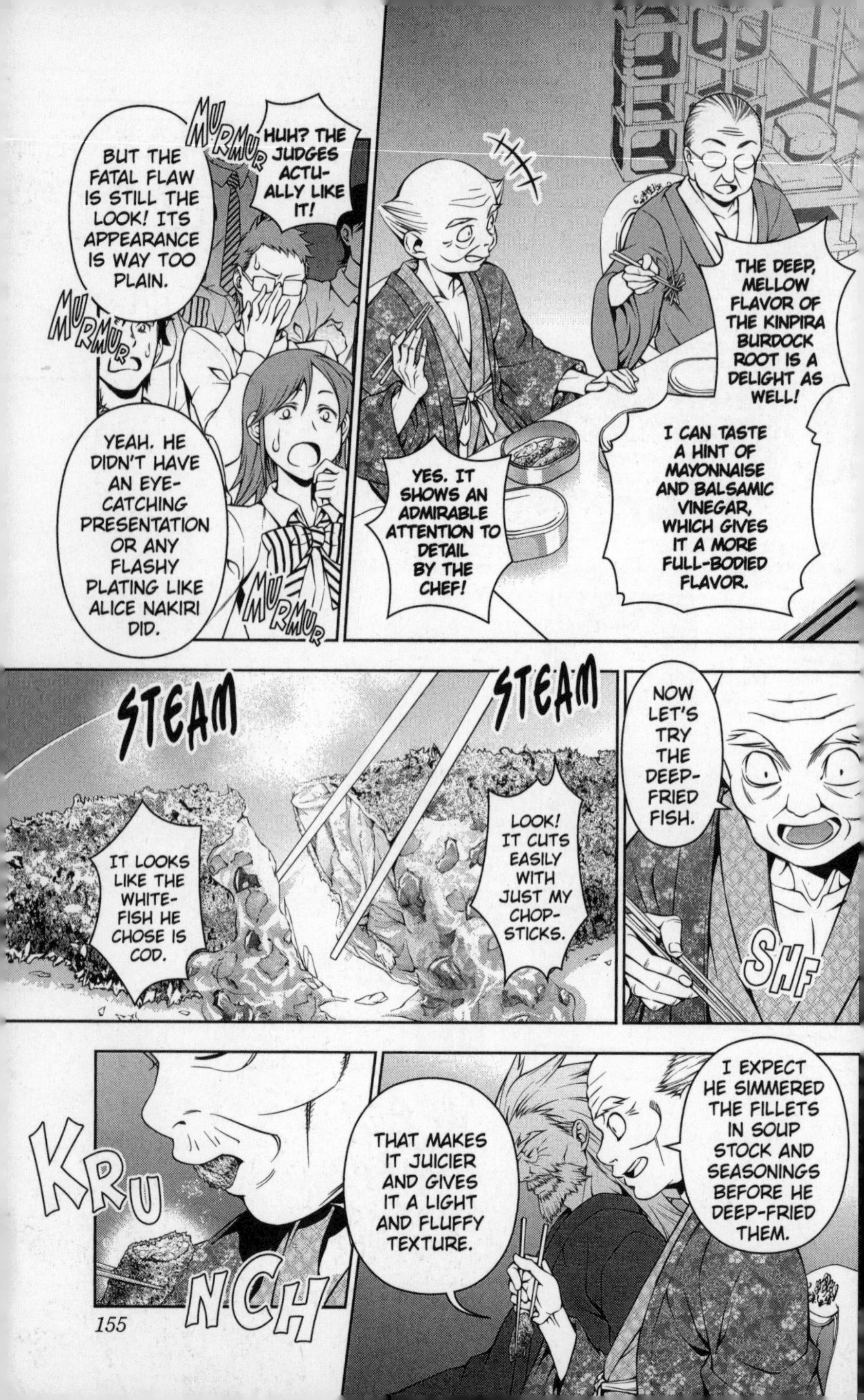
THE DEEP, MELLOW FLAVOR OF THE KINPIRA BURDOCK ROOT IS A DELIGHT AS WELL!
I CAN TASTE A HINT OF MAYONNAISE AND BALSAMIC VINEGAR, WHICH GIVES IT A MORE FULL-BODIED FLAVOR.
YES. IT SHOWS AN ADMIRABLE ATTENTION TO DETAIL BY THE CHEF!
HUH? THE JUDGES ACTU-ALLY LIKE IT!
MURMUR
BUT THE FATAL FLAW IS STILL THE LOOK! ITS APPEARANCE IS WAY TOO PLAIN.
MURMUR
YEAH. HE DIDN'T HAVE AN EYE-CATCHING PRESENTATION OR ANY FLASHY PLATING LIKE ALICE NAKIRI DID.
MURMUR
NOW LET'S TRY THE DEEP-FRIED FISH.
SHF
STEAM
LOOK! IT CUTS EASILY WITH JUST MY CHOP-STICKS.
STEAM
IT LOOKS LIKE THE WHITE-FISH HE CHOSE IS COD.
I EXPECT HE SIMMERED THE FILLETS IN SOUP STOCK AND SEASONINGS BEFORE HE DEEP-FRIED THEM.
THAT MAKES IT JUICIER AND GIVES IT A LIGHT AND FLUFFY TEXTURE.
KRUNCH

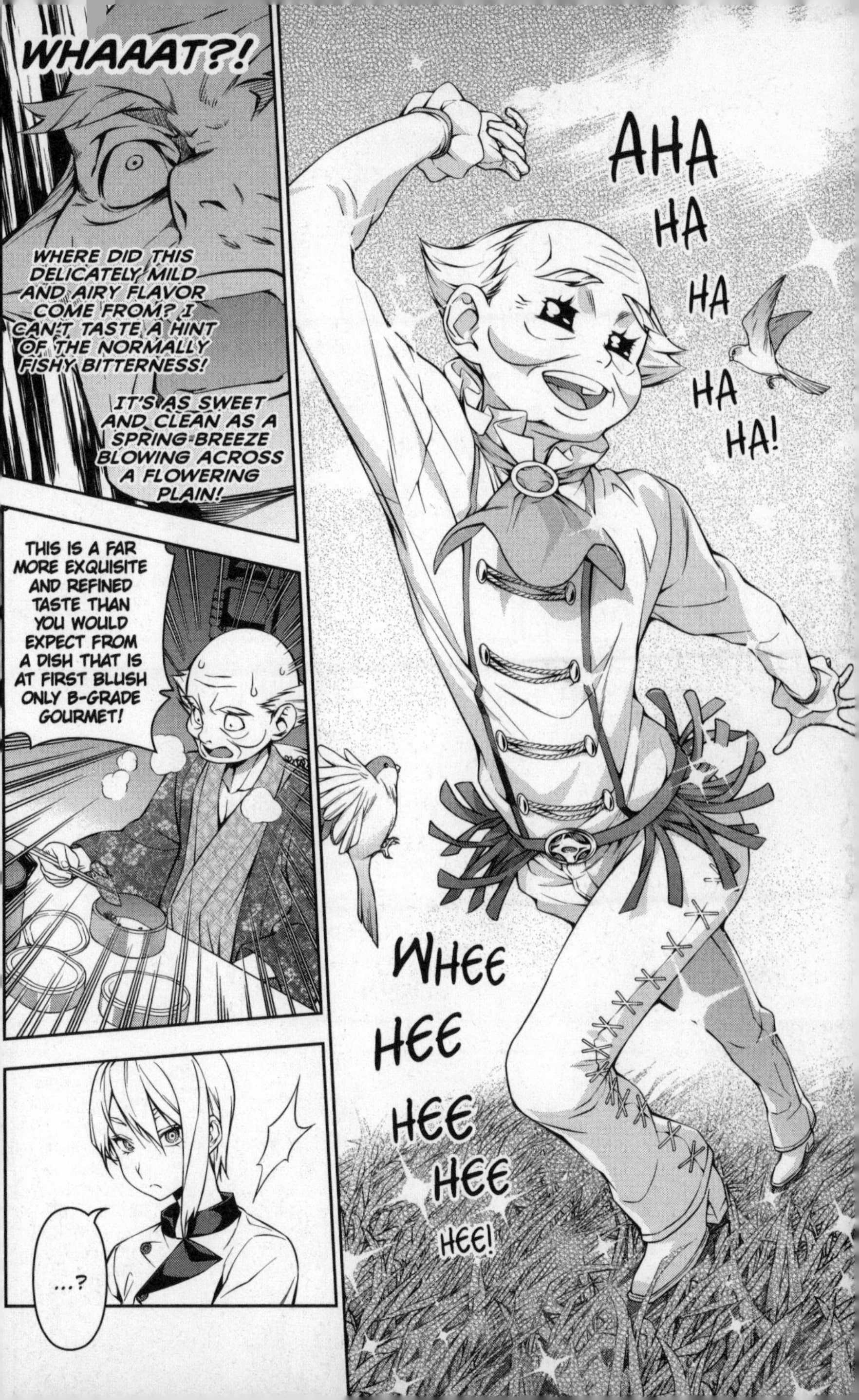
AHA HA HA HA HA!
WHEE HEE HEE HEE HEE!
WHAAAT?!
WHERE DID THIS DELICATELY MILD AND AIRY FLAVOR COME FROM? I CAN'T TASTE A HINT OF THE NORMALLY FISHY BITTERNESS!
IT'S AS SWEET AND CLEAN AS A SPRING BREEZE BLOWING ACROSS A FLOWERING PLAIN!
THIS IS A FAR MORE EXQUISITE AND REFINED TASTE THAN YOU WOULD EXPECT FROM A DISH THAT IS AT FIRST BLUSH ONLY B-GRADE GOURMET!
...?

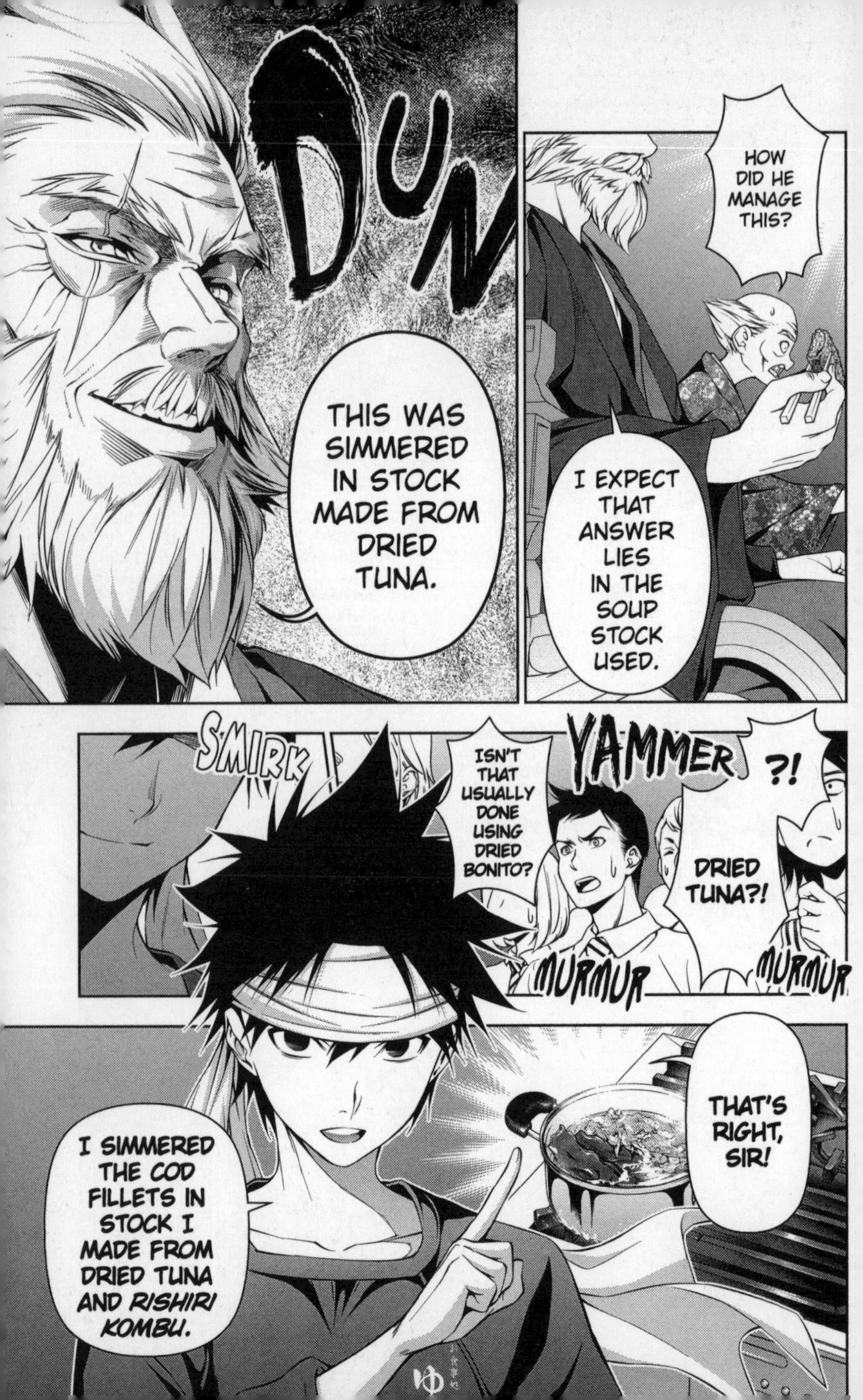
HOW DID HE MANAGE THIS?
I EXPECT THAT ANSWER LIES IN THE SOUP STOCK USED.
DUN
THIS WAS SIMMERED IN STOCK MADE FROM DRIED TUNA.
?!
YAMMER
DRIED TUNA?!
MURMUR
ISN'T THAT USUALLY DONE USING DRIED BONITO?
MURMUR
SMIRK
THAT'S RIGHT, SIR!
I SIMMERED THE COD FILLETS IN STOCK I MADE FROM DRIED TUNA AND *RISHIRI KOMBU*.

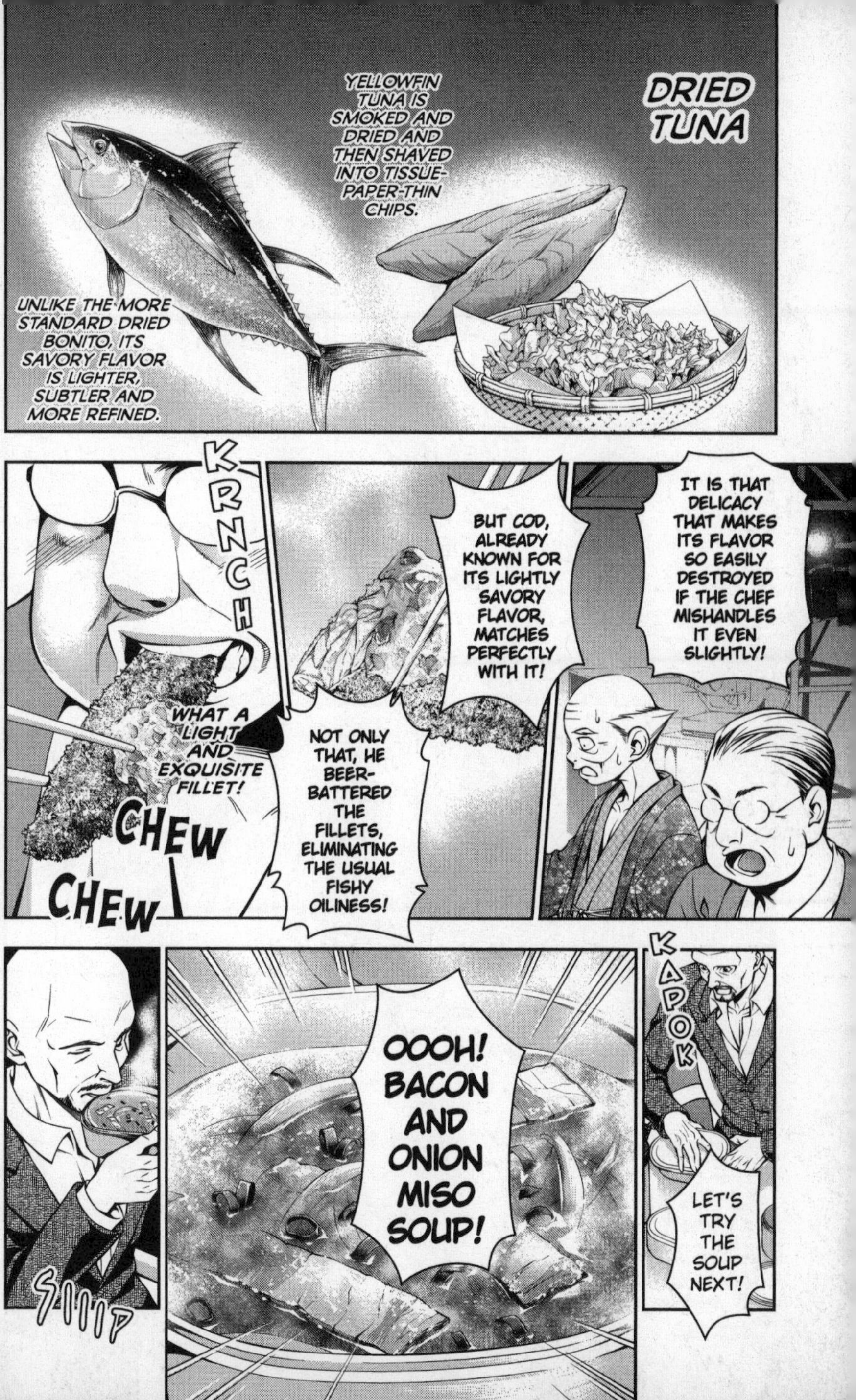
DRIED TUNA
YELLOWFIN TUNA IS SMOKED AND DRIED AND THEN SHAVED INTO TISSUE-PAPER-THIN CHIPS.
UNLIKE THE MORE STANDARD DRIED BONITO, ITS SAVORY FLAVOR IS LIGHTER, SUBTLER AND MORE REFINED.
IT IS THAT DELICACY THAT MAKES ITS FLAVOR SO EASILY DESTROYED IF THE CHEF MISHANDLES IT EVEN SLIGHTLY!
BUT COD, ALREADY KNOWN FOR ITS LIGHTLY SAVORY FLAVOR, MATCHES PERFECTLY WITH IT!
NOT ONLY THAT, HE BEER-BATTERED THE FILLETS, ELIMINATING THE USUAL FISHY OILINESS!
KRNCH
WHAT A LIGHT AND EXQUISITE FILLET!
CHEW
CHEW
KAPOK
LET'S TRY THE SOUP NEXT!
OOOH! BACON AND ONION MISO SOUP!
SIIIP

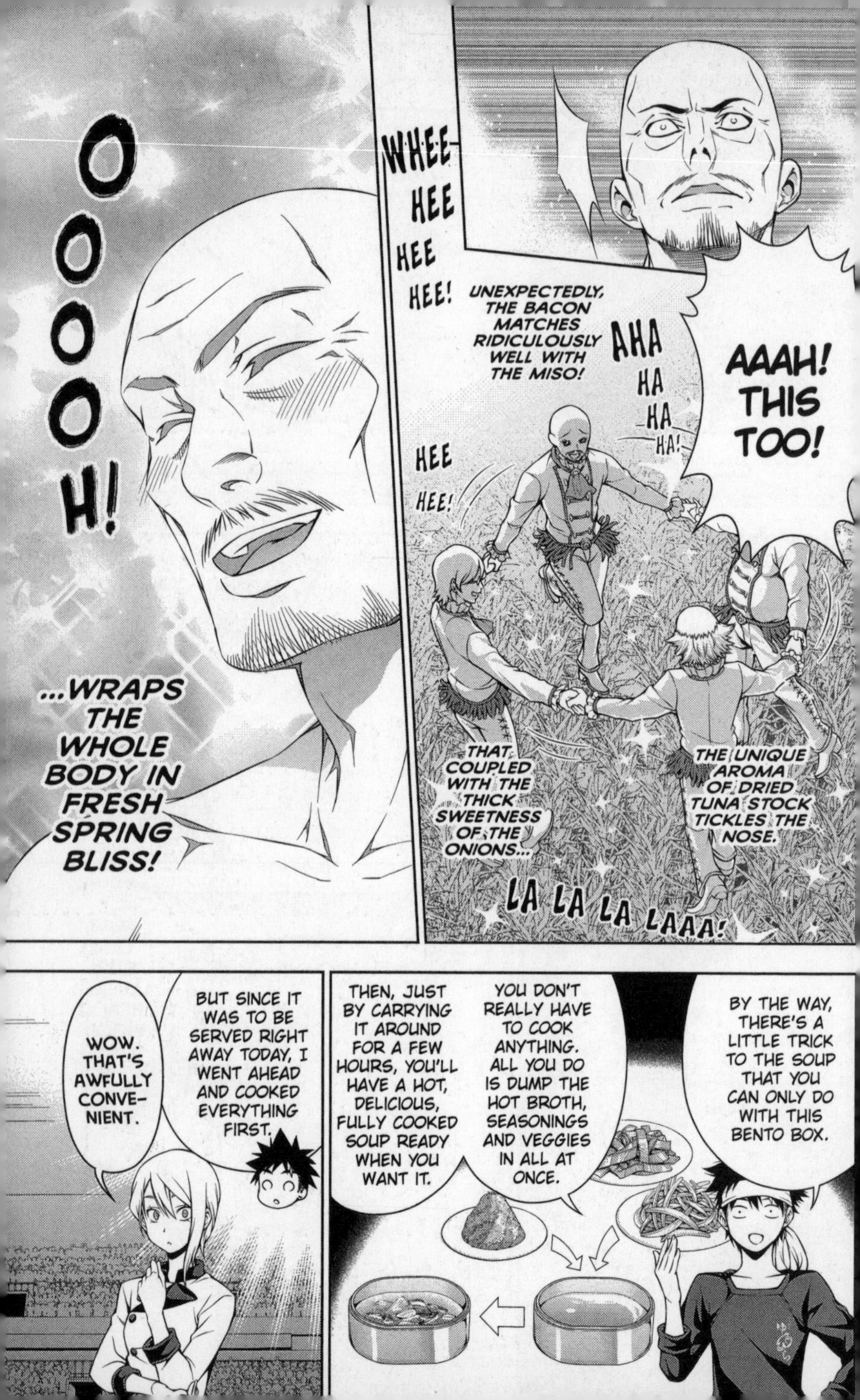
WHEE HEE HEE HEE!
AAAH! THIS TOO!
UNEXPECTEDLY, THE BACON MATCHES RIDICULOUSLY WELL WITH THE MISO!
AHA HA HA HA!
HEE HEE!
THE UNIQUE AROMA OF DRIED TUNA STOCK TICKLES THE NOSE.
THAT, COUPLED WITH THE THICK SWEETNESS OF THE ONIONS...
LA LA LA LAAAA!
OOOOOH!
...WRAPS THE WHOLE BODY IN FRESH SPRING BLISS!
BY THE WAY, THERE'S A LITTLE TRICK TO THE SOUP THAT YOU CAN ONLY DO WITH THIS BENTO BOX.
YOU DON'T REALLY HAVE TO COOK ANYTHING. ALL YOU DO IS DUMP THE HOT BROTH, SEASONINGS AND VEGGIES IN ALL AT ONCE.
THEN, JUST BY CARRYING IT AROUND FOR A FEW HOURS, YOU'LL HAVE A HOT, DELICIOUS, FULLY COOKED SOUP READY WHEN YOU WANT IT.
BUT SINCE IT WAS TO BE SERVED RIGHT AWAY TODAY, I WENT AHEAD AND COOKED EVERYTHING FIRST.
WOW. THAT'S AWFULLY CONVE-NIENT.

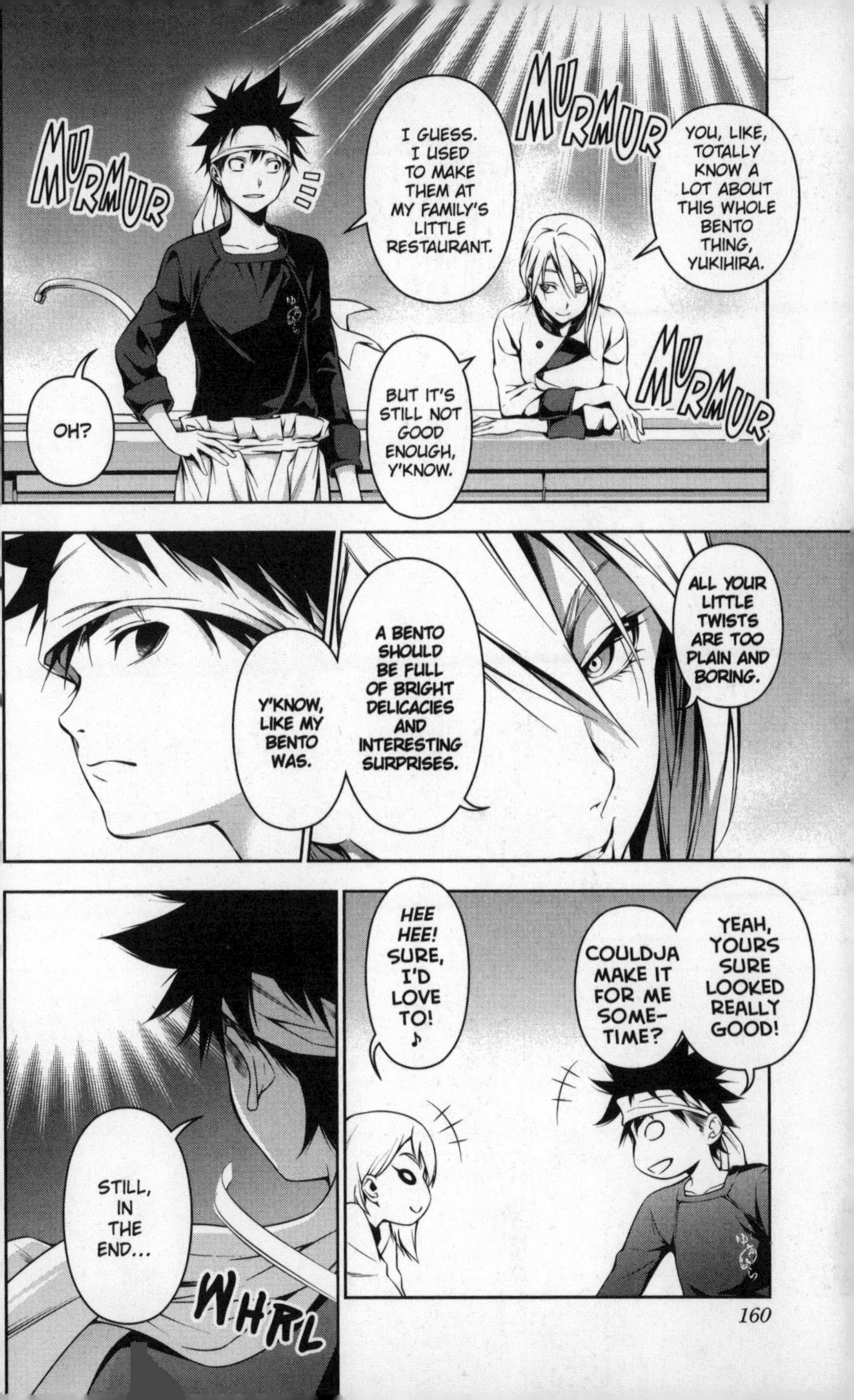
MURMUR
YOU, LIKE, TOTALLY KNOW A LOT ABOUT THIS WHOLE BENTO THING, YUKIHIRA.
MURMUR
I GUESS. I USED TO MAKE THEM AT MY FAMILY'S LITTLE RESTAURANT.
MURMUR
BUT IT'S STILL NOT GOOD ENOUGH, Y'KNOW.
OH?
ALL YOUR LITTLE TWISTS ARE TOO PLAIN AND BORING.
A BENTO SHOULD BE FULL OF BRIGHT DELICACIES AND INTERESTING SURPRISES.
Y'KNOW, LIKE MY BENTO WAS.
YEAH, YOURS SURE LOOKED REALLY GOOD!
COULDJA MAKE IT FOR ME SOME-TIME?
HEE HEE! SURE, I'D LOVE TO! ♪
STILL, IN THE END...
WHRL

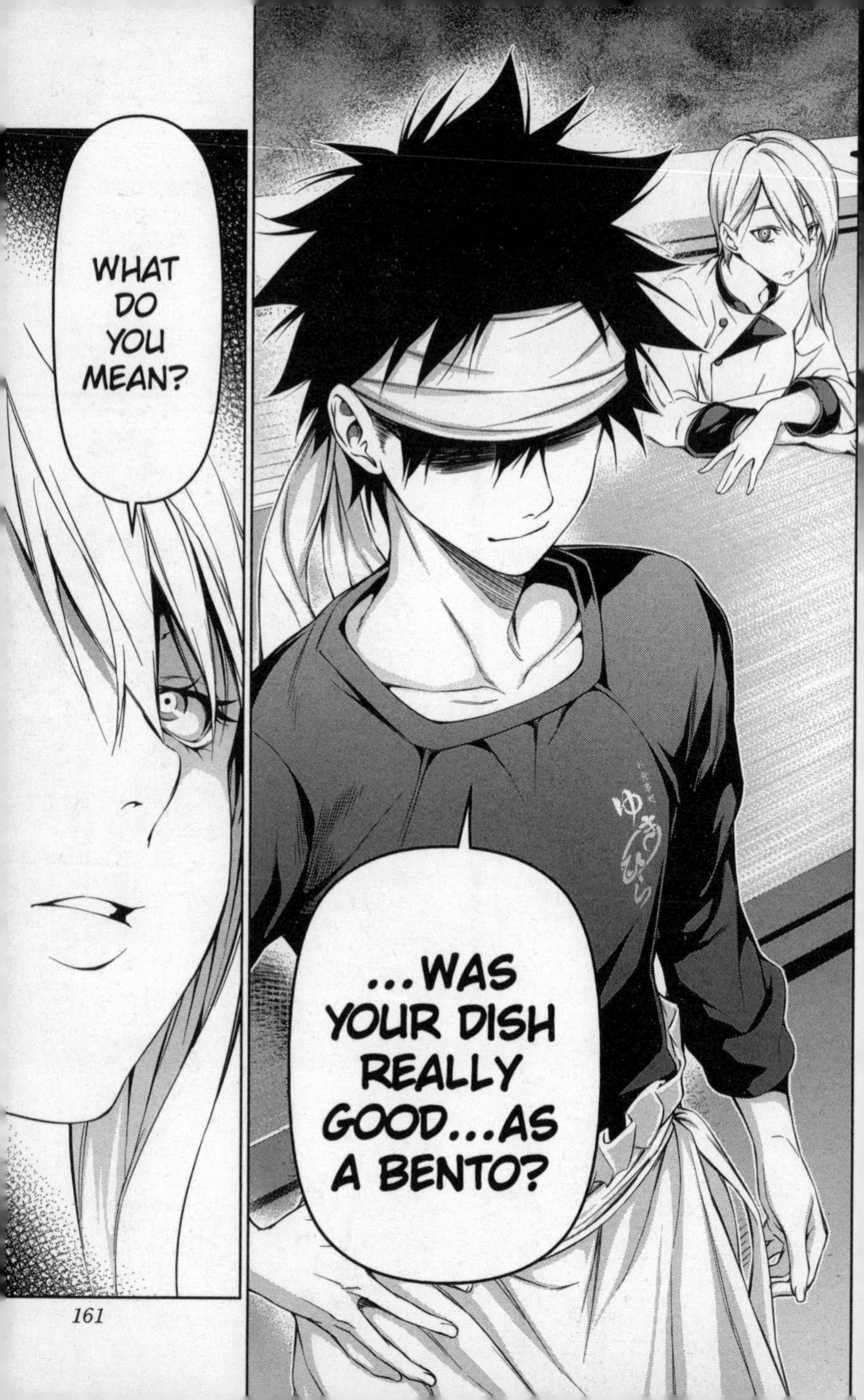
...WAS YOUR DISH REALLY GOOD...AS A BENTO?
WHAT DO YOU MEAN?

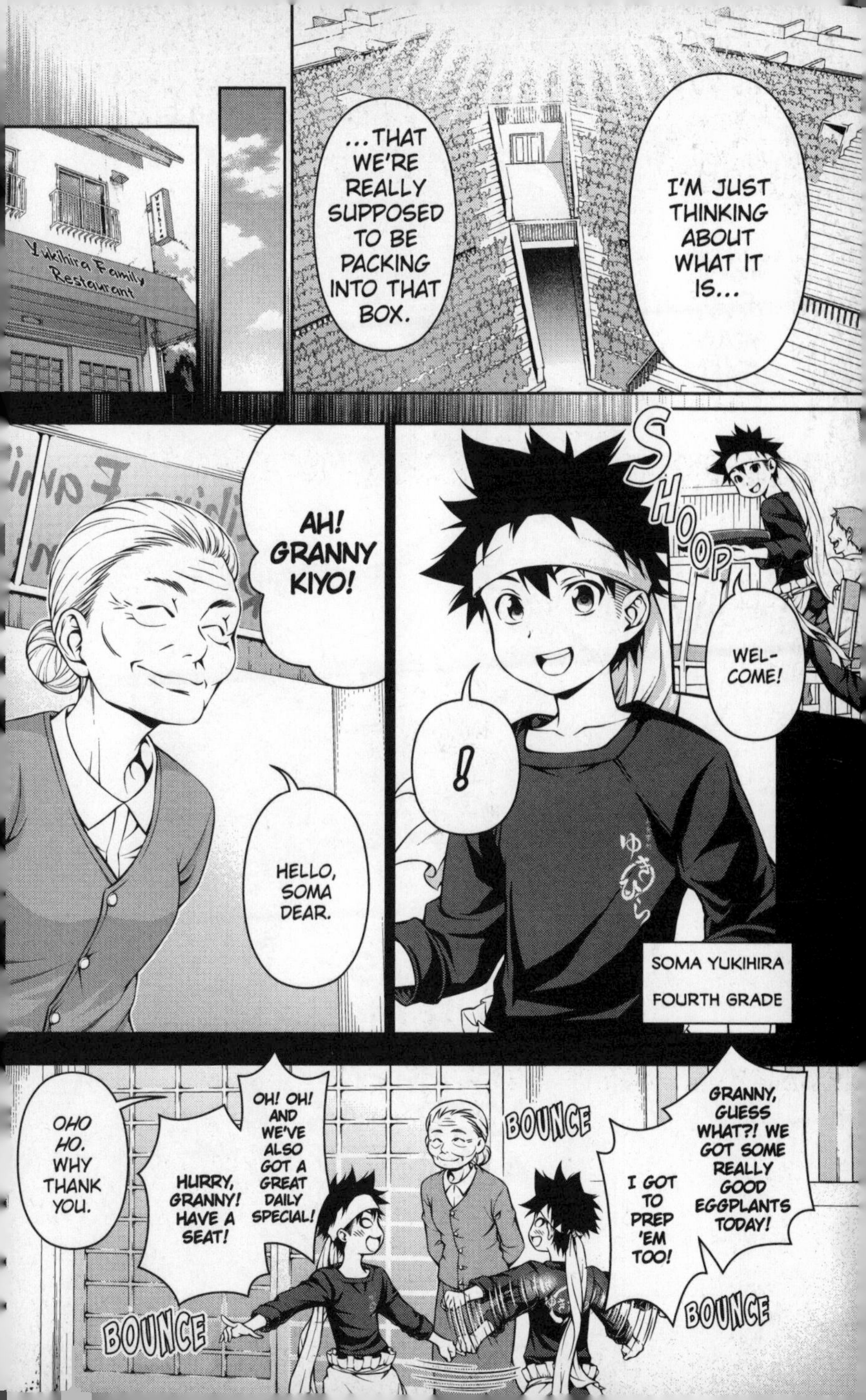
I'M JUST THINKING ABOUT WHAT IT IS...
...THAT WE'RE REALLY SUPPOSED TO BE PACKING INTO THAT BOX.
Yukihira Family Restaurant
SHOOP
WEL-COME!
!
SOMA YUKIHIRA
FOURTH GRADE
AH! GRANNY KIYO!
HELLO, SOMA DEAR.
GRANNY, GUESS WHAT?! WE GOT SOME REALLY GOOD EGGPLANTS TODAY!
I GOT TO PREP 'EM TOO!
BOUNCE
BOUNCE
OH! OH! AND WE'VE ALSO GOT A GREAT DAILY SPECIAL!
HURRY, GRANNY! HAVE A SEAT!
BOUNCE
OHO HO. WHY THANK YOU.

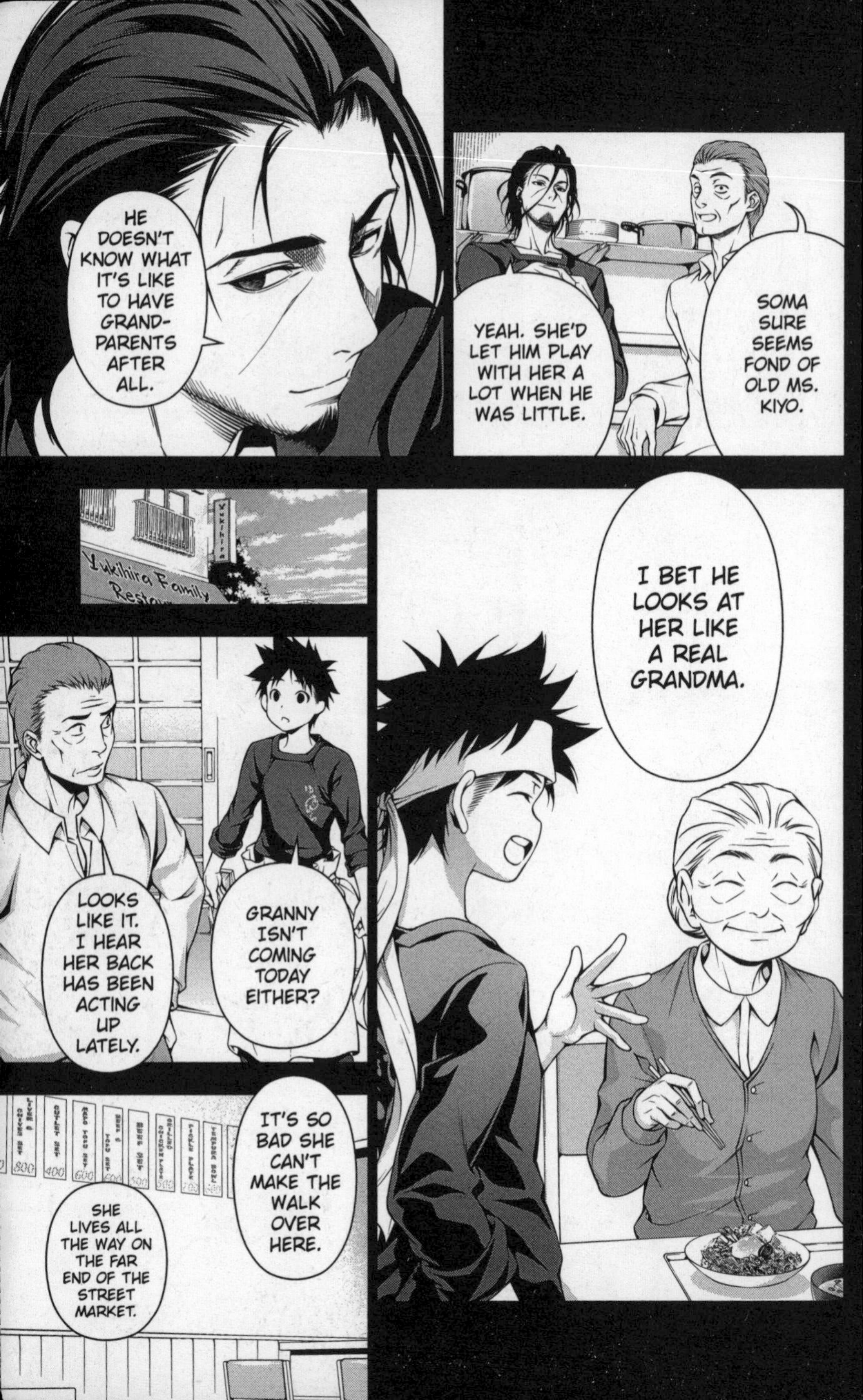
SOMA SURE SEEMS FOND OF OLD MS. KIYO.
YEAH. SHE'D LET HIM PLAY WITH HER A LOT WHEN HE WAS LITTLE.
HE DOESN'T KNOW WHAT IT'S LIKE TO HAVE GRAND-PARENTS AFTER ALL.
I BET HE LOOKS AT HER LIKE A REAL GRANDMA.
Yukihira
GRANNY ISN'T COMING TODAY EITHER?
LOOKS LIKE IT. I HEAR HER BACK HAS BEEN ACTING UP LATELY.
IT'S SO BAD SHE CAN'T MAKE THE WALK OVER HERE.
SHE LIVES ALL THE WAY ON THE FAR END OF THE STREET MARKET.

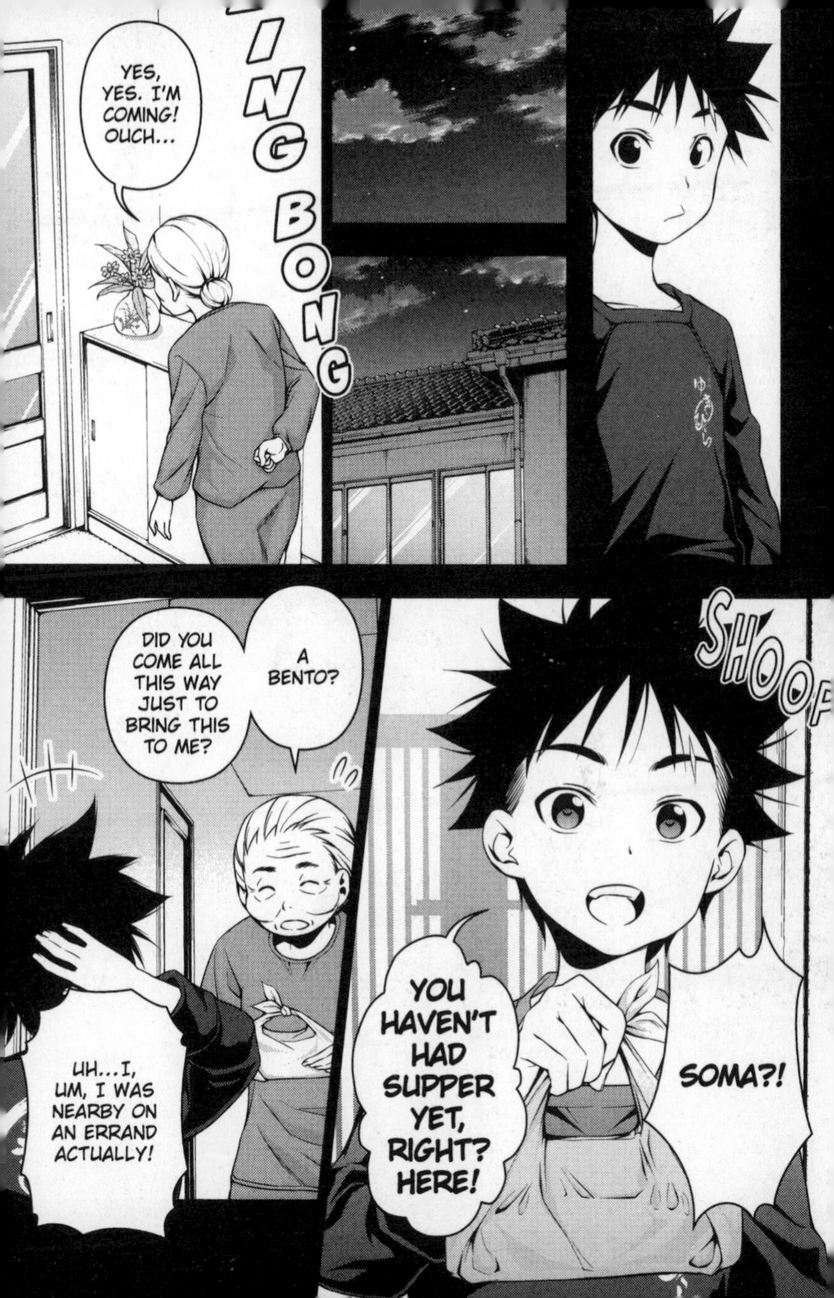
ING BONG
YES, YES. I'M COMING! OUCH...
SHOOF
SOMA?!
YOU HAVEN'T HAD SUPPER YET, RIGHT? HERE!
A BENTO?
DID YOU COME ALL THIS WAY JUST TO BRING THIS TO ME?
UH...I, UM, I WAS NEARBY ON AN ERRAND ACTUALLY!

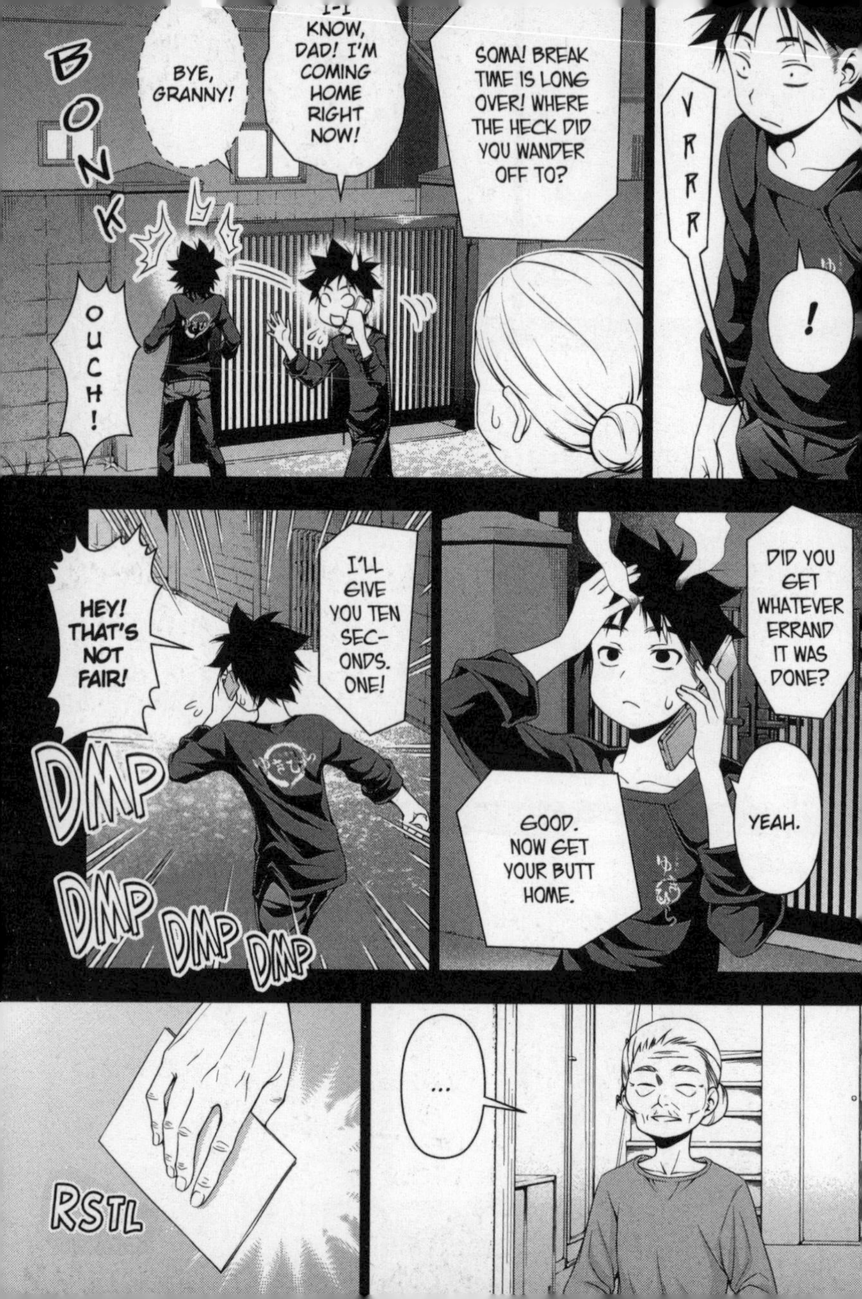
VRRR
!
SOMA! BREAK TIME IS LONG OVER! WHERE THE HECK DID YOU WANDER OFF TO?
I-I KNOW, DAD! I'M COMING HOME RIGHT NOW!
BYE, GRANNY!
BONK
OUCH!
DID YOU GET WHATEVER ERRAND IT WAS DONE?
YEAH.
GOOD. NOW GET YOUR BUTT HOME.
I'LL GIVE YOU TEN SEC- ONDS. ONE!
HEY! THAT'S NOT FAIR!
DMP
DMP
DMP
DMP
...
RSTL

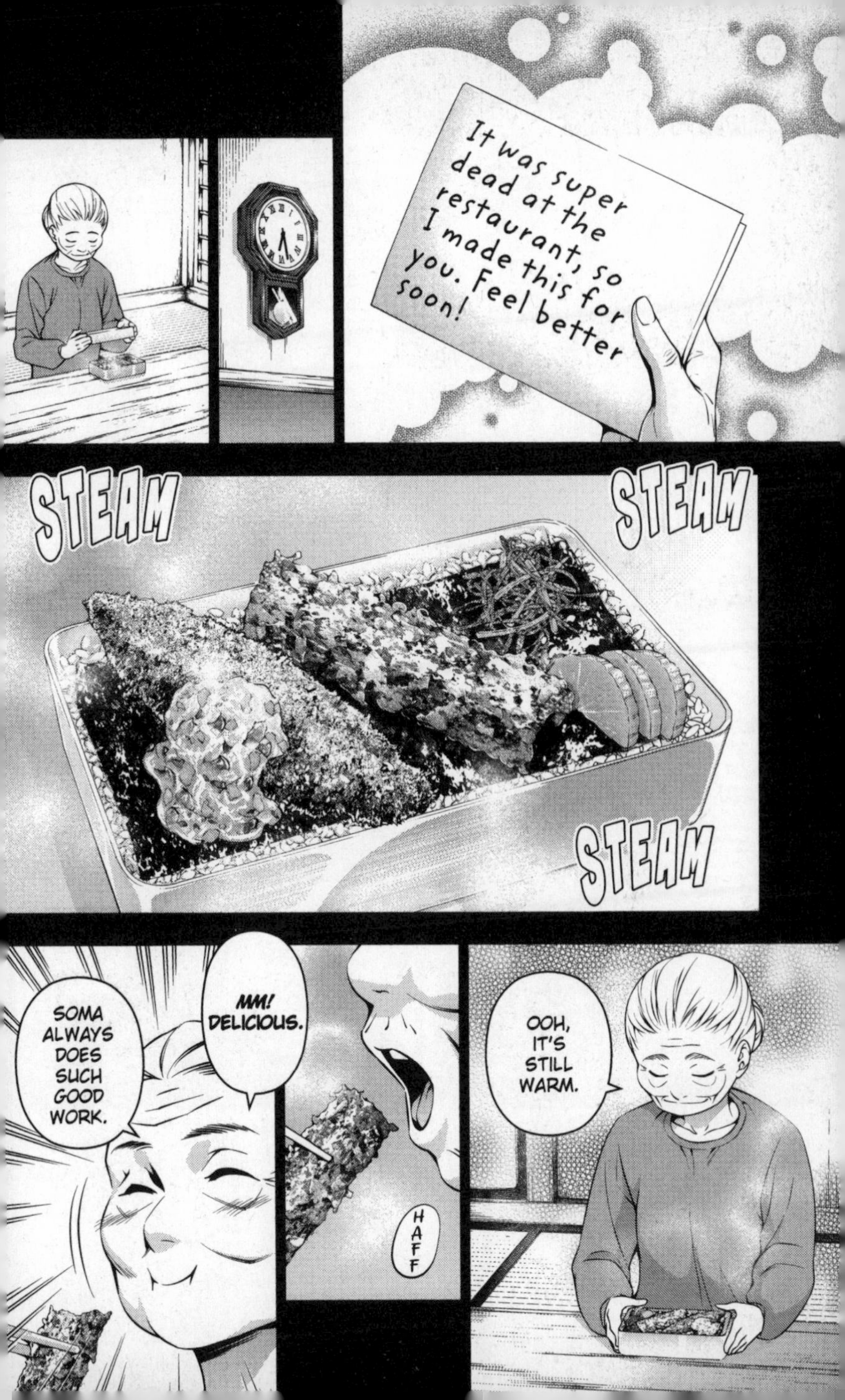
It was super dead at the restaurant, so I made this for you. Feel better soon!
STEAM
STEAM
STEAM
OOH, IT'S STILL WARM.
HAFF
MM! DELICIOUS.
SOMA ALWAYS DOES SUCH GOOD WORK.

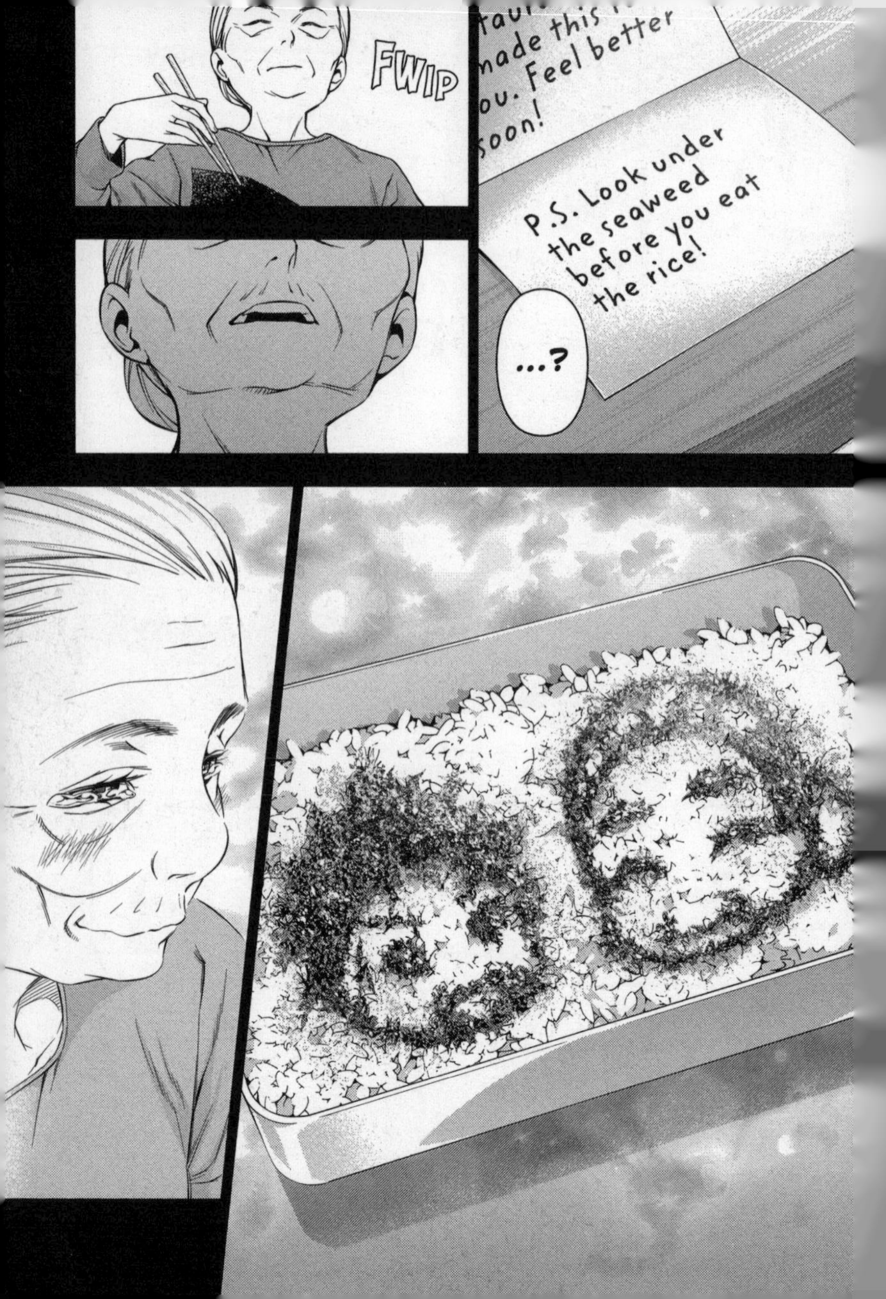

made this
ou. Feel better
soon!
P.S. Look under the seaweed before you eat the rice!
FWIP
...?

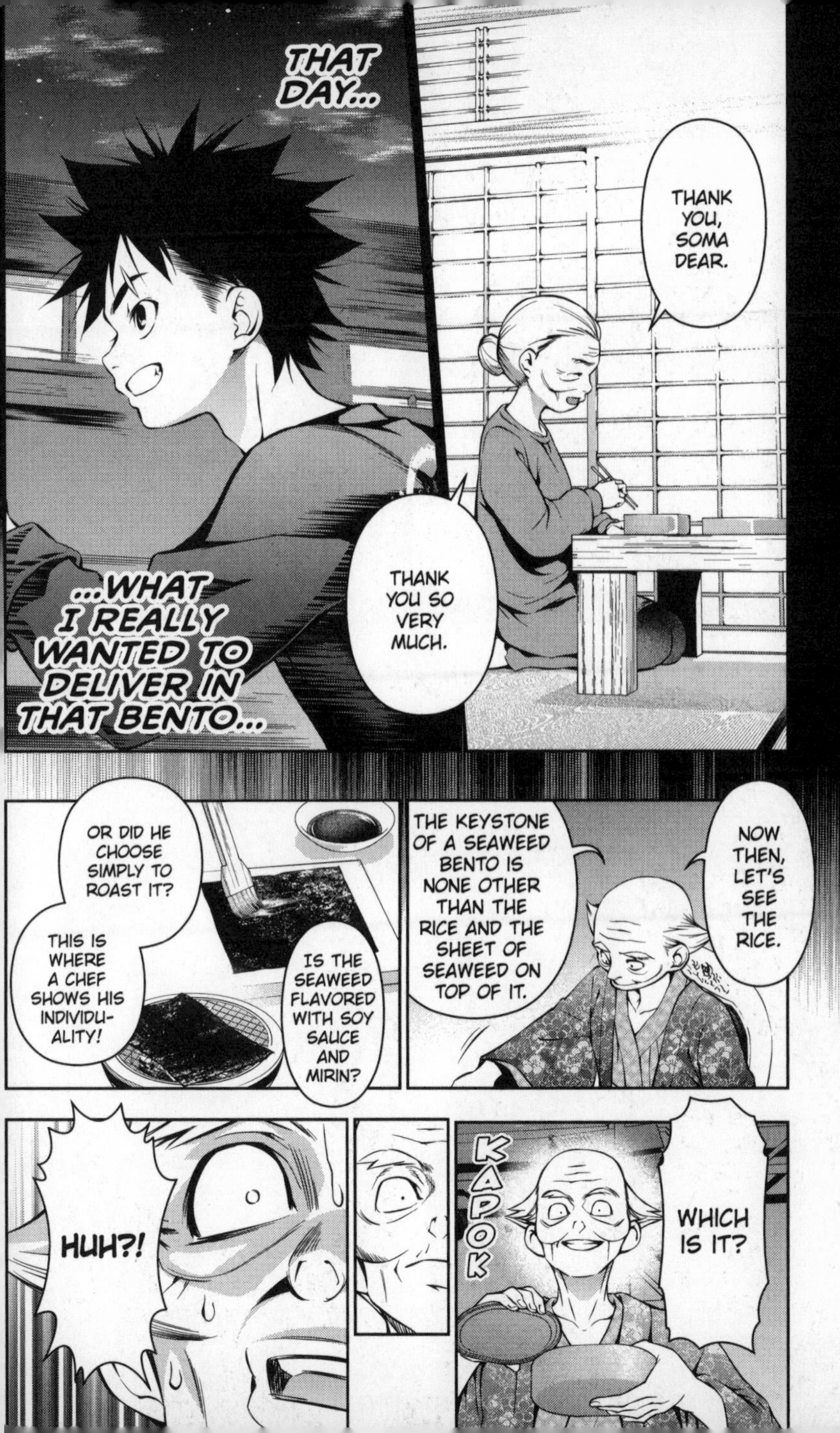
THANK YOU, SOMA DEAR.
THANK YOU SO VERY MUCH.
THAT DAY...
...WHAT I REALLY WANTED TO DELIVER IN THAT BENTO...
NOW THEN, LET'S SEE THE RICE.
THE KEYSTONE OF A SEAWEED BENTO IS NONE OTHER THAN THE RICE AND THE SHEET OF SEAWEED ON TOP OF IT.
IS THE SEAWEED FLAVORED WITH SOY SAUCE AND MIRIN?
OR DID HE CHOOSE SIMPLY TO ROAST IT?
THIS IS WHERE A CHEF SHOWS HIS INDIVIDUALITY!
WHICH IS IT?
KAPOK
HUH?!

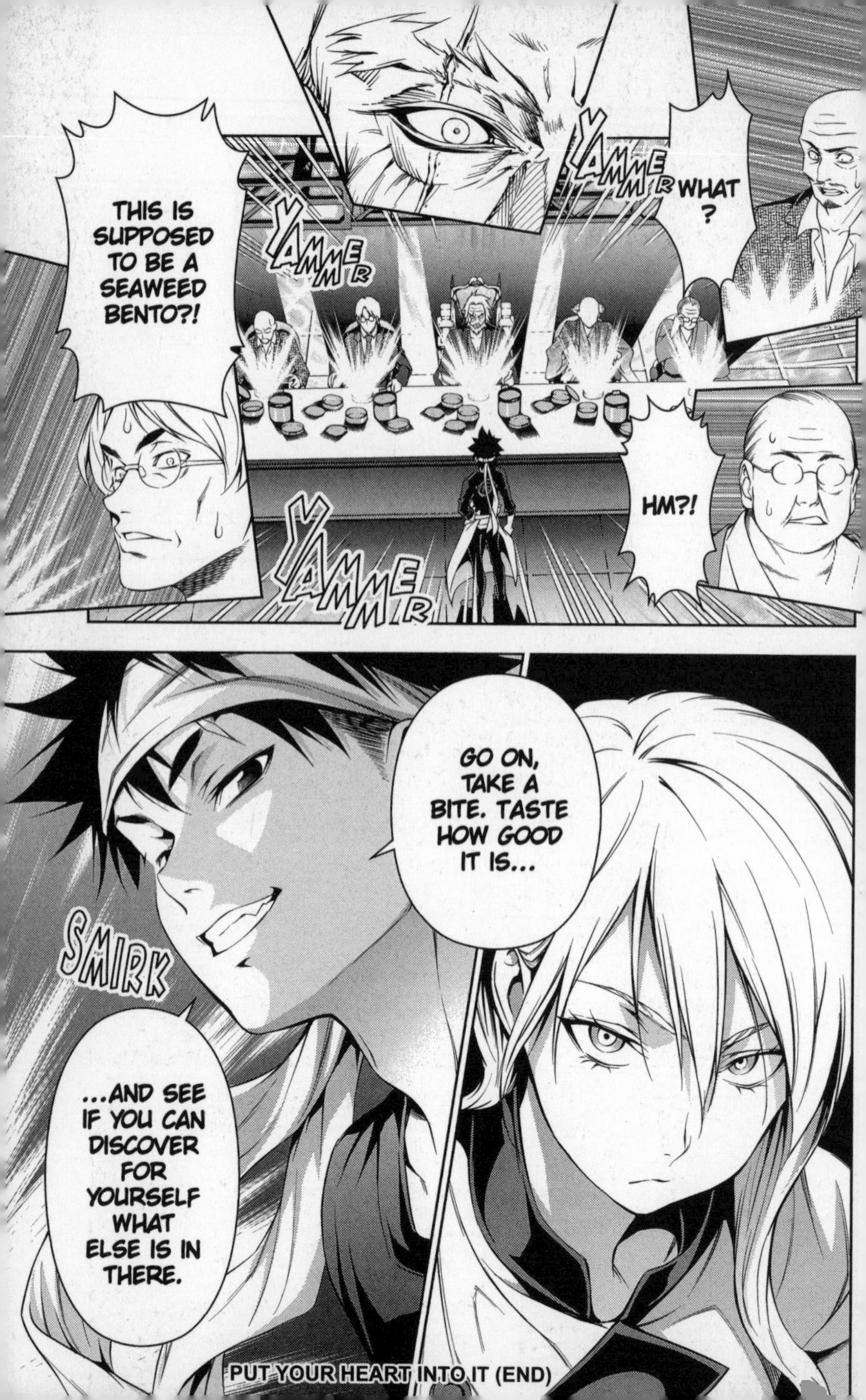
YAMMER
WHAT?
YAMMER
THIS IS SUPPOSED TO BE A SEAWEED BENTO?!
HM?!
YAMMER
GO ON, TAKE A BITE. TASTE HOW GOOD IT IS...
SMIRK
...AND SEE IF YOU CAN DISCOVER FOR YOURSELF WHAT ELSE IS IN THERE.
PUT YOUR HEART INTO IT (END)

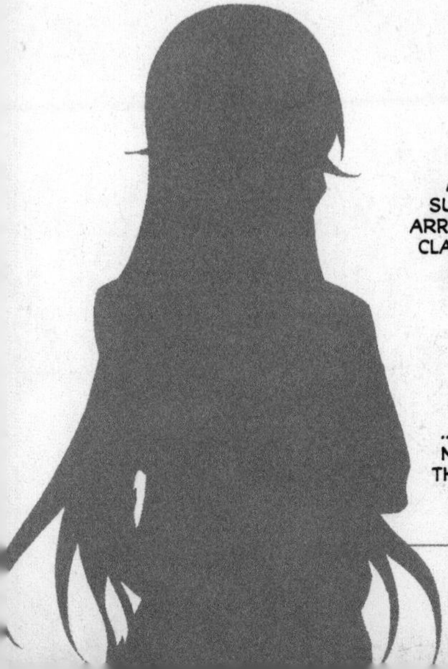

AN OH-SO-BRIEF SUMMER VACATION ARRIVES, WITH THE FALL CLASSIC LOOMING ON THE HORIZON.

WHILE THE STUDENTS TACKLE THE BREAK WITH THEIR VARIOUS PLANS AND DREAMS...

...ONE PERSON WHO'S NOT PARTICIPATING IN THE CLASSIC MUST FIND SOMETHING ELSE TO FILL HER TIME...

SIDE STORY–ERINA'S SUMMER VACATION

RELEASED IN *WEEKLY SHONEN JUMP*'S ISSUE 4/5 OF 2014.

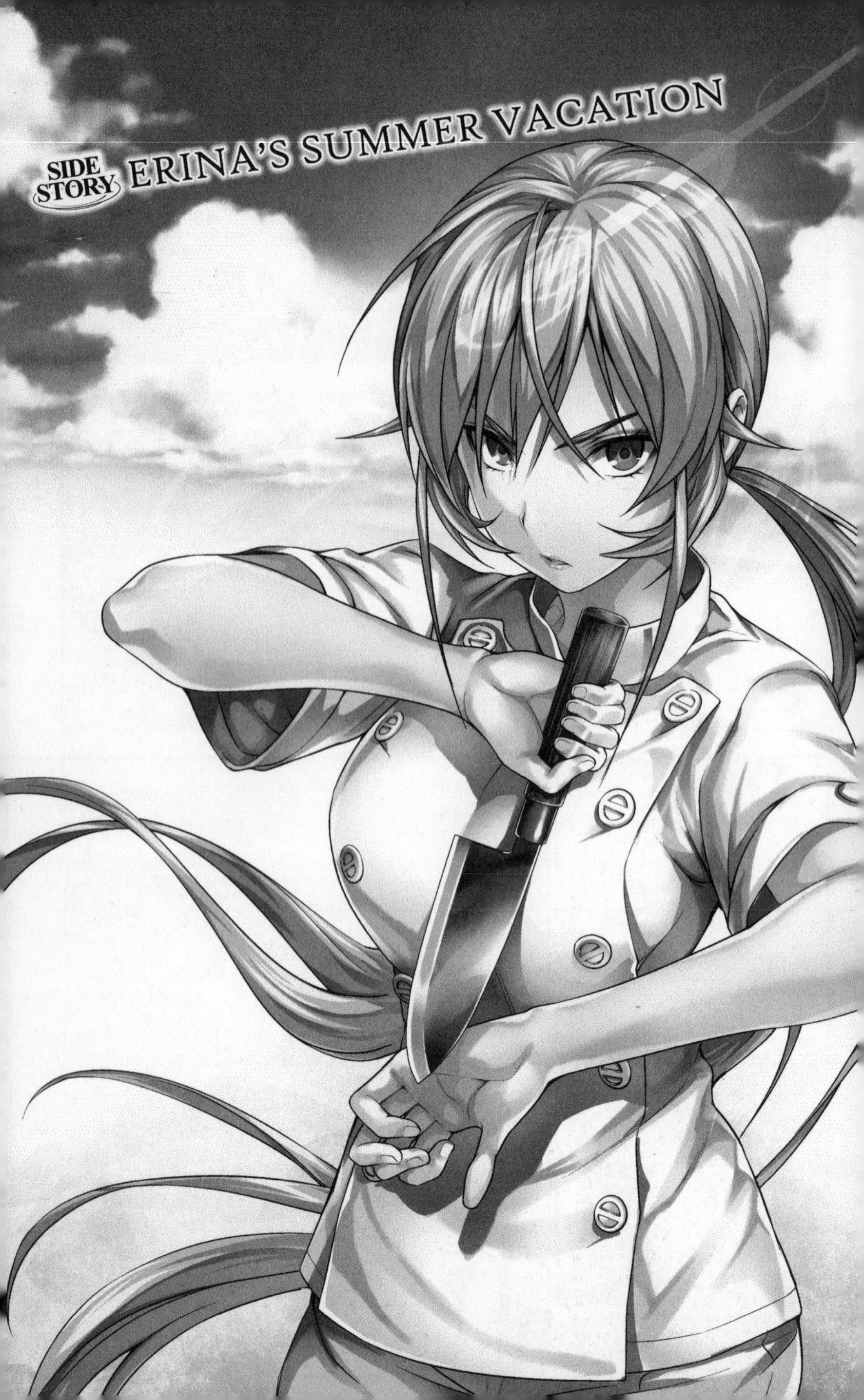
SIDE STORY
ERINA'S SUMMER VACATION

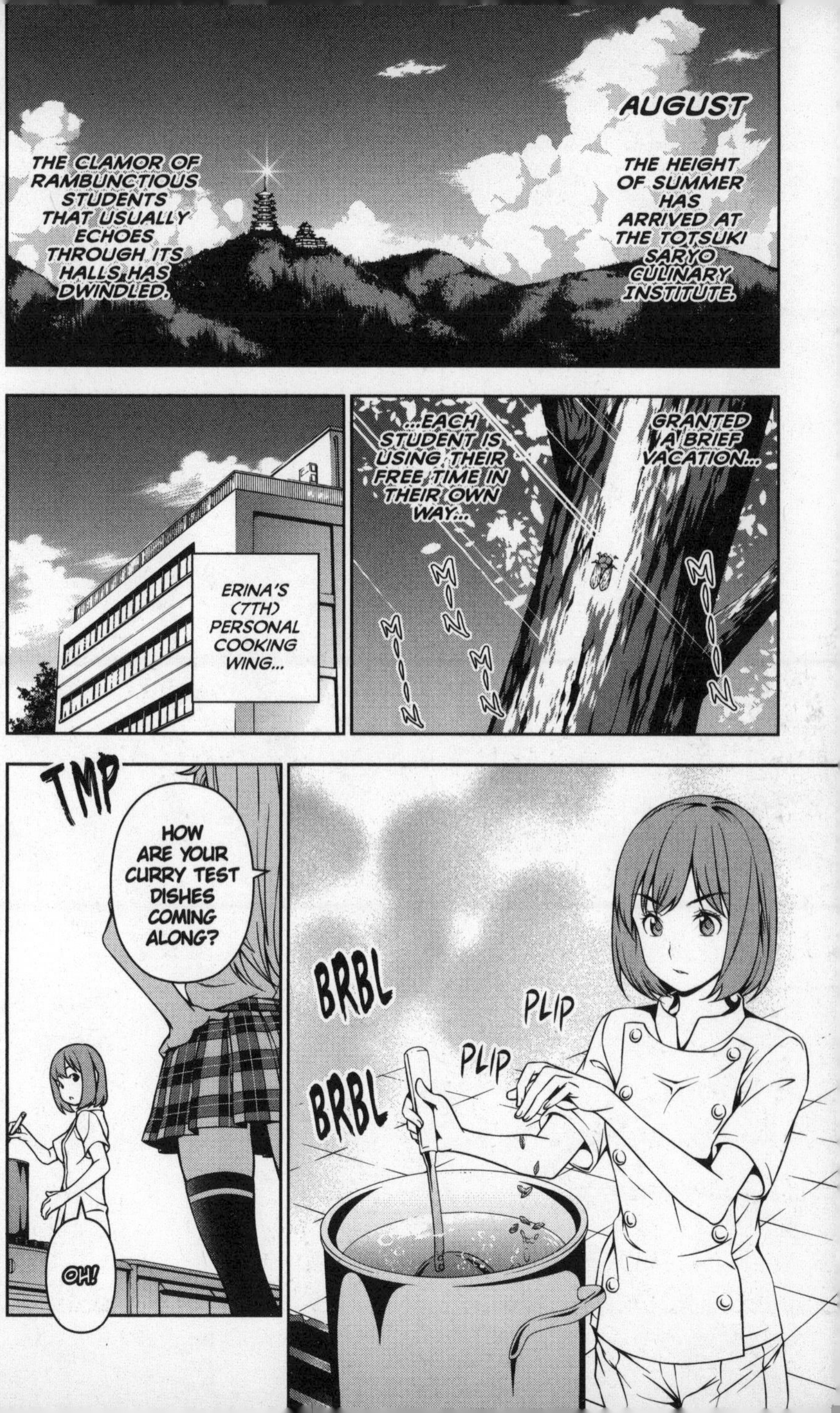
AUGUST
THE HEIGHT OF SUMMER HAS ARRIVED AT THE TOTSUKI SARYO CULINARY INSTITUTE.
THE CLAMOR OF RAMBUNCTIOUS STUDENTS THAT USUALLY ECHOES THROUGH ITS HALLS HAS DWINDLED.
GRANTED A BRIEF VACATION...
...EACH STUDENT IS USING THEIR FREE TIME IN THEIR OWN WAY...
MIIIN
MIN
MIN
MIIIN
ERINA'S (7TH) PERSONAL COOKING WING...
PLIP
PLIP
BRBL
BRBL
TMP
HOW ARE YOUR CURRY TEST DISHES COMING ALONG?
OH!

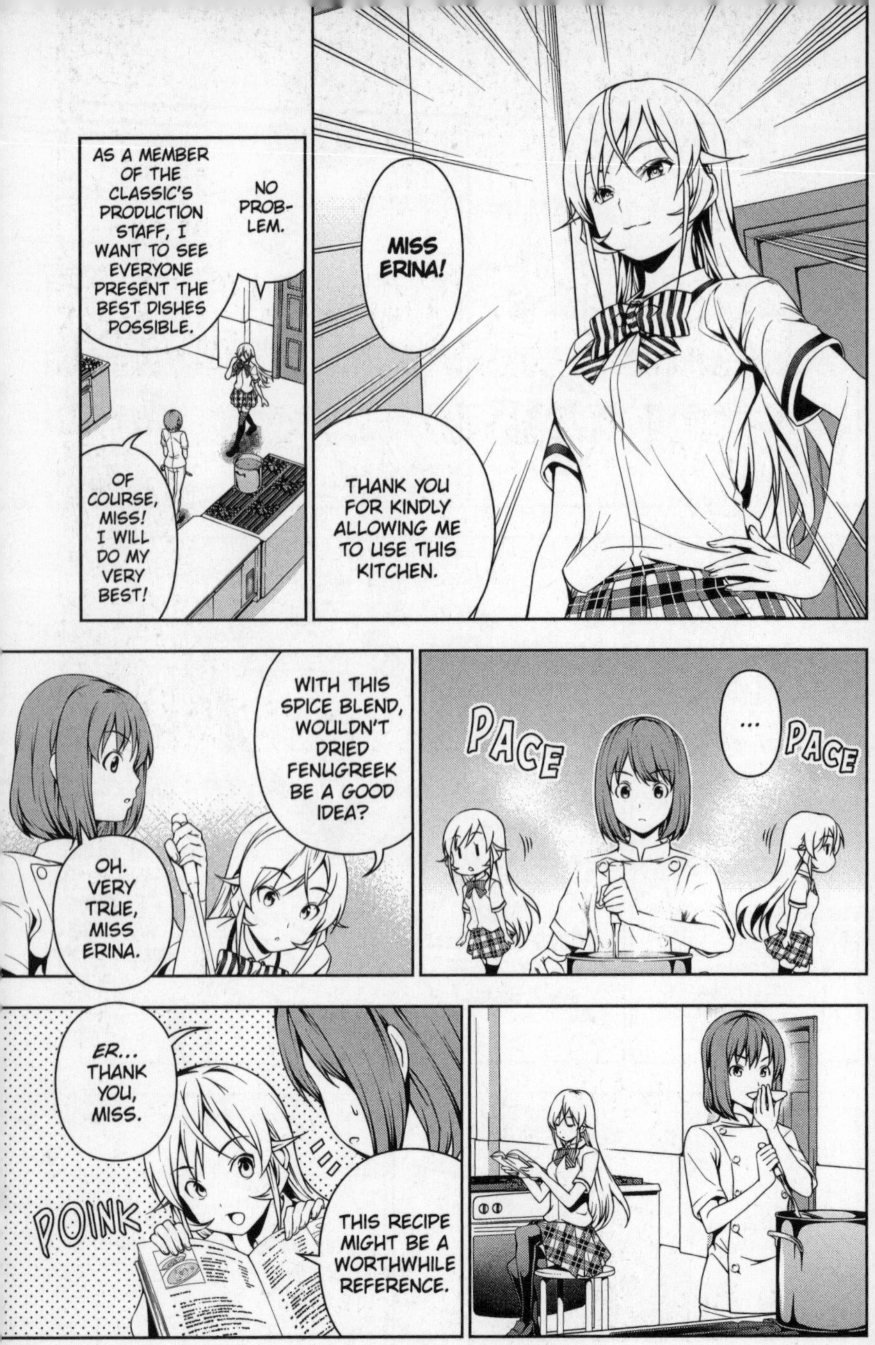
MISS ERINA!
THANK YOU FOR KINDLY ALLOWING ME TO USE THIS KITCHEN.
NO PROBLEM.
AS A MEMBER OF THE CLASSIC'S PRODUCTION STAFF, I WANT TO SEE EVERYONE PRESENT THE BEST DISHES POSSIBLE.
OF COURSE, MISS! I WILL DO MY VERY BEST!
PACE
...
PACE
WITH THIS SPICE BLEND, WOULDN'T DRIED FENUGREEK BE A GOOD IDEA?
OH. VERY TRUE, MISS ERINA.
THIS RECIPE MIGHT BE A WORTHWHILE REFERENCE.
ER... THANK YOU, MISS.
POINK

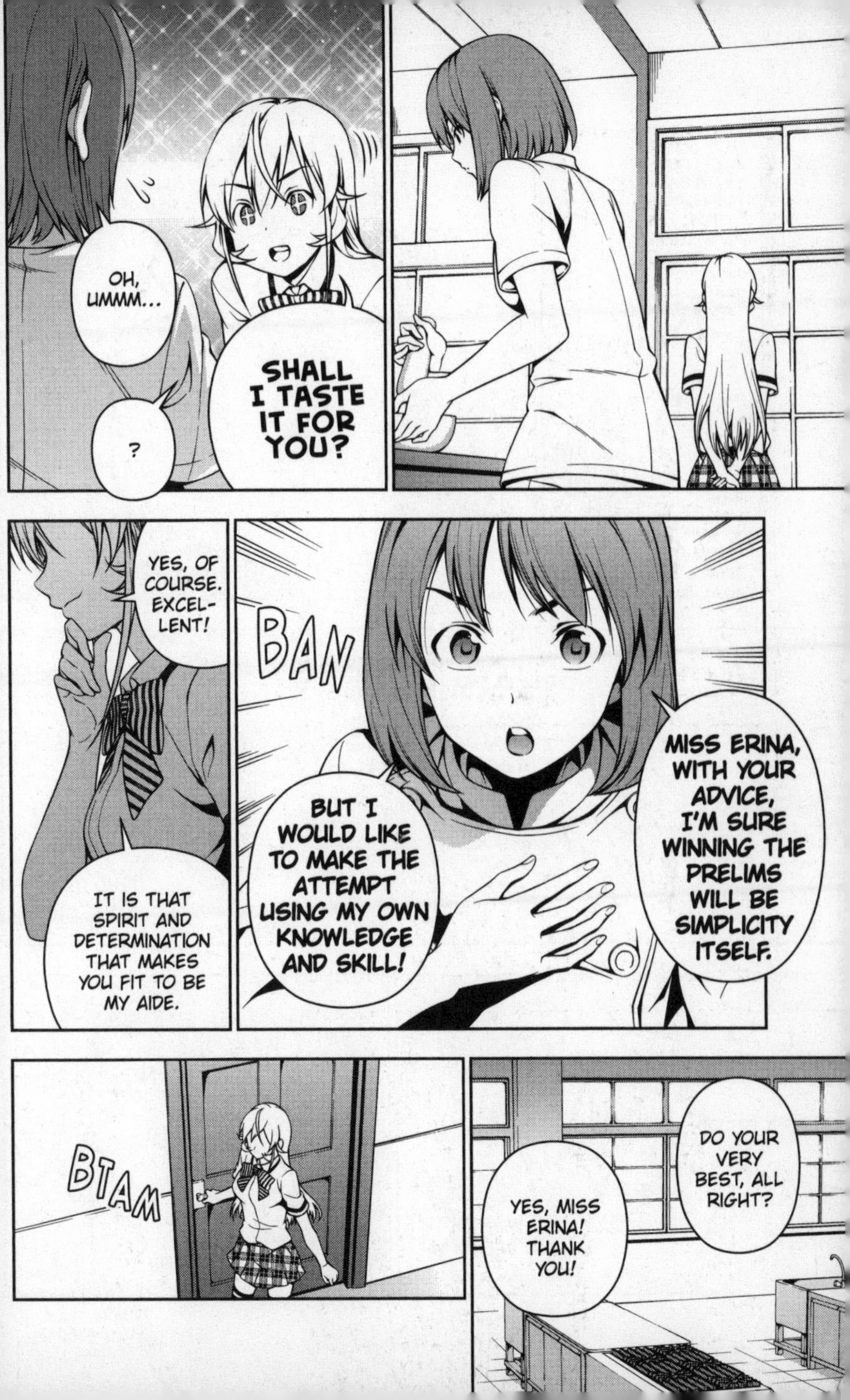
OH, UMMM...
SHALL I TASTE IT FOR YOU?
?
MISS ERINA, WITH YOUR ADVICE, I'M SURE WINNING THE PRELIMS WILL BE SIMPLICITY ITSELF.
BAN
BUT I WOULD LIKE TO MAKE THE ATTEMPT USING MY OWN KNOWLEDGE AND SKILL!
YES, OF COURSE. EXCEL-LENT!
IT IS THAT SPIRIT AND DETERMINATION THAT MAKES YOU FIT TO BE MY AIDE.
DO YOUR VERY BEST, ALL RIGHT?
YES, MISS ERINA! THANK YOU!
BTAM

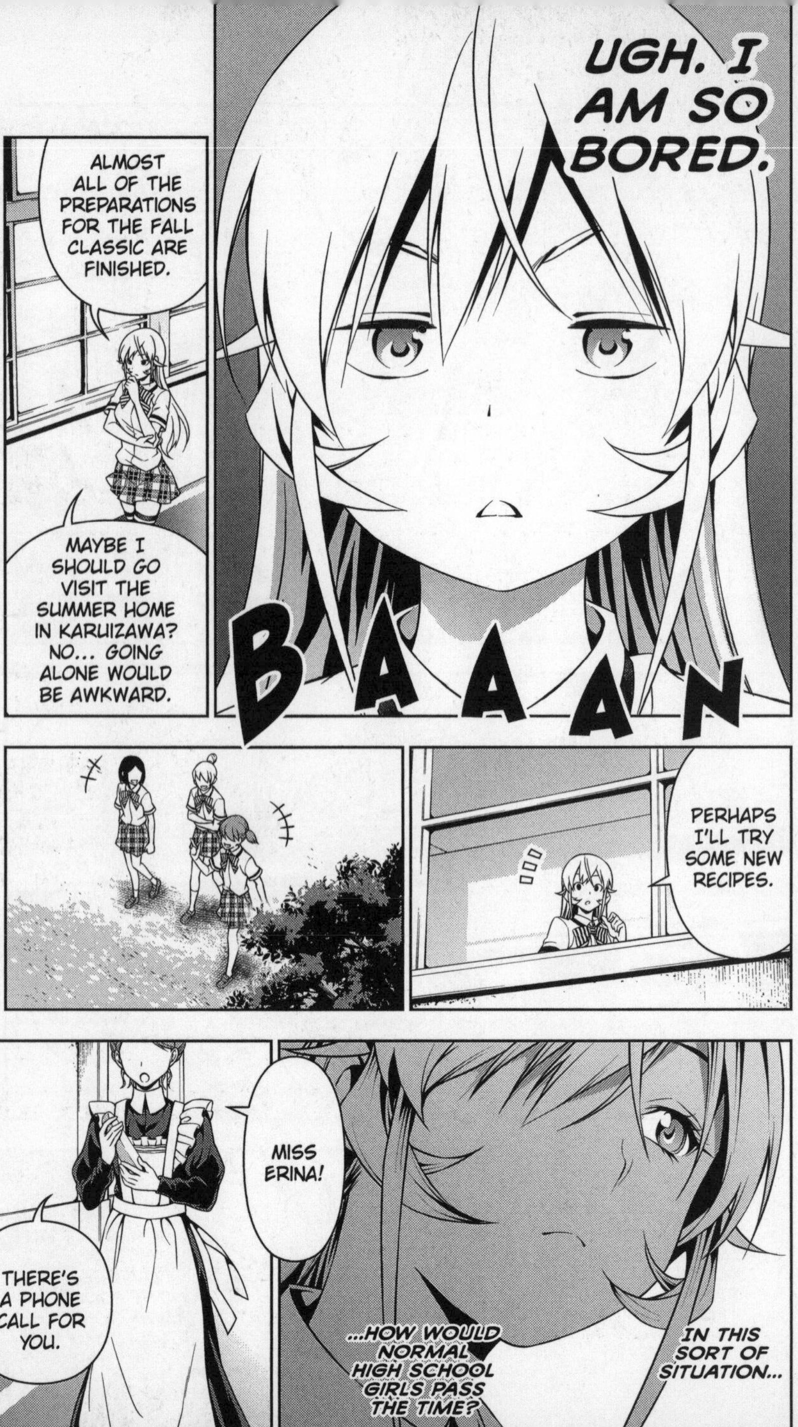
UGH. I AM SO BORED.
BAAAN
ALMOST ALL OF THE PREPARATIONS FOR THE FALL CLASSIC ARE FINISHED.
MAYBE I SHOULD GO VISIT THE SUMMER HOME IN KARUIZAWA? NO... GOING ALONE WOULD BE AWKWARD.
PERHAPS I'LL TRY SOME NEW RECIPES.
IN THIS SORT OF SITUATION...
...HOW WOULD NORMAL HIGH SCHOOL GIRLS PASS THE TIME?
MISS ERINA!
THERE'S A PHONE CALL FOR YOU.

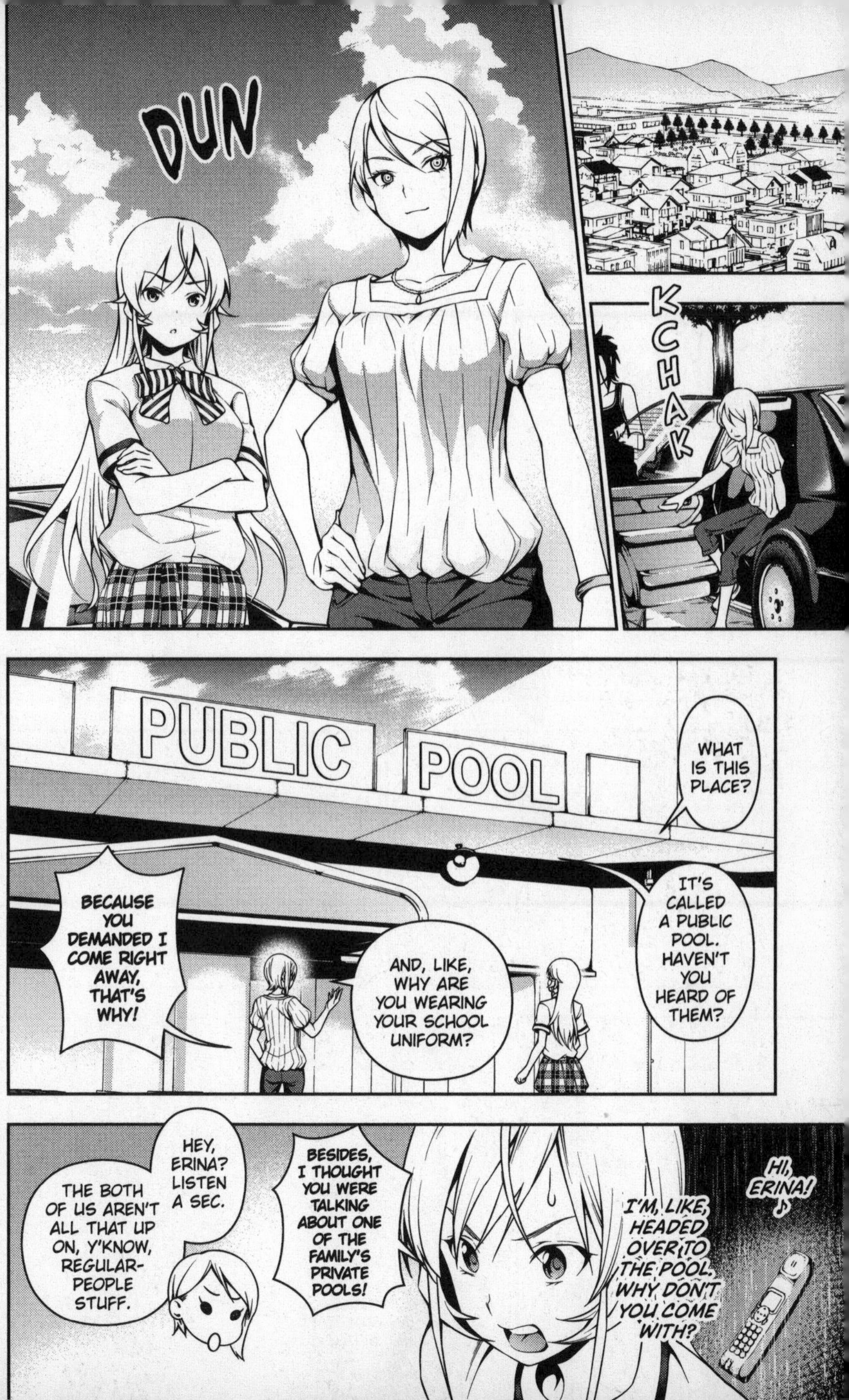
KCHAK
DUN
PUBLIC POOL
WHAT IS THIS PLACE?
IT'S CALLED A PUBLIC POOL. HAVEN'T YOU HEARD OF THEM?
AND, LIKE, WHY ARE YOU WEARING YOUR SCHOOL UNIFORM?
BECAUSE YOU DEMANDED I COME RIGHT AWAY, THAT'S WHY!
HI, ERINA! ♪
I'M, LIKE, HEADED OVER TO THE POOL. WHY DON'T YOU COME WITH?
BESIDES, I THOUGHT YOU WERE TALKING ABOUT ONE OF THE FAMILY'S PRIVATE POOLS!
HEY, ERINA? LISTEN A SEC.
THE BOTH OF US AREN'T ALL THAT UP ON, Y'KNOW, REGULAR-PEOPLE STUFF.

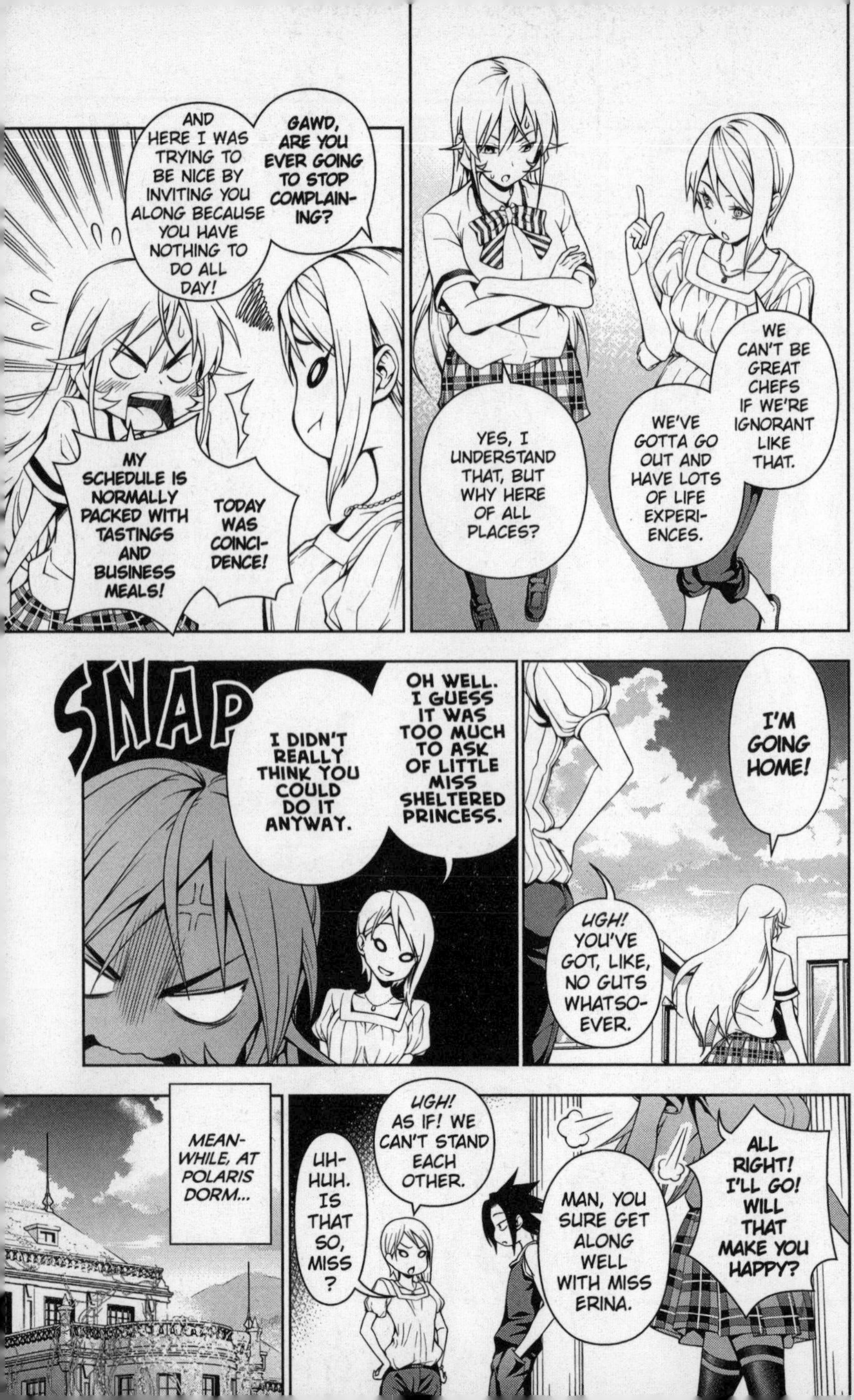
WE CAN'T BE GREAT CHEFS IF WE'RE IGNORANT LIKE THAT.
WE'VE GOTTA GO OUT AND HAVE LOTS OF LIFE EXPERI-ENCES.
YES, I UNDERSTAND THAT, BUT WHY HERE OF ALL PLACES?
GAWD, ARE YOU EVER GOING TO STOP COMPLAIN-ING?
AND HERE I WAS TRYING TO BE NICE BY INVITING YOU ALONG BECAUSE YOU HAVE NOTHING TO DO ALL DAY!
TODAY WAS COINCI-DENCE!
MY SCHEDULE IS NORMALLY PACKED WITH TASTINGS AND BUSINESS MEALS!
I'M GOING HOME!
UGH! YOU'VE GOT, LIKE, NO GUTS WHATSO-EVER.
SNAP
OH WELL. I GUESS IT WAS TOO MUCH TO ASK OF LITTLE MISS SHELTERED PRINCESS.
I DIDN'T REALLY THINK YOU COULD DO IT ANYWAY.
ALL RIGHT! I'LL GO! WILL THAT MAKE YOU HAPPY?
MAN, YOU SURE GET ALONG WELL WITH MISS ERINA.
UGH! AS IF! WE CAN'T STAND EACH OTHER.
UH-HUH. IS THAT SO, MISS?
MEAN-WHILE, AT POLARIS DORM...

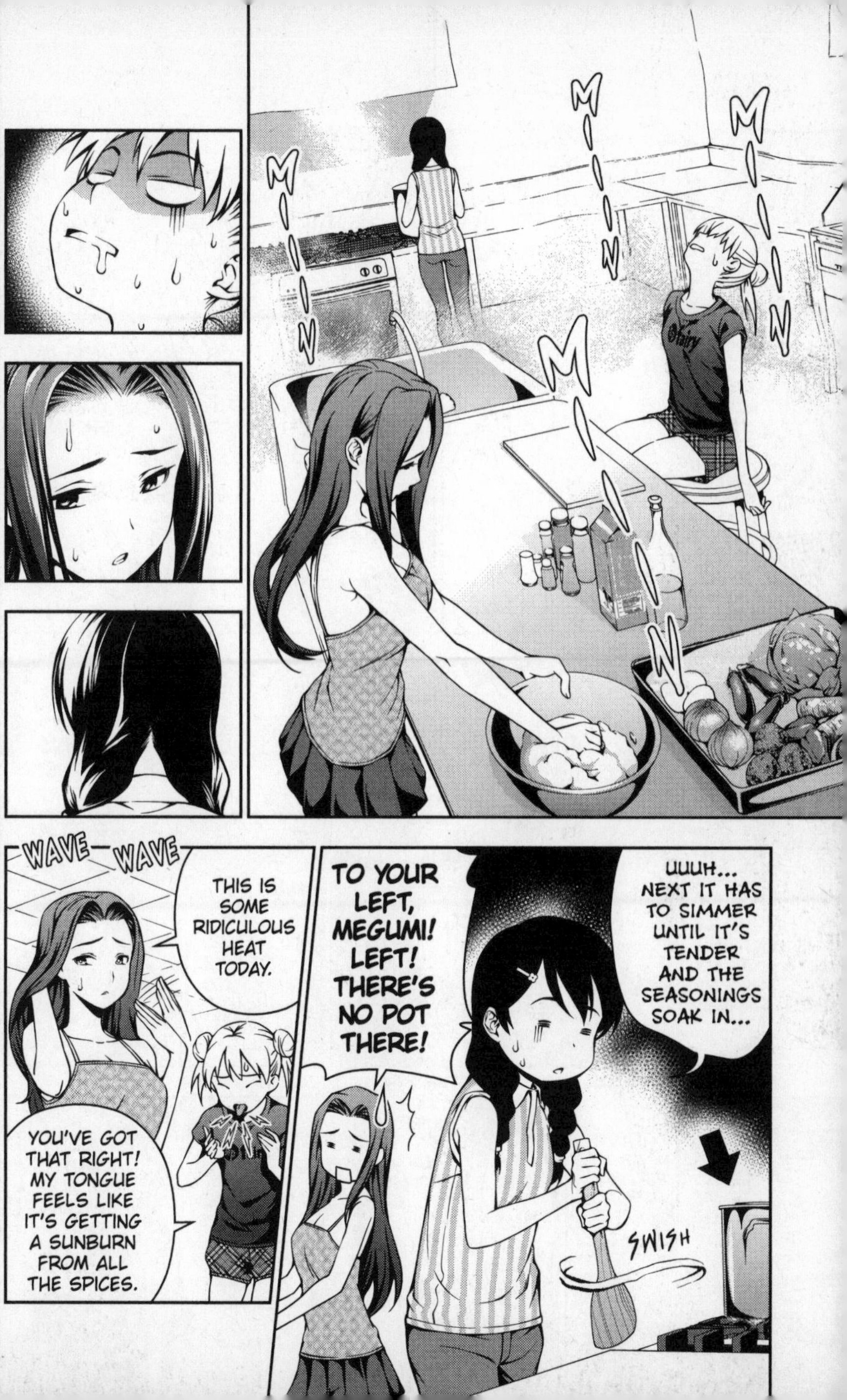
MIIIIN
MIIIIN
MIIIIN
MIIIIN
UUUH... NEXT IT HAS TO SIMMER UNTIL IT'S TENDER AND THE SEASONINGS SOAK IN...
TO YOUR LEFT, MEGUMI! LEFT! THERE'S NO POT THERE!
SWISH
WAVE WAVE
THIS IS SOME RIDICULOUS HEAT TODAY.
YOU'VE GOT THAT RIGHT! MY TONGUE FEELS LIKE IT'S GETTING A SUNBURN FROM ALL THE SPICES.

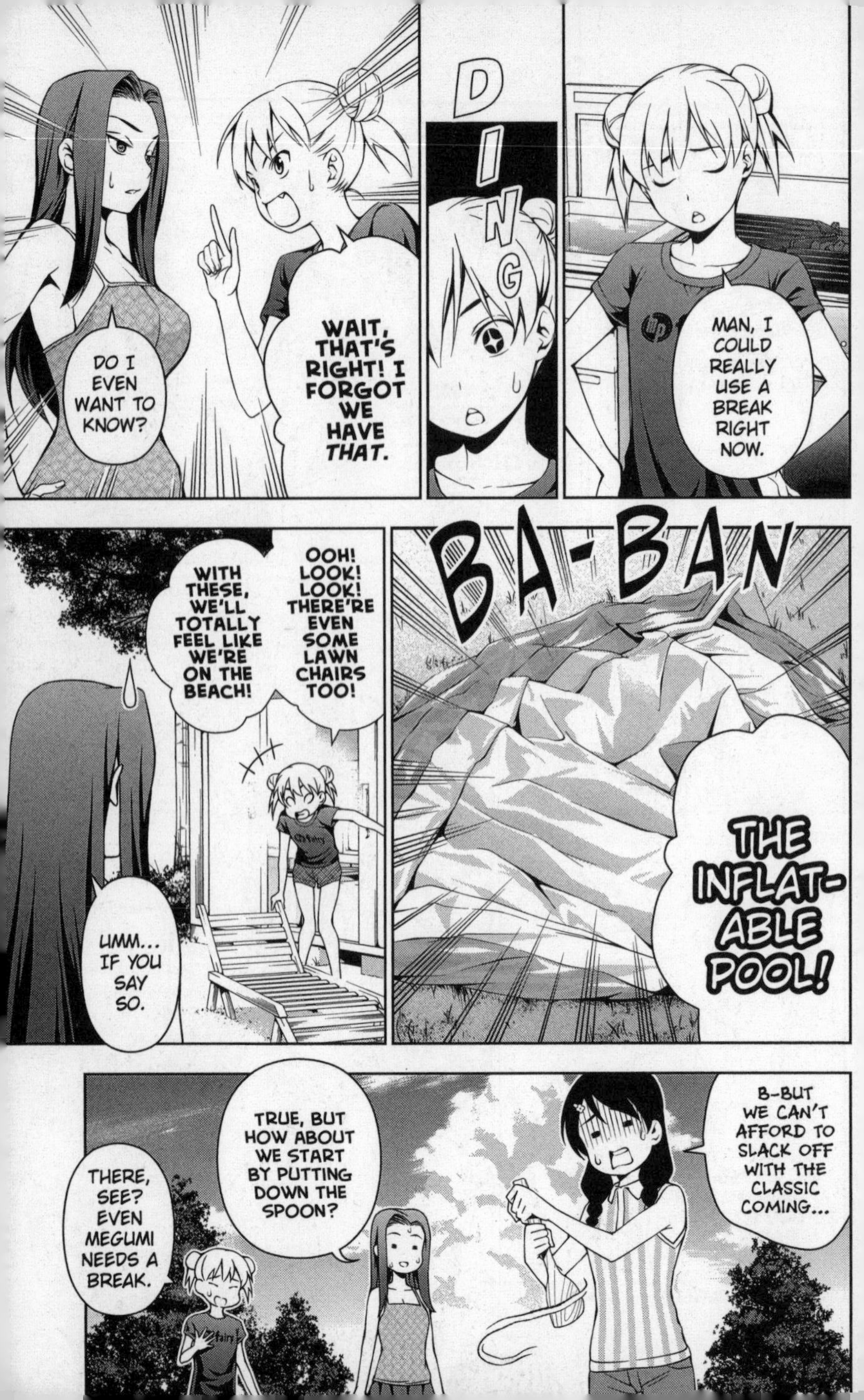
MAN, I COULD REALLY USE A BREAK RIGHT NOW.
DING
WAIT, THAT'S RIGHT! I FORGOT WE HAVE *THAT*.
DO I EVEN WANT TO KNOW?
BA-BAN
THE INFLAT-ABLE POOL!
OOH! LOOK! LOOK! THERE'RE EVEN SOME LAWN CHAIRS TOO!
WITH THESE, WE'LL TOTALLY FEEL LIKE WE'RE ON THE BEACH!
UMM... IF YOU SAY SO.
B-BUT WE CAN'T AFFORD TO SLACK OFF WITH THE CLASSIC COMING...
TRUE, BUT HOW ABOUT WE START BY PUTTING DOWN THE SPOON?
THERE, SEE? EVEN MEGUMI NEEDS A BREAK.

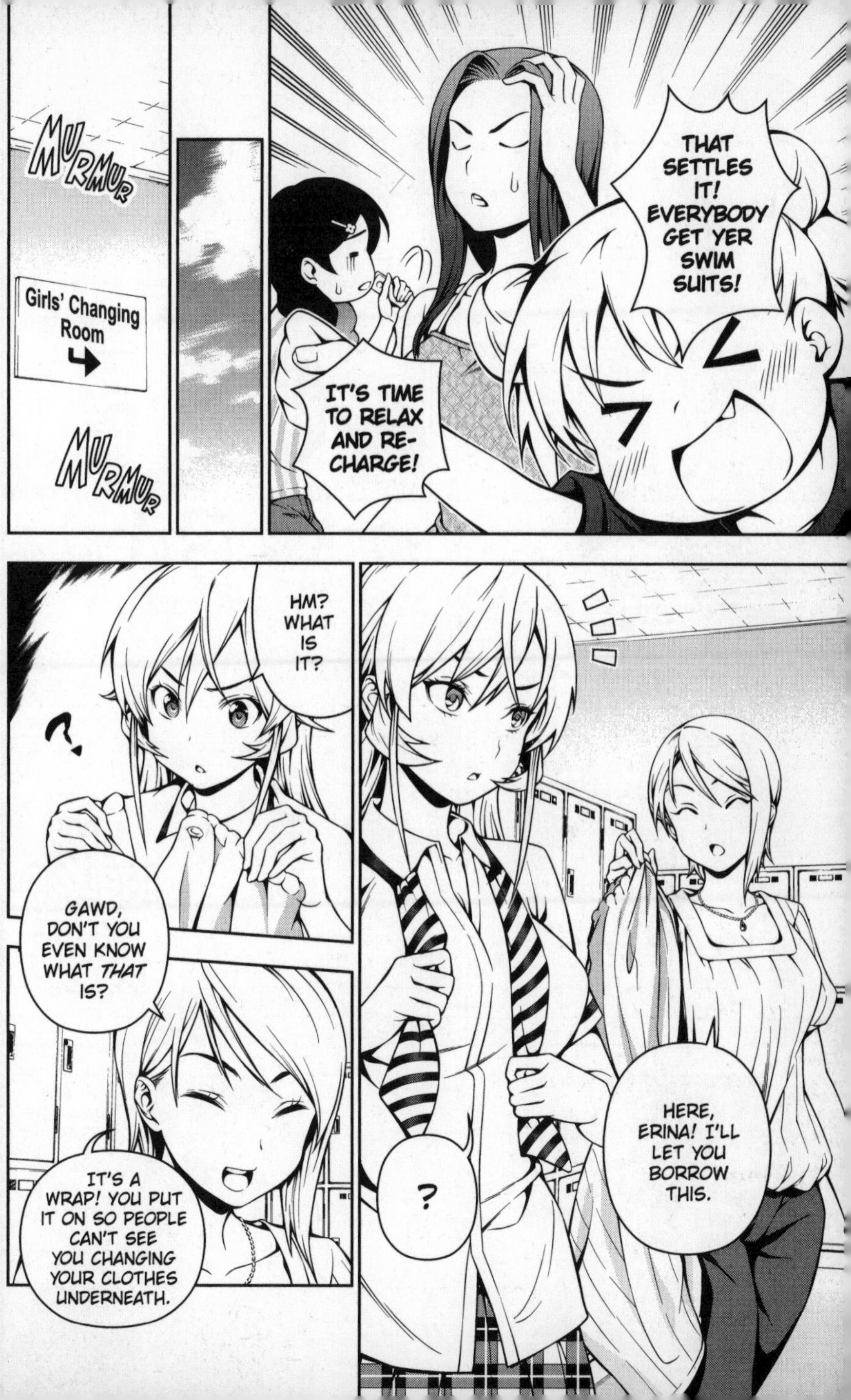
THAT SETTLES IT! EVERYBODY GET YER SWIM SUITS!
IT'S TIME TO RELAX AND RE-CHARGE!
MURMUR
Girls' Changing Room
MURMUR
HERE, ERINA! I'LL LET YOU BORROW THIS.
?
HM? WHAT IS IT?
?
GAWD, DON'T YOU EVEN KNOW WHAT *THAT* IS?
IT'S A WRAP! YOU PUT IT ON SO PEOPLE CAN'T SEE YOU CHANGING YOUR CLOTHES UNDERNEATH.

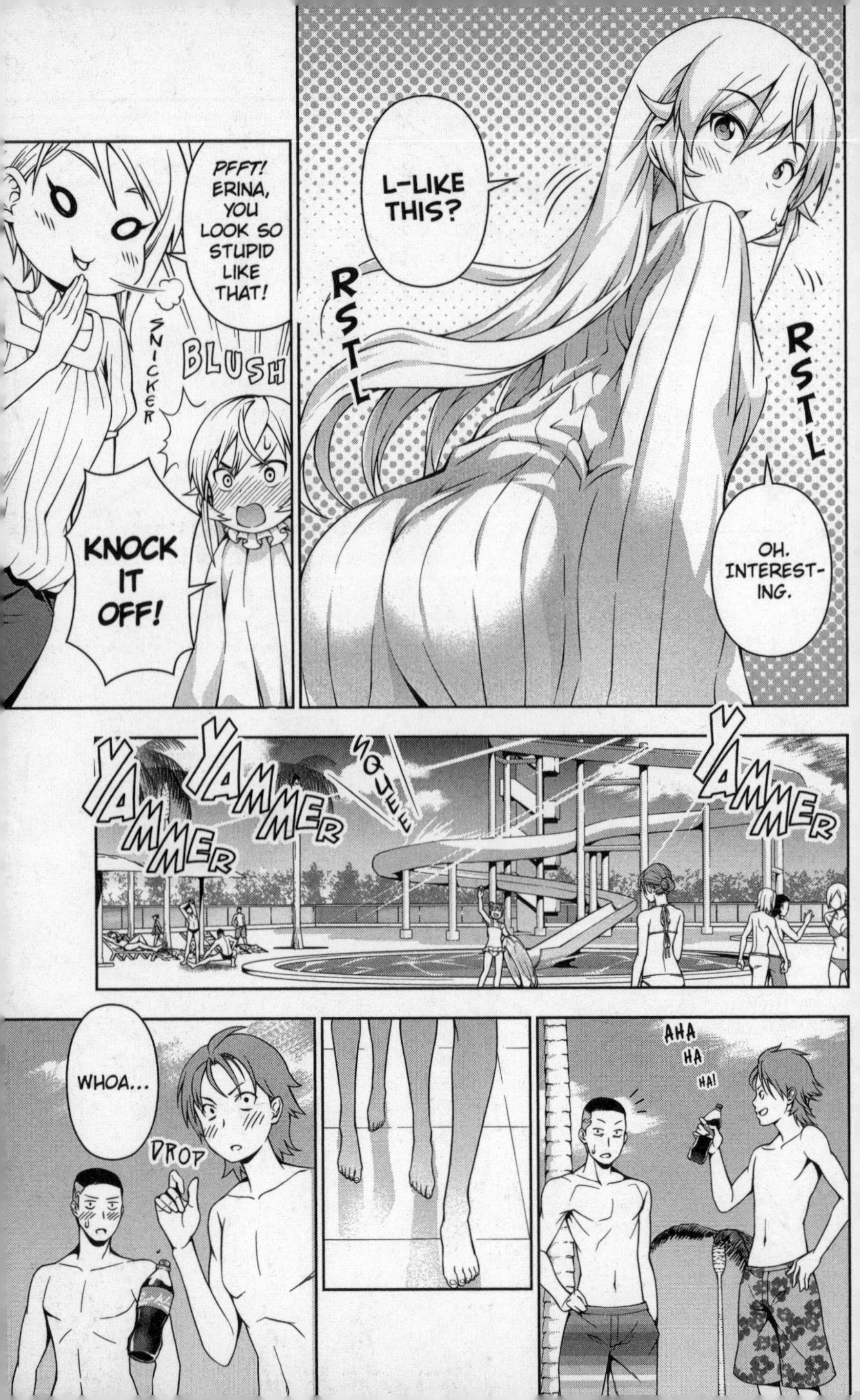
L-LIKE THIS?
RSTL
RSTL
OH. INTERESTING.
PFFT! ERINA, YOU LOOK SO STUPID LIKE THAT!
SNICKER
BLUSH
KNOCK IT OFF!
YAMMER
YAMMER
YAMMER
AHA HA HA!
WHOA...
DROP

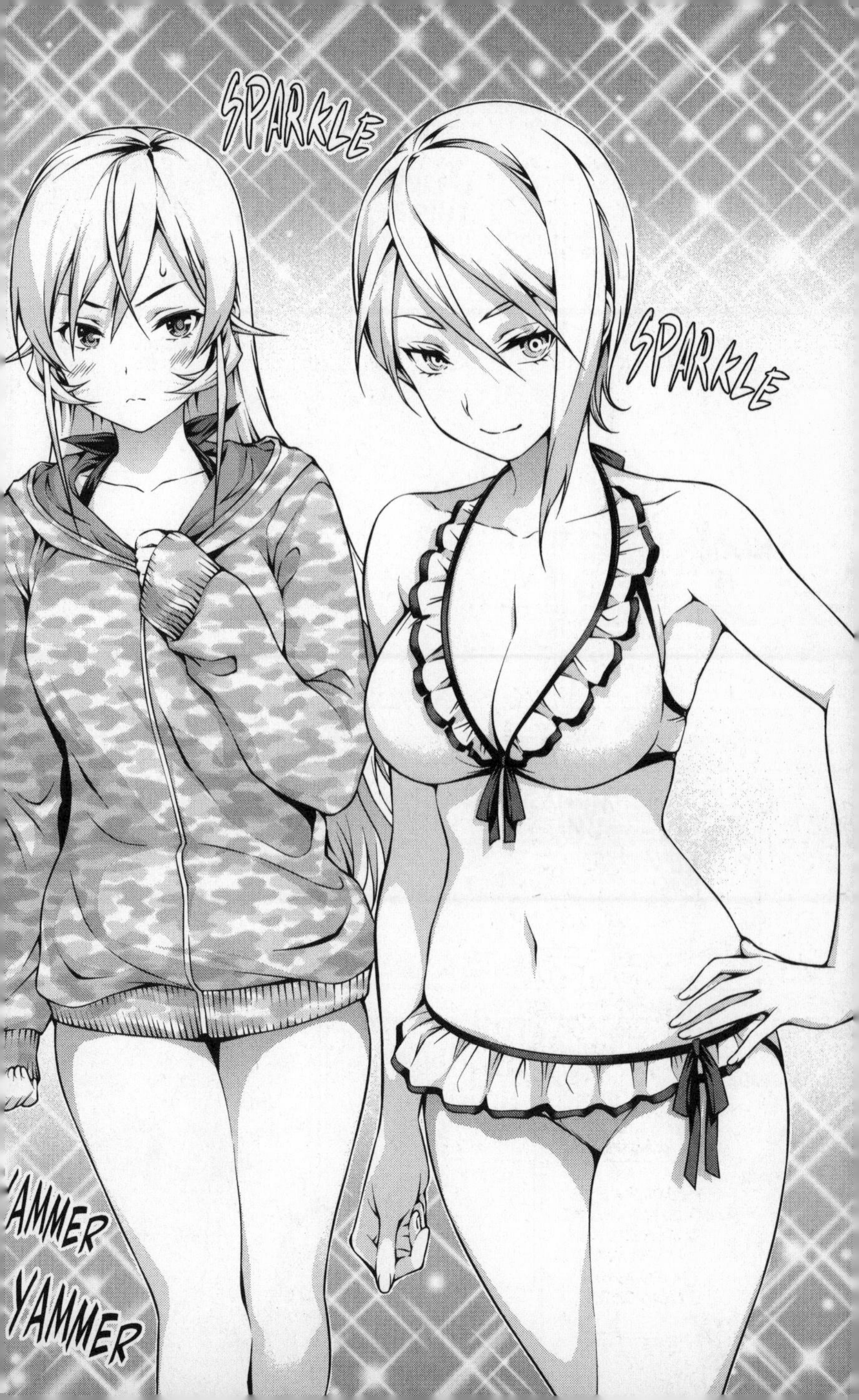
SPARKLE
SPARKLE
YAMMER YAMMER

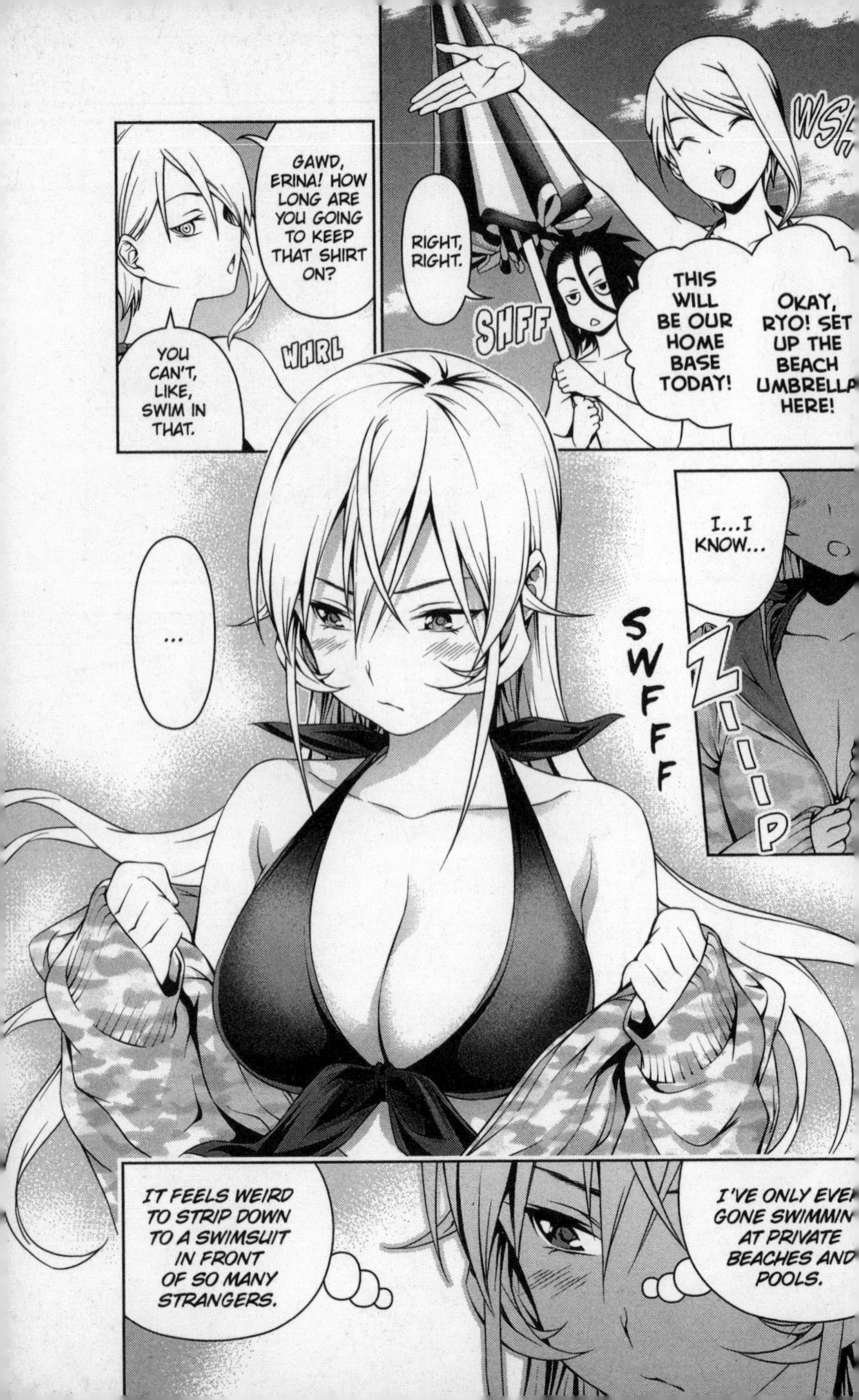
WSH
OKAY, RYO! SET UP THE BEACH UMBRELLA HERE!
THIS WILL BE OUR HOME BASE TODAY!
RIGHT, RIGHT.
SHFF
GAWD, ERINA! HOW LONG ARE YOU GOING TO KEEP THAT SHIRT ON?
WHRL
YOU CAN'T, LIKE, SWIM IN THAT.
I...I KNOW...
ZIIIP
SWFFF
...
I'VE ONLY EVE GONE SWIMMIN AT PRIVATE BEACHES AND POOLS.
IT FEELS WEIRD TO STRIP DOWN TO A SWIMSUIT IN FRONT OF SO MANY STRANGERS.

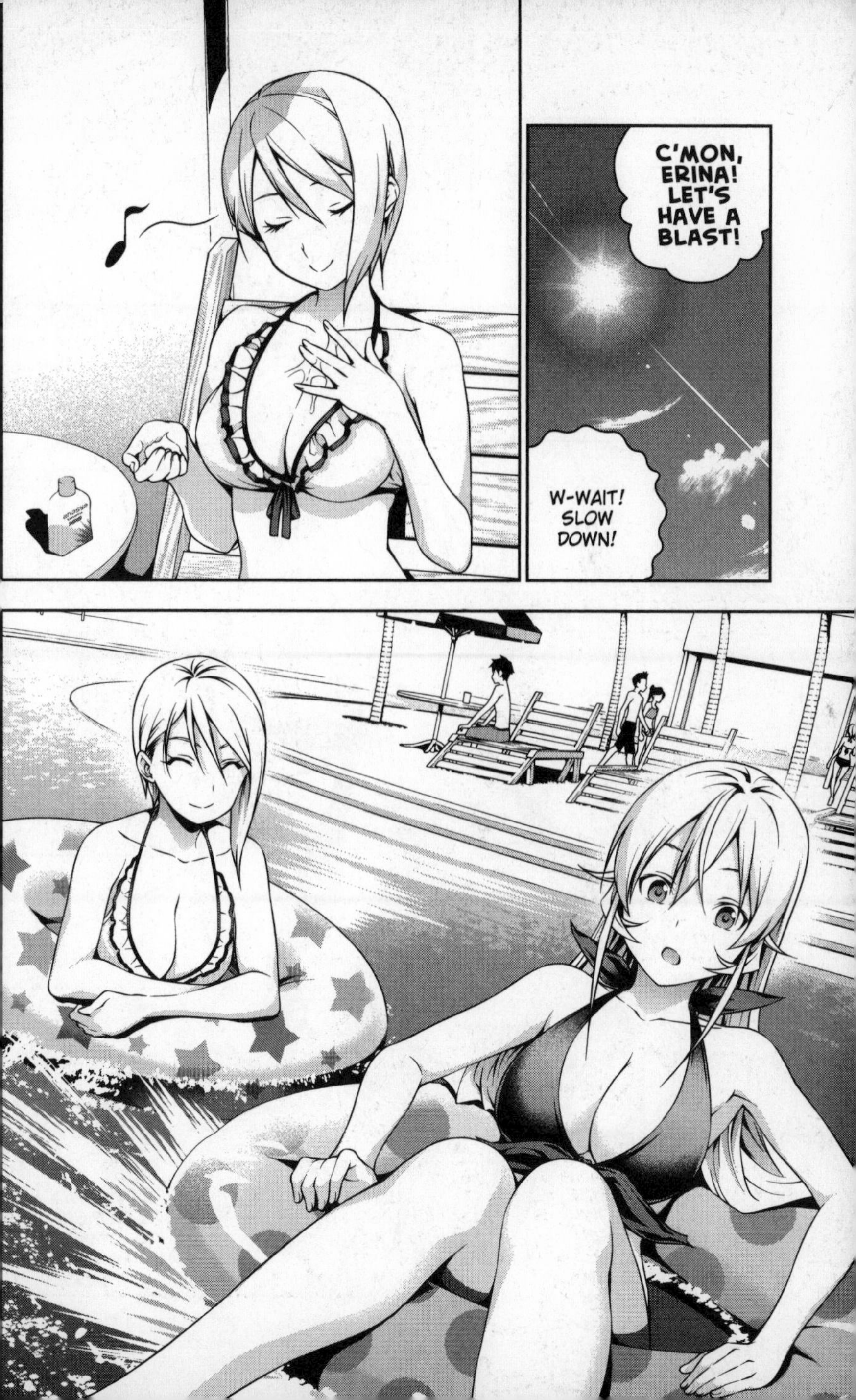
C'MON, ERINA! LET'S HAVE A BLAST!
W-WAIT! SLOW DOWN!

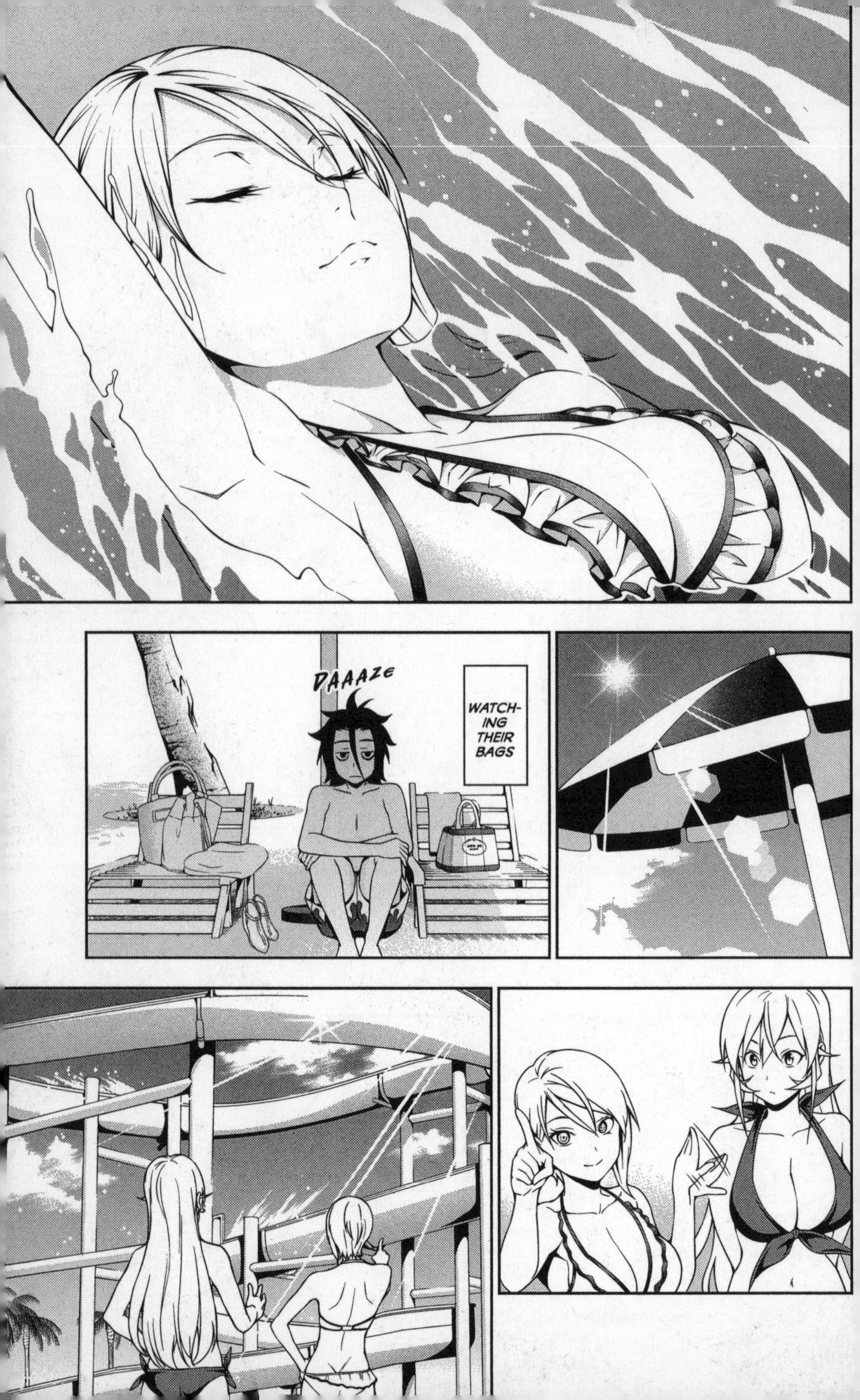
DAAAZE
WATCHING THEIR BAGS

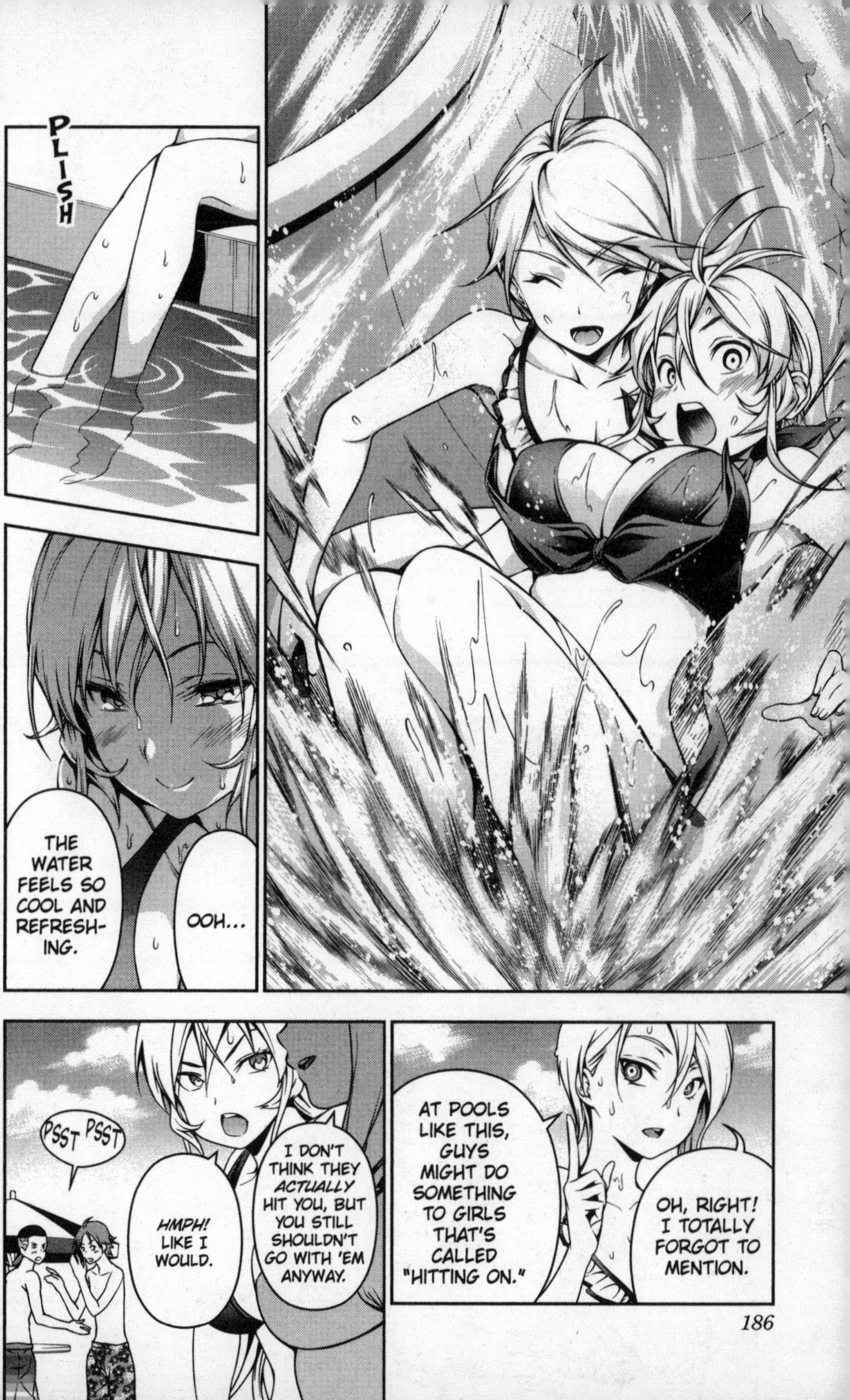
PLISH
OOH...
THE WATER FEELS SO COOL AND REFRESHING.
OH, RIGHT! I TOTALLY FORGOT TO MENTION.
AT POOLS LIKE THIS, GUYS MIGHT DO SOMETHING TO GIRLS THAT'S CALLED "HITTING ON."
I DON'T THINK THEY *ACTUALLY* HIT YOU, BUT YOU STILL SHOULDN'T GO WITH 'EM ANYWAY.
HMPH! LIKE I WOULD.
PSST PSST

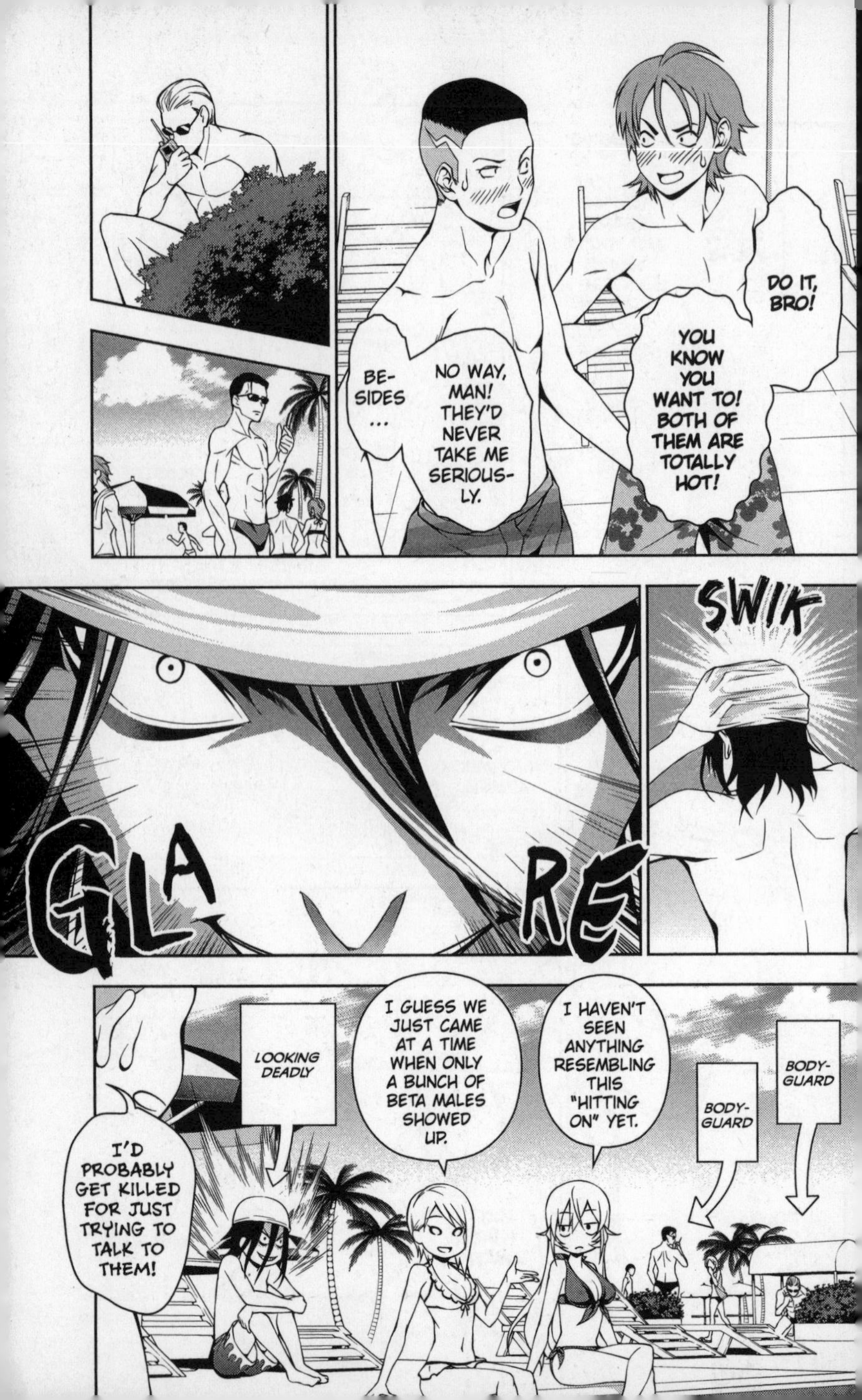
DO IT, BRO!
YOU KNOW YOU WANT TO! BOTH OF THEM ARE TOTALLY HOT!
NO WAY, MAN! THEY'D NEVER TAKE ME SERIOUSLY.
BESIDES...
SWIK
GLARE
BODY-GUARD
BODY-GUARD
I HAVEN'T SEEN ANYTHING RESEMBLING THIS "HITTING ON" YET.
I GUESS WE JUST CAME AT A TIME WHEN ONLY A BUNCH OF BETA MALES SHOWED UP.
LOOKING DEADLY
I'D PROBABLY GET KILLED FOR JUST TRYING TO TALK TO THEM!

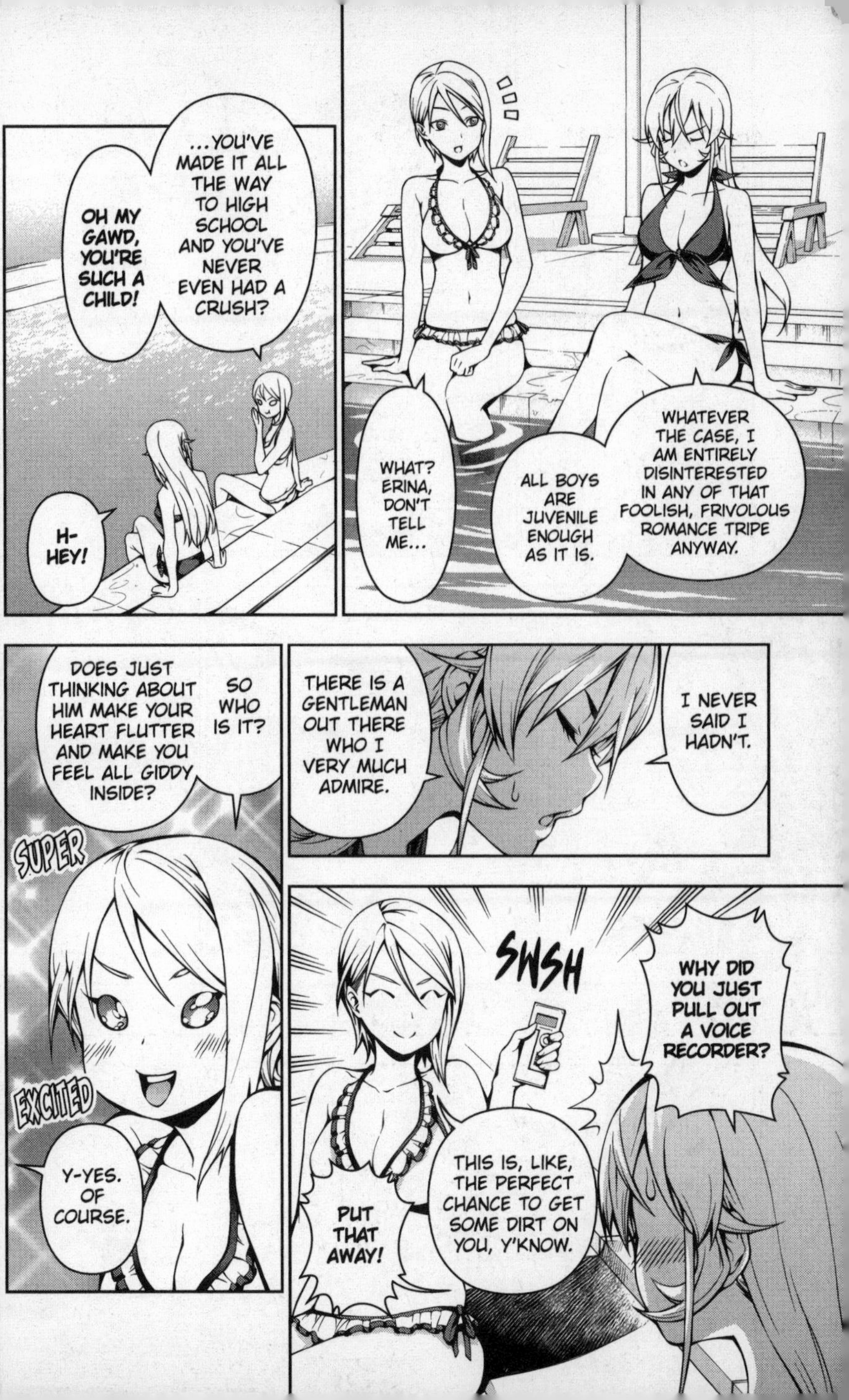
WHATEVER THE CASE, I AM ENTIRELY DISINTERESTED IN ANY OF THAT FOOLISH, FRIVOLOUS ROMANCE TRIPE ANYWAY.
ALL BOYS ARE JUVENILE ENOUGH AS IT IS.
WHAT? ERINA, DON'T TELL ME...
...YOU'VE MADE IT ALL THE WAY TO HIGH SCHOOL AND YOU'VE NEVER EVEN HAD A CRUSH?
OH MY GAWD, YOU'RE SUCH A CHILD!
H-HEY!
I NEVER SAID I HADN'T.
THERE IS A GENTLEMAN OUT THERE WHO I VERY MUCH ADMIRE.
SWSH
WHY DID YOU JUST PULL OUT A VOICE RECORDER?
THIS IS, LIKE, THE PERFECT CHANCE TO GET SOME DIRT ON YOU, Y'KNOW.
PUT THAT AWAY!
SO WHO IS IT?
DOES JUST THINKING ABOUT HIM MAKE YOUR HEART FLUTTER AND MAKE YOU FEEL ALL GIDDY INSIDE?
SUPER
EXCITED
Y-YES. OF COURSE.

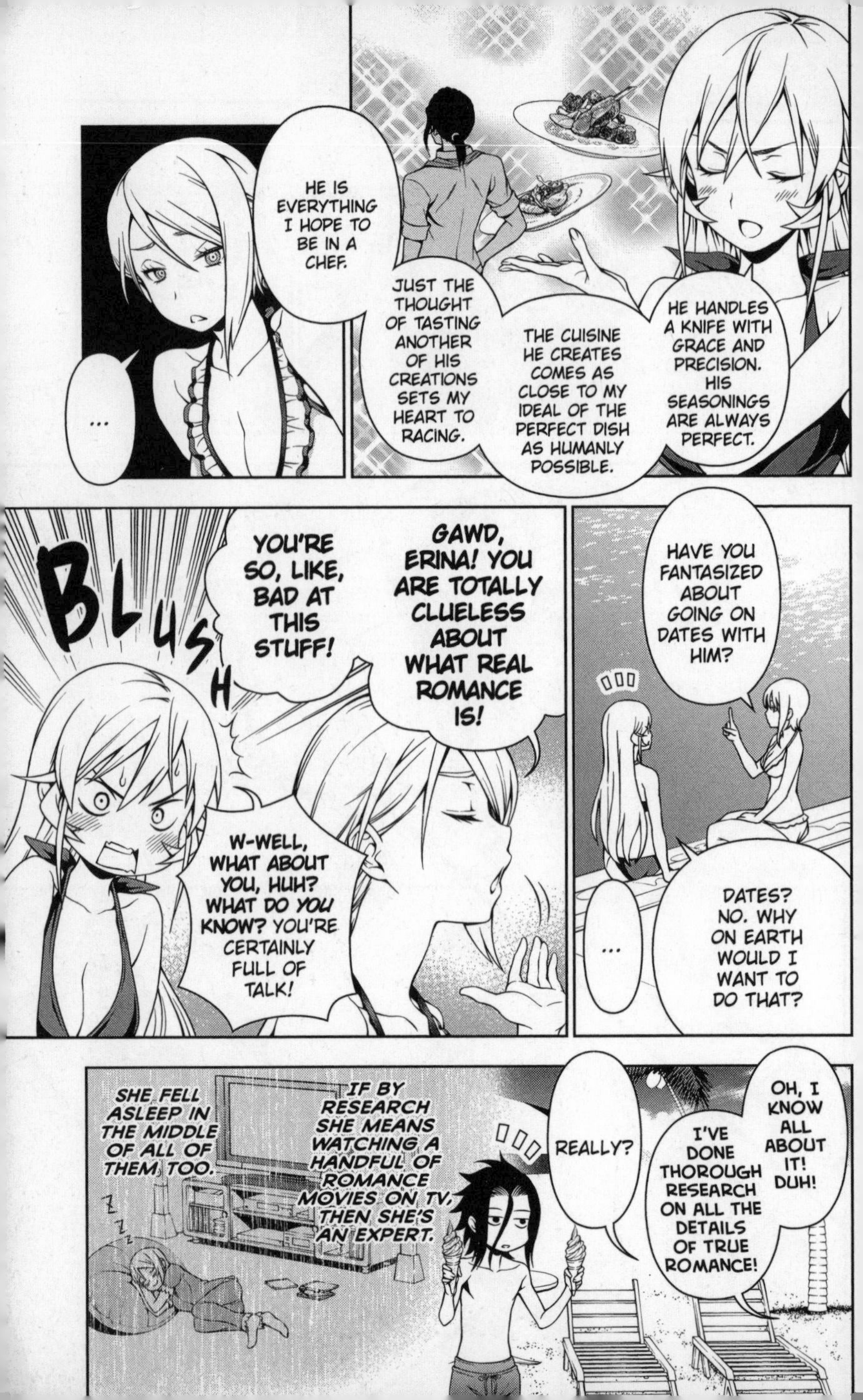
HE HANDLES A KNIFE WITH GRACE AND PRECISION. HIS SEASONINGS ARE ALWAYS PERFECT.
THE CUISINE HE CREATES COMES AS CLOSE TO MY IDEAL OF THE PERFECT DISH AS HUMANLY POSSIBLE.
JUST THE THOUGHT OF TASTING ANOTHER OF HIS CREATIONS SETS MY HEART TO RACING.
HE IS EVERYTHING I HOPE TO BE IN A CHEF.
...
HAVE YOU FANTASIZED ABOUT GOING ON DATES WITH HIM?
DATES? NO. WHY ON EARTH WOULD I WANT TO DO THAT?
...
GAWD, ERINA! YOU ARE TOTALLY CLUELESS ABOUT WHAT REAL ROMANCE IS!
YOU'RE SO, LIKE, BAD AT THIS STUFF!
BLUSH
W-WELL, WHAT ABOUT YOU, HUH? WHAT DO YOU KNOW? YOU'RE CERTAINLY FULL OF TALK!
OH, I KNOW ALL ABOUT IT! DUH!
I'VE DONE THOROUGH RESEARCH ON ALL THE DETAILS OF TRUE ROMANCE!
REALLY?
IF BY RESEARCH SHE MEANS WATCHING A HANDFUL OF ROMANCE MOVIES ON TV, THEN SHE'S AN EXPERT.
SHE FELL ASLEEP IN THE MIDDLE OF ALL OF THEM, TOO.

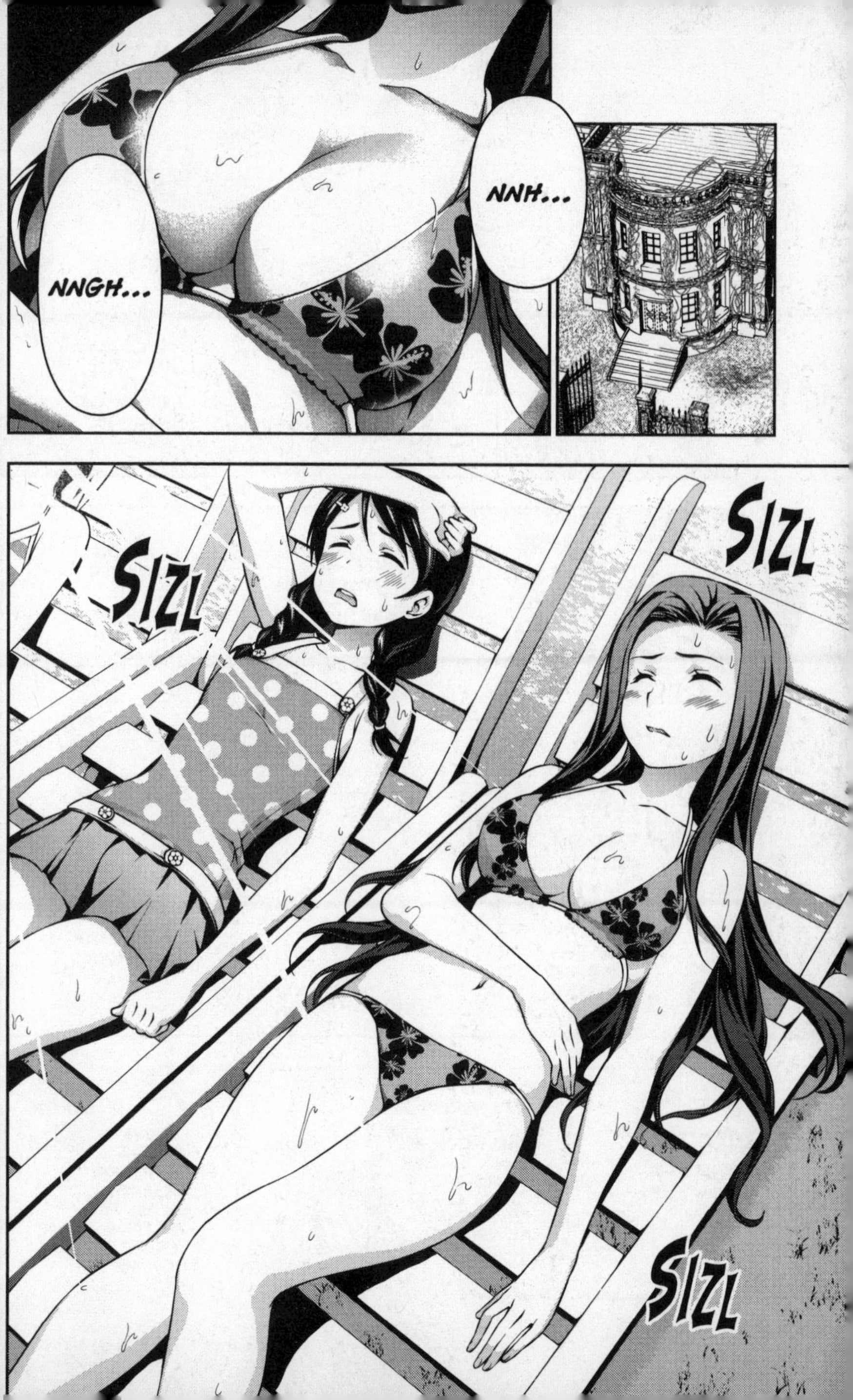
NNH...
NNGH...
SIZL
SIZL
SIZL

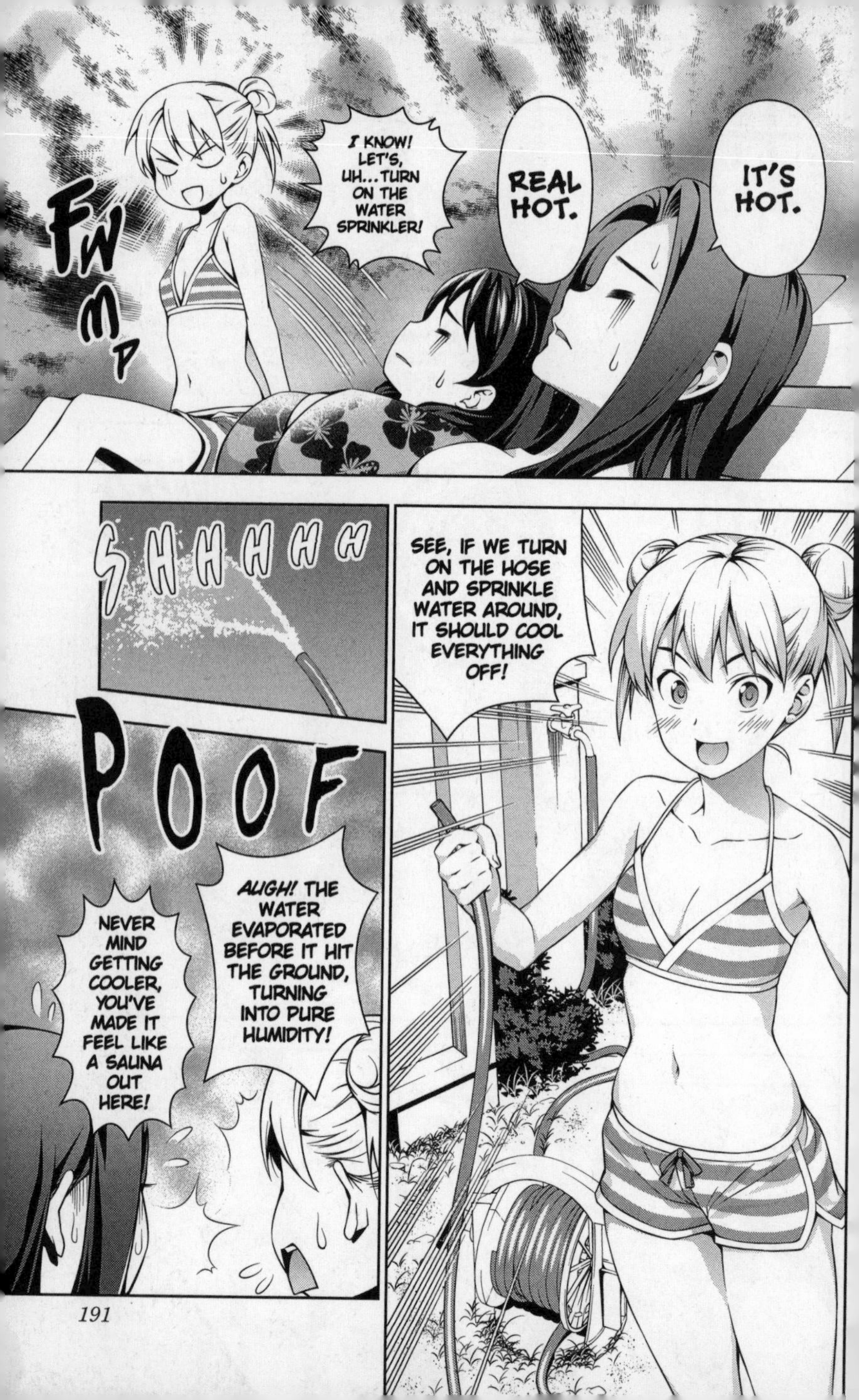
IT'S HOT.
REAL HOT.
I KNOW! LET'S, UH...TURN ON THE WATER SPRINKLER!
FWMP
SEE, IF WE TURN ON THE HOSE AND SPRINKLE WATER AROUND, IT SHOULD COOL EVERYTHING OFF!
SHHHHH
POOF
AUGH! THE WATER EVAPORATED BEFORE IT HIT THE GROUND, TURNING INTO PURE HUMIDITY!
NEVER MIND GETTING COOLER, YOU'VE MADE IT FEEL LIKE A SAUNA OUT HERE!

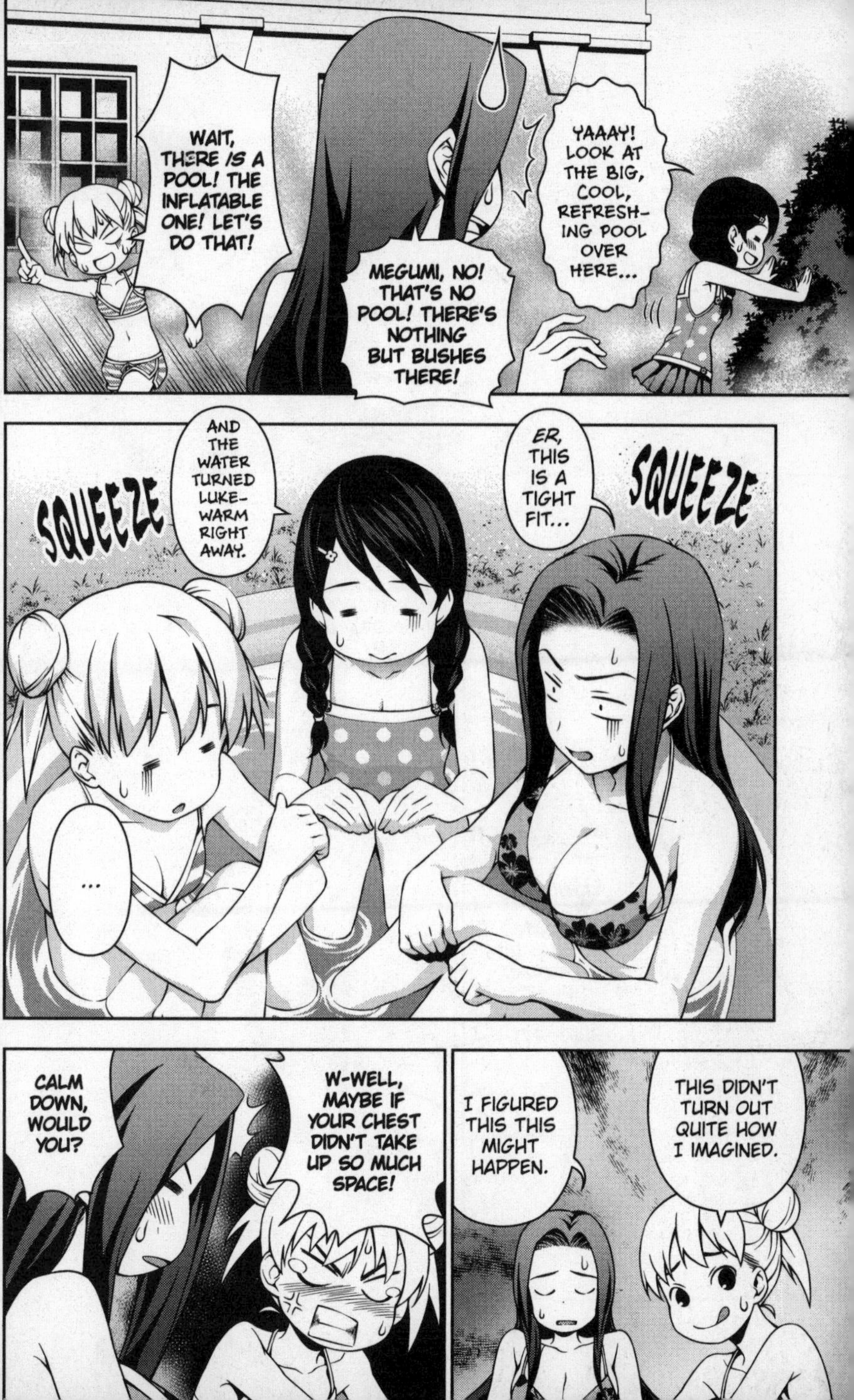
YAAAY! LOOK AT THE BIG, COOL, REFRESHING POOL OVER HERE...
MEGUMI, NO! THAT'S NO POOL! THERE'S NOTHING BUT BUSHES THERE!
WAIT, THERE *IS* A POOL! THE INFLATABLE ONE! LET'S DO THAT!
SQUEEZE
ER, THIS IS A TIGHT FIT...
AND THE WATER TURNED LUKEWARM RIGHT AWAY.
SQUEEZE
...
THIS DIDN'T TURN OUT QUITE HOW I IMAGINED.
I FIGURED THIS THIS MIGHT HAPPEN.
W-WELL, MAYBE IF YOUR CHEST DIDN'T TAKE UP SO MUCH SPACE!
CALM DOWN, WOULD YOU?

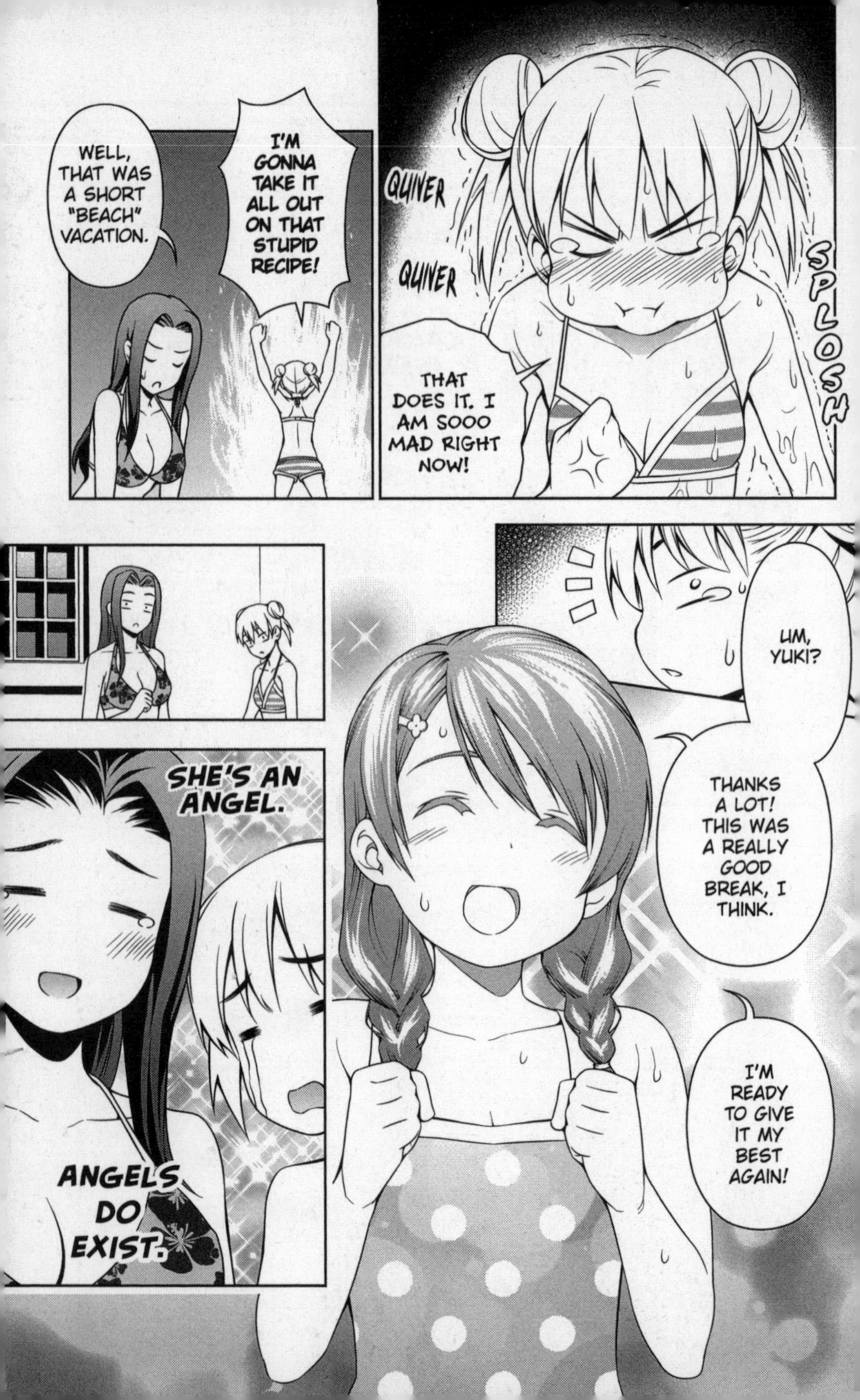
SPLOSH
QUIVER
QUIVER
THAT DOES IT. I AM SOOO MAD RIGHT NOW!
I'M GONNA TAKE IT ALL OUT ON THAT STUPID RECIPE!
WELL, THAT WAS A SHORT "BEACH" VACATION.
UM, YUKI?
THANKS A LOT! THIS WAS A REALLY GOOD BREAK, I THINK.
I'M READY TO GIVE IT MY BEST AGAIN!
SHE'S AN ANGEL.
ANGELS DO EXIST.

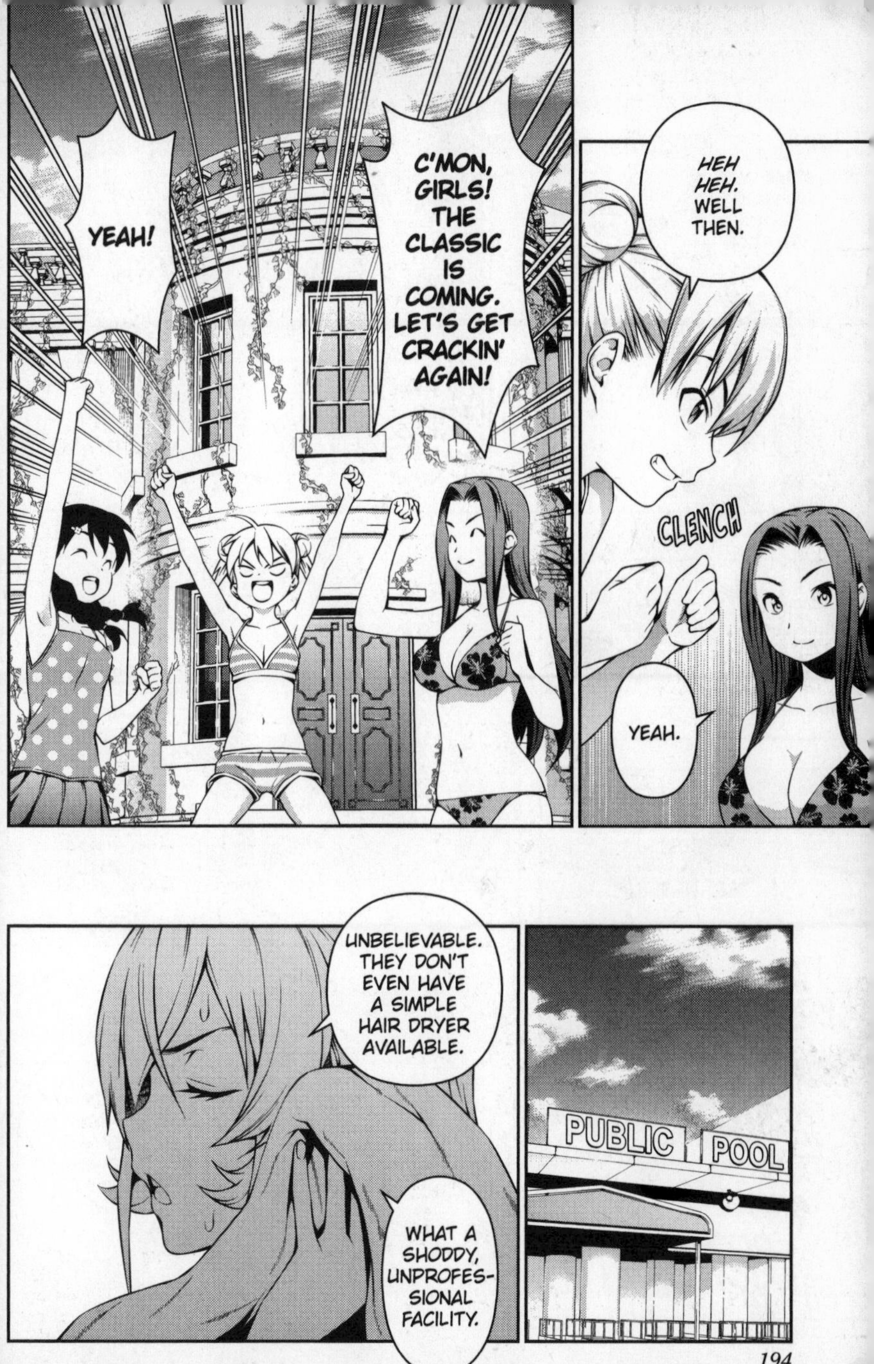
HEH HEH. WELL THEN.
CLENCH
YEAH.
C'MON, GIRLS! THE CLASSIC IS COMING. LET'S GET CRACKIN' AGAIN!
YEAH!
PUBLIC
POOL
UNBELIEVABLE. THEY DON'T EVEN HAVE A SIMPLE HAIR DRYER AVAILABLE.
WHAT A SHODDY, UNPROFES-SIONAL FACILITY.

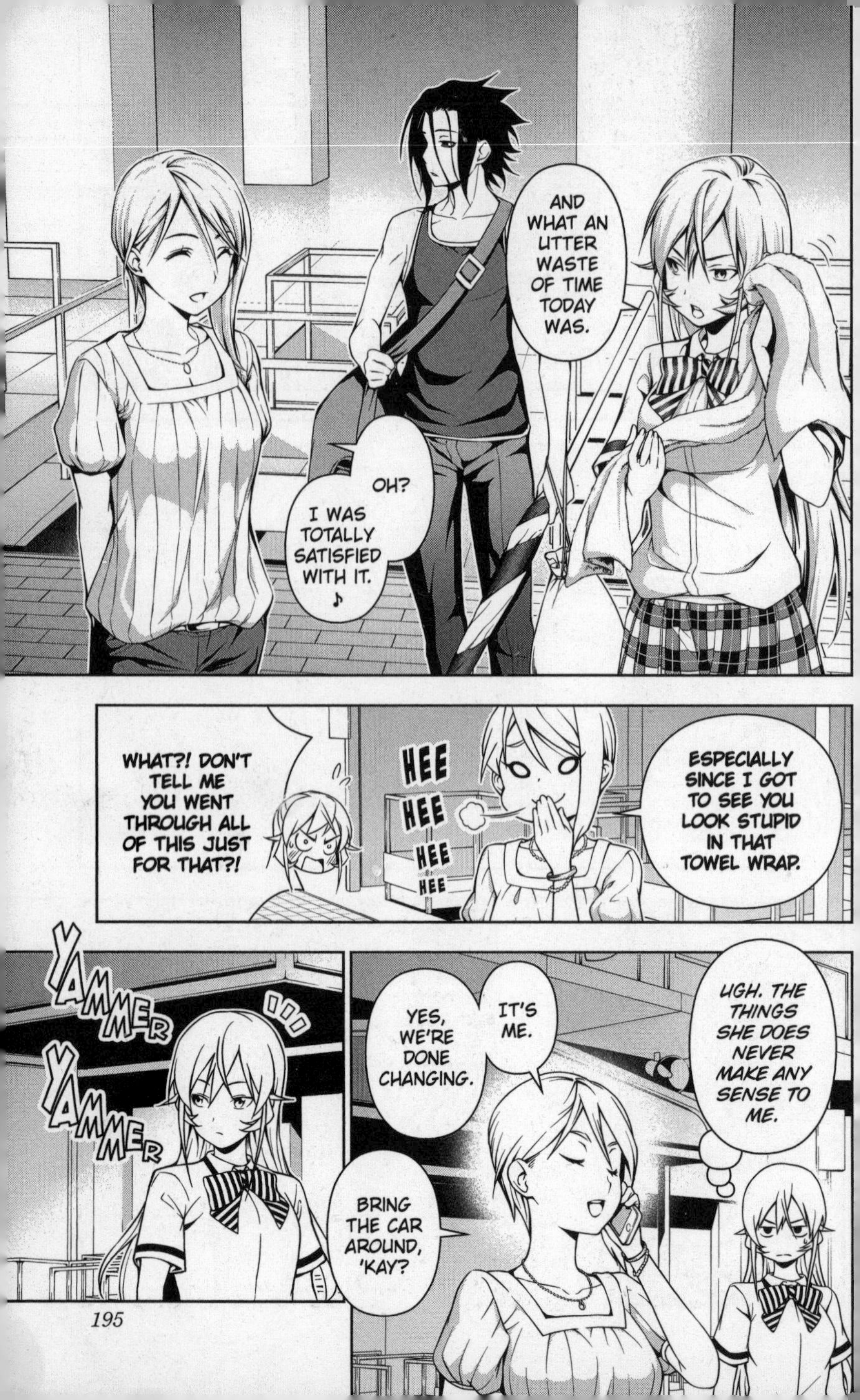
AND WHAT AN UTTER WASTE OF TIME TODAY WAS.
OH? I WAS TOTALLY SATISFIED WITH IT. ♪
ESPECIALLY SINCE I GOT TO SEE YOU LOOK STUPID IN THAT TOWEL WRAP.
HEE HEE HEE HEE
WHAT?! DON'T TELL ME YOU WENT THROUGH ALL OF THIS JUST FOR THAT?!
UGH. THE THINGS SHE DOES NEVER MAKE ANY SENSE TO ME.
IT'S ME.
YES, WE'RE DONE CHANGING.
BRING THE CAR AROUND, 'KAY?
YAMMER YAMMER

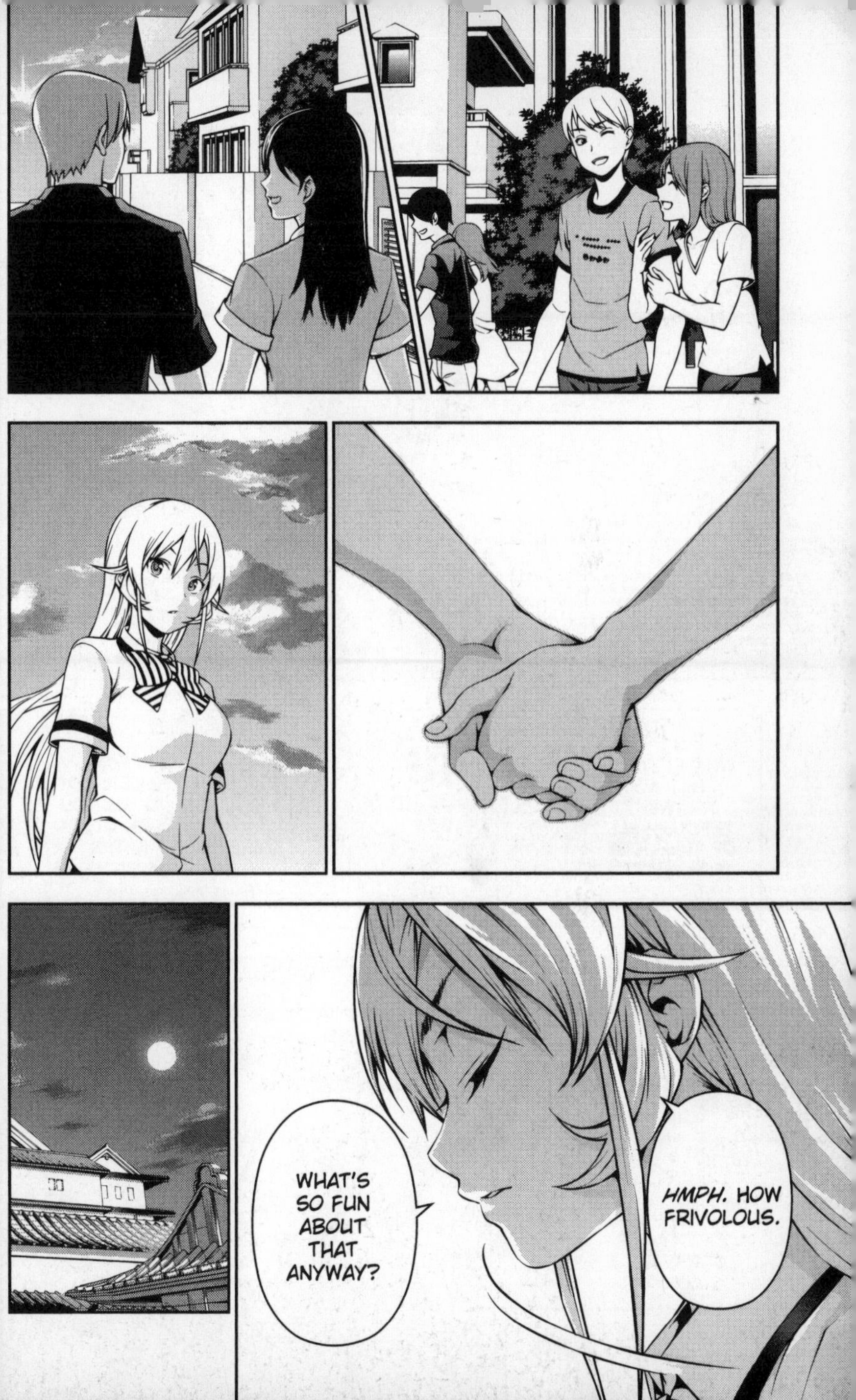
HMPH. HOW FRIVOLOUS.
WHAT'S SO FUN ABOUT THAT ANYWAY?

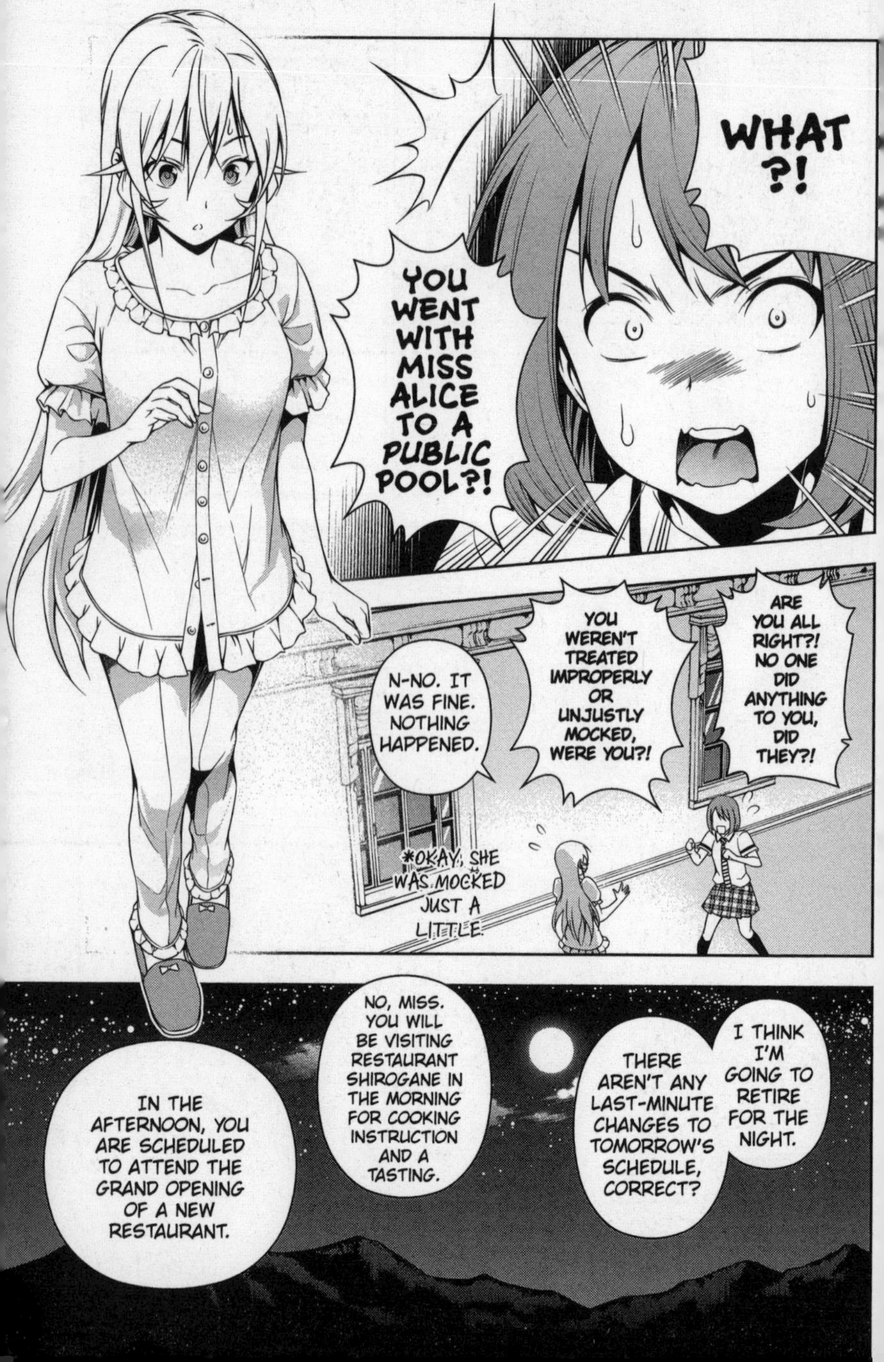
WHAT?!
YOU WENT WITH MISS ALICE TO A PUBLIC POOL?!
ARE YOU ALL RIGHT?! NO ONE DID ANYTHING TO YOU, DID THEY?!
YOU WEREN'T TREATED IMPROPERLY OR UNJUSTLY MOCKED, WERE YOU?!
N-NO. IT WAS FINE. NOTHING HAPPENED.
*OKAY, SHE WAS MOCKED JUST A LITTLE.
I THINK I'M GOING TO RETIRE FOR THE NIGHT.
THERE AREN'T ANY LAST-MINUTE CHANGES TO TOMORROW'S SCHEDULE, CORRECT?
NO, MISS. YOU WILL BE VISITING RESTAURANT SHIROGANE IN THE MORNING FOR COOKING INSTRUCTION AND A TASTING.
IN THE AFTERNOON, YOU ARE SCHEDULED TO ATTEND THE GRAND OPENING OF A NEW RESTAURANT.

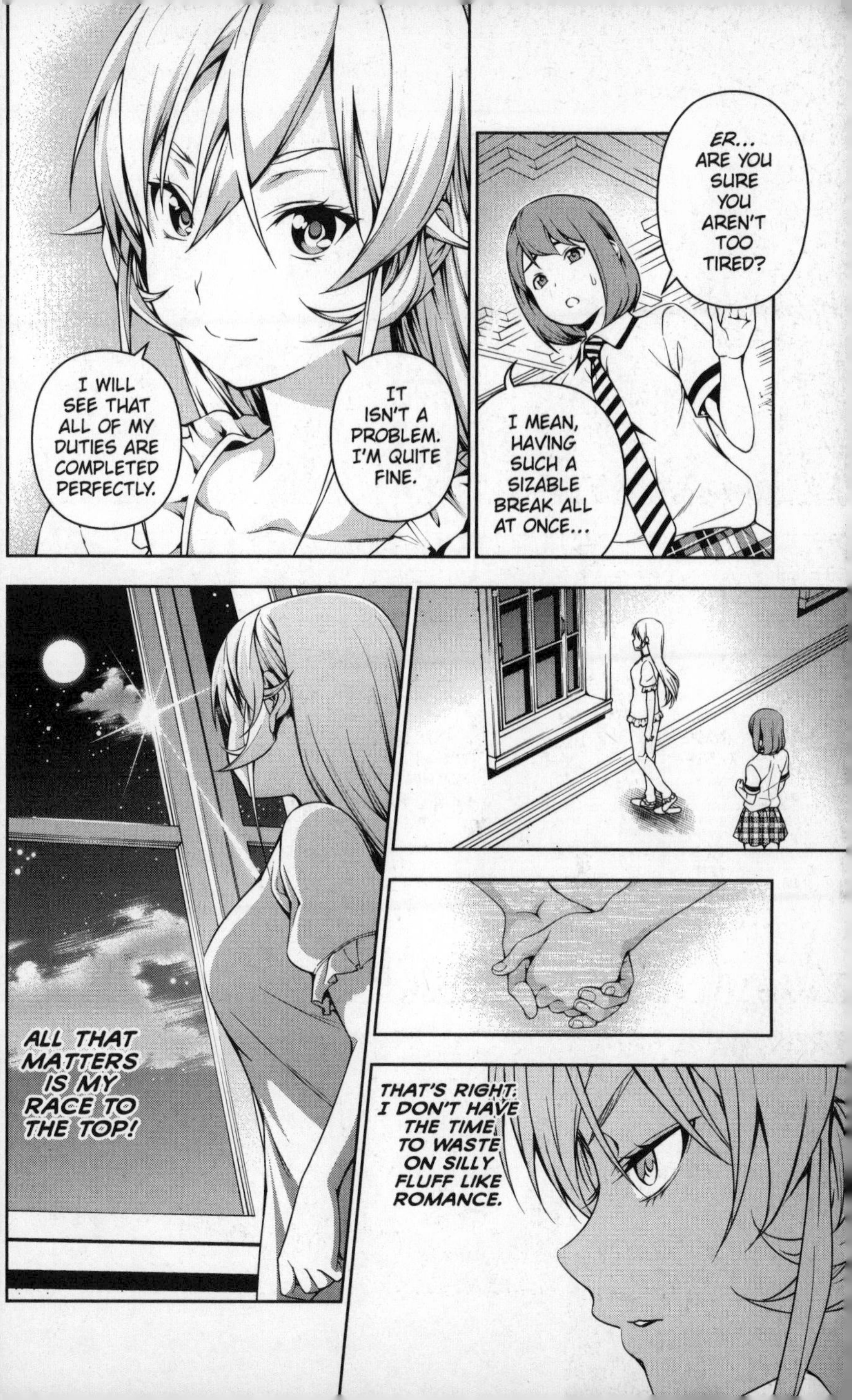
ER... ARE YOU SURE YOU AREN'T TOO TIRED?
I MEAN, HAVING SUCH A SIZABLE BREAK ALL AT ONCE...
IT ISN'T A PROBLEM. I'M QUITE FINE.
I WILL SEE THAT ALL OF MY DUTIES ARE COMPLETED PERFECTLY.
THAT'S RIGHT. I DON'T HAVE THE TIME TO WASTE ON SILLY FLUFF LIKE ROMANCE.
ALL THAT MATTERS IS MY RACE TO THE TOP!

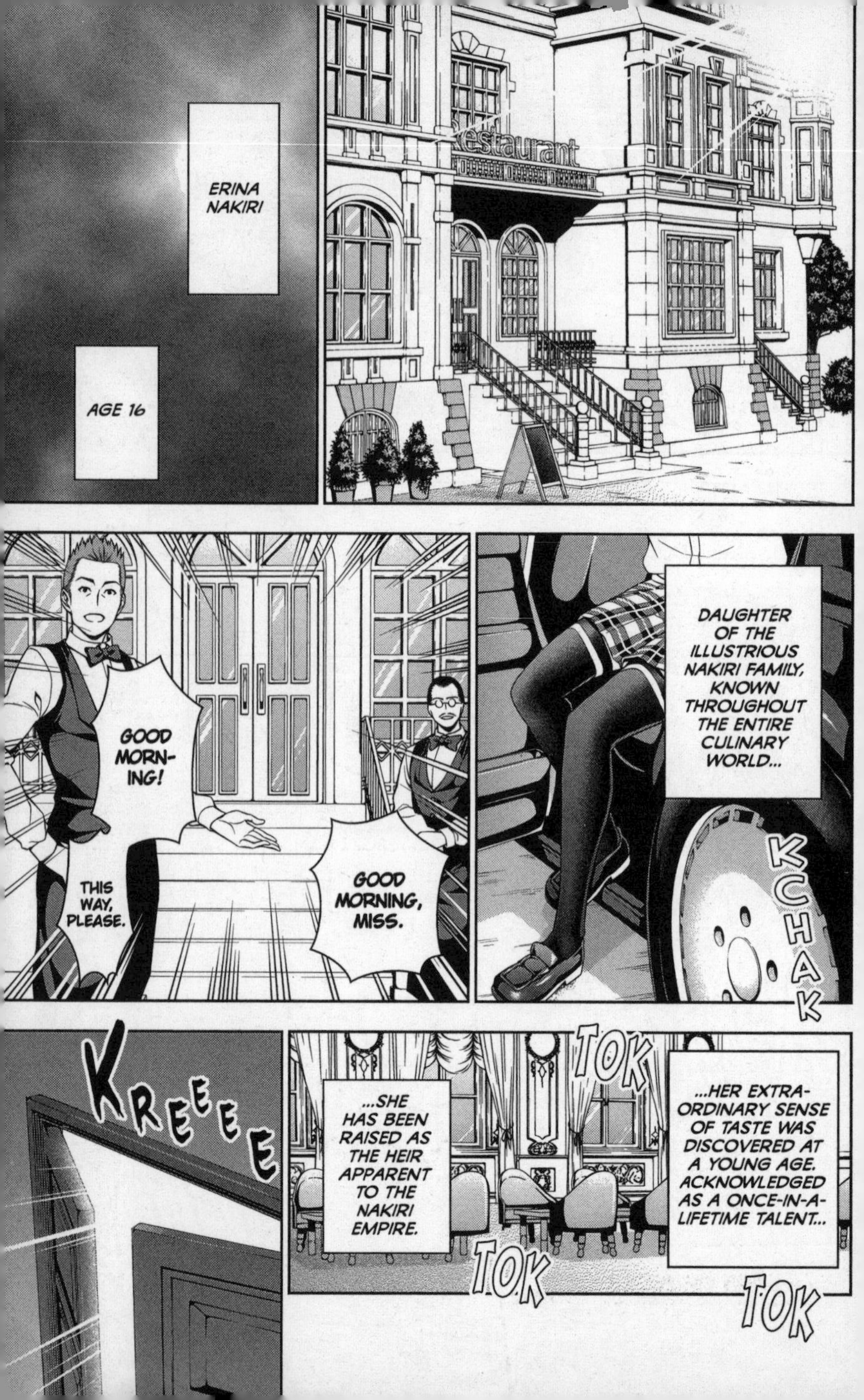
Restaurant
ERINA NAKIRI
AGE 16
DAUGHTER OF THE ILLUSTRIOUS NAKIRI FAMILY, KNOWN THROUGHOUT THE ENTIRE CULINARY WORLD...
KCHAK
GOOD MORN-ING!
GOOD MORNING, MISS.
THIS WAY, PLEASE.
TOK
...HER EXTRA-ORDINARY SENSE OF TASTE WAS DISCOVERED AT A YOUNG AGE. ACKNOWLEDGED AS A ONCE-IN-A-LIFETIME TALENT...
...SHE HAS BEEN RAISED AS THE HEIR APPARENT TO THE NAKIRI EMPIRE.
TOK
TOK
KREEEE

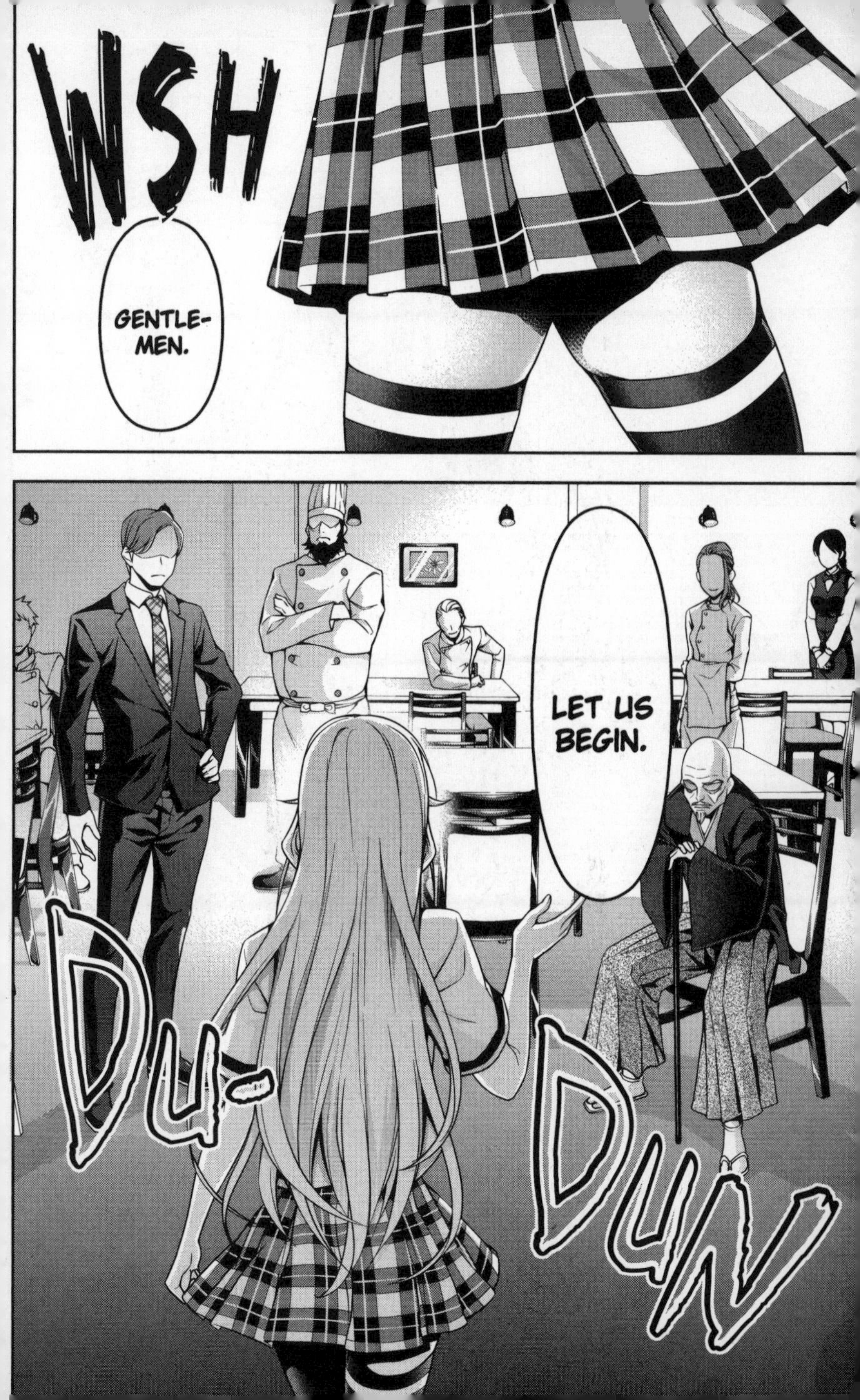
WSH
GENTLE- MEN.
LET US BEGIN.
DU- DUN

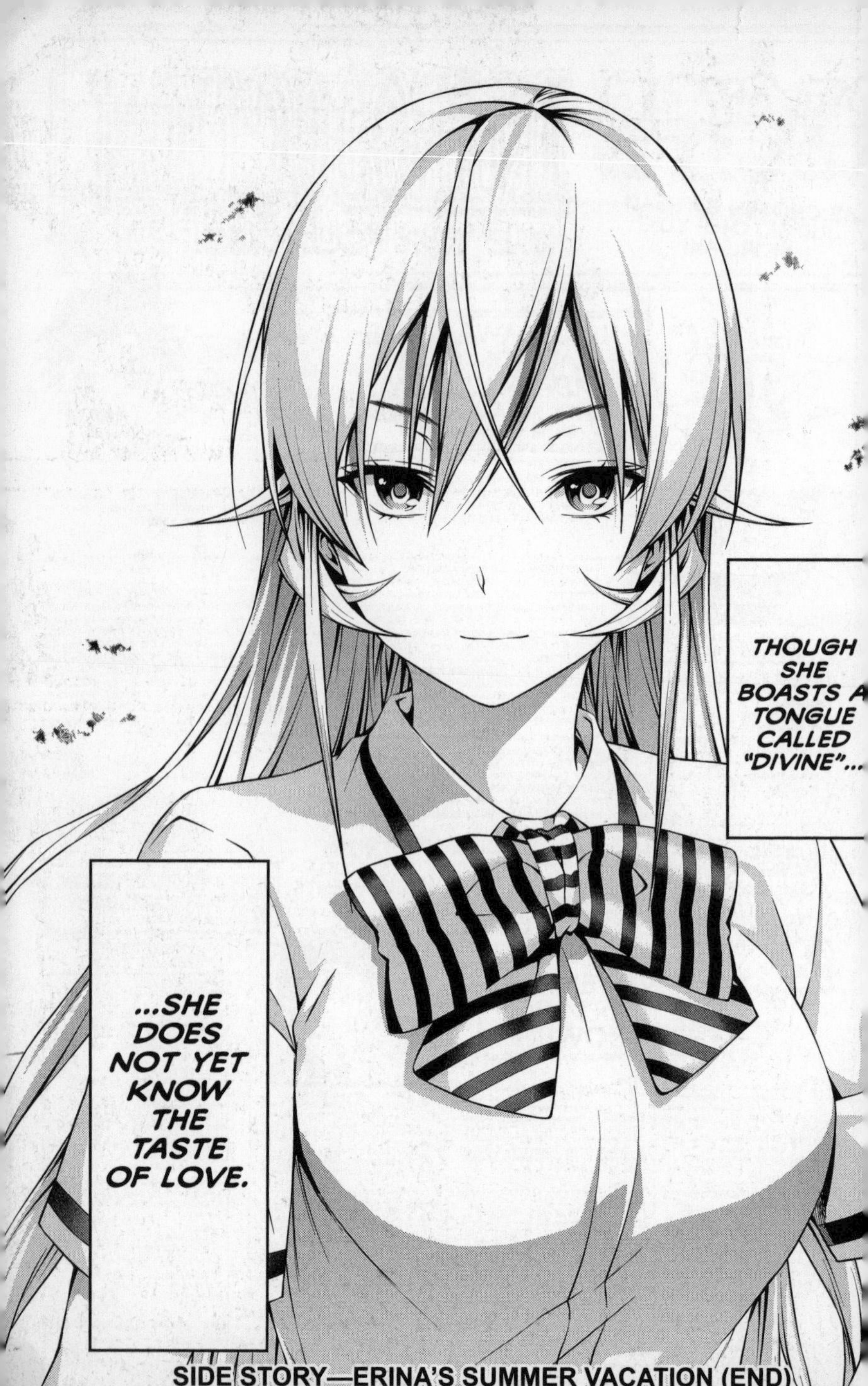
THOUGH SHE BOASTS A TONGUE CALLED "DIVINE"...
...SHE DOES NOT YET KNOW THE TASTE OF LOVE.

SIDE STORY—ERINA'S SUMMER VACATION (END)

RECIPE INTRODUCTION

AS CHOSEN BY HEAD JUDGE, CHEF YUKI MORISAKI

THE TOP FOUR RECIPES!

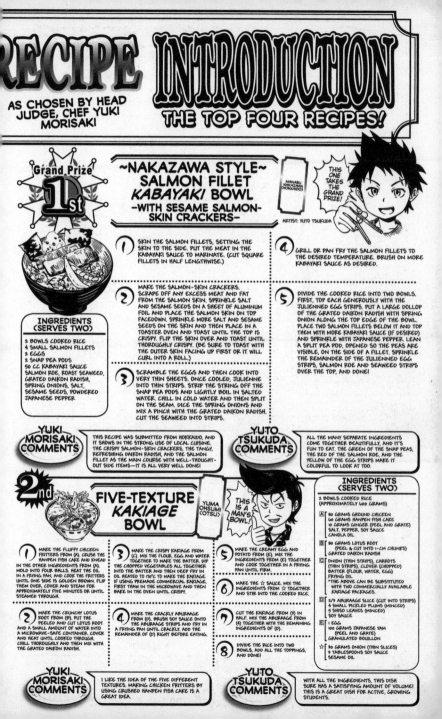

Grand Prize 1st

~NAKAZAWA STYLE~ SALMON FILLET *KABAYAKI* BOWL -WITH SESAME SALMON-SKIN CRACKERS-

MANABU NAKAZAWA (HOKKAIDO)

THIS ONE TAKES THE GRAND PRIZE!

ARTIST: YUTO TSUKUDA

INGREDIENTS (SERVES TWO)

2 BOWLS COOKED RICE
4 SMALL SALMON FILLETS
2 EGGS
2 SNAP PEA PODS
50 CC KABAYAKI SAUCE
SALMON ROE, ROAST SEAWEED, GRATED DAIKON RADISH, SPRING ONIONS, SALT, SESAME SEEDS, POWDERED JAPANESE PEPPER

1. SKIN THE SALMON FILLETS, SETTING THE SKIN TO THE SIDE. PUT THE MEAT IN THE KABAYAKI SAUCE TO MARINATE. (CUT SQUARE FILLETS IN HALF LENGTHWISE.)
2. MAKE THE SALMON-SKIN CRACKERS. SCRAPE OFF ANY EXCESS MEAT AND FAT FROM THE SALMON SKIN. SPRINKLE SALT AND SESAME SEEDS ON A SHEET OF ALUMINUM FOIL AND PLACE THE SALMON SKIN ON TOP FACEDOWN. SPRINKLE MORE SALT AND SESAME SEEDS ON THE SKIN AND THEN PLACE IN A TOASTER OVEN AND TOAST UNTIL THE TOP IS CRISPY. FLIP THE SKIN OVER AND TOAST UNTIL THOROUGHLY CRISPY. (BE SURE TO TOAST WITH THE OUTER SKIN FACING UP FIRST OR IT WILL CURL INTO A ROLL.)
3. SCRAMBLE THE EGGS AND THEN COOK INTO VERY THIN SHEETS. ONCE COOLED, JULIENNE INTO THIN STRIPS. STRIP THE STRING OFF THE SNAP PEA PODS AND LIGHTLY BOIL IN SALTED WATER. CHILL IN COLD WATER AND THEN SPLIT ON THE SEAM. DICE THE SPRING ONIONS AND MIX A PINCH WITH THE GRATED DAIKON RADISH. CUT THE SEAWEED INTO STRIPS.
4. GRILL OR PAN FRY THE SALMON FILLETS TO THE DESIRED TEMPERATURE. BRUSH ON MORE KABAYAKI SAUCE AS DESIRED.
5. DIVIDE THE COOKED RICE INTO TWO BOWLS. FIRST, TOP EACH GENEROUSLY WITH THE JULIENNED EGG STRIPS. PUT A LARGE DOLLOP OF THE GRATED DAIKON RADISH WITH SPRING ONION ALONG THE TOP EDGE OF THE BOWL. PLACE TWO SALMON FILLETS BELOW IT AND TOP THEM WITH MORE KABAYAKI SAUCE (IF DESIRED) AND SPRINKLE WITH JAPANESE PEPPER. LEAN A SPLIT PEA POD, OPENED SO THE PEAS ARE VISIBLE, ON THE SIDE OF A FILLET. SPRINKLE THE REMAINDER OF THE JULIENNED EGG STRIPS, SALMON ROE AND SEAWEED STRIPS OVER THE TOP, AND DONE!

YUKI MORISAKI COMMENTS

THIS RECIPE WAS SUBMITTED FROM HOKKAIDO, AND IT SHOWS IN THE STRONG USE OF LOCAL CUISINE. THE CRISPY SALMON-SKIN CRACKERS, THE TANGY, REFRESHING DAIKON RADISH, AND THE SALMON FILLET AS THE MAIN COURSE WITH WELL-THOUGHT-OUT SIDE ITEMS—IT IS ALL VERY WELL DONE!

YUTO TSUKUDA COMMENTS

ALL THE MANY SEPARATE INGREDIENTS COME TOGETHER BEAUTIFULLY, AND IT'S FUN TO EAT. THE GREEN OF THE SNAP PEAS, THE RED OF THE SALMON ROE, AND THE YELLOW OF THE EGG STRIPS MAKE IT COLORFUL TO LOOK AT TOO.

2nd

FIVE-TEXTURE *KAKIAGE* BOWL

YUMA OHSUMI (OTSU)

THIS IS A MAN'S BOWL!

INGREDIENTS (SERVES TWO)

2 BOWLS COOKED RICE (APPROXIMATELY 600 GRAMS)

A [80 GRAMS GROUND CHICKEN
60 GRAMS HANPEN FISH CAKE
10 GRAMS GINGER (PEEL AND GRATE)
SALT, PEPPER, SOY SAUCE
CANOLA OIL

B [80 GRAMS LOTUS ROOT (PEEL & CUT INTO 1-CM CHUNKS)
GRATED DAIKON RADISH

C [ONION (THIN STRIPS), CARROTS (THIN STRIPS), CLOVER (CHOPPED)
BATTER (FLOUR, WATER, EGG)
FRYING OIL
*THE ABOVE CAN BE SUBSTITUTED WITH TWO COMMERCIALLY AVAILABLE KAKIAGE PACKAGES.

D [2/3 ABURAAGE SLICE (CUT INTO STRIPS)
4 SMALL PICKLED PLUMS (MINCED)
5 SHISO LEAVES (MINCED)
SOY SAUCE

E [1 EGG
100 GRAMS JAPANESE YAM (PEEL AND GRATE)
GRANULATED BOUILLON

☆ [30 GRAMS ONION (THIN SLICES)
3 TABLESPOONS SOY SAUCE
SESAME OIL

1. MAKE THE FLUFFY CHICKEN FRITTERS FROM (A). CRUSH THE HANPEN FISH CAKE AND KNEAD IN THE OTHER INGREDIENTS FROM (A). MOLD INTO FOUR BALLS. HEAT THE OIL IN A FRYING PAN, AND COOK THE FRITTERS UNTIL ONE SIDE IS GOLDEN BROWN. FLIP THEM OVER, COVER AND STEAM FOR APPROXIMATELY FIVE MINUTES OR UNTIL STEAMED THROUGH.
2. MAKE THE CRUNCHY LOTUS ROOT FROM (B). PUT THE PEELED AND CUT LOTUS ROOT AND A SMALL AMOUNT OF WATER INTO A MICROWAVE-SAFE CONTAINER. COVER AND HEAT UNTIL COOKED THROUGH. CHILL THOROUGHLY AND THEN MIX WITH THE GRATED DAIKON RADISH.
3. MAKE THE CRISPY KAKIAGE FROM (C). MIX THE FLOUR, EGG AND WATER TOGETHER TO MAKE THE BATTER. DIP THE CHOPPED VEGETABLES ALL TOGETHER INTO THE BATTER AND THEN DEEP FRY IN OIL HEATED TO 170°C TO MAKE THE KAKIAGE. IF USING PREMADE COMMERCIAL KAKIAGE, FIRST THAW IN THE MICROWAVE AND THEN BAKE IN THE OVEN UNTIL CRISPY.
4. MAKE THE CRACKLY ABURAAGE FROM (D). BRUSH SOY SAUCE ONTO THE ABURAAGE STRIPS AND FRY IN A FRYING PAN UNTIL CRACKLY. ADD THE REMAINDER OF (D) RIGHT BEFORE EATING.
5. MAKE THE CREAMY EGG AND POTATO FROM (E). MIX THE INGREDIENTS FROM (E) TOGETHER AND COOK TOGETHER IN A FRYING PAN UNTIL FIRM.
6. MAKE THE ☆ SAUCE. MIX THE INGREDIENTS FROM ☆ TOGETHER AND STIR INTO THE COOKED RICE.
7. CUT THE KAKIAGE FROM (3) IN HALF. MIX THE ABURAAGE FROM (4) TOGETHER WITH THE REMAINING INGREDIENTS OF (D).
8. DIVIDE THE RICE INTO TWO BOWLS, ADD ALL THE TOPPINGS, AND DONE!

YUKI MORISAKI COMMENTS

I LIKE THE IDEA OF THE FIVE DIFFERENT TEXTURES. MAKING CHICKEN FRITTERS BY USING CRUSHED HANPEN FISH CAKE IS A GREAT IDEA.

YUTO TSUKUDA COMMENTS

WITH ALL THE INGREDIENTS, THIS DISH SURE HAS A SATISFYING AMOUNT OF VOLUME! THIS IS A GREAT DISH FOR ACTIVE, GROWING STUDENTS.

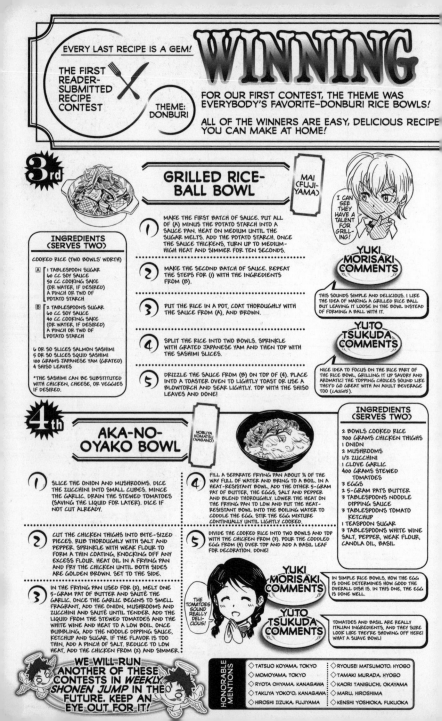

EVERY LAST RECIPE IS A GEM!

THE FIRST READER-SUBMITTED RECIPE CONTEST

THEME: DONBURI

WINNING

FOR OUR FIRST CONTEST, THE THEME WAS EVERYBODY'S FAVORITE—DONBURI RICE BOWLS!

ALL OF THE WINNERS ARE EASY, DELICIOUS RECIPE YOU CAN MAKE AT HOME!

3rd

GRILLED RICE-BALL BOWL

MAI (FUJIYAMA)

I CAN SEE THEY HAVE A TALENT FOR GRILLING!

INGREDIENTS (SERVES TWO)

COOKED RICE (TWO BOWLS' WORTH)

A
- 1 TABLESPOON SUGAR
- 60 CC SOY SAUCE
- 50 CC COOKING SAKE (OR WATER, IF DESIRED)
- A PINCH OR TWO OF POTATO STARCH

B
- 2 TABLESPOONS SUGAR
- 60 CC SOY SAUCE
- 40 CC COOKING SAKE (OR WATER, IF DESIRED)
- A PINCH OR TWO OF POTATO STARCH

6 OR SO SLICES SALMON SASHIMI
5 OR SO SLICES SQUID SASHIMI
100 GRAMS JAPANESE YAM (GRATED)
4 SHISO LEAVES

*THE SASHIMI CAN BE SUBSTITUTED WITH CHICKEN, CHEESE, OR VEGGIES IF DESIRED.

1. MAKE THE FIRST BATCH OF SAUCE. PUT ALL OF (A) MINUS THE POTATO STARCH INTO A SAUCE PAN. HEAT ON MEDIUM UNTIL THE SUGAR MELTS. ADD THE POTATO STARCH. ONCE THE SAUCE THICKENS, TURN UP TO MEDIUM-HIGH HEAT AND SIMMER FOR TEN SECONDS.
2. MAKE THE SECOND BATCH OF SAUCE. REPEAT THE STEPS FOR (1) WITH THE INGREDIENTS FROM (B).
3. PUT THE RICE IN A POT, COAT THOROUGHLY WITH THE SAUCE FROM (A), AND BROWN.
4. SPLIT THE RICE INTO TWO BOWLS. SPRINKLE WITH GRATED JAPANESE YAM AND THEN TOP WITH THE SASHIMI SLICES.
5. DRIZZLE THE SAUCE FROM (B) ON TOP OF (4). PLACE INTO A TOASTER OVEN TO LIGHTLY TOAST OR USE A BLOWTORCH AND SEAR LIGHTLY. TOP WITH THE SHISO LEAVES AND DONE!

YUKI MORISAKI COMMENTS

THIS SOUNDS SIMPLE AND DELICIOUS. I LIKE THE IDEA OF MAKING A GRILLED RICE BALL BUT LEAVING IT LOOSE IN THE BOWL INSTEAD OF FORMING A BALL WITH IT.

YUTO TSUKUDA COMMENTS

NICE IDEA TO FOCUS ON THE RICE PART OF THE RICE BOWL, GRILLING IT UP SAVORY AND AROMATIC! THE TOPPING CHOICES SOUND LIKE THEY'D GO GREAT WITH AN ADULT BEVERAGE TOO (*LAUGHS*).

4th

AKA-NO-OYAKO BOWL

NOBUYA KOMATSU (NAGANO)

INGREDIENTS (SERVES TWO)

2 BOWLS COOKED RICE
300 GRAMS CHICKEN THIGHS
1 ONION
2 MUSHROOMS
1/2 ZUCCHINI
1 CLOVE GARLIC
400 GRAMS STEWED TOMATOES
3 EGGS
2 5-GRAM PATS BUTTER
3 TABLESPOONS NOODLE DIPPING SAUCE
3 TABLESPOONS TOMATO KETCHUP
1 TEASPOON SUGAR
3 TABLESPOONS WHITE WINE
SALT, PEPPER, WEAK FLOUR, CANOLA OIL, BASIL

1. SLICE THE ONION AND MUSHROOMS. DICE THE ZUCCHINI INTO SMALL CUBES. MINCE THE GARLIC. DRAIN THE STEWED TOMATOES (SAVING THE LIQUID FOR LATER). DICE IF NOT CUT ALREADY.
2. CUT THE CHICKEN THIGHS INTO BITE-SIZED PIECES. RUB THOROUGHLY WITH SALT AND PEPPER. SPRINKLE WITH WEAK FLOUR TO FORM A THIN COATING, KNOCKING OFF ANY EXCESS FLOUR. HEAT OIL IN A FRYING PAN AND FRY THE CHICKEN UNTIL BOTH SIDES ARE GOLDEN BROWN. SET TO THE SIDE.
3. IN THE FRYING PAN USED FOR (2), MELT ONE 5-GRAM PAT OF BUTTER AND SAUTÉ THE GARLIC. ONCE THE GARLIC BEGINS TO SMELL FRAGRANT, ADD THE ONION, MUSHROOMS AND ZUCCHINI AND SAUTÉ UNTIL TENDER. ADD THE LIQUID FROM THE STEWED TOMATOES AND THE WHITE WINE AND HEAT TO A LOW BOIL. ONCE BUBBLING, ADD THE NOODLE DIPPING SAUCE, KETCHUP AND SUGAR. IF THE FLAVOR IS TOO THIN, ADD A PINCH OF SALT. REDUCE TO LOW HEAT, ADD THE CHICKEN FROM (2) AND SIMMER.
4. FILL A SEPARATE FRYING PAN ABOUT ¾ OF THE WAY FULL OF WATER AND BRING TO A BOIL. IN A HEAT-RESISTANT BOWL, ADD THE OTHER 5-GRAM PAT OF BUTTER, THE EGGS, SALT AND PEPPER AND BLEND THOROUGHLY. LOWER THE HEAT ON THE FRYING PAN TO LOW AND PUT THE HEAT-RESISTANT BOWL INTO THE BOILING WATER TO CODDLE THE EGG. STIR THE EGG MIXTURE CONTINUALLY UNTIL LIGHTLY COOKED.
5. DIVIDE THE COOKED RICE INTO TWO BOWLS AND TOP WITH THE CHICKEN FROM (3). POUR THE CODDLED EGG FROM (4) OVER TOP AND ADD A BASIL LEAF FOR DECORATION. DONE!

THE TOMATOES SOUND REALLY DELICIOUS!

YUKI MORISAKI COMMENTS

IN SIMPLE RICE BOWLS, HOW THE EGG IS DONE DETERMINES HOW GOOD THE OVERALL DISH IS. IN THIS ONE, THE EGG IS DONE WELL.

YUTO TSUKUDA COMMENTS

TOMATOES AND BASIL ARE REALLY ITALIAN INGREDIENTS, AND THEY SURE LOOK LIKE THEY'RE SHOWING OFF HERE! WHAT A SUAVE BOWL!

WE WILL RUN ANOTHER OF THESE CONTESTS IN *WEEKLY SHONEN JUMP* IN THE FUTURE. KEEP AN EYE OUT FOR IT!

HONORABLE MENTIONS

- TATSUO KOYAMA, TOKYO
- MOMOYAMA, TOKYO
- RYOTA OHYAMA, KANAGAWA
- TAKUYA YOKO'O, KANAGAWA
- HIROSHI IIZUKA, FUJIYAMA
- RYOUSEI MATSUMOTO, HYOGO
- TAMAKI MURADA, HYOGO
- KAORI TANIGUCHI, OKAYAMA
- MARU, HIROSHIMA
- KENSHI YOSHIOKA, FUKUOKA

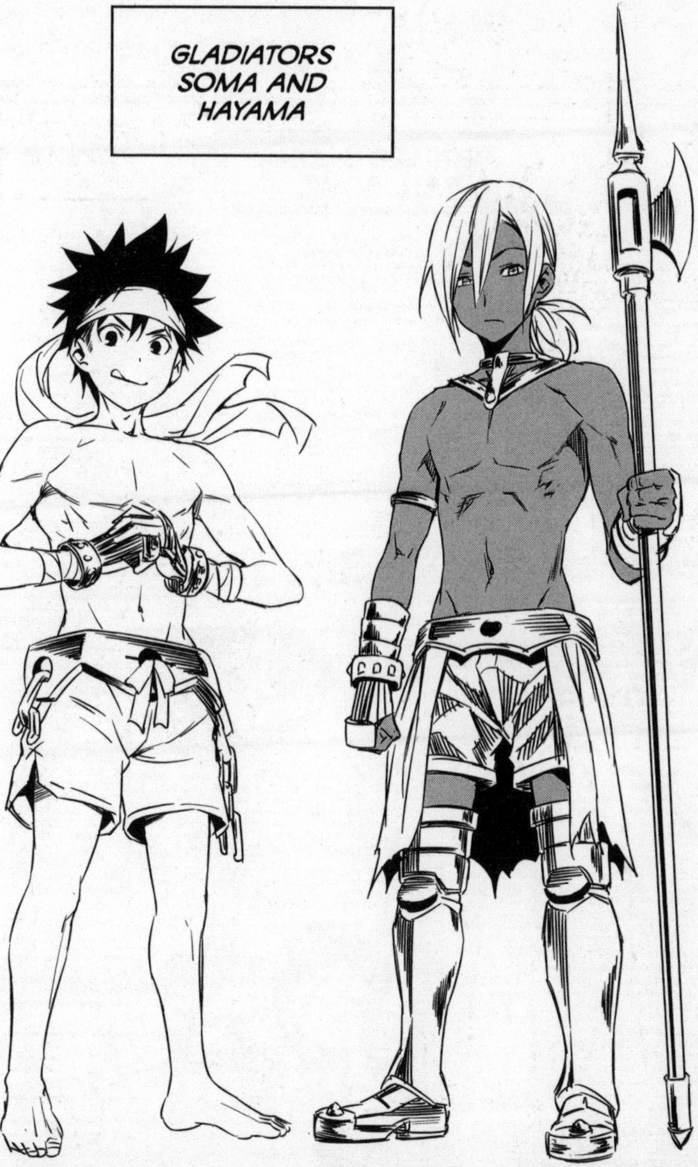
GLADIATORS SOMA AND HAYAMA

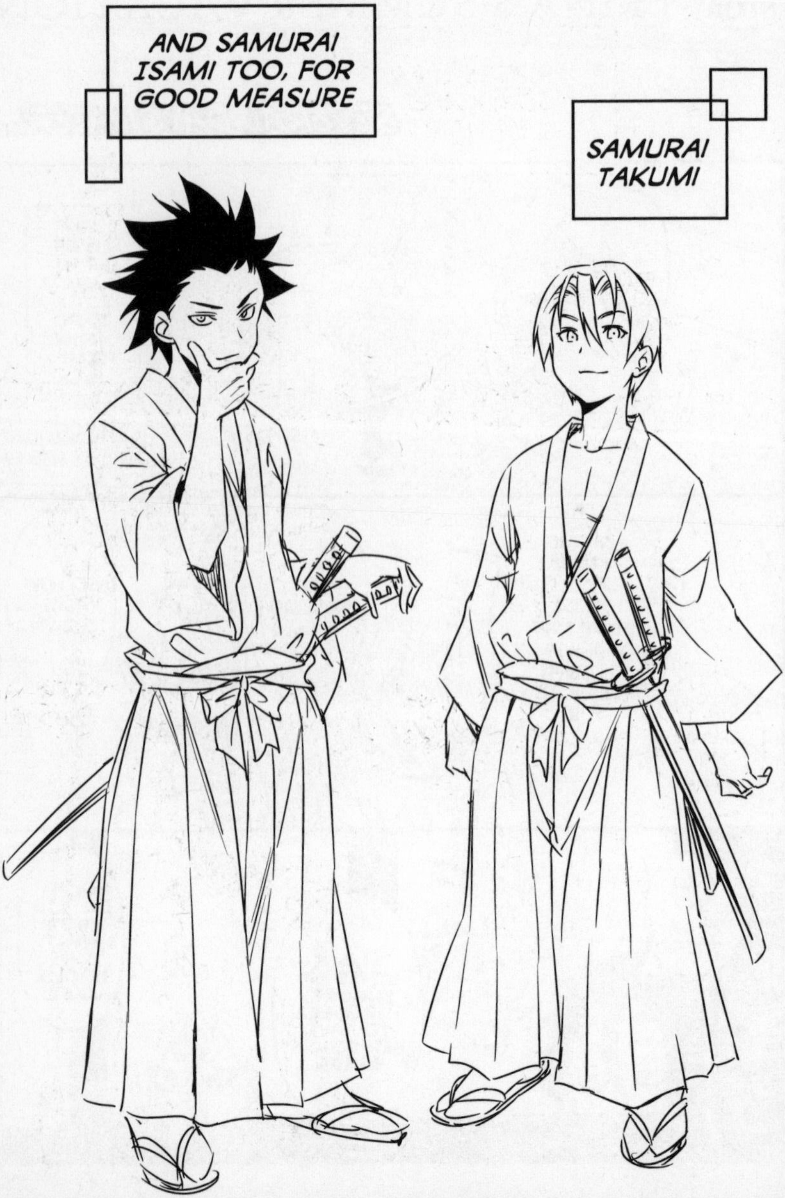
SAMURAI TAKUMI
AND SAMURAI ISAMI TOO, FOR GOOD MEASURE

SIDE STORY ERINA'S SUMMER VACATION

SEVERAL DAYS LATER...

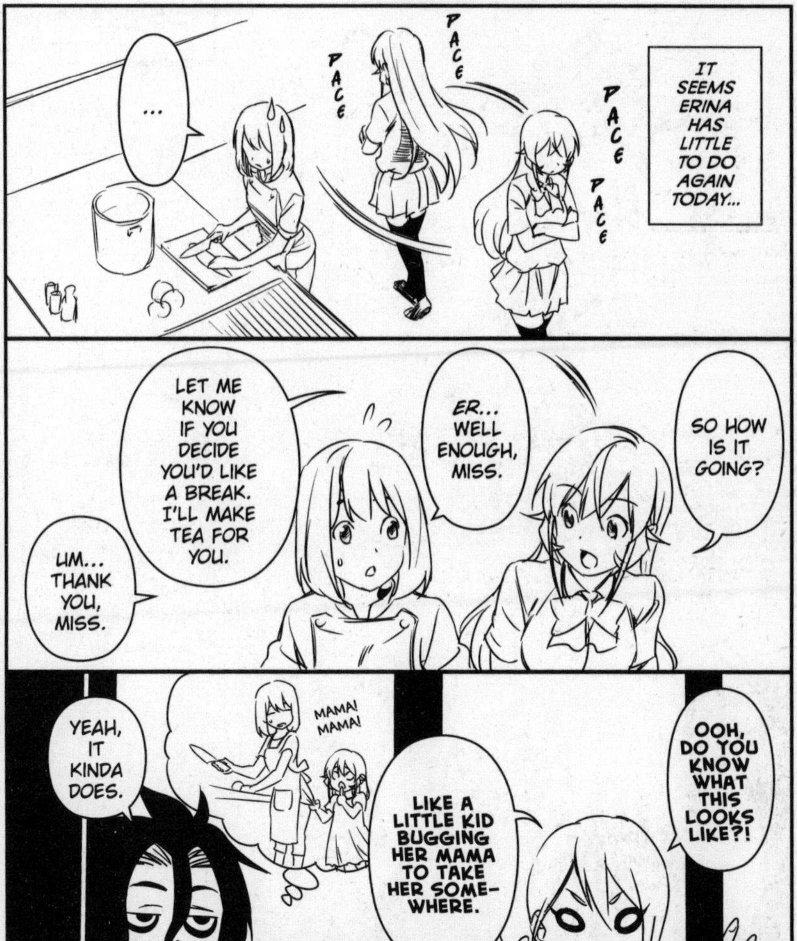
IT SEEMS ERINA HAS LITTLE TO DO AGAIN TODAY...
PACE PACE
PACE PACE
...
SO HOW IS IT GOING?
ER... WELL ENOUGH, MISS.
LET ME KNOW IF YOU DECIDE YOU'D LIKE A BREAK. I'LL MAKE TEA FOR YOU.
UM... THANK YOU, MISS.
OOH, DO YOU KNOW WHAT THIS LOOKS LIKE?!
LIKE A LITTLE KID BUGGING HER MAMA TO TAKE HER SOME-WHERE.
MAMA! MAMA!
YEAH, IT KINDA DOES.

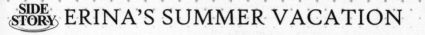

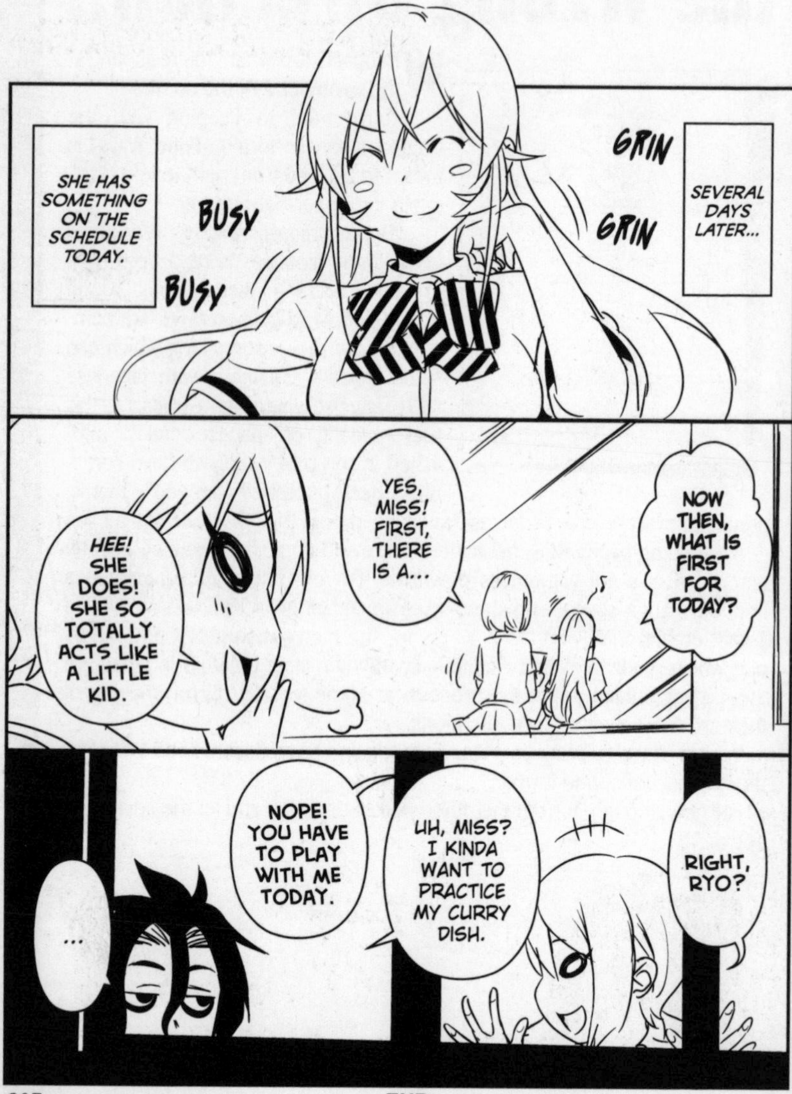
SEVERAL DAYS LATER...
GRIN
GRIN
BUSY
BUSY
SHE HAS SOMETHING ON THE SCHEDULE TODAY.
NOW THEN, WHAT IS FIRST FOR TODAY?
YES, MISS! FIRST, THERE IS A...
HEE! SHE DOES! SHE SO TOTALLY ACTS LIKE A LITTLE KID.
RIGHT, RYO?
UH, MISS? I KINDA WANT TO PRACTICE MY CURRY DISH.
NOPE! YOU HAVE TO PLAY WITH ME TODAY.
...

END

You're Reading in the Wrong Direction!!

Whoops! Guess what? You're starting at the wrong end of the comic!

...It's true! In keeping with the original Japanese format, **Food Wars!** is meant to be read from right to left, starting in the upper-right corner.

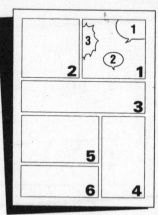

Unlike English, which is read from left to right, Japanese is read from right to left, meaning that action, sound effects and word-balloon order are completely reversed... something which can make readers unfamiliar with Japanese feel pretty backwards themselves. For this reason, manga or Japanese comics published in the U.S. in English have sometimes been published "flopped"—that is, printed in exact reverse order, as though seen from the other side of a mirror.

By flopping pages, U.S. publishers can avoid confusing readers, but the compromise is not without its downside. For one thing, a character in a flopped manga series who once wore in the original Japanese version a T-shirt emblazoned with "M A Y" (as in "the merry month of") now wears one which reads "Y A M"! Additionally, many manga creators in Japan are themselves unhappy with the process, as some feel the mirror-imaging of their art skews their original intentions.

We are proud to bring you Yuto Tsukuda and Shun Saeki's **Food Wars!** in the original unflopped format.

For now, though, turn to the other side of the book and let the adventure begin...!

—Editor

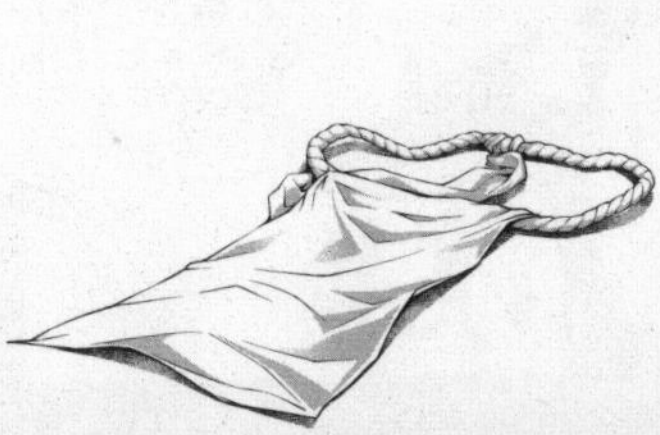